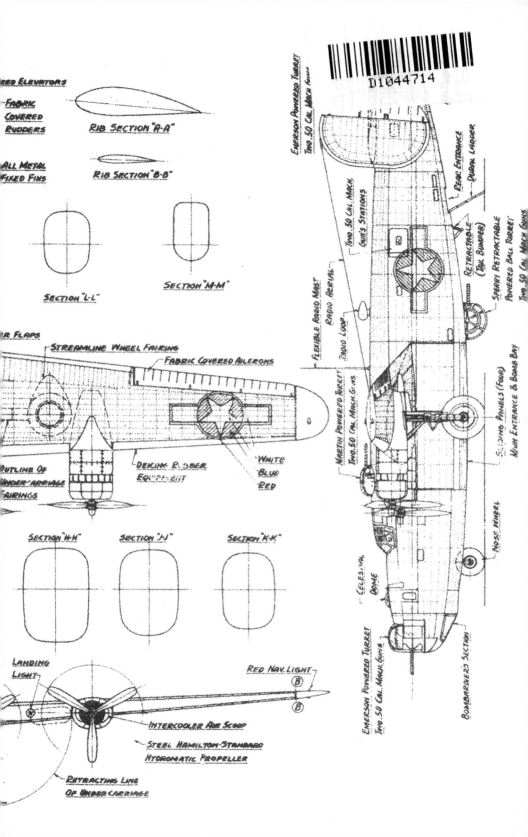

The Arsenal
of Democracy

Books by A. J. Baime

*Go Like Hell: Ford, Ferrari,
and Their Battle for Speed and Glory at Le Mans*

Big Shots: The Men Behind the Booze

The Arsenal of Democracy

FDR, Detroit,
and an Epic Quest to Arm
an America at War

A. J. BAIME

HOUGHTON MIFFLIN HARCOURT
BOSTON | NEW YORK

www.hmhco.com

Library of Congress Cataloging-in-Publication Data
Baime, A. J. (Albert J.)
The arsenal of democracy : FDR, Detroit,
and an epic quest to arm an America at war / A. J. Baime.
pages cm
Includes bibliographical references and index.
ISBN 978-0-547-71928-3
1. Ford Motor Company — History — 20th century. 2. Industrial mobilization —
United States — History — 20th century. 3. Automobile industry and trade —
Military aspects — United States — History — 20th century. 4. Willow Run
(Manufacturing plant) — History — 20th century . 5. B-24 (Bomber) — Design and
construction — History. 6. Ford, Edsel, 1893-1943. 7. Ford, Henry, 1863-1947.
8. Ford, Henry, II, 1917-1987 9. World War, 1939-1945 — Economic aspects —
United States. 10. World War, 1939-1945 — Michigan. I. Title. II. Title: FDR,
Detroit, and an epic quest to arm an America at war.
HD9710.U54B35 2014
940.53'1 — dc23
2013045019

Printed in the United States of America
DOC 10 9 8 7 6

Every single man, woman, and child is a partner in the most tremendous undertaking of our American history.

— Franklin D. Roosevelt

I refuse to recognize that there are impossibilities. I cannot discover that anyone knows enough about anything on this earth definitely to say what is and what is not possible.

— Henry Ford

Cover image: B-24 Liberator bombers in flight on May 19, 1942. Maximum speed: 303 miles per hour. Range: 2,850 miles. Engines: four Pratt & Whitney R-1830s totaling 4,800 horsepower. Armament: ten .50 caliber machine guns and 8,000 pounds of bombs.

Contents

Introduction

THIS BOOK IS ABOUT many things. It's about World War II. It's about the rise of airpower, an apocalyptic science when applied to military action. It's about an American president confined to a wheelchair who sought to teach the world how to walk again during the Great Depression, only to find himself facing a losing war against unconscionable evil. It's about Detroit — "the biggest wartime boom-town of all" — and its automobile industry, which in 1941 had a bigger economy than any foreign nation except Britain, France, Germany, and possibly the Soviet Union. Ultimately, this book is about a father and a son who more than any other figures in the first half of the twentieth century symbolized Americanism all over the world — their love, their empire, and the war that tore them apart.

In 1941 Henry Ford and his only child, Edsel, launched the most ambitious wartime industrial adventure ever up to that point in history.* They attempted to turn their motorcar business into an aviation powerhouse, to build four-engine bombers, the weapon the Allied leaders thirsted for above all others. The older Ford (Henry was seventy-six when the war began) was one of the nation's richest and most controversial men, an ardent antiwar activist and accused Nazi sympathizer. His only child, Edsel, was a tragic Gatsby-esque character who was dying of a disease that all his riches couldn't cure.

With the help of "Cast Iron" Charlie Sorensen, Detroit's heralded Hercules of the assembly lines, and the aviator Charles Lindbergh, the Fords attempted to turn the US Air Corps' biggest, fastest, most destructive heavy bomber into the most mass-produced American aircraft of all time. Their quest captured the imagination of a nation

---

* The advent of the Manhattan Project was still many months in the future.

and came to illuminate all that could go wrong on the home front during the war — and all that could go right.

At the same time, the Fords were being quietly investigated by US Treasury agents, who believed the family's ties to its French division — which was cooperating with the Nazi high command to help build Hitler's arsenal — may have violated the Trading with the Enemy Act. An investigation kicked into high gear in 1943, the day a "strictly confidential" memo landed on Roosevelt's desk in the White House detailing "amazing and shocking correspondence" between Edsel Ford and a key French operative. Did the family have a dark secret?

Honor, betrayal, sacrifice, death — all of it is woven into a father-son drama that, in the larger context of the war, has never fully been explored.

In the climactic scenes of this book, the reader will be transported into battle aboard bombers built by the Fords. "Here was the power," Lindbergh said of these 60,000-pound machines (fully loaded), "the efficiency, the superhuman magic of which we had dreamed." Henry Ford's vision in the early part of the century, "Fordism," had fueled the rise of cities, suburbs, and industries. Now — inside enemy territory — that same vision would tear it all down.

Today Detroit gets trotted out as a symbol of a superpower in decline. The city has lost more than half its population since the war, and it is the largest American city ever to declare bankruptcy. Its main artery, the Edsel Ford Expressway, runs right into it, though the man it is named for is all but forgotten. There was a time, however, when Detroit was a "city of destiny," "a city forging thunderbolts." This is a book about World War II and the Motor City — its heroes, its villains, and its legacy.

Prologue

ON THE NIGHT OF December 29, 1940, a few moments before 9:00 PM, Franklin Delano Roosevelt wheeled himself in his chair through the White House warrens and into the Diplomatic Reception Room on the first floor. He wore a gray wool suit and a face that, for an eternal optimist, appeared grim. An incongruous audience stood in the room. The President's mother was there, as were some White House guests, actors Clark Gable and Carole Lombard. Roosevelt was preparing to deliver an address that generations hence would deem one of the most important pieces of political rhetoric in modern history. It was called "The Arsenal of Democracy."

At that very moment, in London, bombs were raining from the night sky. Adolf Hitler's air force was subjecting London to the worst pounding since the start of the Battle of Britain — a night of terror planned specifically to steer attention away from Roosevelt's speech, which promised to solve a great mystery: what was the President prepared to do about the Nazis and their conquering armies? With most of Europe already subjugated, would Washington remain neutral? Or was Roosevelt prepared to support the effort to defeat Hitler with American-made tanks, guns, ships, and bomber aircraft?

All week long the White House had stirred with activity in anticipation of the President's "fireside chat." On the Sunday of the address, Roosevelt worked over every word in his office, complaining to his secretary, Grace Tully, who went heavy on the punctuation when she typed.

"Grace!" he yelled. "How many times do I have to tell you to stop wasting the taxpayers' commas?"

When he was satisfied, he sent the speech to the State Department for comment. He had his throat sprayed to ease his sinuses. White

House workers removed the gold-trimmed presidential china from the Diplomatic Reception Room, and as Roosevelt sipped cocktails and ate dinner, they tested the broadcasting equipment, the wires snaking across the floor onto a desk on which a cluster of microphones stood — the ears of the world.

At the stroke of nine, the largest radio audience ever gathered tuned in. Over five hundred stations were broadcasting the speech in the United States. This was the "Golden Age of Radio," with popular shows like *Jack Benny* and *Amos 'n' Andy,* and yet no broadcast had ever lured more attention than the President's speech. The only one that had come close was the Joe Louis–Max Schmeling fight at Yankee Stadium two years earlier.

Amid the rubble of Britain's cities, at 3:00 AM London time, thousands, including Prime Minister Winston Churchill, crowded around their radios. Roosevelt's address would be broadcast in South America, China, the Soviet Union, and in six languages in Europe.

Roosevelt began. "My friends, this is not a fireside chat on war. It is a talk on national security; because the nub of the whole purpose of your President is to keep you now, and your children later, and your grandchildren much later, out of a last-ditch war for the preservation of American independence and all of the things that American independence means to you and to me and to ours," the President said. And then, gravely: "Never before since Jamestown and Plymouth Rock has our American civilization been in such danger as now."

The events leading up to that night had placed the President in an impossible situation.

For eleven years, the Great Depression had plagued the global economy. The United States was a nation paralyzed by its economy. In 1940 about 17 percent of Americans were unemployed, over 7 million able-bodied people. Only 48,000 taxpayers out of 132 million earned more than $2,500 a year (the rough equivalent of $40,000 today). Nearly one-third of American homes had no running water. Americans had no unemployment insurance or antibiotics.

Since he came to power in 1933 (five weeks after Hitler became chancellor of Germany), Roosevelt had fought tirelessly to meet the basic needs of the masses. Recoiling from the horror of World War I, Congress had passed numerous Neutrality Acts, based in the idea that the oceans protected American soil from foreign attack, like some giant moat. With no funding, the US military had grown anemic. The army ranked sixteenth in the world in size, with fewer than 200,000 men, compared to 7 million Nazi soldiers. No legitimate munitions industry existed. The Army Air Corps had fewer than 1,300 combat planes, and most of them were technologically obsolete.

In Europe, Hitler's rise had caused consternation at first. An artist and an ex-convict, he had brilliantly harnessed the power and will of the German people using modern communications such as film and radio. He had been secretly building his military for years using American-style principles of mass production. It was a futuristic kind of fighting force, with unprecedented amounts of horsepower built on assembly lines in factories and mounted on wheels and wings.

As Britain's spymaster William Stephenson (code name: Intrepid) confided in Roosevelt: "The Fuehrer is not just a lunatic. He's an evil genius. The weapons in his armory are like nothing in history. His propaganda is sophisticated. His control of the people is technologically clever. He has torn up the military textbooks, and written his own."

It was the Luftwaffe that the Americans and British feared most, the first-ever fully crafted air force, headed by Hitler's most trusted confidant, Hermann Goering, a World War I ace pilot turned morphine addict who had spent time in a sanitarium locked in a straitjacket. By the late 1930s, German factories were birthing more warplanes than all other nations combined. The German Air Force, it seemed, could turn the Nazis into Nietzschean supermen. As the British statesman Sir Nevile Henderson put it, "If one makes a toy, the wish to play with it becomes irresistible. And the German Army and Air Force were super toys."

When Hitler invaded Poland in 1939, he declared: "I am putting on the uniform, and I shall take it off only in death or victory." On May 10, 1940, the Nazis invaded France, Holland, Luxembourg, and Belgium. The French — who had the finest army of the European Allies — surrendered within five weeks. According to French premier Paul Reynaud, his forces were like "walls of sand that a child puts up against waves on the seashore."

Great Britain was next. The Luftwaffe's dive-bombers tore into England's cities. Centuries-old buildings crumbled. "The London that we knew was burning," one local wrote. "The London which had taken thirty generations a thousand years to build . . . and the Nazis had done that in thirty seconds." Reporting over CBS radio from London, Edward R. Murrow brought the terror into America's living rooms. "There are no words to describe the thing that is happening," he reported on September 18, 1940.

Suddenly Americans couldn't help but imagine the destruction of New York, Washington, Los Angeles.

On October 22, 1940, the White House received a most chilling letter from a Jewish doctor from Baden, Germany, via a refugee activist with contacts inside Nazi-occupied territory. It told of being taken by the Nazis and delivered to a concentration camp, where thousands of Jews were herded "like criminals behind barbed wire." Five hundred refugees had died already of starvation and pestilence, according to this shocking missive. "If the United States continues to work so slowly the number of dead here is going to increase in a most deplorable manner."

In the White House, it began to sink in: the unparalleled depth of Hitler's evil, and what it would take to defeat him.

The President crystallized his plan. Hitler was fighting an engineer's war, and there would be no escaping the maelstrom. To win, Roosevelt would need to harness the complete capacity of American industry — all its resources — in a way never done before and as soon as possible. As one Washington insider, future War Production Board chief Donald Nelson, put it: "The whole industrial strength of the United States, should it be directed toward war-making, would constitute power never dreamed of before in the history of Armageddon. . . . It would be a struggle in which all our strength would be needed — and the penalty for being unable to use all our strength would be the loss of everything we had."

During Christmas week of 1940, Roosevelt prepared for the fireside chat he hoped would ignite the nation's industrial flame. His chief speechwriters, the playwright Robert Sherwood and adviser Samuel Rosenman, moved into the White House so that they could work around the clock on the address. On December 29, from the White House's Diplomatic Reception Room, the President delivered it flawlessly, the microphones picking up the percussion of his lips and the turning of pages.

"The Nazi masters of Germany have made it clear that they intend not only to dominate all of life and thought in their own country," Roosevelt said, using the word "Nazi" for the first time in a public address, "but also to enslave the whole of Europe, and then to use the resources of Europe to dominate the rest of the world."

Roosevelt quoted Hitler: "I can beat any other power in the world."

The President then called upon private industry, the heart of his defense plan:

Guns, planes, ships, and many other things have to be built in the factories and the arsenals of America. They have to be produced by workers and managers and engineers with the aid of machines which in turn have to be built by hundreds of thousands of workers throughout the land. . . . As President of the United States, I call for that national effort. I call for it in the name of this nation which we love and honor and which we are privileged and proud to serve.

"We must be," the President said, "the great arsenal of democracy."

In London, as the bombs dropped, civilians could be heard roaring with confidence from basement shelters, empowered by Roosevelt's words. "When I visited the still-burning ruins today," Churchill told Roosevelt the next morning, "the spirit of the Londoners was as high as in the first days of the indiscriminate bombing in September, four months ago."

In Berlin, Hitler's propaganda chief Joseph Goebbels scoffed at the American president's bravado. If the war was going to be a contest of industrial prowess, the Nazis believed they could not be beaten.

"What can the USA do faced with our arms capacity?" he wrote in his diary. "They can do us no harm. [Roosevelt] will never be able to produce as much as we, who have the entire economic capacity of Europe at our disposal. The USA stands poised between war and peace. Roosevelt wants war, the people want peace. . . . We must wait and see what he does next."

PART I

THE MOTOR CITY

1

Henry

With his Model T, Henry Ford affected the world more than
any other man in fifteen hundred years.

— HISTORIAN NORMAN BEASLEY

THERE WAS NOTHING GLAMOROUS about the invention, nothing
to suggest that it was destined to revolutionize human life. It stood
awkwardly on its four wheels, a Frankenstein machine made out of
bicycle pieces, a wooden box that looked like the bottom half of a
pauper's coffin, and an array of minutiae from the hardware store. It
had a bench atop, under which sat its heart and soul, an engine that
produced the power equivalent of four horses. Sometime after midnight on June 4, 1896, in a dingy brick shed that stank of gasoline
behind a row house at 58 Bagley Avenue in Detroit, a gray-eyed inventor labored over its final touches with the tenderness of a father
caring for a newborn.

Henry Ford was thirty-two years old, not young considering that
the average life span in America at the time was forty-nine. He was
a man of almost no formal education, and he had little in the bank
but a dream. With his friend Jim Bishop standing by, he wheeled his
invention — a horseless carriage, what he called a "Quadricycle" — out
of the Bagley Avenue shed into the humid night, a light spring rain
beading in his mustache.

At roughly 4:00 AM, he ran into his home and woke his wife Clara — or Callie, as he called her. It was time, he said. Everything was ready. She rushed from bed, grabbing a cloak, an umbrella, and their two-year-old son Edsel. Together the family moved to the back-yard and into the rain. Clara held the cloak over baby Edsel with one hand and the umbrella over Henry with the other. As Henry would later tell the story:

"Mr. Bishop had his bicycle ready to ride ahead and warn drivers of horse-drawn vehicles — if indeed any were to be met with at such an hour. I set the choke and spun the flywheel. As the motor roared and sputtered to life, I climbed aboard."

The Quadricycle had come to Henry as an epiphany six years earlier, in 1890. He was a newlywed living comfortably on a Dearborn farm about eight miles from downtown Detroit. It was a quiet life in those days. There were no cars driving by, no airplanes overhead, no air conditioners whirring, not even a tractor in the barn. The loudest sounds Henry would hear on a given day were an occasional thunder crack, the smack of an ax on a log, his wife's fingers on the piano keys. Henry's future was set. He would spend his years tilling this land in quiet obscurity, as his father had done before him.

But he felt the tug of ambition. He had an obsession with mechanical objects — with clocks in particular. What made them move? How could a mechanism function with such immaculate precision, with no interference from human hands? It seemed to have an intelligence all its own, one that surpassed human capability in a way. Even as a child, Henry couldn't keep his curious fingers out of timepieces. As a neighbor put it: "Every clock in the Ford home shuddered when it saw him coming."

He had likely learned of the internal combustion engine while reading about the pioneering work of Germany's Karl Benz and Gottlieb Daimler, who built the first gasoline-powered horseless carriages in Europe in 1885 and 1886. Not long after Henry and Clara settled on the farm, he saw a gas engine in a soda bottling plant. One night, while Clara was playing the piano, he blurted out a prophecy.

"I've been on the wrong track," he said. "What I would like to do is make an engine that will run by gasoline and have it do the work of a horse." He grabbed a sheet of music and sketched the Quadricycle on the back. "But I can't do it out here on the farm. I need money for tools and money to pay for other things."

Henry and his wife moved from the farm to the teeming city in search of their dream. Their odyssey had begun.

Over the next five years, they struggled with finances while Henry worked day and night. They moved from one apartment to the next, smaller each time. Clara had to plead with the clerk at the hardware store to extend their $15 credit. Henry began to call his wife "The Believer." He found a job at the Edison Illuminating Company for $40 a week — good money, but he needed every penny for parts and experiments.

Henry worked night shifts at Edison from 6:00 PM to 6:00 AM. He'd gotten the position under dubious circumstances. The man before him had been killed on the job. But here among the steam engines and Edison dynamos, Henry was in his element. The plant powered some 5,000 streetlamps in the city and brought electricity into the homes of over 1,000 Detroiters for the first time. To see an Edison bulb flicker on at sunset was proof that an idea could change the world.

When Clara got pregnant, the couple's finances grew more complicated. On November 6, 1893, a doctor arrived at their apartment on a bicycle with a bag of equipment tied to the handlebars. Clara gave birth to a healthy boy. "Mrs. Ford didn't give me any trouble at all," the doctor told Henry. "She never complained one bit." And the child? "He was born without circumstance."

Henry entered the bedroom and saw Clara with the baby in her arms. Here was a son whose destiny would ride alongside his own. The child had his mother's chocolate brown eyes and delicate mouth. Henry reached out one of his long, calloused fingers, and the baby curled a fist around it.

"You can see he's smart, Callie, by the way he knows me," Henry said. "He cost twice as much as Grandpa Holmes paid to get me safely into this world, but he'll be worth it."

Though the couple had little money, they named the child Edsel, which in Old English meant "rich."

Soon after, the family moved yet again — to Bagley Avenue, which had a brick shed in the back where Henry could work on his machine. Things were looking up: he'd been named chief engineer at the main Edison plant, working the day shift. His new apartment was just three blocks from his work, and the apartment was wired for electricity supplied by Edison. After dinner each night the Fords moved to the shed out back, Clara keeping Henry company while Edsel crawled around, burning his little hands on occasion on hot valves.

Then came the night of June 4, 1896. At 4:00 AM, with Clara and two-year-old Edsel watching in the rain, Henry sat in his throbbing invention for the first time, not knowing what the engine of fate had in store, incapable of imagining that he would see millions upon millions of automobiles with his name on them spring to life in the coming decades.

Henry hit the gas and rolled down the cobblestone alley. He made his first historic drive through the streets of Detroit.

Locals grew accustomed to seeing "Crazy Henry" and his family motoring through the city. The Fords cruised over the bumpy cobbles at twenty miles per hour, past the gutters full of horse manure and the electric-powered streetcars that crisscrossed downtown Detroit. Henry wore a bow tie, the wind brushing back his side-parted brown hair and mustache. Clara sat beside him in a bonnet, veil, and flowing dress, cradling Edsel in her lap. Kids gave chase, pumping away on bicycles. Along the streets, saloons emptied and necks craned. Always a friend rode ahead on a bike to clear a path and warn carriage riders, whose horses would get spooked.

"Here comes that crazy Henry Ford," Henry heard time and again over the engine's song.

"Yes, crazy," he muttered, smiling at his little boy Edsel. "Crazy like a fox."

With the help of investors, Henry launched the city's first automobile manufacturing outfit, the Detroit Automobile Company, on August 5, 1899. He quit his job at Edison, and that winter he introduced his first commercial car. It made the front page of the *Detroit News-Tribune*: "Thrilling Trip on the First Detroit-Made Automobile When the Mercury Hovered About Zero."

The company ran out of money within the year. Now out of a job,

Henry continued to look for investors. The Fords moved into cheaper quarters again, living with Henry's seventy-six-year-old father William on West Grand Boulevard. William Ford urged his son to get a real job.

"You'll never make a go of it," he said of the horseless carriage business. "They'll never sell."

Henry pushed on. In 1903 he managed to gather eleven investors, who raised the phenomenal sum of $150,000. At 9:30 AM on June 16, 1903, at 68 Moffat Street in Detroit, the official forms were signed. Henry took 255 shares, each at $100, while most others signed on for 50 shares. Ford Motor Company was born. With a crew of about seventy-five men, Henry rented a wooden single-story space on Mack Avenue. He was forty years old. It had been twelve years since he moved to Detroit to chase his dream, and now everything was in place.

The first customer was a Chicago dentist, who paid $850 for his Ford automobile. In the next twelve months, 1,000 more automobiles rolled out of Mack Avenue. Customers were willing to pay for Henry's cars because they were reliable, affordable, and easy to maintain, and Henry had an uncanny talent to produce one just like the one before. His genius lay not in the product he produced but in the production itself—an integrated factory system as precise as a timepiece. Every spring and cog and hook had sprung from the imagination of the factory's creator and his team, and the factory functioned as if it possessed its own sentience. Thanks to its efficiency, the product could be created cheaply, and that savings was passed on to the customer.

In 1904, Henry moved into a bigger space on Piquette Avenue, a three-story brick building measuring 56 feet wide and 402 feet long. The day he stepped inside, he had visions of grandeur that would soon be eclipsed again.

"Let's run it!" he shouted, his footsteps echoing down the cavernous space, his son Edsel racing alongside on his bicycle.

All over the world, thousands of dreamers and tinkerers were competing to be the first successful automaker. Henry read about their experiments in *Horseless Age* and *Motor World* magazines; their crude steam-, battery-, and gasoline-powered vehicles were almost all doomed to history's junkyard. It was a race of ambition, ideas, and audacity — a race that Henry Ford won. Each car he produced in Detroit was a rolling ambassador of a new machine age, spreading the gospel through the streets of American cities and towns, and eventually overseas.

After four years in business, Henry's salary dwarfed that of Detroit's new baseball star Ty Cobb fifteen times over. That didn't include dividends, which paid investors 100 percent of their original money down in the first year. Company profits went from $283,037 in 1904 to $1,124,675 in 1907. Henry knew he had hit it big the day his wife came to him with consternation on her face. She was doing laundry one day and had found a forgotten uncashed check for $75,000 in the pocket of his pants.

Reporters from the newspapers swarmed Henry's factory, where they often found the gray-eyed man with his son Edsel by his side, the boy shyly looking up at his beaming father with wonder in his eyes. Despite all of Henry's success and money, he told his friends and employees, it was his boy that mattered most. With his Ford car, he was becoming an icon. But with Edsel, he was a father. Edsel was destined to be his crowning achievement.

2

The Machine Is the New Messiah

There is in manufacturing a creative joy that only poets are supposed to know. Some day I'd like to show a poet how it feels to design and build a railroad locomotive.

— WALTER CHRYSLER

DETROIT WAS ON THE VERGE. No city had ever grown so pregnant with fortune as Detroit at the turn of the twentieth century. Not San Francisco during the Gold Rush, not New York in the Gilded Age. This was the city where the age of coal and steam was about to end.

The village of Detroit was founded in 1701 by a French explorer named Antoine Laumet de La Mothe sieur de Cadillac, on the banks of what is now called the Detroit River. By the nineteenth century, the city had gained a reputation for its metal workers. Over 250 metal shops had opened by the Civil War. Decades before a car ever appeared in the Motor City, urban planners prophetically designed Detroit's downtown in the shape of a wheel, with a city center and grand boulevards fanning out like spokes, thoroughfares that carried horse-and-buggy traffic from downtown out into the sprawl.

By the time Henry Ford sold his first car, Detroit was home to 286,000 people. It was the thirteenth-largest metropolis in the country, spread out over seventeen square miles. Like most northern cities, it was vastly Caucasian and homogeneous, with dirt and macadam roads filled with horse traffic. A post–Civil War lumber boom in Michigan made Detroit a shipping and railroad hub. With iron mines to the north (Michigan's mines produced 80 percent of the nation's iron ore at the turn of the century) and coal just about everywhere, the city was a perfect place for a new industry to explode. All it needed was a spark.

Ransom Olds launched his auto company around the same time as Henry Ford's. By 1904, 5,000 Curved Dash Oldsmobiles had rolled out of the Olds Motor Works at $650 apiece. John and Horace Dodge launched the Dodge Brothers Company in 1900 with the most sophisticated machine shop in town. Hard-drinking sons of a fish shop owner, and known for pulling pistols if they weren't paid on time, the Dodges always got what they wanted. David Dunbar Buick, Louis Chevrolet, Walter Chrysler — they all found their way to Detroit, the Silicon Valley of the early twentieth century.

Nightly a new breed of auto men gathered at the bar of the Pontchartrain Hotel on Cadillac Square. As one local described the Pontchartrain: "Excitement was in the air. A new prosperity was in the making. Fortunes were being gambled. Men played hard, but they worked desperately. It was not an uncommon sight to see four or five men carry a heavy piece of machinery into the room, place it on the floor or table and set it in motion. There, men began to talk a strange new language."

Meanwhile, Detroit's bus and train stations unloaded daily thousands of laborers, who were lured by work in the factories. Detroit welcomed the first stretch of paved road and the first public parking garage.

"Detroit in those days was seething with intensity," wrote one Motor City chronicler. "Millions were tossed into a pot, and lost; pennies were tossed into a different pot, and came out millions." Though David Buick's name graced innumerable automobiles in his lifetime, he died a pauper in Detroit. Louis Chevrolet's life ended in hardship in the Motor City; after helping start the company that bore his name, he had dropped out of the venture because he thought it had no future.

On the other end, no auto man's fortune skyrocketed like Henry Ford's.

Early one morning in the winter of 1906–1907, Henry arrived at his Piquette Avenue plant hunting for a $3-a-day pattern worker and rising production man, Charles Sorensen. A twenty-five-year-old Danish immigrant with big fists and an even bigger temper, Sorensen was so handsome that people called him Adonis. Two fingertips were missing from his right hand, not rare for a man in his line of work.

Henry said to Sorensen, "Come with me, Charlie. I want to show you something."

They climbed the stairs to the north end of the third floor.

"Charlie," Henry said, "I'd like to have a room finished off right in this space. Put up a wall with a door big enough to run a car in and out. Get a good lock for the door. . . . We're going to start a completely new job."

Soon this secret room — only Henry, Sorensen, and a small handful of engineers were allowed inside — was electric with activity. A large blackboard dominated the space. Henry spent endless hours in his lucky rocking chair staring at it. On that blackboard, the Model T was born. Sorensen would always remember the glint he saw in Henry's eye — a look of genius and determination, the knowledge that something great was about to happen.

Henry famously summed up the idea of this car: "I will build a motorcar for the great multitude. It will be so low in price that no man making a good salary will be unable to own one," he explained, adding that every owner of this automobile would enjoy "the blessing of hours of pleasure in God's greatest open spaces." Model Ts would soon cover every major city on earth like ants on an anthill.

Mass production was still a new idea; it had been put into practice at Ford's Detroit factory, the Singer sewing machine factory, and the Colt firearms works, among other examples. But Henry revolutionized the notion by imagining it on an exponentially larger canvas. The idea of fully integrated mass production came to him like the burst of light in an Edison bulb.* As he described it:

---

* Charlie Sorensen and others have staked a claim to the idea of the moving assembly line. Nevertheless, history has given Henry Ford the credit.

The man who places a part does not fasten it. The man who puts in a bolt does not put on the nut; the man who puts on the nut does not tighten it. Every piece of work in the shop moves. It may move on hooks, on overhead chains. . . . It may travel on a moving platform or it may go by gravity.

Henry contacted Detroit's finest architect, a German-born son of a rabbi named Albert Kahn, who had built Detroit's Children's Hospital and the Packard factory. Together they ventured to an old horse-racing track at the corner of Woodward and Manchester in a Detroit neighborhood called Highland Park.

"When Henry Ford took me to the old race course and told me what he wanted," Kahn later recalled, "I thought he was crazy."

Detroiters watched in awe as the building went up. Four stories tall, the factory covered twelve acres. Henry called it Highland Park, but the press dubbed it "Crystal Palace" because of its rows of windows that sparkled in the sunlight. When it was completed, Henry filled it with laborers from all over the world and breathed life into it. One writer who ventured into Highland Park in those early days captured its magnitude:

Fancy a jungle of wheels and belts and weird iron forms — of men, machinery, and movement — add to it every kind of sound you can imagine: the sound of a million squirrels chirping, a million monkeys quarreling, a million lions roaring, a million pigs dying, a million elephants smashing through a forest of sheet iron . . . and you may acquire a vague conception of that place.

Highland Park produced 19,000 Model Ts its first year, 34,500 its second, and 78,440 its third. Its efficiency and vastness struck beholders as nothing short of a miracle, and the man whose name was on the building gained a reputation as a singular character who could achieve the impossible.

By the "Roaring Twenties," Fordism — mass production and the Model T — had rewoven the fabric of a nation. Fordism had democratized mobility, created new industries, and powered an economic boom as if by engine and throttle, crystallizing the emergence of a new American middle class. It had changed the way people worked, dressed, shopped, farmed, worshiped, and vacationed. It had also reshaped cities and connected them to farms, enabling the rise of the suburb.

Fordism was the crowning invention of a new machine age. Americans living through the first two decades of the twentieth century saw an incredible array of new mechanisms that inspired their collective imagination and changed their quotidian lives: the telephone, electric passenger elevator, radio, phonograph, motion picture machine, electric railway, and flying machine. But it was the car that powered the United States to the forefront of the community of nations. It was mass production that defined Americans in their own minds as masters of the new machine age.

Meanwhile, the Model T spread the gospel of Fordism overseas. It was used as a taxi in Cuba, Japan, and all over Europe. In Russia it was called "the Universal Car." As Ford offices and assembly plants were erected all over the world, populations celebrated the arrival of mobility and its economic power.

Henry was just beginning. Already an industrialist, he sought to become a social engineer, using his factory as a laboratory. Highland Park swelled with Poles, Russians, Romanians, Hungarians, Maltese, and Serbs — a total of forty-nine nations were represented. These men couldn't communicate with each other, but they could communicate with the machine, working their piece of the assembly line. Highland Park moved faster and faster. By 1919 a substantial number of Henry's 45,000 workers were handicapped in some way. One had no hands, four had no feet, four were blind, thirty-seven were deaf and dumb, sixty were epileptics — but all were doing jobs specifically designed to accommodate their circumstances, like cogs in the machine.

On January 5, 1914, Henry invited a handful of reporters to his offices. He knew that the sheer audacity of the announcement he was about to make would send it clear across the globe. Never comfortable with public speaking, he stood by a window while Ford's chief finance man read a statement.

"The Ford Motor Company, the greatest and most successful automobile manufacturing company in the world, will, on January 12, inaugurate the greatest revolution in the matter of rewards for its workers ever known to the industrial world. At one stroke it will reduce the hours of labor from nine to eight, and add to every man's pay a share of the profits of the house. The smallest to be received by a man 22 years old and upward will be $5 a day."

In the space of a paragraph, Henry had just doubled the pay of tens of thousands of workers. Given the pay that prevailed in other industries (an average of $1.75 for a nine-hour day for steelworkers, for example), the "$5 Day" was a shock.

"He's crazy, isn't he?" *New York Times* publisher Adolph Ochs said when he heard of Henry's $5 Day. "Don't you think he's crazy?" The *Wall Street Journal* called the $5 Day an "economic crime" and a misapplication of "Biblical principles."

To understand the genius behind the idea one had to read between the lines. By doubling his workers' pay, Henry knew the first thing each of those thousands of workers would do was buy a Model T.

Later that same year, Henry showed up at Highland Park with a black man named William Perry and instructed a foreman to "see to it that he's comfortable." In the United States, black people were prohibited from most jobs, from serving in the military to working in most schools and public offices. But they were not forbidden in Henry Ford's factory. William Perry was the first skilled black worker in a Detroit plant. With his hiring, Henry triggered a historic exodus of poor African Americans from the South.

"Five dollars a day was what Mr. Ford said," Amiri Baraka wrote in *Blues People,* "and Negroes came hundreds of miles to line up outside his employment offices."

There were 5,000 African Americans in Detroit at the turn of the century. By 1920, there were 40,000, with a thousand more arriving every month, most headed to the gates of "Ford's."

By 1918 Henry had begun to conceive his ultimate mechanical masterpiece. It would not be a car, but a new factory — an industrial megalopolis so intimidatingly vast that it would seem otherworldly to anyone but Henry himself. "We are going to make it at the Rouge," he confided to one of his top production men, speaking of the little river that wound through Dearborn, a river named by explorers a century earlier for the red wild flowers that grew from its banks.

"What are you going to do—have everything at the Rouge?" replied Henry's employee.

"Eventually."

"If we are going to move everything down there, someday you will have 100,000 people working there."

"That's what I suspect."

Construction began in 1918. By dredging the little River Rouge, Henry enabled big ships to steer down its path, thus connecting this inland spot in Dearborn to the major ports of the world. From the riverbank, a factory rose, an industrial marvel straight out of an H. G. Wells novel. It would be called "The Rouge."

Meanwhile, when Henry looked out his office window, he saw thousands of men at the gates asking for work. Black, white, deaf, blind, and dumb, they came from cities and small towns, from nations abroad, a sea of broad shoulders, men who would make his cars and earn enough doing so to buy one themselves. Henry was beatified, cast as the new industrial savior, "the Zeus of American mythology." When a group of college students were asked to name the greatest figures of all time, they ranked Henry Ford third behind Napoleon and Jesus Christ.

But it wasn't Henry Ford that had ushered in this new age of prosperity, Henry claimed. It wasn't any man at all. It was the machine. The machine was the impetus for the new utopia. The machine would bring about the brave new world.

"The machine," Henry said, "is the new Messiah."

"Machinery is accomplishing in the world what man has failed to do by preaching, propaganda, or the written word," said Henry. The machine "will soon bring the world to a complete understanding. Thus may be envisioned a United States of the World. Ultimately," he naively preached, "it will surely come."

3

Edsel

There is not a scrap of artificiality about Mr. Edsel Ford's smile.
It just happens.

— A LOCAL DETROITER

EDSEL BRYANT FORD WAS too young to recall his first ride
through the streets of Detroit in his father's Quadricycle. "I don't
remember the first automobile that my father made," he later said.
"My father told me that I rode in it, but of course, I now recall nothing about it. But I do well remember that the Mayor of Detroit came
to see . . . because I was standing at the window, watching for him
to come in." Edsel was old enough, however, to remember his father
as a backyard tinkerer short on money. Through his childhood, he
would watch his father grow from a broke dreamer into the most famous man in the world. In Edsel's adult life, he would look back on
the simplicity of his childhood with longing and, at times, despera-
tion.

His earliest memories were of sledding in winter and playing
checkers at home. With little money, life was simple. He had a small
table for himself in the family kitchen where he studied his ABCs in
a bowl of his mother's alphabet soup. When he wanted to take violin
lessons, his father could afford the lessons but not the violin, so the
teacher let him have it on credit.

In an era when fathers were diffident — many worked six days a week, nine hours a day — Henry showered affection on his only child. Early family photographs show them embracing, playing in the snow, Henry turning cartwheels to make Edsel laugh. The family letters and diaries reveal an adoration for one another and an innocence that would soon vanish.

"Snowed all day," Henry wrote in January 1901. "Edsel got soaking wet. He and Grandpa played checkers. Edsel cheated awful and beat every game. Went to bed so full of laughs he could not say his prayers."

At Christmas that same year, young Edsel wrote a letter: "Dear Santa Claus, I haven't had a Christmas tree in four years. And I have broken all my trimmings. And I want some more. I want a pair of rollar [sic] skates. And a book. I can't think of anything more. I want you to think of something. Good by, Edsel."

As Ford Motor Company grew, it became a kind of family religion. It was "all the family talked about," Edsel recalled. He got his first Ford car at age ten and began driving himself to school, after which he joined his father at work. He was a fixture by Henry's side in the afternoon, trotting along on his short legs to keep up.

Edsel liked to sit with his father's rising star, the Dane Charlie Sorensen, who turned out wooden toys for the boy from the lathes. Everyone in the plant was terrified of temperamental Sorensen, a mechanical genius when his hands weren't curled into fists. But he was like a proud uncle to young Edsel.

At the Detroit University School (a private high school — Henry could now easily afford the $70 per semester tuition), Edsel's classmates called him "Brainy." He joined the track team, but his real love was automobiles. He doodled them in class and kept thick scrapbooks of pictures he cut out of magazines, pasting them in at perfect right angles. These scrapbooks remained among his keepsakes for his entire life. Unlike his father, for whom the democratization of affordable mobility was an obsession, Edsel was mesmerized by the luxury chariots of Europe: Bugatti, Rolls-Royce, Hispano-Suiza. He was emblematic of the next generation of Americans, whose dreams and desires were loftier and more cosmopolitan than those of the one before.

Henry saw poetry in machines and mass production. Edsel saw it in the beautiful lines of a Mercedes-Benz.

Each afternoon Henry awaited the arrival of his son at the factory. "Have you seen Ed?" he would say. "Oh, yes, he's here. I see his books!"

"I told Edsel that he ought to know everything that was going on in the place," Henry later said. "I told him that he would do better to spend two or three years just wandering around seeing how everything was done and getting acquainted with the men, always keeping in mind that, someday, he would be called upon to administer it all."

As Edsel later put it: "Father put me through the mill."

When Edsel graduated from high school and his friends went off to Harvard and the University of Michigan, he went to work full-time for his father. Employees called him Mr. Edsel; his father and Sorensen called him by his first name. In his office, Edsel kept an old engine that Henry had built in the Bagley Avenue shed — a reminder of the innocence of his childhood and how far the Fords had come.

Once he became a fully grown man, Edsel stood in a glare of spotlight — the Motor City's princeling son. Elegant in a suit tailored by Detroit's most prominent haberdashery, Dunn & Company, and wearing handmade shoes from London, he had an eye for aesthetics. Upon meeting the Detroit artist Irving Bacon, Henry introduced his son as "the artist in the family." (Bacon would remember Edsel being "extremely interested in his father's affairs, the kind of son any father would be proud of.") Lacking his father's height (he was five-foot-four), Edsel made up for it with acuity and a smile that illuminated a room. He was "handsome enough to charm the dogs off a meat wagon," one young woman said of him.

Unlike Henry, a teetotaler who was uncomfortable in social situations, Edsel enjoyed his nights as much as his days. When the family visited Europe in 1912, the eighteen-year-old wrote in his diary: "Bad headache — too much Paris." While Henry wouldn't be seen at the Pontchartrain bar, Edsel introduced Detroit to the rumba in this noisy watering hole. (His father called this kind of nightlife "sex dancing.") Edsel was a regular at Detroit Tigers games, and he developed a taste for yacht racing. He smoked his cigarettes like he played his golf: left-handed and with panache.

On the occasion of his twenty-first birthday, Henry gave Edsel a gift. Together they went to the bank.

"Bill, I have a million dollars in gold here," Henry said to the teller. "This is Edsel's twenty-first birthday, and I want him to have it."

Edsel was visibly shaken. Afterward, he returned to his desk, exemplifying the dutifulness that would define him in later years. An adored child of wealth and intelligence, Edsel was raised to be the man any young American would want to be, in an era that promised a bright future for most. But as was engraved on his cuff links, OMNIUM RERUM VICISSITUDO.

All things change.

On the evening of November 1, 1916, a who's who of the new automotive aristocracy filed into a mansion on Boston Boulevard in Detroit to attend the wedding ceremony of Edsel Ford. Henry's friends Thomas Edison, Harvey Firestone of the Firestone Tire Company, and the Dodge brothers took their places. Edsel appeared in a black tuxedo with his bride, Eleanor Lowthian Clay, the niece of the founder of Detroit's most prominent department store chain, Hudson's. Edsel was twenty-two years old, his bride just nineteen. The wedding was held at the bride's family manse. Guests were surprised by the event's lack of pomposity ("I don't think I saw $1,000 worth of jewels among the crowd," one man present remembered) and its sheer speed. The ceremony was over in minutes.

"I don't envy you one bit but that boy of yours," John Dodge told Henry Ford.

"Yes, I have a fine son to carry on," Henry said. "If he keeps on as he is now, the company will be in good hands some day."

The newlyweds honeymooned in Hawaii. ("You wouldn't know us, we are so healthy," Edsel wrote his parents. "I am getting very good on the surfboard.") When he returned, Edsel had a surprise for his parents. Henry and Clara Ford had built a bucolic mansion called Fair Lane in Dearborn, which bordered the Detroit city line. Their new home was a shrine to their son. Edsel had a suite of rooms, a $30,000 pipe organ, his own bowling alley, and an indoor swimming pool lined with heated benches. The mansion was a young man's paradise, designed to keep Edsel by his father's side. But Edsel chose not to live at Fair Lane, or even on the property next door. He moved his bride into the city. Together they began to hatch a plan to build a home an hour's drive away in Grosse Pointe — the fashionable center of a new wealthy social set on Lake St. Clair, the Motor City's answer to Gatsby's West Egg.

Edsel and Eleanor eventually built their new home on Gaukler Pointe, a sprawling piece of property along the rocky lake front. The home was designed to resemble a cottage in the Cotswolds, a rural section of southwestern England. Pieces of the structure were imported from Europe, some dating back centuries. Edsel built a dock for his yachts. On September 4, 1917, Edsel and Eleanor gave birth to a boy they christened Henry Ford II — the name of obvious symbolism.

In Detroit, gnarled hands sticking out of suit jacket sleeves signified honor and success, but Edsel fit more into the sophisticated world of New York and Washington, where Victorian standards of wealth and aristocracy were woven into the fabric of a new modernist sensibility. He befriended Jews, poured money into charities, and educated himself in the arts and literature. At secluded Gaukler Pointe, protected from harm by his security staff and the tall stone walls that surrounded the property, he had built a sanctuary.

When he read the headlines of the coming war in Europe — the Great War, what would soon be called World War I — the violence seemed a world away. Nevertheless, each new headline — the assassination of the Archduke Ferdinand in 1914, the sinking of the *Lusitania* with so many Americans aboard a year later — was difficult to grasp as reality. As the war came closer to home, Edsel, like all Americans, read these news stories with quivering hands.

He did not know it at the time, but World War I was about to kick his life into the long, tragic spiral that would define him to the end.

One November morning in 1915, Henry Ford sat in the swaying belly of a Pullman car with his publicity chief, Louis Lochner.* They were headed for Washington to meet President Woodrow Wilson. Throughout the train, passengers turned worried eyes on their news-

---

* Lochner would later become a major figure in journalism, winning a Pulitzer Prize in 1939 for his reporting on Nazi Germany.

papers. Germany was dropping bombs on England from zeppelins. The British were using poison gas against the Germans. (One young German soldier named Adolf Hitler was temporarily blinded by gas weaponized by the British, forcing a long hospital stay.) Henry hoped to talk the President into participating in a peace crusade, to keep America out of the war. As the locomotive steamed southward, he worked over some maxims he hoped would grab headlines.

"Men sitting around a table, not men dying in a trench, will finally settle differences," he said over the sound of the railcar's clattering. He turned to Lochner. "Make a note of that. We'll give it to the boys in the papers when we get to New York."

At the White House, his legs crossed in a chair, Henry found the President amiable — but unwilling to commit to any peace crusade. The political situation was far too complex. So Henry delivered an ultimatum.

"Tomorrow at ten in New York," he told President Wilson, "representatives of every big newspaper will come to my apartment for a story. I have today chartered a steamship. I offer it to you to send delegates to Europe. If you feel you can't act, I will."

On December 4, 1915, at 2:00 PM, the *Oskar II* — Henry's "Peace Ship" — set sail out of New Jersey across the Atlantic. Aboard Henry had gathered an eclectic assemblage of activists. Before leaving, he unleashed a litany of peace aphorisms.

"War is murder."

"The word 'murderer' should be embroidered in red letters across the breast of every soldier."

"I will devote my life to fight this spirit of militarism."

The most news-making personage in the world even wrote to the pope and made the missive available to the papers.

Henry's Peace Ship proved an international embarrassment and failed to save a single life. After reaching Europe, he realized that his mission was misguided. He turned around and headed home. The press called him "God's fool" and "a clown." His *Oskar II* was "a loon ship."

Henry didn't bear the biggest brunt of the criticism, however. Edsel did.

When Woodrow Wilson asked Congress for a declaration of war on Germany on April 6, 1917, Edsel was twenty-three years old — draft age. Henry mobilized his lawyers to keep his son out of it. Edsel received his exemption on March 11, 1918, on the grounds that he was more valuable to the country at home building military equipment in Ford's factories. In Europe, he would stop one bullet. At home, he could contribute more. Still, he became the target of every saber-rattler in the nation.

"Young Ford should take his medicine just like the rest of the boys," declared *Detroit Saturday Night*. While young men stood "ready to pay with their lives for the honor and the interest of the American people," said former president Theodore Roosevelt (whose four sons all served, one losing his life), "the son of wealthy Mr. Ford sits at home in ignoble safety."

Edsel was stuck between his father's will and his own integrity. For the first time, he understood the isolation and impotence that came with his position.

"I want no stay-at-home appointment," he said. "I will accept none. I don't want to don a uniform with the assurance that I will be expected to do nothing but sit in a swivel chair. There is one job in this war I do not want and will not take, and that is the job of a rich man's son."

Everywhere Edsel went, he saw judgment in people's eyes. He could not escape the ignominy. Throughout the war, he helped build military boats, helmets, and Liberty aircraft engines. But the effort was not enough to erase the smear on his reputation. "All his life he will be singled out as a slacker and a coward," one reporter said of him.

Was Edsel a coward? Henry Ford's prodigal son? One of the most idolized young men in America suddenly had everything to prove.

4

Learning to Fly

More than electric lights, more than steam engines, more than telephones, more than automobiles, more even than the printing press, the airplane separated past from future. It had freed mankind from the earth and opened the skies.

— STEPHEN E. AMBROSE, *The Wild Blue*

AT 11:00 AM PARIS time on the eleventh day of the eleventh month of 1918, World War I ended with the Allies victorious. A little more than one month later, on New Year's Day in 1919, Detroit's prince was crowned.

Henry announced his retirement and named Edsel the president of Ford Motor Company, a job he would hold until the end of his life. Edsel's face appeared in newspapers all over the globe next to headlines quoting his salary at an amazing $150,000 a year. At twenty-five years old, he was the top man of the world's most influential corporation. His first move on the job was to give 28,000 employees a 20 percent raise, from $5 to $6 a day. He was now so famous that couples named their baby boys after him. In the 1920s, Edsel Fords were born in Georgia, in Alabama, in Michigan.

Quietly, behind the scenes, Edsel negotiated to buy out all the stockholders. It cost him $105 million. When Henry got the news, he shrugged and said, "Well, if Edsel has bought it, I can't help it." In private, he danced a jig around a room. The Fords owned their family empire outright.* At his height with Standard Oil, John D. Rockefeller owned no more than 27 percent. The Ford stock was split 55 percent to Henry, 42 percent to Edsel, and 3 percent to Clara.

Then, one chilly May morning in 1920, a crowd gathered at the Fords' new River Rouge factory. Years in construction, the almighty Rouge was complete, a city of brick buildings and thick stacks rising off the Rouge River's bank. Entering at Gate 4 on Miller Road, reporters and dignitaries stared wide-eyed at their surroundings—the inner sanctums of the world's largest factory. If Ford Motor Company was a family religion, this was its Vatican.

Once again, the Ford plant was envisioned to function with all the precision of a timepiece. Only it was part man, part machine. Picture a timepiece filled with laborers as well as self-propelled mechanical pieces. And then picture that timepiece as big as a metropolis, with 100 miles of interior railroad, 330 acres of windows, and an electric power plant big enough to power all the homes in Chicago. When it was fully operational, the River Rouge plant would churn out 4,000 Model Ts every day.

In a display of solidarity, the Ford clan appeared, and the crowds applauded them: Henry, his son Edsel, and Edsel's son, two-and-a-half-year-old Henry Ford II, who wore a beaver fur cap atop his chubby toddler face. Henry clutched his grandson in his arms as Edsel watched. Young Henry II was given a match, and with some help, he lit the coke in Blast Furnace A—igniting not just this industrial mecca but a new era. The crowds cheered, the photographers clicking away as the little boy stood "clapping his hands and shouting gleefully," as one person present remembered.

"The fun of playing with matches was almost too much for Henry II," reported the *Detroit News*.

Standing by watching his son perform his first rite of passage as a member of the Ford clan, Edsel beamed, the proud father playing the role that his own father had once played. All this would one

* Not that the investors didn't make out themselves. One investor who put in $2,500 in 1903 walked away with well over $29 million.

day belong to Henry II, whose destiny, like his father's, would be the Rouge.

The factory's sheer vastness struck fear in beholders. According to a *Vanity Fair* exposé, the Rouge

> could lay claim to being the most significant public monument in America, throwing its shadow across the land probably more widely and more intimately than the United States Senate, the Metropolitan Museum of Art, and the Statue of Liberty. In hyperbole and anathema, it has been compared, lyrically, reverently, vindictively, to the central ganglion of our nation, to an American altar of the God-Objective of Mass Production.

And the Ford family owned it all.

By 1927, Henry and Edsel's fortune together was estimated in the *New York Times* at $1.2 billion, putting them on the top of the list of the world's richest men. At Gaukler Pointe, Edsel's garage filled with exotic, one-of-a-kind automobiles and the walls of his house grew crowded with works by the European masters. Rare objects dated back before the birth of Christ. Edsel and Eleanor Ford's collection of art pieces, rare Chinese objects, rugs, and sculptures would soon become renowned, worth over $4 million (the equivalent of over $70 million today).

The Edsel Fords became the nucleus of a moneyed social set. Throughout Prohibition, they kept a well-stocked bar for their cocktail parties. Through friends, Edsel met Franklin Delano Roosevelt for the first time in the early 1920s. Roosevelt had recently come down with polio and lost the use of his legs. Unprompted, Edsel wrote a check for $25,000 for a polio charity. When the future New York governor and United States president saw the check, he said, "Well, I'm just flabbergasted!"

Henry bristled at the idea of his son as a society figure. He once declared that he would rather repair automobiles in a Detroit garage for sixty hours a week than socialize with the likes of Edsel's friends. "A Ford can take you anywhere," he famously said, "except into society." The difference of opinion foreshadowed the rift that was about to tear father and son apart.

But at the time, the two men presented a unified front to the world. They spent hours together every day conducting business. At night, their dialogue continued over a private phone line that connected Henry's Fair Lane home directly to Edsel's study at Gaukler Pointe.

"My father is a great man," Edsel told one reporter. To another, he said, "I have not worked out for myself anything in the nature of a business philosophy. I see no reason why I should for I cannot imagine a better one than my father has held."

Privately, like his father, Edsel felt the tug of ambition and a need for public accomplishments that would push his World War I embarrassment permanently into the shadows. The legacy of Ford Motor Company — Fordism and the Model T — belonged to Henry. So, at the age of twenty-eight, Edsel went in search of a legacy of his own. It was the Roaring Twenties, a time when science was king and anything felt possible.

When it came to the Fords, not even the sky was the limit.

Years earlier, when Edsel was fourteen years old, he had set out to build Detroit's first airplane, in a barn on Woodward Avenue. He was part of a small team that included a friend named Charles Van Auken, a sweeper who worked in his father's Highland Park factory, and two other employees of his father's. In the barn, Edsel and his friends unloaded their tools and parts and milled pieces of lumber. It was the adolescent's answer to his father's shed behind Bagley Avenue, where Henry built his first Quadricycle.

Like so many boys who had read of the Wright brothers' adventures — including the first controlled human flight, over the dunes of Kitty Hawk, North Carolina, in 1903 — Edsel dreamed the immortal dream: to harness power and take flight. But unlike so many boys who dreamed of airplanes, Edsel had the means to build one.

Barely a teenager, and just six years after the Wright brothers made their first flight, Edsel hurled himself into a wild adventure. At the time, only a few men had successfully accomplished controlled, machine-powered flight. The Brazilian inventor Alberto Santos-Dumont debuted a flying machine he called Oiseau de Proie (French for "bird of prey"). In the Parisian neighborhood of Bois de Boulogne, he flew 200 feet in 1906. Frenchman Louis Blériot, an inventor who wore a mustache like a set of wings, was active at the same time as the Wrights, pioneering a monoplane design. He made the first flight across the English Channel in the summer of 1909, moving the *London Daily Express* to declare that "Great Britain is no longer an island."

That same year, in Dearborn, Edsel and Van Auken modeled their flying machine after Blériot's. It had a single fabric wing, a wooden skeleton, and a tricycle landing gear, the parts machined at the Highland Park Ford factory. For power, they mounted a Model T engine, drilled full of holes to lighten the weight, in the plane's nose.

On the day of the maiden flight, Edsel and Van Auken towed the airplane to a field behind a Ford car. Van Auken agreed to pilot the thing (Edsel was forbidden by his father). As Edsel stood by holding his breath, Van Auken motored along the grass and lifted off, sailing six feet over the earth as the Model T engine buzzed like a gnat. A gust of wind caught the aircraft sideways and sent it crashing into a tree. Van Auken got out dazed and slightly injured, having banged his head.

"The thing did leave the ground," Edsel later recalled, "and probably it is just as well that it did not get too high, for it might have fallen and killed somebody."

When a local Detroiter named William Stout launched the Stout Metal Airplane Company some years later, Edsel saw opportunity. By this time, he was president of Ford Motor Company, the boss of tens of thousands of men. Stout, meanwhile, was a wildly coiffed inventor and former Packard engineer who built the first all-metal airplane in the United States, *Maiden Detroit* ("Made in Detroit"). Edsel invested $2,000 in the fledgling company and tried to convince his father to partner with him and build an airfield that would lure aviators from across America. What Detroit had been for motorcars, Edsel argued, it could be in the future for airplanes.

Henry was against it. Edsel swayed him on one condition: he would not pilot a plane himself. He would leave the flying to men who had less responsibility than the president of Ford Motor Company. Still an infant science, aviation was simply too dangerous. One example: of the first forty pilots to fly for the US Air Mail Service during those years, thirty-one died in crashes.

Once Henry gave the venture his blessing, Edsel became a partner in the Stout Metal Airplane Company. A series of unprecedented events unfolded, with Edsel leading the charge.

Edsel and his father cleared 240 acres and built the most modern airport in America, with a factory for Stout to build aircraft. "They were pioneering," said William Mayo, who became Ford's chief aviation engineer. "Nobody knew in those days just how long a runway should be." The Fords were the first in the country to lay a concrete landing strip, the first to build an airport hotel for out-of-town flyboys (the 108-room Dearborn Inn, which is still there), and the first private company to take on a US Air Mail Service contract. They were also the first to launch a commercial airline with regularly scheduled flights, to carry cargo. (Scheduled passenger flights did not exist.) Starting in 1925, pilots flew back and forth between Dearborn, Cleveland, and Chicago. Via the first scheduled flight, Edsel sent a letter to Ford's Chicago branch manager. "This letter is to wish you greetings by Air Mail. I am posting the letter in Detroit at 8:15 AM this morning, and it will be transported to Dearborn by motor and flown to Chicago on the first privately operated Air Mail Service flight for the United States Post Office Department."

When Henry and Edsel bought out Stout and built their own factory in 1925, they quickly became the top-producing airplane manufacturer in the country. Though there were many models, the Ford Tri-Motor — nicknamed the "Tin Goose," a revolutionary flying machine due to its three engines — became the bestseller. At roughly $50,000, it was purchased by Hollywood stars, the US military, and later by nascent airlines like TWA and Pan American. Its slogan: "The Highways of the Sky."

Edsel became aviation's greatest benefactor, and this more than his position at Ford thrust him into the public eye. Passenger flight, Edsel proclaimed, would soon become quotidian, just as other inventions had become part of daily life in recent years — the radio and its newscasts, the supermarket, and branded food products like Hostess cupcakes and Gerber baby food.

"There are sound economic reasons for believing that a great epoch of air transportation is being born," Edsel said. "A new commercial and industrial era is beginning with the airplane just as surely as new eras began with steamships, railroads, and automobiles. . . . It is truly the Age of the Air."

To prove that airplanes were not suicide machines, Edsel created the "Ford Reliability Tour," which became known as the "Edsel Ford Trophy." Pilots gathered at Ford Airport and flew to cities around the country, drumming up publicity with each stop. At its height, the Tour's finishing ceremonies lured 175,000 spectators to Ford Airport. Edsel was also the major backer behind the expedition of US Navy commander Richard Byrd, who in 1926 became the first pilot to fly over the North Pole — in a plane named *Josephine Ford,* after Edsel's young daughter. Three years later, Byrd flew over the South Pole and named a series of mountain ranges after Edsel (still called the Ford Ranges).

On August 11, 1927, a crowd of some 75,000 spectators gathered at Ford Airport, the cars parking in the fields around the main terminal, the hangars, and the Ford airplane factory. They could see the new Sperry Beacon searchlight on the southeast corner of the hangar, which aided pilots landing by night. The searchlight produced a higher-watt beam than 9 million Ford cars, the "nearest approach to intensity of that coming from the sun yet to be produced," Ford Motor Company claimed.

Henry and Edsel stood on the airfield at the center of it all, and along with the crowds they craned their necks with eyes glued to the skies. There in the blue ether, at roughly 2:00 PM, he appeared — a speck in the distance, accompanied by an engine's song. Charles Lindbergh's *Spirit of St. Louis* came into focus, circling above the concrete runway. Amid roars and whistles from the crowd, Lindbergh came in for a graceful landing. Henry and Edsel were there to meet him.

Just three months earlier, the pilot had captured the hearts and minds of the world by flying solo across the Atlantic, from Long Island to Paris. Entire generations looked up at the sky upon hearing of his feat, as if seeing it for the first time. "The news just saturated all the conversation, newspapers, the radios," remembered former South Dakota senator George McGovern, who was five years old at the time and would go on to become an accomplished pilot as well as a presidential candidate. "Pictures of Lindbergh with his helmet and goggles were on the front pages. I just thought he was the most glamorous creature on God's earth. I grew up thinking Lindbergh was our greatest American."

Now here was Lindbergh at Ford Airport, twenty-five years old, tall, slim, and blond. Together the Fords and "Lucky Lindy" — along with Lindbergh's mother, a Detroit schoolteacher — smiled for photographers. Afterward, Lindbergh took Henry for his first airplane ride. The *Spirit of St. Louis* lifted off with Henry crunched inside awkwardly (there was only one seat).

"This was the finest ride I ever had," Henry declared upon landing. "Why, it is just like going on a picnic."

When it was Edsel's turn, he climbed aboard. Cruising at over 100 miles per hour, the view from the sky was breathtaking. Detroit's smokestacks looked like cigarettes sticking out of brick buildings. Up here Edsel rode on the wings of his lofty dreams. Up here one felt like a superman. Lindbergh himself put it best: to feel "the godlike power man derives from his machines — the strength of a thousand horses at one's fingertips; the conquest of distance through mercurial speed; the immortal viewpoint of the higher air."

Upon landing, Edsel felt more certain of his destiny than ever. His future was taking flight. "I believe that 1928 will go down in history as the year in which American business accepted the airplane," he told reporters.

When American business accepted the airplane, Edsel believed that he would be the first man approached. If ever there was a way to live up to his father's legacy and expectations, the airplane was it.

5

Father vs. Son

For all their ambition for Edsel to make a name for himself, Father and Mother Ford never wanted their son to grow up. They wanted to keep him close to themselves and guide his every thought.

— CHARLIE SORENSEN

AT 1:00 PM ONE day in the early 1920s, Henry Ford appeared in the "Roundtable" lunchroom of the company's stately Engineering Laboratory, offering his limp handshake to his most trusted employees, about a dozen men total — the engineering brain trust of Ford Motor Company. It was tradition for these men to lunch together each day at exactly the same time, with waiters in ties serving them strange concoctions that Henry had his chef dream up using soybeans. Edsel took his seat to Henry's right at the table, and Charlie Sorensen sat on Henry's left.

Business matters were off-limits at these lunches, but Edsel brought up business anyway. There were problems with the Model T's brakes, which paled in comparison to the competition's. Customers were angry, and government men in Washington were calling, saying the car was unsafe. There were complaints from abroad too.

"Father," Edsel said, "I believe the time has arrived for us to give serious consideration to a hydraulic brake system."

The men at the table leaned in, awaiting Henry's response.

"Edsel, you shut up!" Henry barked. He stood and left the room, leaving his son red-faced and humiliated.

For months Edsel had been having trouble communicating with his father. Something was coming between them. Edsel was now a man with four kids of his own, and he was attempting to establish himself as a trailblazing corporate officer. When he tried to bring in a new breed of college-educated executives and a corporate flow chart, his father would not allow it.

"Mr. Ford didn't go along with that line of thinking," recalled Henry's secretary, Ernest Liebold. "He often said that if he wanted a job done right he would always pick the man who didn't know anything about it."

When Edsel started on a new building to house a team of trained accountants, his father came looking for him.

"What's going on here?" he asked, pointing at the construction site.

Henry didn't believe in accountancy. When he learned of Edsel's plans, he ordered the construction stopped and had the site fenced off. He had all the accountants fired, and all their desks and chairs removed from their offices on the fourth floor of the old Administration building. Then he went looking for his son.

"Edsel," Henry said. "If you really need more room you'll find plenty of it on the fourth floor."

As company president, Edsel was ahead of his time. He sought to modernize everything he saw — from styling to corporate structure to engineering. "The next big development will be rear-engine designs, with all driving mechanism behind," he told one reporter, predicting an engineering movement that would revolutionize the auto racing world thirty years later.

Most importantly, Edsel continued to build on his father's work to expand and strengthen the company's foundation abroad, turning Ford Motor Company into one of the first modern international corporations, along with American powerhouses like Standard Oil, Eastman Kodak, and Detroit rival General Motors. With his son Henry II standing beside him, Edsel broke ground with a gold shovel on Dagenham, "the Detroit of Europe" — the largest factory on the continent when it opened its doors in 1931, located on the Thames River twelve miles outside London. In Germany he moved operations from a small plant in Berlin to a full-fledged factory in Cologne that same year. In France the company added a new assembly plant in Asnières to its homebase in Bordeaux, with plans for further expansion at a site in Poissy.

Always impeccably dressed, Edsel presented a levelheaded and eloquent persona. "He attained a kind of greatness that Henry was utterly incapable of understanding," one biographer wrote of Edsel. He had "a statesmanlike quality that reached far beyond the industrial confines of his day."

His father, meanwhile, had changed. Now in his early sixties, Henry no longer worked with his hands. When his curious fingers became idle, a darkness emerged. No one defined this transformation better than a Detroit minister named Samuel Marquis, whom Henry hired to "put Jesus Christ in my factory," and who later fled the company out of fear of what the Rouge was becoming.

"There rages in him," the Reverend said of Henry, "an endless conflict between ideals, emotions and impulses as unlike as day and night — a conflict that at times makes one feel that two personalities are striving within him for mastery." The one Henry was "a dreamer, an idealist." When the darkness emerged, "the affable, gentle manner has disappeared. There is a light in the eye that reveals a fire burning within altogether unlike that which burned there yesterday."

In 1919, Henry bought a newspaper — the *Dearborn Independent*. In these pages, to Edsel's horror, his father's alter ego made its debut on an international stage. On May 22, 1920, an article appeared, taking up the entire front page, headlined "The International Jew: The World's Foremost Problem." For the next ninety-one issues, the *Dearborn Independent* published anti-Semitic tirades, with headlines like "Jewish Jazz — Moron Music — Becomes Our National Music" and "Does Jewish Power Control the World Press?" The articles ran without a byline, but because the newspaper branded itself "The Ford International Weekly," readers assumed that Henry was responsible.

In truth, Henry hadn't the formal education to write any article, nor the sophistication to understand the power of the pen. The stories were written by former *Detroit News* scribe William Cameron and Henry's secretary Liebold, a portly anti-Semite who later said that the impetus came from "Mr. Ford's wishes in carrying out the idea of revealing to the public the facts pertaining to Jewish activities."

For Henry, anti-Semitism was a part of everyday life. It was all around him, even in the schoolbooks kids read. By giving a voice to the sentiment, he must have believed that his newspaper was expressing what people around him felt but couldn't voice themselves. He used his car dealerships to distribute the *Independent,* pushing them to sell quotas of subscriptions.

Edsel begged his father to stop. He had close Jewish friends. Besides, he argued, the articles were costing the company customers. Both he and his mother Clara removed their names from the paper's masthead.

In 1922, the articles were anthologized in a book called *The International Jew: The World's Foremost Problem.* Readers consumed the book assuming that the sentiments inside were Henry's own. An enthusiastic audience embraced the volume in Germany. One avid reader was an up-and-coming thirty-three-year-old militant named Adolf Hitler, who kept a dog-eared copy of *Der Internationale Jude* in his office, as well as a portrait of Henry Ford. When rumors surfaced in the United States of a Ford run for president before the 1924 election, Hitler offered his support.

"I wish I could send some of my shock troops to Chicago and other big American cities to help in the elections," he told a *Chicago Tribune* reporter. "We look to Heinrich Ford as the leader of the growing Fascist movement in America. . . . We have just had his anti-Jewish articles translated and published. The book is being circulated in millions throughout Germany."*

Henry ended the rants in January 1922. Following a devastating

---

* When Hitler published *Mein Kampf* in 1925–1926, Henry Ford was the only American mentioned: "It is Jews who govern the stock exchange forces of the American Union. Every year makes them more and more controlling masters of the producers in a nation of one hundred and twenty millions; only a single great man, Ford, to their fury, still maintains full independence" (Neil Baldwin, *Henry Ford and the Jews,* pp. 180–81).

lawsuit, and under extreme pressure from friends (including the *New York Times* columnist Arthur Brisbane, who certainly did understand the power of the pen), Henry relented and stopped the articles. "No one can charge that I am an enemy of the Jewish people," he said. "I employ thousands of them." Soon after, he released an apology that ran on full pages in newspapers across the country. Meanwhile, sales of the book attributed to him boomed in Germany. Henry's malice was metastasizing out of control.

By the time Edsel turned thirty years old, the Detroit he had known as a child had disappeared. When he walked the streets, he recalled as a boy seeing nothing but horses and carriages and "the bicycle craze," people of all ages pedaling on the new two-wheeled fad. Now the place teemed with motorcar traffic and swelling crowds, with engines throbbing and horns honking. Detroit was America's thirteenth-largest city when Edsel was born; now it was the fourth-largest (behind New York, Chicago, and Philadelphia). New factories sprawled across city blocks: Chrysler's Lynch Road plant, the Fisher Body factory, the Cadillac plant. The stacks cast their shadows across the city's bourgeois emblems of prosperity: the Cadillac Theater, Hudson's flagship department store (owned by Edsel's in-laws), the Detroit Institute of the Arts (of which Edsel was president).

Nothing struck fear in Edsel's heart, however, like the sight of General Motors' majestic new downtown headquarters, a towering structure designed by Albert Kahn. For the first time — and the timing could not have been worse — the Ford family was facing serious competition from across town.

Founded in 1908, General Motors had by the 1920s developed a tiered lineup of brands — rising from the Chevrolet through the Oakland, Oldsmobile, Buick, and luxury Cadillac, not to mention GMC trucks and the Pontiac, introduced in 1926. (The Fords made Ford, Lincoln, and later Mercury cars.) It was the Chevrolet in particular that America lusted for in increasing numbers.

Thus was inaugurated the great corporate rivalry of the twentieth century, a capitalist slug match for the heavyweight title of America's car brand. Banner headlines called out the biggest business story in American history: "Ford-Chevrolet War Looms," "Ford-Chevrolet Battle for Supremacy."

GM's chairman, Alfred Sloan, was reinventing his corporation, just as Edsel was trying to do, only in Sloan's case there was no one in his way. Sloan saw in the new American customer the whim of desire. With a new styling chief named Harley Earl, Sloan came up with "Dynamic Obsolescence" — an annual model change coupled with heavy advertising campaigns for cars that would always be "completely new" and "priced so low." It was a strategy to keep customers coming back for more "Hollywood styling." Sloan also launched a banking unit (GMAC) that allowed customers to buy cars on credit — a stroke of genius.

In 1924, two out of every three automobiles sold in America were Model Ts. Two years later, Chevrolet was outselling Ford two to one, knocking the Ford family into second place for the first time in twenty years. As president of Ford Motor Company, Edsel saw his family empire spiraling on his watch.

Ultimately, the Model T became the rope that separated father and son in an awkward tug-of-war over the future. Ford needed an all-new model, Edsel argued. But Henry refused. He held on to his obsolete Model T, dropping the price so low that it cost less per pound than a wheelbarrow.

Edsel orchestrated an executive group in an attempt to gain influence, headed by his most trusted confidant and best friend, Ernest Kanzler, who was married to his wife's sister. The two spent hours together huddled in the private study adjoining Edsel's office, smoking cigarettes. (Henry didn't approve of smoking.)

"I have responsibility but no power," Edsel told Kanzler. "I can't even face people. The whole thing is so silly and unfair."

"Why doesn't Mr. Ford take his goddamn fiddle and go somewhere and play?" Kanzler came back. "And let us run the plant?"

Edsel could no longer communicate with his father. So Kanzler penned a daring six-page memo to Henry on the need for a new model. It was dated January 26, 1926. The pair heard nothing. Days later, Edsel set sail for a vacation in Europe.

"Well," Henry told one of his men, "by this time I think Edsel is several miles out to ocean, so I think tomorrow we can get rid of Kanzler."

While abroad with his family, Edsel learned by telegram that Kanzler — his best friend — had been fired from Ford Motor Company.

He was devastated.

To escape the pressure, Edsel receded from the public eye. He asked public relations men that his name not appear in the press, nor his picture. "Please be advised," he wrote Sorensen, "that my personal photograph is to be withheld from distribution or publication for any purpose." When asked about his father publicly, Edsel said: "It's his business. He built it from nothing. He has a right to run it as he pleases."

Edsel avoided his father at work. Henry, in turn, paid Edsel's staff to spy on him at home. At one point, Henry let himself into Gaukler Pointe and smashed all the liquor bottles.

"The next time you see Edsel," Henry told his secretary Liebold, "tell him you don't approve of the people he goes around with."

"That's going a bit far," Liebold came back. "I think Edsel would consider it an affront for me to make a suggestion of that kind."

"Well, you tell him. That's what I want him to know."

The tug-of-war over the Model T came to a head in 1926. Edsel was carefully convincing his father to release a new model (the Model A of 1928, which would become one of the most iconic automobiles of all time). One day after an argument over modernizing the design, Henry stormed off. He went to a secretary's office and demanded to see Sorensen, telling him to order Edsel to leave the premises. He wanted Edsel to take a trip to California.

"Make it a long stay," Henry said to Sorensen, "and tell him I will send him his paycheck out there. I'll send for him when I want to see him again."

Edsel refused to go. And then, just when the situation seemed like it had hit bottom, it got considerably worse.

Henry Ford had hired a new employee who was to become a kind of nemesis to Edsel. His name was Harry Bennett, though over the next three decades he would be called other things — Ford's super-policeman, Henry's pistol-packing errand boy, the "Company

Rasputin," a gangster, a Nazi, or simply "the Little Man in Henry's Basement." His rise in the 1920s would change the trajectory of Detroit forever.

"You know, gentlemen," Henry said to a gathering of reporters, "in an organization as big as ours we must have an occasional son of a bitch. Naturally, we are so big we must have the very best in certain positions that we can get."

6

The Ford Terror

During the thirty years I worked for Henry Ford, I became his most intimate companion, closer to him even than his only son.

— HARRY BENNETT

HENRY FORD WAS RELAXING in a New York hotel room one day when he met a man named Harry Bennett. He was a little figure — five-foot-seven, 145 pounds, with hard blue eyes, receding brown hair, and a bulldog jaw. The *New York Times* columnist Arthur Brisbane introduced the two. Bennett was from Ann Arbor, Michigan, not far from where Henry lived. The twenty-four-year-old was just out of the navy, where he had served as a deep-sea diver and had boxed under the name "Sailor Reese."

Henry took a liking to Bennett. The little man had sly eyes that were calculating and fearless and a picaresque past that made him sound like a character out of a gritty detective novel. Every scar on his face had a story. Harry Bennett had learned to brawl as a kid from his father. In fact, his father had been killed in a barroom fight.

"I could use a man like you at the Rouge," Henry said. "Can you shoot?"

"Sure I can," said Bennett.

The men at the Rouge were "a pretty tough lot," Henry said. "I haven't got any policemen out there."

Soon after, Henry hurled Bennett into the iron jungle. "There may be a lot of people over there who want to fire you," he told Bennett, "but don't pay any attention to them. I'm the only one who can fire you. Remember, you're working for me."

Born in 1892, Bennett was a year older than Edsel. In his basement office in the Rouge, he kept a small desk, a fireplace, and a couch. He hung a picture of his daughter on the wall. Other than that, the office was spare. It had two doors, one in front of him controlled by a button under his desk, and another secret door behind him so that Henry could come and go without being noticed. Bennett hung a target in his office for .32 caliber target pistols. He and his boss Henry sat for hours firing away. According to Bennett, "Mr. Ford was a dead shot."

Each morning Bennett dressed in a suit, his trademark bow tie (a hanging tie could be grabbed and used in a fight), a fedora, and a holster in which he packed a handgun at all times. He picked up Henry at his Fair Lane estate and took him to work. Whatever Henry needed done, Bennett was there for the doing. The fact that he couldn't change the oil of an automobile stirred confusion among the ranks. When asked what his job was, Bennett answered, "I am Mr. Ford's personal man." And then: "If Mr. Ford told me to blacken out the sun tomorrow, I might have trouble fixing it. But you'd see a hundred thousand sons-of-bitches coming through the Rouge gates in the morning, all wearing dark glasses."

Henry paid Bennett "peanuts for a salary," according to the ex-navy man. But he had access to a safe full of cash for special expenses. He moved into a winged Gothic home owned by Henry on the Huron River in nearby Ypsilanti, where he threw wild parties and showed pornographic films with titles like *The Casting Director* and *A Stiff Game*. He called his home "The Castle."

In the 1920s, Bennett began to amass a private security force called the Service Department — a group of ex-boxers and ballplayers, cons, bad cops kicked off the force, and characters from Detroit's La Cosa Nostra, which during Prohibition ran a thriving booze trade, smuggling liquor over the Detroit River from Canada. Service Department men were noticeable for their size, rough language, and cauliflower ears, and for the fact that they hung around without doing any work.

"They're a lot of tough bastards," Bennett described his burgeoning Gestapo, "but every one of them is a goddamn gentleman."

By the end of the 1920s, Bennett had become Henry Ford's closest confidant. When asked by reporters one day who the greatest man in the world was, Henry smiled and pointed at the bow-tied brute. With Henry's power behind him, Bennett's star skyrocketed. Suddenly, if a reporter wanted to talk to someone at Ford Motor Company, he had to talk to Harry Bennett first. Nothing got done without Bennett's approval.

"You couldn't get a message to anybody without him seeing," Ford engineer Laurence Sheldrick said of Bennett. "One could not hire, fire, or transfer a man. I could not send a man on a trip. I could not make a long-distance telephone call. I could not send a telegram if he did not wish me to do so. Regardless of where you were, he knew it. He had a spy system that was that thorough."

Edsel regarded Bennett as a curiosity at first. He saw plenty of Harry and his "Service Men," as his father put Bennett in charge of all security detail. For Edsel, kidnapping threats were routine, for himself and his four kids. "I can replace factories, but not grandchildren," Henry said. Edsel had his own bodyguards. Curiously, however, he began to notice that he was being followed. When he played golf, he saw men in the woods in suits and fedoras, watching him. When his eldest son Henry II drove his Lincoln Zephyr (he was at Yale now), he saw cars trailing him in his rearview.

The more Edsel learned about Harry Bennett, the more he realized the kind of things of which the Little Man in Henry's Basement was capable. Once, when a hoodlum threatened Henry II, Bennett said he would handle it. "Later on," remembered Edsel's youngest, William, "the guy was found floating face down in the river."

An astute political creature, Edsel began to see Bennett as a rival for his father's affections. Edsel was an only child, but suddenly there were two sons in the Ford empire.

The stock market crash of 1929 fomented chaos in Detroit. No city was hit as hard with such immediacy in the first years of the Great Depression. From Black Tuesday on, America stopped buying cars. For three years, economists in Washington struggled for control over the monetary system. But in the end, Detroit's banks failed first, sending the ailing economy off a cliff in 1933.

In February, spurred by the insolvency of Detroit's banks, Michigan governor William Comstock declared a bank holiday, closing the doors to customers desperate to pull out their cash. Indiana's banks followed on February 23, Maryland's on the 25th, Arkansas's on the 27th, and Ohio's on the 28th. Banks in Alabama, Arizona, California, Kentucky, Louisiana, Mississippi, Nevada, and Oregon all locked their doors within the next week.

By this time, the auto industry had laid off more than half its workers. Detroit parking lots turned into shantytowns. Any business open all night became a homeless shelter. The jobless rate hit 40 percent by the time the banks closed; 125,000 Detroit families had no financial relief whatsoever.

When reporters sought Henry out at Ford offices, they found that his dark alter ego had taken complete control. Henry called the Depression "a good thing, generally."

"Let them fail," Henry said on one occasion. "Let everybody fail! I made my fortune when I had nothing to start with, by myself and my own ideas. Let other people do the same."

The *New York Times* sent Anne O'Hare McCormick, one of the first powerful female journalists, to interview Henry. In a glass-walled office, he fidgeted for two hours. "Henry Ford is the only American name more potent internationally than that of a movie star," she wrote. "To the world at large, his is the image in which we live and move.

"Something has happened to Ford," she concluded, "and perhaps through him to the America which he represents."

One reporter called Henry "the Mussolini of Detroit."

Henry saved his most sour vitriol for the new president, Franklin Roosevelt. In a fury of activity during Roosevelt's first one hundred days in the White House, he introduced his National Industrial Recovery Act, which dictated rules for businesses to function in a paralyzed economy. Henry went on the attack. He told reporters that Roosevelt was a leader "whose particular genius is to try to run other people's businesses." The government, Henry said, "has not any too rosy a record running itself so far."

When the President invited Henry to the White House in an attempt to mend fences, Henry refused to meet him.

"If Henry Ford would quit being a damn fool about this matter and call me on the telephone," Roosevelt told a friend during his first term, "I would be glad to talk to him."

Henry finally agreed to meet Roosevelt on April 27, 1938. The meeting made the cover of *Newsweek*. Walking out of the White House afterward, Henry said, "Well, he took up the first five minutes telling me about his ancestry." Henry had no idea why, "unless Roosevelt wanted to prove he had no Jewish blood."

Edsel faced the bank crisis with optimism: not long after Black Tuesday, he gave everyone a raise. "Ford Motor Company employees of every grade began working under an increase wage scale Monday," he announced, his statement making the front page of the *New York Times*.

But as the nation sank deeper into despair, Edsel fell into its grip. He was financially leveraged and had to ask his father for help bailing out a Detroit bank in which he was heavily invested.

Even worse, his dreams of a future as an aviation pioneer crashed to the ground, literally. The Fords had allowed the US military to experiment with a Ford Tri-Motor to see if the airplane could carry the weight of bombs. While in flight, one of the plane's wings sheared off, and the fuselage became a missile, exploding on impact and killing its two pilots. Soon after, Edsel was in the Engineering Laboratory working over a new airplane design when his father entered the room. He showed the new plane to Henry.

"That's no good," Henry said. "No, don't do that."

When Edsel watched his father walk out of the room that day, he saw his defining ambitions vanish. Henry was sickened by the death of the pilots, by the idea of Ford airplanes being used for military purposes, and perhaps by the sales charts too. The peak year for the aviation venture was 1929, when Ford sold ninety-four airplanes. By 1932, that number shrank to four. Henry ended the company's aviation venture. He turned Ford Airport into a motorcar test track.

"Edsel Ford is more depressed than I've ever seen him," a Ford friend wrote in his diary in 1933.

Harry Bennett, however, found opportunity in the Depression. As head of personnel, Bennett ruled the Rouge. People were desperate for work. If a man wanted a job — well, then, maybe he'd have to do somebody a favor. Maybe he'd have to vote a certain way in an election. Maybe he would have to wax one of Harry Bennett's yachts, if he didn't want to get his teeth knocked out. By 1937, Bennett had succeeded in building the Service Department into what H. L. Mencken's *American Mercury* magazine called "the most powerful private police force in the world."

"There are about eight hundred underworld characters in the Ford Service Department," labor leader Benjamin Stolberg said. "They are the Storm Troops. They make no pretense of working, but are merely 'keeping order' in the plant community through terror."

Among the Service Men employed by Bennett: Norman Selby, an ex-pugilist who fought as "Kid McCoy," married ten times, paroled to Bennett after serving twenty years for murdering his sweetheart. Joseph "Legs" Laman, admitted serial kidnapper, nicknamed for his ability to evade the law on foot. Joe Adonis, a mobster called by the *New York Post* "a gang punk" and "dope king." Sicilian mob boss Chester LaMare, the "Al Capone of Detroit," who controlled Detroit's waterfront during Prohibition. Former journeyman pugilist Elmer "One Round" Hogan, Sicilian gangster Joe Tocco, Jack Dempsey's former manager Leonard Saks. . . .

Under constant intimidation by Bennett's Service Men — the "Ford Terror" — workers at the Rouge suffered nervous breakdowns and an anxiety-induced ailment known as "the Ford stomach." "I think it was just fear that caused this tension in the company," recalled engineer Roscoe Smith. "A lot of people, when [Bennett's men] came around and started taking them apart, just couldn't take it. They couldn't stand the pressure."

Meanwhile, the speed of the assembly line increased.

"*Go like hell,*" was the call of the foremen. "*If you're gonna get that raise, you gotta increase production.*"

Once the best place to work in the country, Ford was becoming the worst. "Henry had a way of getting his work done through fear," said Jack Davis, a longtime Ford sales executive. "The loyalty you had, you had because of Edsel. You hoped and prayed for the day when Edsel could be in charge."

As Edsel lost control of the company, he found solace in his own role as a father. There were football games at Gaukler Pointe and sailing trips on the lake. Though he indulged his four kids and shielded them from the Ford Terror, his oldest, Henry II, saw the worry lines deepen into his father's face. The split between Henry and Edsel was, in the words of one of Henry II's schoolmates, "the dirty little secret of the Ford family."

Edsel knew that Henry II was next in line. The young man would soon be the center of this drama. Edsel took an active role in grooming Henry II, in his education at Yale and his future at the Rouge. He made sure that Henry II had a relationship with his grandfather.

Then, one day, Edsel was on a train from Maine to Detroit when he was overcome by a stabbing pain in his gut. He had to be removed from the train and taken to a hospital. The next day he told reporters that he was "all right," that the ailment was "not serious." But it was serious. The malignancy Edsel would battle for the rest of his days had struck for the first time. Locked in a power struggle with Bennett and his father, he began to suffer vomiting episodes at work, sometimes retreating to the private suite connected to his office, where his secretary brought him glasses of milk and crackers.

Clara Ford asked Sorensen to come to Fair Lane and explain what was happening to her son. What was happening between Henry and Edsel?

"Who is this man Bennett," she asked Sorensen, "who has so much control over my husband and is ruining my son's health?"

Sorensen was one of the hardest men in Detroit. He walked away in tears.

The empire had split into rivaling factions: Henry and Bennett on one side, Edsel on the other. Cast Iron Charlie Sorensen—who ran the production day to day—lived in the gray area between. The two factions rivaled like tectonic plates in a fault line. It was clear that something drastic was about to occur. And then one day it did.

On the morning of May 26, 1937, a union leader named Walter Reuther organized a gathering outside the Rouge's main entrance, Gate 4, to hand out United Auto Workers union literature—mostly quotes pulled out of Roosevelt's Wagner Act, which dictated by federal law for the first time that labor could organize. The Wagner Act changed the playing field in Detroit like nowhere else, putting unprecedented amounts of power in the hands of the workingman.

It was a typical spring morning in southern Michigan, warm and humid, with a drab, acid-stained sky. As more union men gathered, reporters and photographers showed up, as well as clergymen. Union activity was the source of mounting tension in the Motor City, but nowhere was that tension as fraught with danger as it was at the Rouge. Ever since Roosevelt had signed the Wagner Act in 1935, Harry Bennett's Service Department thugs had mercilessly harassed anyone who dared to voice union sympathy. Reuther had worked in the Rouge — he had the scars to prove it — and he was the union's loudest voice in the Motor City. On this day, as he handed out union literature, he knew that the possibility for violence was high.

Earlier that morning, a union man named Ed Hall had gotten a call from one of Bennett's top Service Men, former Detroit police commissioner John Gillespie. "I don't want you to go out there today," Gillespie warned. "Something is going to happen — it's going to be extremely unpleasant."

"I have a license to carry two revolvers," the union man came back. "If any of your stooges out there lay a hand on me, I'll blow them so full of holes they won't make a good sieve."

The early hours outside the Rouge passed without incident. But then Reuther spotted the mob: a gang of forty Service Men walking his way, guys in fedoras and baggy suits. Among them, later identified in federal court documents, were Joe "Legs" Laman, ex-prizefighter Sam Taylor, mobster Angelo Caruso, and former "Black Sox" pitcher Eddie "Knuckles" Cicotte, banned from baseball for helping to throw the 1919 World Series.

"This is Ford property," one of the toughs shouted at Reuther. "Get the hell out of here."

Before Reuther could answer, the men attacked. The historic "Battle of the Overpass" had begun.

For months Henry Ford had stoked the fire in the Rouge. All of the Detroit companies had resisted union activity (General Motors, by this time the largest company in the world, paid $1 million to detective agencies in the mid-1930s to infiltrate the plants and rid them of labor leaders), but Henry had gone a step further. The advent of the union, a keystone of Roosevelt's New Deal, incited rage in Henry.

"Labor unions are the worst thing that ever struck the earth," he said in a statement in 1937. "Financiers are behind the unions and their object is to kill competition so as to reduce the income of the workers and eventually bring on war. We will never recognize the United Auto Workers union or any other union."

Both General Motors and Chrysler signed union contracts in 1937, leaving Ford as the holdout—union enemy number one. Henry wanted "a strong, aggressive man who can take care of himself in an argument" to handle the union problem. In a meeting one day with Edsel, Sorensen, and Harry Bennett, Henry Ford put his aide-de-camp Bennett in charge of labor relations, igniting a shouting match between father and son.

"If you want to fight the union," Edsel argued, "then let's do it in the proper manner, and let's fight it within the law. Let's hire a good constitutional lawyer to assist Mr. Bennett, and let me sit in on the negotiations to offer my advice."

Henry wanted none of it. Bennett stockpiled weapons and tear gas. As one Service Department goon said, "If it takes bloodshed, we'll shed blood right down to the last drop."

That morning in May 1937, as Reuther and his fellow unionizers passed out literature at the Rouge's Gate 4, Bennett unleashed his Service Department goons. "They picked up my feet and my shoulders and slammed me down on the concrete," Reuther later said. "And while I was on the ground, they kicked me again in the face, head and other parts of my body."

Shattered noses, guts stomped, groins kicked in. Priests came shouting in the name of the Lord. Reporters stood helpless, their knees weak at the sight of the beatings. "My head was like a piece of raw steak," union leader Richard Frankensteen later said. "I do not know how many times I was conscious or unconsciousness." Another union man, William Merriweather, had his back broken. "Oh my God, he looked as if he were dead," one witness later said in federal testimony. "Blood was coming out of his nose and mouth." Beaten senseless, Reuther was thrown down a flight of concrete stairs. "The end of my spine hit every one," he later recalled.

Service Men grabbed cameras from photographers, but one *Detroit News* shooter named James Kilpatrick made a sprint for it. "There is a cameraman," yelled one of Bennett's men. "Get that son of a bitch." Following a foot chase, the photographer made it to a police station and took refuge, the evidence safe in his hands.

The next day, Edsel flipped through the pages of his newspaper, his brown eyes glazing over at the stark pictures of the Battle of the Overpass. (The pictures were later published all over the nation; they would inspire the Pulitzer Prize committee to create a category for photography.) The Battle of the Overpass was more than a brawl to Edsel; it symbolized the failure of the promise of industrial America, the destruction of the utopian dream that was supposed to be his destiny.

Edsel was forty-three years old and struggling with his health. As president of his family empire, he had watched it shrink and stiffen, as if, like himself, it suffered from some kind of disease. It was the largest automaker in the world when Edsel was made president; now it was America's third-largest behind GM and Chrysler Corporation, with just 18.6 percent of the US market. Edsel had earned the respect of everyone in Detroit with the exception of his own father, who had chosen the affection of another "child." Even the union men respected Edsel Ford.

"His soul bled," said Reuther. "I felt sorry for him. I still do."

Edsel could quit, walk away, and live out his life with his wife and his kids, whom he adored, in a state of quiet repose. He could devote his life freely to his passions — racing his yacht, curating the collections at the Detroit Institute of the Arts, crafting the minds of his children. Or he could continue down this lonely road, fighting for his empire.

Ford Motor Company was the family religion. It was impossible to separate the family from the empire, the flesh of the men from the metal of the machine that bore their name. Besides, Edsel had a growing son, Henry II, now nineteen years old. Henry II's birthright was this empire. If Edsel absconded, his firstborn's future would be lost, whatever that future might be.

"It was like a family tragedy," one person close to the Fords said. "At this point Edsel had the tragic recognition — that there was no way out of his dilemma except by death, his father's or his own."

7

Danger in Nazi Germany

The German Air Force is a guarantor of German peace. But I openly confess that terrible will be the result when the command for an attack comes. Then, we swear to the German people, we shall become the terror of our enemy. Nothing shall halt us from unreserved recklessness. . . . In defiance of all foes, this air force is invincible.

— HERMANN GOERING, *Hitler's second in command and head of the Luftwaffe, March 1, 1938*

ON A SEPTEMBER DAY in 1938, a fifty-nine-year-old Detroit auto man named William Knudsen stood on the deck of the German ocean liner *Bremen,* watching the New York skyline disappear into the horizon. Knudsen was a giant, his frame rising well over six feet with heavy bulk stretching out of a finely stitched suit. Though his silver hair and mustache were finely groomed, he had the gnarled hands of a boilermaker.

Knudsen was the president of the world's largest corporation, Detroit-based General Motors, which controlled an amazing 10 percent of the entire productive capacity of the United States, the most industrialized nation on earth. His $300,000-plus salary trumped that of any American who worked outside of Hollywood. As the *Bremen* steamed for Europe, two women recognized the towering auto man.

"Is there going to be war, Mr. Knudsen?"

"No, ma'am."

"But the steward says there is going to be war."

"No, there's not going to be any war at all," Knudsen said, his Danish accent still noticeable nearly forty years after he had immigrated to the United States. The production man saw things practically. During the Great Depression, Knudsen figured, war was too expensive. "Nobody could afford it."

He was headed to Europe to check on GM's factories, which were in danger given the precarious political situation. GM owned Opel, the largest car brand in Germany. Much to Knudsen's surprise, given the lingering Depression in the United States, business at Opel was booming as never before. Under Hitler, Germany had by far the strongest economy in Europe, and sales of Opel cars were on the rise. Earlier in the 1930s, long before any threat of war, Opel had agreed to make trucks for the Nazi government, the contracts quite lucrative. By the time of Knudsen's 1938 journey to Germany, over a quarter of Opel's "Blitz" trucks were being sold directly to the Nazi army, the Blitz's biggest customer by far. Recently, however, Hitler's speeches and his political posturing had grown more ominous, sending shock waves of fear across the continent.

What did it all mean? Knudsen aimed to find out.

When the *Bremen* reached port in Britain, he received a message from US ambassador Joseph Kennedy instructing him to return to the States. Americans were being advised to flee the continent. Knudsen pushed on. In London he found the population "scared stiff."

"Airplanes! Airplanes! Airplanes!" Knudsen reported back to the United States. "That is all they think about, and bombs go with them." Gas masks were being handed out. Children were being evacuated from cities. "It was really bad," Knudsen later said. "They were just hysterical."

In Paris, Knudsen was awoken in the middle of the night by air raid drills. Sirens all over the city howled furiously. Citizens ran for their basements, and all electric switches were flipped off, leaving "the City of Lights" empty in the ink-black night.

When Knudsen finally reached Berlin, the city didn't resemble the one he remembered. He could recall arriving here in 1932 to find the streets filled with vagabonds. Six million German men had been out of work. The Depression hit Europe even harder than it did the States. Now the bums were gone. New roads, called autobahns, had been laid; they were wide enough to drive tanks down. All over Berlin, Knudsen saw anti-aircraft guns on the roofs of buildings. Signs on shop and restaurant windows warned Jews to keep out: JUDEN UNERWUENSCHT (JEWS NOT WELCOME). Everywhere Knudsen looked, people offered the Fuehrer's salute on command, barking "Heil Hitler!" like automatons.

When Knudsen checked into the Adlon Hotel in the city center, opposite the Brandenburg Gate, a local General Motors man named Winter showed up to meet him. Hermann Goering, Hitler's second in command, wished to meet with Knudsen the following day, Winter reported.

"Where is Goering?" Knudsen asked.

"At Karin Hall, his lodge."

Would Winter be coming along?

"No," Winter said. "You are to go alone."

Goering's reputation was monstrous. He was a man of insatiable appetites — for power, food, art, jewels. He was a World War I ace pilot who had squandered away years trying to get into the airplane business before riding Hitler's coattails into the limelight. Goering liked to wrap his nearly three-hundred-pound body in bizarre capes. He rouged his face. He often had conspicuously tiny black dots where the pupils of his eyes were supposed to be — the telltale sign of a morphine addict. Goering was not only the head of the German economy but a military reich marshal, commander in chief of the Luftwaffe (air force), and head of the Gestapo, the secret political police, an organization he had himself founded.

The following day, at 9:00 AM, a German military car pulled up in front of the Adlon Hotel. Inside was a driver and Ernst Udet, one of Goering's key Luftwaffe deputies, a pilot who owned the world speed record in an airplane. Knudsen climbed in, wearing a blue suit and derby hat. The car lurched into traffic and headed north to Goering's lodge.

• • •

When Knudsen arrived at Karin Hall, a gate opened onto a property of 105,000 acres. The driveway wove past stately columns of oaks and a fountain with a statue of a horse and a nude rider. Outside the mansion's front door, storm troopers in black uniforms clicked their heels as Knudsen walked by, lifting his derby hat uncomfortably.

Inside sculptures, paintings, and a collection of assorted weaponry crowded the walls. "It would be difficult to find an uglier building or [one] more intrinsically vulgar in its ostentatious display," as the American statesman Sumner Welles once described this property. Following a short wait, the famed reich marshal appeared, Nazi Germany's second-most-powerful figure, wearing a hunting coat with a dagger strapped around his thigh. A three-hour conference followed, with Goering's deputy Udet doing the translating. Goering began by asking if the political situation was causing General Motors problems in Germany.

"Not that I know of," Knudsen said.

"Well, you will not be permitted to take any money out of Germany."

Knudsen squirmed. GM had invested over $40 million in Opel operations. At any moment, Hitler could seize it all—and with what recourse?

After a long silence, Goering got to the point. General Motors was building an aircraft engine called Allison out of its factory in Indianapolis. What did Knudsen know about it?

Knudsen tried to hide his surprise. The engine was being developed for the US Army Air Corps—and it was top-secret. Twelve cylinders, liquid-cooled—the US government had high expectations for the Allison engine.

"I don't know much about it," Knudsen lied.

Goering smiled. "I do." His deputy Udet rolled out blueprints of an aircraft engine that bore a stunning resemblance to the Allison. Goering asked Knudsen if GM's Opel was capable of building such an engine in Germany.

Knudsen studied the blueprints. "Yes," he responded, "that can be made."

"We will get 1,250 horsepower out of it," said Udet.

Goering's smile widened. "We will build the plant," he said. "We will furnish all the money you need, in American dollars, to buy the machines and tools to make it. We will pay you a fee, besides."

Knudsen said, "That is a matter I would have to take up with the Board of Directors of General Motors."

Goering proceeded to brag about his Luftwaffe, displaying his renowned hubris. These great fleets of mechanical birds were the most powerful weapon in the history of the world, Goering said. Soon the German airplane factories would produce 35,000 planes per year. Germany, Goering said, was better equipped for war than any other nation. Ever.

The conference ended with a tour of Karin Hall. How, Knudsen wondered, with a published government salary of $12,000 a year, was Goering able to afford such luxury? And what of this air force? Was it all true?

Knudsen spent the rest of his time in Germany in distress. Before he left, Hitler and the leaders of Britain, France, and Italy signed the historic Munich Pact, allowing the Nazis to essentially take over a critical chunk of Czechoslovakia without a shot fired — anything to avoid war. It was a brilliant political victory for Hitler, and proof that amazing things could be accomplished through schoolyard bullying.

That Goering knows airplanes, Knudsen said to himself upon his departure from Nazi Germany. *So does Udet. I wonder how they got copies of the Allison engine. Goering knows something about machinery, too . . . knows more about people — the German people, anyway, the way he has those storm troopers clicking their heels. No, he doesn't want war — what the Hell! Ten years ago, he was nothing but a fellow trying to sell airplanes in Denmark.*

In the fall of 1937, the head of Ford Motor Company's German division, Dr. Heinrich Albert, arrived for a meeting in Dearborn on a politically dangerous mission. Dr. Albert had traveled a long way to convince Edsel Ford to agree to build trucks for the Nazi government in Germany. Charlie Sorensen welcomed the executive into the Administration Building.

Dr. Albert was a sixty-four-year-old German auto man with an acne-scarred face and a strange history. He had served as a German spy in the United States during World War I and had gotten himself tangled in a scandal when he accidentally left a briefcase full of top-secret German documents on a train in New York City. He later admitted that the loss of those documents was "as big a loss as the loss of the battle of the Marne." A domineering man of quick intelligence, he had moved on to a position of power in Germany, serving as minister of the national economy and then chairman of Ford-Werke AG in Cologne, where for many years he worked to protect the interests of the Ford family in Europe. The Cologne plant was the second-largest Ford manufacturing site outside of the United States, behind Dagenham in England. Along with Dr. Albert that day in Dearborn came an engineer named V. Y. Tallberg, the only American working at Ford's German factory.

According to a source that came forward later, the room at the hotel where Dr. Albert stayed when he arrived in the States was "rigged with microphones" by the FBI, and "Dr. Albert was shadowed from the moment he stepped on American soil to the moment he left" by J. Edgar Hoover's Washington-based Federal Bureau of Investigation.

In Sorensen's office (either Edsel was out of town or he thought it politically astute not to attend this meeting), Dr. Albert stated his case. He had already detailed his plan through correspondence, so the agenda moved quickly. The German government had designed a truck and had asked Ford-Werke AG to build a factory in the middle of the country, far from any foreign borders, to mass-produce it. Dr. Albert was adamant: the company had to sign this contract with Hitler's government.

"According to the official conception of the duties and obligations of the private industry," Dr. Albert said, "all German manufacturers are bound to execute such orders."

Sorensen turned to the American, Tallberg, who was chief engineer of the Ford plant in Cologne. "How do you feel about that?" he asked.

"Mr. Sorensen, I think that this thing is entirely out of our class," said Tallberg. "As far as the engine is concerned, we can't machine it. We haven't got the machinery for it. It would mean millions of dollars of investment to get the necessary machinery before doing this job."

Sorensen turned to Dr. Albert. "See what he said? He ought to know what he's talking about. You don't know what you're talking about."

Dr. Albert reiterated his case: The Ford family had invested heavily in their works in Germany—far and away the most thriving economy in Europe. And if Hitler wanted Ford to build trucks, Ford would build trucks—or else. The government would pay for the new machinery necessary to do the job. The contract would result in a great increase in profits. The consequences of angering the Nazi high command would be severe. As Tallberg later remembered: "[Dr. Albert] said that if we wanted to stay in business in Germany, we must do that for the German government."

"There's going to be a war over there," Tallberg said.

"You don't know what you're talking about," Sorensen retorted.

"Mr. Sorensen, you're misinformed. They've been stockpiling for years."

Dr. Albert left Dearborn without a commitment, but he continued to pressure Edsel and Sorensen. He assured them that the trucks would not be used for military purposes. "Government orders do not concern war material," he cabled from Germany a month later. "They will not be used for military purposes more than any other private car or truck requisitioned by the government in case of war. . . . Refusal would greatly antagonize."

Could Dr. Albert be trusted? Edsel viewed him as a longtime confidant, a man who had worked doggedly in his family's interest for years. Dr. Albert had always served as the one man above all others in Germany who could be relied upon to give advice when the stakes were high. But now? The rules had changed, though how was not yet apparent. Edsel did not have the benefit of retrospection, of understanding what such a deal could mean. If the trucks would not be used for war purposes, then what would be the downside? Hitler was clearly a dangerous man. But who knew, in 1938, that he would prove to be the most demonic figure of the twentieth century? No one at the time.

Dr. Albert was not in fact a member of the Nazi Party, but he and his Cologne cronies were desperate to please Hitler—just like everyone else in Germany. Dr. Albert's letters and cables poured into Dearborn throughout 1938, each more urgent than the last.

Edsel and Sorensen had a decision to make in which there was no right choice. They could either agree to a deal with Hitler's regime or risk losing their entire investment in Nazi Germany—in the middle of the Great Depression, when every penny and reichsmark counted.

Up to that point in 1938, Hitler had been good to the Fords. When he took power during the Depression, he chose Henry Ford as his inspiration.

"I am a great admirer of his," Hitler said of Ford. "I shall do my best to put his theories into practice in Germany."

In 1933, the year Hitler took power, he launched *Volksmotorisierung*—his rough translation of "Fordism," and a centerpiece of his economic policy. What Fordism had done for America in the earlier part of the century, it could do for Germany in 1933.

"The Government of the Reich will give all support to the development of the motor car industry," Hitler declared at the 1933 Berlin Auto Show. He promised a public works program that would build an "enormous network of automobile roads" and announced Germany's answer to the Model T: the Volkswagen ("people's car"). "If we can only succeed in winning the masses to adopt this means of transportation, the economic as well as the social profit will be undeniable."

German auto production sextupled in the first four years under Hitler (though he himself never learned to drive) and did in fact succeed in lifting the German economy out of the Depression. Massive unemployment gave way to a labor shortage. At Ford's fifty-two-acre factory on the Henry Fordstrasse in Cologne, the stacks spewed smoke over the Rhine River, to Dr. Albert's great pleasure. Since Ford's German company was founded in 1925 (the Cologne plant was completed in 1931), never had it seen such success. Sales of cars, trucks, and buses shot up 600 percent between 1932 and 1938. Since Hitler forbade any profits from leaving the country, all of those reichsmarks were reinvested in the factory. Ford's Cologne plant became one of the most technologically advanced in all of Europe—an industrial jewel, right under Hitler's nose.

That was when the Gestapo swarmed in. That was when the Nazi government began to bend Ford's German division to its will.

A number of American companies had large investments in Nazi Germany at the time, most notably General Motors with its Opel division, Standard Oil, F. W. Woolworth, and International Telephone & Telegraph (ITT). The Nazis took particular interest in the car factories, however, as they were making products that could be used for military purposes. At the time, Ford was the third-largest car company operating in Germany, behind Opel and Daimler-Benz. Ford's investment in Germany neared $9 million in Depression-era dollars (the equivalent of over $147 million today), in a time when the company's global operations were losing money.

In the months after Dr. Albert visited the United States, he began complaining to Edsel about political problems. Ford had not signed the contract to build trucks for the Nazi government, and the company had failed to meet other mandates in Germany. The consequences were immediately apparent. "No one who is in the public service or on the staff of a Party Department or any semi-official department" would be seen in a Ford, Dr. Albert wrote Dearborn. "No officer in the Army, Navy, or Air Force, no member of any undertaking financed by the Government or any of the industries with which Government orders are placed would dare to buy a Ford car."

To gain favor with the Nazi regime, Dr. Albert made it his mission to turn Ford of Germany into a truly German company. He had the name changed from Ford AG to Ford-Werke AG, to make it sound more Teutonic. He negotiated to increase the amount of stock held inside Germany, decreasing the American company's ownership to 55.75 percent. The remaining Americans and Britons, including Edsel Ford, were removed from Ford-Werke's board of directors.

Then Dr. Albert negotiated a complex bartering deal for the Nazi government, which eventually caught the eye of US Treasury Department investigators. He used the American Ford company in Dearborn to import critical raw materials, such as rubber and pig iron, in exchange for exporting cars and parts. According to declassified Treasury Department documents, "the Reich was able to extort" for its own use some 30 percent of the rubber and 20 percent of the pig iron from Ford-Werke. The Nazi government could then use that material as it wished during the key years of Hitler's "Four Year Plan"—

an economic campaign that, in retrospect, was a thinly veiled and highly coordinated plan to prepare for war.

Nazi officials began paying regular visits to Ford's Cologne plant. "We had not only one visit," said the American chief engineer, Tallberg. "But there was constantly Government personnel that more or less watched over us." Nazi salutes and swastika signage became de rigueur at the factory. Ford-Werke gave Hitler a gift of 35,000 reichsmarks on his fiftieth birthday. At the same time, Dr. Albert grew secretive about the operations in Germany.

After an extended visit home to the United States, Tallberg returned to Cologne to find that a new building had appeared beside the Ford factory. As an American, he was not allowed inside.

"What kind of building is that over there that's been put up since I left here?" Tallberg asked his German assistant.

"I'm sorry," came the answer, "I can't tell you that."

"My God," Tallberg said, "I've been in this organization for twelve years and now that building is going up and you can't tell me what it is. Is it a new factory?"

He later learned that German Ford executives had started a secret company using Ford machines to build material for the Nazis. "They were machining parts for the Junkers Airplane Works, or I suppose, any airplane parts," Tallberg later said.

The Ford family was losing control of its German operations.

A master of propaganda, Hitler chose a strategic day in 1938 to make a public statement about his admiration for Henry Ford. On the occasion of Henry's seventy-fifth birthday, the motor magnate attended an event in Detroit where — to his surprise — German officials were in attendance. They presented Henry with the Grand Cross of the German Eagle. The highest award Hitler ever offered to any non-German, the Cross was made of gold and adorned with four swastikas.

Henry stood emaciated in his old age at this Detroit function, unaware of the extreme political maelstrom he was tumbling into. He stood smiling in a light tan suit as a cameraman froze his image in celluloid at the very moment a member of the German consulate pinned the Eagle to his breast. The Fuehrer sent Henry a personal note thanking him for his "humanitarian ideals" and for his work toward "the cause of peace." (Soon after, the famed aviator Charles Lindbergh received a similar award, as did General Motors' head of European operations, James Mooney, who met personally with Adolf Hitler about business conditions in Germany on more than one occasion.)

Photos of Henry wearing the Nazi medal drew outrage. "I question the Americanism of Henry Ford," the Jewish entertainer Eddie Cantor said in a statement to the press, "for accepting a citation from the biggest gangster in the world. . . . Doesn't he realize that the German papers, reporting the citation, said all Americans were behind Nazism? Whose side is Mr. Ford on?"

Henry released a statement, saying there was "no sympathy on my part with Nazism. . . . Those who have known me for many years realize that anything that breeds hate is repulsive to me."

Nevertheless, Henry refused to give the award back, likely for fear of angering Hitler personally. When Henry was asked by a reporter one day what to do about Hitler, he nodded toward his aide-de-camp Harry Bennett.

"Do you really want to get rid of Hitler?" Henry said. "I'll send Harry over there with six of his men. They'll get rid of Hitler for you in no time."

At a board meeting on April 20, 1938, in Germany, Charlie Sorensen agreed to a contract to build trucks for the Nazi government under careful circumstances. The company would partner with another German concern, Ambi-Budd, which would furnish much of the labor and be the face of the venture. The plant would be built in Berlin, far from any foreign border, according to Hitler's wishes. And access to the plant by Americans would be heavily restricted.

At the time, no one in America could imagine that the greatest catastrophe in human history was at hand. Hitler's speeches had grown more ominous through the 1930s, and his book, *Mein Kampf,* had presaged incredible events. But who in America had read *Mein Kampf*? Campaigns against Jews had occurred before — pogroms in Poland, Russia, even France. How would another one be different? In fact, according to a Gallup poll taken in 1939 (the year after Ford Motor Company signed contracts to make trucks for the Hitler regime), 25 percent of Americans believed that a campaign against Jews was imminent *inside the United States.*

In Europe, it was clear that Germany had by far the strongest economy and that Hitler's interests would soon expand outside his borders. The financial boon of investing in this economic power-house during the Depression was difficult for American businessmen to resist. And if there was war in Europe, it seemed clear that Germany would win, no matter the opponent.

"Whatever the political settlement may be," Dr. Albert advised, "not only in official quarters but also in business circles, the opinion prevails that a radical change will take place . . . and that the German sphere of interest will be immensely enlarged. It is assumed that the greater part, if not the whole, of Europe will economically form one unit . . . Germany taking the lead."

It was best to be in Hitler's good graces.

In the fall of 1938, Dr. Albert supervised the opening of the new factory in Berlin to build trucks for the Nazi government. GM's Opel was already building trucks for the regime. With no knowledge of the impending war, no crystal ball that could foresee violence and geno-cide, the Detroit auto companies were now heavily invested in build-ing the Nazi arsenal.

Without the Internet and modern communications, few in Amer-ica took notice of these overseas deals. And they were not entirely unique; other industries, such as banks and technology companies, were functioning similarly in Nazi Germany. When one GM stock-holder raised concern, the company's chairman, Alfred Sloan (Wil-liam Knudsen's boss), defended the contracts and the profits, which were critical to the balance sheets, especially during the Depression. The politics of Nazi Germany "should not be considered the busi-ness of the management of General Motors," Sloan said. "We must conduct ourselves [in Germany] as a German organization." GM had obligations to its stockholders, Sloan said. "We have no right to shut down the plant."

The events that followed shocked the world. November 1938 brought *Kristallnacht,* the "night of broken glass," an orgy of terror that left innumerable synagogues in flames inside Germany. Nearly

10,000 Jewish stores were looted and destroyed, and at least 91 Jews murdered. On March 15, 1939, the Nazis violated the Munich Pact by taking the entirety of Czechoslovakia.

Then, on September 1, 1939, Goering unleashed his Luftwaffe over Poland, while the Nazi Panzer tanks and trucks rolled over the border—a highly coordinated brand of warfare that Hitler called *Blitzkrieg* ("lightning war"), powered by unprecedented amounts of horsepower, some of it built by Ford and GM. Goering offered a definition of *Blitzkrieg* for the newspapers.

"Our enemies should take note," he said. "Aerial attacks, stupendous in their mass effect, surprise, terror, sabotage, assassination from within, the murder of leading men, overwhelming attacks on all weak points in the enemy's defense, sudden attacks, all in the same second, without regard for reserves or losses."

World War II had begun. Though the Nazis were adept at utilizing all forms of weaponry, it was the airplane that revolutionized military engagement on that first morning of the war. Never had a weapon dealt death and destruction with such economy, nor had one proved so capable of distilling a psychology of fear. To mark the occasion, Hitler mounted cameras on his Stuka dive-bombers. When he sat later to watch the film, he marveled at the velocity of the machines, the power of the engines, the impact of the bombs.

"That is what will happen to them!" he cried out. *"That is how we will annihilate them!"*

PART II

THE LIBERATOR

I was a ball turret gunner on a B-24 Liberator. My first experience in a ball turret was in combat. It was not exhilarating. It was terrifying. All just flak. Flak — that's what killed most of our people. In the ball turret, you had a good view. It was hell. You could see the bombs land. We weren't sending enough of the bombs down as far as I was concerned. I didn't care what we did to the people on the ground. They were shooting at me and I wanted them gone. I flew thirty missions. We flew the old B-24s with open windows in back. The noise was horrific. We took terrible beatings. We lost an engine, two engines, and still the plane would fly. The Liberator was a very sturdy plane. It got me out alive.

— MARVIN GRAHAM, *Shreveport, LA*

8

Fifty Thousand Airplanes

Spring 1940

If Roosevelt took this country into war and won, he might be
one of the great figures of all history. But if we lost, he would be
damned forever. The cards are now stacked against us.

— CHARLES LINDBERGH, *January 7, 1941*

ON THE EVENING OF May 9, 1940, Franklin Roosevelt sat in his
second-floor study in the White House in his high-backed red leather
chair, a precise replica of Thomas Jefferson's favorite chair during his
presidency. Roosevelt heard his phone ring at 11:00 PM. On the line,
his Belgian ambassador, John Cudahy, reported jolting news.

Under a veil of darkness, Hitler had launched an all-out attack.
Nazi warplanes were sweeping low over Belgium, Holland, Luxembourg, and parts of France. At that moment, Europe's old citadels
were crumbling, Cudahy reported. Women and children were pan-
icking in the streets.

Roosevelt hung up the phone. For years he had anticipated this
moment — all-out war in Europe. As he knew from experience, war
had a magnetic force, a way of sucking in ever-greater populations.
Would the United States of America be capable of resisting this force?

He spent a sleepless night on the phone with his advisers. At 10:30 the next morning, the doors to the Oval Office burst open and the President appeared, sleepless but alert, wheeled in his chair by an aide. Roosevelt's cabinet was already assembled around a mahogany conference table — trusted confidants like Henry Morgenthau, secretary of the treasury; Cordell Hull, secretary of state; and General George C. Marshall, the grim-faced and gimlet-eyed army chief of staff. Roosevelt had the walls of the Oval Office crowded with pictures of ships, a tribute to his love of sailing and his navy days. Though he was a crippled man, he was a wellspring of charisma, a man whose mere presence heightened the sentience of everyone in the room.

Roosevelt took command. He was fifty-eight years old, a man of peerless prestige, with blazing blue-gray eyes and a voice that boomed from his big chest with all the intonations of a patrician education: Groton, Harvard (where he was editor of the newspaper), Columbia Law. Raised the son of wealthy sixth-generation Americans in Hyde Park, New York, he had traveled often as a boy in Europe and could speak French and German. He was a distant cousin of Theodore Roosevelt, the twenty-sixth president of the United States. During World War I, before he was elected governor of his home state of New York, Roosevelt had served as assistant secretary of the navy, and while he had spent most of the war in Washington, he had seen enough of the battlefield in Europe to envision the gutters of Brussels and Rotterdam flowing with blood that morning in 1940.

"I have seen war on land and sea," he said about his experience during World War I. "I have seen blood running from the wounded. I have seen men coughing out their gassed lungs. I have seen the dead in the mud. I have seen cities destroyed. . . . I hate war."

With his staff that morning, the President examined the American armed forces, a military drained of all resources by the Great Depression. The fighting forces had little weaponry. There was no legitimate munitions industry. In one embarrassing instance in the year past, General George Patton had needed nuts and bolts to repair some rusty tanks. The army had none, so he had to order his own from a Sears, Roebuck & Co. catalog. The US Army was smaller than that of Belgium, a nation that could fit inside Maryland. On that very morning, in Louisiana, the army was carrying out war games — using broomsticks in place of guns and eggs in place of grenades.

"We Americans treat our Army like a mangy old dog," said General Marshall.

The group had themselves to blame. Most had supported Congress's Neutrality Acts in the 1930s, all of which the President had signed. These laws were meant to isolate the United States from its allies in the event of war — to essentially make war illegal in America. "It was born of the belief that we could legislate ourselves out of war," said Robert Sherwood, Roosevelt's chief speechwriter, "as we had once legislated ourselves out of the saloons (and into the speakeasies). Like Prohibition, it was an experiment 'noble in motive' but disastrous in result."

What frightened Roosevelt most was the military's critical lack of airplanes. The airplane had played a role in World War I many years earlier, but hardly a big one. In traditional warfare, troops and ships moved at five or ten miles per hour. In traditional warfare, the oceans protected the American mainland from attack.

"But the new element — air navigation — steps up the speed of possible attack to 200, to 300 miles an hour," Roosevelt said. "From a base in the outer West Indies, the coast of Florida could be reached in 200 minutes. The Azores are only 2,000 miles from parts of our eastern seaboard and if Bermuda fell into hostile hands it is a matter of less than three hours for modern bombers to reach our shores."

The most accurate intelligence on the Nazi Luftwaffe made the spine of Washington tingle with fear. Goering, it was estimated, could manufacture some 18,000 airplanes a year.

And American airpower?

"Well, to be realistic, we were practically nonexistent," General Henry Harley "Hap" Arnold, head of the US Army Air Corps, later said of the situation in 1940.

As Roosevelt's cabinet meeting continued, more bad news arrived over the wire. "I remember the dismay with which we heard of the crumbling of the fortresses along the Belgian eastern frontier," recalled Undersecretary of State Sumner Welles, who sat uncomfortably in the Oval Office that morning. "Worst of all was the increasing apprehension that the German war machine was so overwhelmingly superior in might, quality, strategy, material, and morale."

The President ordered his staff to assess everything it would need to reinvent the American military and turn it into a force that could match the Nazi war machine — and with terrific speed. Then he steeled himself, digging deep and summoning the facade — his famous optimism. "You know," he once told Orson Welles, "you and I are the two best actors in America." He ordered the doors to the Oval Office opened. When reporters swarmed, they found the President smiling calmly and confidently, his cigarette holder sticking out from between his tobacco-stained teeth.

"Good morning," Roosevelt began as photographers clicked and pencils scribbled. "I hope you had more sleep than I did. I guess most of you were pretty busy all night." The President met question after question. Not once did he mention the words "Nazi" or "Hitler." There was one question he refused to answer.

What were the chances of America entering the war?

The truth was that Roosevelt knew war was inevitable. And he had already come up with a plan. As Sears, Roebuck executive Donald Nelson, who would soon be appointed head of the War Production Board, later wrote of the spring of 1940: "Who among us, except the President of the United States, really saw the magnitude of the job ahead, the awful mission of the United States in a world running berserk?

"I can testify that all the people I met and talked to, including members of the General Staff, the Army and Navy's highest ranking officers, distinguished statesmen and legislators, thought of the defense program as only a means for equipping ourselves to keep the enemy away from the shores of the United States. None of us — not one that I know of, except the President — saw that we might be fighting Germany and Japan all over the world."

One week later, on May 16, 1940, the President sat in his limousine en route from the White House to the Capitol Building. As he passed the Labor Department and the Justice Department, the buildings appeared dull and gray, soaked in a heavy rain. The sullen mood of the city that morning reflected the overall mood of the nation. This was a country still in the grip of depression, with 8 million people out of work and 7.5 million more making less than the minimum wage (30 cents an hour).

Inside the House chamber — that dramatic setting where presidents delivered State of the Union Addresses — Roosevelt stood at the rostrum with steel buckles locking his lifeless legs in place. Always, there existed an elaborate production around the President to conceal his disability and any hint of weakness from the American public. Standing upright, he smiled as two hundred of Washington's most powerful men gave him an ovation that lasted two full minutes. Despite the applause, they were a grim-looking lot. As one journalist described the scene, "Every Cabinet member present appeared sunk in serious thought."

"These are ominous days," Roosevelt began. "The clear fact is that the American people must recast their thinking about national protection. The brutal force of modern offensive war has been loosed in all its horror. New powers of destruction, incredibly swift and deadly, have been developed; and those who wield them are ruthless and daring."

Roosevelt was prepared to challenge the nation as it had never been challenged before in its 164-year history. "This means [the creation of] military implements — not on paper — which are ready and available to meet any lightning offensive against our American interest," he said. "It means also that facilities for production must be ready to turn out munitions and equipment at top speed."

Standing before his political friends and foes, he asked Congress for $1.28 billion for the military. Then he dropped a number that confounded all experts: "I believe that this nation should plan at this time a program that would provide us with 50,000 military and naval planes."

The crowd erupted in roars and applause, on both sides of the aisle. But silently, everyone present came to the same conclusion: Fifty thousand military planes? Impossible.

Even before the war had started, Roosevelt had envisioned the future of modern combat. Control of the skies, with the threat of instant apocalyptic devastation, would win the day. Even the threat of it would be enough to change the course of political action among nations.

As early as 1938, he had argued in a meeting with military advisers for a fleet of state-of-the-art aircraft. US Army Air Corps chief Hap Arnold remembered the meeting as airpower's "Magna Carta." "The President came straight out for air power," Arnold recalled. "Airplanes — now — and lots of them!" Roosevelt spoke most about "mass production" on American assembly lines — making airplanes like they made cars in Detroit. His closest aide, Harry Hopkins, later recalled, "The President was sure then that we were going to get into war and he believed that airpower would win it."

"Pounding away at Germany from the air," Roosevelt had said, would crack "the morale of the German people.... When I write to foreign countries I must have something to back up my words. Had we had this summer [in 1938] 5,000 airplanes and the capacity to produce 10,000 per year ... Hitler would not have dared to take the stand that he did."

The President, his military chiefs, and his cabinet had all come to agreement: not only would airpower play the most critical role in the future of military aggression, but the four-engine bomber would be the most critical weapon of all. As Air Corps chief Hap Arnold said in 1940: "The United States must build, as quickly as possible, an Air Force capable of waging a decisive air offensive against the Axis powers in Europe, and this Air Force must consist predominantly of Heavy Bombers."

And yet, mired in economic priorities, Washington had failed to build any semblance of airpower. Some progress had been made: aviation firms had produced prototypes of new military planes. Boeing had developed the B-17 four-engine bomber. The first B-17 had a short and ominous history: three months after its first shakedown flight, it had crashed, killing its two test pilots, but it had since progressed in design. The Army Air Corps had ordered a fleet of 360-mile-per-hour Curtiss-Wright P-40 Warhawk single-engine fighters after seeing the first prototype in 1938. And Consolidated Aircraft Corporation out of San Diego had unveiled the prototype for the B-24 four-engine bomber in 1939 — the Liberator, the biggest and most powerful of them all.

None of these airplanes, however, existed in any numbers. Most of the progress in American aviation during the 1930s was aimed at civilian travel. Still, in 1940, if a person wanted to fly from New York to Los Angeles, he would spend twenty-four hours in a DC-3, flying at low altitude (cabins were not pressurized) at a mere 155 miles per hour, at his own peril (no radar), stopping three times to refuel. And only if weather permitted.

By the time the President announced his 50,000-airplane plan, America's European allies were clamoring for flying machines from the United States. They needed weapons that could stand up to the Nazi Luftwaffe. If the British couldn't get American warplanes soon, "You'd have the Germans eating breakfast with us," said the Air Ministry's Patrick Hennessy. France's premier, Paul Reynaud, cried for "clouds of airplanes" from the United States — planes that could not be offered to the French because they did not exist and there was no US company capable of building them in time.

Now the air war was on in Europe, democratic nations were crumbling under the onslaught of Hitler's warplanes, and America had no airpower.

The day after Roosevelt's 50,000-airplane speech, his critics attacked. Congress had already approved $7 billion in military expenditures, Senator Bennett Clark of Missouri said. "We hear now that the Army has only 58 airplanes that are not obsolete." Clark wanted to know how the rest of that money "was squandered." The man emerging as Roosevelt's loudest critic, the aviator Charles Lindbergh, called the 50,000-airplane plan "hysterical chatter." In Germany, Hermann Goering burst out laughing when he heard Roosevelt's plan.

"What is America," commented Adolf Hitler, "but beauty queens, millionaires, stupid records, and Hollywood?"

Ultimately, the President's strategy would be a test of the democratic system itself. If this war would be fought not just with soldiers but with assembly lines, the United States would seem to have a terrific advantage. America's foundries, refineries, and factories turned out more steel, aluminum, and cars than all the other major powers combined, and the nation had larger reserves of oil than any other country. The question became: how could Roosevelt convince American industry to put its free-enterprise interests aside and build the weapons that could arm the Allies, when most of America still believed the war in Europe would never touch them?

The President needed the nation's titans of industry in his corner. Throughout his years in the White House, however, his politics had made enemies of these powerful industrialists. The New Deal had inserted government into big business as never before. "They are unanimous in their hate for me," he said of Wall Street and industrial tycoons in a campaign speech for his second term in 1936. "And I welcome their hatred." Now those titans of industry were the figures that Washington needed most.

Roosevelt needed a man on the inside, a liaison who understood mass production and who could oil the hinge that joined big industry and its assembly lines to the nation's capital. He invited the Wall Street legend Bernard Baruch to the White House. Baruch had played this kind of role under Woodrow Wilson during World War I. The financier had three suggestions.

"First, Knudsen. Second, Knudsen. Third, Knudsen."

When the phone rang in the office of the president of General Motors in downtown Detroit, Knudsen was expecting the call.

"Mr. Knudsen," an operator said, "the President of the United States wants to talk to you. Here he is."

"Knudsen?"

"Yes, Mr. President."

"I want to see you in Washington. I want you to work on some production matters. When can you come down here?"

That night Knudsen went home to his family and explained that he was leaving his $300,000-plus salary behind. His flabbergasted twenty-year-old daughter asked why. "This country has been good to me," Knudsen said. "And I want to pay it back." He had arrived from Denmark via Ellis Island forty years earlier with $30 in his pocket; left to find his way alone, he had fought with his fists on the docks in New York just to get by. Now he was a rich sixty-one-year-old man being appointed to the most important production job in the world.

On his way south, Knudsen stopped in New York to see his boss, General Motors chairman Alfred Sloan, who detested Roosevelt and his New Deal politics. "They'll make a monkey out of you down there in Washington," Sloan warned. Sloan told Knudsen that if he was going to work for Roosevelt, he need not come back. His days at GM were through. When Knudsen arrived at La Guardia Field to fly to Washington, reporters were waiting for him.

"Can you build those fifty thousand planes?" they asked.

"I can't," said Knudsen. "But America can."

Knudsen moved into a Washington apartment and took an office in the Federal Reserve Building on Constitution Avenue across from the Army and Navy Departments. Roosevelt placed him in full command of defense manufacturing – "tanks, airplanes, engines, uniforms, and the multifarious items needed in the program after the first processing stage," the official announcement read. For this Knudsen would receive a salary of $1. He was the first of World War II's so-called dollar-a-year men.

His square head and blue eyes made the cover of *Life* magazine the following week. A reporter from *The New Yorker* trailed him for a series of three profiles. Knudsen's appointment signified a historic moment in American history: the attempt to turn a democratic government, free enterprise, and the military into one giant fighting machine.

The President was very clear on what would be Knudsen's most important task. "The effective defense of this country and the vital defense of other democratic nations requires that there be a substantial increase in heavy bomber production," Roosevelt wrote on May 4, 1941. "I am fully aware of the fact that increasing the number of heavy bombers will mean a great strain upon our production effort. It will mean a large expansion of plant facilities and the utilization of existing factories not now engaged in making munitions. But command of the air by the democracies must and can be achieved. We must see to it that the process is hastened and that the democratic superiority in the air be made absolute."

When Knudsen met George Marshall, the army chief of staff, the General said to him, "Your responsibility and my responsibility are much alike. Your responsibility is to produce; my responsibility is to use. Our greatest need is time."

Knudsen promised "speed, speed, and more speed."

At the first meeting of what was now called the National Defense

Advisory Commission, headed by Knudsen and US Steel chief Edward Stettinius, Knudsen boldly took the floor.

"Our immediate problem is to make 50,000 airplanes a year," he said. "We haven't got a lot of airplane factories. And we haven't got time to wait for them to be built. As I see it, an airplane is pretty big. A bomber weighs from 20,000 to 40,000 pounds. Standing in a field, it looks pretty big. And it is big. But when an airplane is taken apart, it is nothing but a lot of little pieces. With that in mind, I figure the automobile business can make parts for airplanes, and sections for planes that we can glue together. In the automobile industry they understand mass production."

Knudsen and Secretary of the Treasury Henry Morgenthau came up with a plan. Who had both aviation experience and mass production know-how? Why not call the family who pioneered aviation through the 1920s, the family who invented the idea of fully integrated mass production on a grand scale in the first place?

When it came to the Ford family, as one government official put it, "nothing was ever impossible."

9

"Gentlemen, We Must Outbuild Hitler"

Spring to Fall 1940

England's battles, it used to be said, were won on the playing fields of Eton. This plan is put forward in the belief that America's can be won on the assembly lines of Detroit.

— WALTER REUTHER, *1940*

AT THE ROUNDTABLE LUNCHEON in Dearborn, with Henry Ford sitting between Edsel and Sorensen and waiters in white coats hovering, the conversation turned to the war in Europe.

The situation overseas sent Henry into fits of rage, which he unleashed at the Roundtable. He was "obsessed with the European situation," according to Sorensen. "It was on his mind night and day. Anything pertaining to Europe would upset him. The likelihood of [America's] involvement upset him almost to incoherence." Now seventy-seven, Henry had suffered a minor stroke. He was so waifish, he looked like his skeleton was trying to crawl out of him. His eyes appeared as if someone had "dimmed the power behind them," according to Harry Bennett. Henry had begun to show serious signs of senility. He was often confused, mentally volatile, and paranoid. All through the 1930s, he had clashed publicly with the Roosevelt administration. Now all his paranoia was fixated on the President.

"The people are looking for a leader," Henry said. "And they've got a leader who is putting something over on them, and they deserve it." Henry was sure the President had his own agenda and lives would be lost as a result. "They don't dare have a war," Henry said of the Roosevelt administration. "And they know it."

But the war in Europe had already begun; the political situation was completely out of control. France had already been conquered, and Britain was left to fight the Nazis alone. It had fallen to Edsel and Sorensen to protect the family's assets overseas, however possible. Ford Motor Company was straddling nations at war. In fact, the company was at war with itself, in more ways than one.

Ford plants in Germany, France, Belgium, Holland, and Denmark were now in Nazi-occupied territory. Ford of Britain, on the other hand (the Ford empire's greatest power abroad), was serving Churchill's campaign against the Nazis. A new factory outside Manchester was tooling up to churn out complex Rolls-Royce Merlin aircraft engines for Britain's marvelous Spitfire fighter planes, while Dagenham outside London was making military trucks and ambulances.

Edsel couldn't discuss these issues frankly at the Roundtable— his father was too volatile. Henry's physician, Dr. McClure, had cautioned Edsel not to bring the stress of the war upon his father. Back in his corner office, Edsel wrote careful letters to his executives abroad, hoping to obtain information. Were the factories in Nazi-occupied territory damaged? Were they running at all?

Dr. Albert had cabled Edsel from Germany to say that Ford-Werke in Cologne would do its best "to safeguard your interests in plants in occupied territory." The plants in Europe were up and running, he reported. "You realize, of course," Dr. Albert wrote Edsel, "that as soon as a victorious army occupies foreign territory, according to international law (convention of the Haag), the occupying forces have the right to use all plants for manufacturing war matériel."

"We are producing normal trucks only" in Germany, Dr. Albert promised—an obvious lie. (As Cologne's former chief engineer Tallberg put it: "Of course those trucks were going to the military.") Further information, Dr. Albert wrote, could not be disclosed "under the restrictions imposed on communicating with foreign countries."

Meanwhile, the family had received word that their Antwerp assembly plant had been bombed by the British. Given the lack of communication from abroad, the information came from Washington. Secretary of State Cordell Hull had cabled Edsel to inform him that "four Belgian employees were wounded" and that "damage to the plant was principally broken glass."

A key source of information for Edsel was Maurice Dollfus, the head of Ford of France, a chain smoker with a bad heart and a "pyrotechnic eloquence," as one auto man described him. A loyal, longtime friend of the Ford family, Dollfus wrote Edsel a series of long letters after the start of the war. He could reveal facts, but "very often not *all* the truth," owing to the Nazi censors who would surely be reading the letters before delivery.

With Paris conquered, Dollfus was forced to continue running the Ford facilities in France as part of the Nazi arsenal, delivering trucks to the *Wehrmacht*. Hitler had an insatiable thirst for machinery and horsepower; the Nazis were taking all the trucks Ford of France could build, and paying for them.

"Our trucks are in very large demand by the German authorities," Dollfus wrote Edsel in August 1940, "and I believe that as long as the war goes on and at least for some period of time all that we shall produce will be taken by the German authorities."

"In order to safeguard our interests," Dollfus wrote Edsel, "and I am here talking in a very broad way — I have been to Berlin and have seen General von Schell himself." General Adolf von Schell was the Nazis' plenipotentiary for automotive affairs, in charge of taking over the continent's car factories for military purposes. "My interview with him has been by all means satisfactory," Dollfus wrote. In the margin of his letter, he scribbled in longhand: "I was the first Frenchman to go to Berlin."

On July 30, 1940, Edsel cabled a simple note to Dollfus: "Glad you are safe also plants looking forward to fuller reports regards." Two months later, he wrote Dollfus again, thanking him for his hard work. "I also appreciate your great effort to keep the organizations intact and desire to produce something. . . . You are doing a fine job in cooperating with the other companies in the allocation of raw materials for the various Ford companies."

The idea of allegiance had become a complex entanglement. Doll-fus was doing everything he could to please the Nazis; otherwise, they would kick him out and take control. It was a matter of survival. Privately, Edsel grappled with the idea that his company was willfully serving the Nazi war machine. His factories were building the arse-nals that were destroying each other. As Dollfus wrote Edsel: "The history of our company during this war seems like a novel." Only the evil they faced was all too real.

Edsel ventured south to Washington in late May 1940 to attend meetings about airplane production. This was "Washington Won-derland," the cherry-blossomed asylum, tangled in rivaling ambi-tions and red tape and dotted with its famous edifices — the Capitol Building, the White House, the Supreme Court Building. The roads crisscrossed with motorcar traffic — every car made in America. Ed-sel arrived at Treasury Secretary Henry Morgenthau's office at 8:30 AM on May 31.

The news from Europe that morning was profoundly disturb-ing. Ships were evacuating 200,000 stranded British and another 140,000 French and Belgian soldiers from the shores of Dunkirk, beaten back in France by the Nazi juggernaut. At any moment, the British expected an invasion. No foreign power had successfully in-vaded the Isles since the Norman French in 1066. So sure were Brit-ish leaders of the impending Nazi invasion that they had removed street signs from cities and towns along the coastline, hoping the Na-zis would get lost upon arrival.

Unlike his father, Edsel was a friend and ally of President Roos-evelt and his administration. Conversation was informal in Morgen-thau's mahogany-paneled office. The airplane situation was grave, Morgenthau explained. The President had promised thousands of aircraft engines to the British. Somebody had to build them — and fast! The President was receiving desperate missives from Winston Churchill. ("The enemy have a marked preponderance in the air," Churchill had written. "The small countries are simply smashed up, one by one, like matchwood. . . . I trust you realize, Mr. President, that the voice and force of the United States may count for nothing if they are withheld too long. You may have a completely subjugated Nazified Europe established with astonishing swiftness.")

Morgenthau wanted to know: Could Edsel Ford build aircraft engines on his assembly lines? What would it entail, and how long would it take?

"Sure, we can do it," said Edsel. "We will make all the studies we can in a preliminary way and see what can be done." As Morgenthau later recalled, Edsel said he would take on the job "for patriotic reasons."

Four days later, just before midnight, an armored car pulled up to Gate 4 of the Rouge. Two soldiers unloaded top-secret blueprints for the Rolls-Royce Merlin aircraft engine, the British-designed power plant that was the jewel of the Royal Air Force. Following the blueprints, the Fords received the aircraft engine itself. Knudsen arrived in Dearborn from Washington to help study the project.

On June 13, Edsel returned to Washington with Sorensen to finalize the deal. They arrived at 8:30 AM and headed to the Mayflower Hotel for breakfast. Knudsen met them there. All talk was of aviation engines — the scintillating technical challenge of producing them en masse, according to automobile manufacturing principles.

Edsel appeared tired that morning. Not long before, he had checked himself into Henry Ford Hospital with crippling stomach pain; doctors had run uncomfortable tests, making him imbibe barium solutions and forcing tubes down his throat. They were unable to diagnose anything. "I was concerned about Edsel," Sorensen later remembered. "The doctors were keeping tabs on him. . . . When he showed signs of indigestion, from which he suffered a great deal, his father would be impatient about that. He would criticize Edsel unmercifully."

In Washington, Edsel and Sorensen negotiated a contract for 9,000 Rolls-Royce Merlin aircraft engines. Six thousand would go to the British, and the other 3,000 to the US military. The government would pay Ford a provisional price of $16,000 per engine (about $10 per horsepower). Edsel kept his father abreast of negotiations by phone, carefully explaining the situation so as not to upset him. To Edsel's amazement, he was able to convince his father that the family should take on the project. As Sorensen later wrote in his diary: "I am surprised . . . Henry Ford had stated that he would not make any war supplies for any foreign nation. . . . No one could have been more careful in keeping him fully informed than Edsel and I had been."

When Edsel and Sorensen left Washington, news of the agreement made headlines all over Europe and North America. In Britain's House of Commons, the announcement raised roars from crowds of politicians, who believed that Ford magic from the United States would be a huge boon to their campaign against the Nazis. Churchill's top aircraft production man, Lord Beaverbrook, made his own announcement that Ford of Dearborn would make engines for the Royal Air Force. The news brought relief to all of Britain, where morale had sunk to an all-time low. In the newspapers that same week were pictures of Hitler's triumphant march into Paris. Time was running out; with France conquered, the Nazis were just twenty-six miles from England.

Two days after the Fords agreed to produce the Rolls-Royce Merlin, Henry changed his mind. He called Edsel and Sorensen into his office. Edsel appeared with a smile on his face, unaware of the pitfall he had just stepped into. His father explained the situation: in a fit of paranoia, he was now refusing to make the engines, claiming that Roosevelt was trying to lead the country into the fray. "They want war!" Henry said. He would build the motors for American defense, but not for Britain. Sorensen had never heard Henry shout louder in forty years of employ.

This was Edsel's deal. He had negotiated the contract. News of it had been reported all over the world. "We wouldn't have made these commitments if you hadn't expressed yourself in favor," Edsel said, in the strongest tone he could speak with his father.

"I don't care," Henry responded. "Call up Knudsen and tell him we've changed our mind."

Edsel was crestfallen. He headed to his office and picked up the phone. It was one of the most difficult calls he ever made.

"Bill," Edsel said, "we can't make those motors for the British."

"Why?"

"Father won't do it."

Knudsen was incredulous. "But you are the president of the company."

"I know, but father won't do it, and you know how he is."

Knudsen phoned some military powerbrokers and secured himself an airplane to fly directly to Detroit. He hurried to the Rouge. In Edsel's office, he shook Henry's hand.

"Mr. Ford," Knudsen burst out, "this is terrible about those motors."

"You are mixed up with some bad people in Washington," Henry said. "I won't make motors for the British government. For the American government, yes; for the British government, no."

"But, Mr. Ford," Knudsen said, "we have your word that you would make them. I told the President your decisions, and he was very happy about it."

The mention of Henry's nemesis, Roosevelt, was a mistake. "We won't build the engine at all," Ford said. "Withdraw the whole order."

Knudsen's face grew purple with rage. He stormed out of the Rouge. His phone call to Henry Morgenthau's office in Washington was humiliating.

"Edsel said that his father said that if he sold engines to the British government that that would rush the United States into the war," Knudsen told Morgenthau. "We argued back and forth for an hour and a half," he continued. "I don't understand their attitude. They have been selling trucks to the French." Edsel had personally given his word, Knudsen reiterated. "You know, the old man and him — they sort of cross wires once in a while."

After the phone call, Morgenthau called one of his colleagues. "Edsel definitely gave his word to Mr. Knudsen," the Treasury secretary said.

"I guess Edsel isn't old enough yet to have a view of his own," came the answer. "I guess when he grows up and gets about twenty-one his father will back him more."

"Well, I don't know how," Morgenthau said. "I guess he'll have to wait until he hasn't got a father."

Morgenthau grew suspicious of the whole affair. Henry Ford was an accused Nazi sympathizer, who had received the Grand Cross from Hitler himself, who had financial concerns inside Nazi-occupied territory. Now he was refusing to build engines that would be used to attack Germany. Was he prioritizing his family empire above his patriotism? Or was he really just a pacifist?

When Edsel returned home to Gaukler Pointe that night, his driver motoring through the estate's security gates, he faced the painful task of explaining to his wife that his name was about to be brutally maligned all over the world in the newspapers. The Roosevelt administration put out a devastating statement, faulting Edsel. The Canadian government attacked, calling the Fords "a menace to democracy." In Britain—where the Nazi invasion seemed closer with every hour—the news stirred fury.

In Germany, however, Dr. Albert was most pleased. The Nazis couldn't be happier if the Fords refused to build aviation engines for their enemies. In fact, Henry Ford's refusal to build the Merlins, along with his anti-Semitism and his Nazi medal (the Grand Cross of the German Eagle), was perceived by many as further evidence of Nazi sympathies. "The 'Dementi' of Mr. Henry Ford concerning war orders for Great Britain has greatly helped us," Dr. Albert wrote Edsel.

The international embarrassment weighed heavily on Edsel—having his patriotism compromised on the world stage. He was suffering through the indignity of World War I all over again. Of all the feuds that he had suffered through with his father, this one hurt the most.

One month after Henry Ford's aircraft engine debacle, the Battle of Britain began—the first battle ever fought entirely by air forces. The Luftwaffe had gone relatively unchallenged in the air by the rest of Europe. The British were the first to take the Nazis on. Churchill's Royal Air Force brawled with Goering's "birds of hell" in slug matches at astounding speeds, fulfilling the Wellsian prophecy of all-out war in the air between national superpowers.* "Mankind is Franken-

---

* For centuries, intellectuals had written of flying machines engaged in warfare, from Leonardo da Vinci at the turn of the sixteenth century to the British poet Lord Tennyson in the nineteenth, to the most harrowing and prophetic

stein," wrote one British journalist. "Science, especially the science of aviation, is his monster." Churchill's Air Ministry was estimating some 2.5 million casualties on the ground in Britain, including women and children.

The Luftwaffe's numbers proved astounding. Hundreds of Messerschmitts attacked in packs — 350-mile-per-hour single-engine fighters. Following them were Heinkel bombers powered by sophisticated twin Daimler-Benz engines. The Stuka dive-bombers nosed toward the ground at such speeds that the Nazi pilots often fainted while dropping their explosives; the plane could then pull itself out of the dive automatically as the pilot regained consciousness.

"We could feel the shock of the bombs a mile away," said a Ford factory worker at Dagenham, twelve miles outside London. "The noise was terrific. Gunfire commenced at dusk and ended at dawn."

On August 13, 1940, Goering ordered *Adlertag* — "Eagle Day." The Luftwaffe swarmed in even greater numbers. Churchill and his chief military assistant, Lord Ismay, stood in the operations room of Britain's Fighter Command over a map showing the positions of Nazi flying machines.

"There had been fighting throughout the afternoon," Lord Ismay recalled, "and at one moment every single squadron in the Group was engaged. There was nothing in reserve, and the map table showed new waves of attackers crossing the coast." All of England braced for the blow. Said Lord Ismay: "I felt sick with fear."

Without a single ally in military support, Churchill promised to battle to the end. No one believed the British had even a remote chance against the Nazi war machine. As George Orwell put it: "We saw our soldiers fighting their way desperately to the coast, with one aeroplane against three, with rifles against tanks, with bayonets against tommy-guns." Privately, Churchill turned to the United States and quite literally begged Roosevelt for help.

"We shall need the greatest production of aircraft which the United States . . . are capable of sending us," Churchill wrote. "May I invite you then, Mr. President, to give earnest consideration to an im-

account: H. G. Wells's *The War in the Air* of 1908, with its startling imagery of New York City consumed in flames because of bombs dropped from above.

mediate order on joint account for a further 2,000 combat aircraft a month? Of these . . . the highest possible proportion should be heavy bombers, the weapon on which above all others we depend to shatter the foundations of German military power."

"Mr. President," Churchill wrote in another letter, "with great respect I must tell you that in the long history of the world, this is a thing to do now."

With haste, Knudsen put his plan into action — to make the Motor City ground zero for war preparedness.

On October 15, 1940, five hundred of Detroit's most powerful auto men gathered at the Waldorf-Astoria Hotel in New York, where Knudsen was scheduled to deliver a keynote speech following the New York Auto Show. The auto business in America was the centerpiece of the nation's industrial prowess. Either directly or indirectly, over 1,000 auto plants contributed in the United States, in forty-four states, to an industry that was worth over $3 billion and employed one of every nineteen people nationwide. These men in suits mingling at the Waldorf — among them Edsel Ford, General Motors' Alfred Sloan, Chrysler's K. T. Keller, and Packard's Alvan Macauley — were the ones driving this machine.

Standing with a carnation and a US flag pinned to the lapel of his suit coat, Knudsen stumbled through his opening. "As a report on the state of the nation," said one person present, "his speech outranked in importance many a presidential message to congress." Starting this current month, Knudsen said, Washington was going to push through defense contracts at a rate of $600 million a week. Yes, it seemed like the war was far away, across a mighty ocean. But it was coming, Knudsen argued. His words drew gasps from the crowds. It was all simply unbelievable.

"Fifty thousand airplanes," Knudsen said, "130,000 engines, 17,000 heavy guns, 25,000 light guns, 13,000 trench mortars, 33 million shells, 9,200 tanks, 300,000 machine guns and ammunition, 400,000 automatic rifles and ammunition, 1.3 million regular rifles and ammunition, 380 Navy ships, 200 mercantile ships, 210 camps and cantonments, 40 government factories, clothing and other equipment for 1.2 million men . . ."

To fill these orders, Knudsen said, would require 18 billion man-hours. The nation, indeed all those who opposed the Nazis, could count on Detroit, Knudsen said. It would be nothing short of "the greatest production problem of any country in modern times. . . . Give us speed and more speed. Talk to your men — make them feel that it is their responsibility as well as yours. Ask them what they think of a civilization that drives women and children to live in cold and wet holes in the ground."

What America needed most was heavy bombers. "We need more bombers — more big bombers — than we can hope to get," Knudsen pleaded. "Even the British now agree with General Arnold that they cannot win the war with fighter planes. It had been a bitter, bloody experience for them, this realization. Bombers, big bombers, are needed sooner than we dare hope to get them under present circumstances. We must build them at once! You've got to help!"

The President had recently signed a conscription act, the first peacetime draft in history. Millions of young men were registering to do their part. American boys had little to fight with, few tools of war.

"The first half of 1941 is crucial," Knudsen concluded. "Gentlemen, we must outbuild Hitler."

10

The Liberator

Fall 1940 to Spring 1941

> I think it well for the man in the street to realize that there is no power on earth that can protect him from being bombed, whatever people may tell him. The bomber will always get through.
>
> — British politician Stanley Baldwin, *1932*

KNUDSEN AIMED TO FIND out just what Detroit was made of. One of his first calls was to K.T. Keller, the head of Chrysler, which had pulled ahead of Ford during the Depression as the number two automaker in the United States.

"K.T., this is Knudsen. I need your help."

"Sure, Bill," said Keller. "What do you want?"

"I want you to make tanks."

The next day Keller arrived in Knudsen's Detroit office to look over blueprints of the M2A1 tank. Keller was a bowling ball of a man with a vicelike handshake and hair that looked like it was slicked with motor oil. His engineering talents were legendary, and he had been handpicked to take over Chrysler following the retirement and death of Walter Chrysler himself. Keller looked at the tank blueprints and paced around Knudsen's office. Then he turned and said, "I don't know, Bill. I've never seen one of these things."

The next day Keller traveled to the Rock Island Arsenal in Illinois so he could see a tank with his own eyes. Then he called Knudsen back.

"We can make them," Keller said.

"How much will they cost?"

"Damned if I know. Maybe $20,000, maybe $30,000. They weigh about thirty tons apiece. Where do you want us to make them, and when do you want us to get going?"

"Make them in Detroit, and get going now. You have to have a plant and a test ground. I figure they will cost you about $30 million."

"Okay, whatever it figures," Keller said. "What about guns?"

"The Army will furnish them."

"Good. Then we won't have to worry about that. Anything else?"

"Yes," Knudsen said. This was government business, he said. For auto men like Knudsen and Keller, a handshake was something you could take to the bank. But in Washington you had to make things official. "Send me a little piece of paper, showing me what you spend," Knudsen said. "We've got to make it formal, K.T."

Knudsen contacted Alvan Macauley at Packard Motor Car Company, which had just rolled out the first air-conditioned automobile (the 1940 Packard One Eighty, "cooled by mechanical refrigeration"). McCauley agreed to build Rolls-Royce Merlin liquid-cooled V12 aircraft engines — the technological marvel of the British air fleet (and the same engines that Henry Ford refused to build). Knudsen called Harold Vance, head of Studebaker, the maker of the new "Deluxetone" line of automobiles, and other engineering brains at Willys, Nash, and Fisher Body. All agreed to get on the defense bandwagon.

GM's chairman Alfred Sloan had publicly attacked Roosevelt's defense plan. "I believe the greatest danger and the most difficult part of our defense . . . is a protection of the American way of living against attacks from within, not from without"— insinuating clearly that the President and his New Deal politics were graver threats to the US Constitution than the Nazis were. "We haven't got enough 'economic royalists' among us to do this job for national defense," Sloan said sarcastically in a radio interview.

Nevertheless, by the end of 1940, GM had undertaken tens of millions in defense orders. The first of these contracts went to Chevrolet, for 75-millimeter high-explosive shells.

On December 12, 1940, the Fords received word of a potential new venture. Major Jimmy Doolittle — soon to be famous for his "Doolittle Raid" on Tokyo — called asking if Ford Motor Company could help supply machine parts for a four-engine bomber the army was planning on investing heavily in. The British were desperate for them. Consolidated Aircraft out of San Diego had designed the four-engine B-24 Liberator — the largest and most expensive American aircraft in existence at the time. But Consolidated moved too slowly; the company had no production know-how.

Edsel went to see his father at Fair Lane. He tried to explain: The family had to get on the defense bandwagon. The other motor companies in Detroit were accepting military contracts. It was their patriotic duty. Besides, if the Fords didn't work with Washington, the President could try to take over the Rouge. There were rumors. First Lady Eleanor Roosevelt had said as much in a recent speech at Yale. "The President could take over Mr. Ford tomorrow," she'd said, "if an emergency existed."

The situation called for action, Edsel pleaded. Already, the Nazis had bombed Ford's Dagenham plant outside London. Ford workers had been wounded there, and surely there'd be more bombs. The time for action was now.

"Those planes will never be used for fighting," Henry argued. "Before you can build them, the war will be over."

Edsel sent Sorensen to try to talk sense into Henry. "I was over the barrel," Sorensen later remembered. "On one side a mightily determined old man racked by hallucinations. On the other hand, a Franklin Roosevelt Administration, able, even eager, should occasion arise, to take over Ford Motor Company."

Finally Henry relented. He agreed to take on an aviation job — not for war and not for any foreign nation, but "for the defense of the United States only," he said.

From that moment on, Edsel hurled his family empire headlong into the defense effort. As Sorensen put it: "Our organization moved fast — and dangerously."

On December 29, 1940, President Roosevelt delivered his "Arsenal of Democracy" speech from the White House. The following week, Edsel, Sorensen, and a small team of Ford production men flew aboard a US Army aircraft to the Consolidated Aircraft Corporation factory in San Diego to see the four-engine B-24 Liberator for the first time.

Edsel brought his sons with him. Henry II and Benson—both graduated from college now—had never flown in an airplane. They were excited to see a big bomber, and yet they were intimidated by the idea of rubbing elbows with military big shots. Before they left, Edsel confided in Sorensen. It was time to bring his boys into the company. He asked Sorensen if he would help groom them. Someday soon the empire would be theirs. Edsel could not realize at the time how soon their inheritance would come to them, and how hard they would have to fight for it.

"They've had enough school," Edsel told Sorensen. "And they want to go to work. I hope you'll help me place them where they may learn how our departments run."

The oldest, Henry II, was expected to lead the clan someday. Now he was joining his father, taking his rightful place in the empire. He had long understood what the Ford Terror was doing to Edsel. With nervous anticipation, he boarded a flight bound for the West Coast.

Upon landing in San Diego, Edsel and his group found a crowd of reporters waiting for them. The trip was just for exploration, Edsel told them. "We are dealing with a 50,000 pound plane," he said. "Now, if you gentlemen will excuse me, I'll get going. And the quicker I do, the faster the Ford company's national defense effort will take shape."

At the Consolidated airplane factory, Major Reuben Fleet, the white-haired pilot and chief executive, welcomed the Ford team and led them on a tour of his operation. Edsel followed Fleet into the bomber plant, with his sons and Sorensen by his side. The plant was the size of three football fields — nearly half a million parts were manufactured here. The pieces were trucked outside, where the planes were built on a steel bed beneath the hot sun.

Squinting his eyes in the bright California light, Edsel took in the B-24. The bomber was a new machine, the prototype completed just one year earlier. It appeared a monstrosity. The Liberator stood 66 feet 4 inches long and 17 feet 11 inches tall, with the longest wingspan of any airplane of any kind in America—110 feet. The wing, which was designed by an aeronautical engineer named David R. Davis, was oddly shaped — exceptionally long and unusually narrow, with a high-aspect ratio that provided extraordinary lift. It was mounted shoulder-level on the fuselage so that it looked like arms outstretched, and the four engines hung down. One look at the radial engines was enough to know that they possessed awesome amounts of power.

As Fleet explained, the B-24 was America's fastest heavy bomber, with a top speed over 300 miles per hour. It had greater range — nearly 3,000 miles — than any other American airplane. It could carry a bigger payload than any other American flying machine — 8,000 pounds of TNT. With a takeoff weight of nearly 60,000 pounds, it was simply colossal.

Edsel climbed aboard. For over three decades, he had studied the evolution of aviation from afar, his file cabinets crowded with papers on the latest innovations and airplane models. Now he was inside the B-24. The interior was cramped and claustrophobic. A crew of between seven and ten would man the aircraft in battle. In the cockpit, Edsel fingered the instrument panel's twenty-seven gauges and twelve levers for controlling speed and fuel. Four radial engines combined for a total of 4,800 horsepower, the equivalent of a fleet of fifty-six Ford V8s. The view out the windscreen from inside the cockpit made the engine in Edsel's rib cage race. He could only imagine what it would be like to steer this gargantuan machine at low altitude over Hitler's Berlin.

Down in the belly of the aircraft, the bombardier manned the payload doors. Machine gun turrets were affixed in the nose, tail, spine, and belly. Edsel looked closely at the Liberator's tricycle landing gear. It was just like the landing gear he and his friend Van Auken had built on their airplane, back in that barn on Woodward Avenue thirty-two years before. Only, on this aircraft, the front tire was three feet high and capable of holding a load of nearly 27,000 pounds on its own.

In 1939 the military had ordered seven B-24s, and the first Liberators had been delivered to Churchill's Royal Air Force. The Ford men wanted to know how the plane got its name. Major Fleet explained that he was the one who had named it. As he told the British: "We chose the name Liberator because this airplane can carry destruction

THE LIBERATOR · 91

to the heart of the Hun, and thus help you and us to liberate those millions temporarily finding themselves under Hitler's yoke."

At the end of the day, Edsel and Sorensen came to a conclusion: Consolidated had created a hell of a weapon. But the aviation firm didn't have the ability to produce it. The airplanes were pieced together by hand in a standing position, the parts brought to the plane rather than the other way around. There was no understanding of metallurgy, nor any real assembly line at all. Under the hot San Diego sun, the metal would expand and contract by night and day. Under these conditions, there was no way to make one plane exactly like another. Each aircraft was a tailor-made object, its production an incredibly time-consuming affair.

As young Henry II stood by watching, his father and Sorensen criticized the operation unmercifully. Major Fleet bristled with anger.

"How would you do it?" he asked.

The answer: The Fords would make bombers like they made cars. Mass production. Fordism.

That night, Edsel, Sorensen, and Edsel's sons turned over the production problem for hours at a dinner table at San Diego's Coronado Hotel. The idea presented a scintillating challenge. As Knudsen had said, what was a bomber but a large machine made of small pieces? Pieces that could be crafted just like automobile parts? Like a car, an airplane was a frame built with seats for humans, housing an engine that provided propulsion. The leap from a car to an airplane required the added theory of aerodynamics to supply liftoff and control of the skies, and heaps of horsepower to put that theory into practice. A car could conquer time and space. The airplane increased the distance exponentially and added an all-important dimension: altitude.

Edsel loved talking through these engineering puzzles with his sons sitting next to him. It was as if this dinner table were a pulpit and the boys were learning their family religion.

After dinner, Sorensen stayed up thinking the job through in his bed. Cast Iron Charlie was now sixty years old, the age at which he had promised himself and Henry Ford that he would retire. The man they used to call "Adonis" had white hair and tired, wrinkle-creased eyes, though he had lost only a little of his musculature. He had come to America as a young man with almost nothing in his pockets; now his fortune was estimated to be in the eight-figure range, in Depression-era dollars. For nearly four decades he had worked in Henry Ford's factories. He would describe it as "the greatest industrial adventure in history," one that took him and Henry "from a backyard machine shop to a billion dollar worldwide enterprise and creation of a magic name."

Now he sat with his notes spread out on the bed in the middle of the night in San Diego, his watch ticking away the hours. Little did he know at that moment that he was about to embark on a new adventure more ambitious than any Henry Ford had experienced.

"To compare a Ford V-8 with a four-engine Liberator bomber was like matching a garage with a skyscraper," Sorensen figured. "But despite their great differences I knew the same fundamentals applied to high-volume production of both, the same as they would to an electric egg beater or to a wrist watch. I saw no impossibility in such an idea even though mass production of anything approaching the size and complexity of a B-24 never had been attempted before."

All night Sorensen worked over his notes, imagining "the biggest challenge of my production career — bigger than any Model T assembly line sequence for Highland Park, more momentous than the layout and construction of the great River Rouge plant. . . . Now, in one night, I was applying 35 years of production experience to planning the layout for building not only something I had never put together before, but the largest and most complicated of all air transport and in numbers and at a rate never before thought possible."

The next morning, at breakfast in the hotel, Sorensen passed Edsel a sketch of a factory. It showed the outline of a building a mile long and a quarter of a mile wide, with railroad tracks running into it and a vast parking lot. Sorensen's idea: to build the largest airplane factory in history — a factory that would roll out one heavy bomber every hour, spelling doom to the Nazi regime.

There in the dining room Edsel examined the sketch that was about to throw his life into unimaginable upheaval. To Edsel, the airplane represented the dream that he had lost — the ambition, the identity, the innocence of his youth. He saw in the drawing, and in the bomber-an-hour proposal, a shot at redemption.

For not serving in World War I.

For the assaults on his patriotism.

For enduring his father's incessant attacks on his dignity and character.

For Harry Bennett.

With his sons at the table, Edsel pronounced that they would build such a factory. Everyone at the table — Edsel, his boys, and Sorensen — put their signature on the sketch, as if making some pact with the devil. They discussed the idea for an hour, then headed to meet Major Fleet with a $200 million proposition backed by nothing but a pencil sketch and the promise of Ford magic. Henry II nervously asked if he could stay behind. His father insisted he come along.

In the meeting, Major Fleet listened to the proposal. He shook his head.

"Get serious," he said.

He didn't want Ford to build airplanes; he wanted help making parts so that *he* could build airplanes. "Why not make units for us, and we'll assemble them?"

"We are not interested in assemblies," Sorensen boldly told Major Fleet. "We'll make the complete plane or nothing." If the Air Corps was willing to spend $200 million — an unfathomable gamble at the turn of 1941 — "we will build and equip a plant capable of turning out one Liberator bomber an hour," Sorensen said.

Edsel smiled at the audacity of it all. Sorensen looked at him. Then he glanced over at Edsel's son, Henry II, who was following the meeting silently. He saw something in young Henry's eyes — the same look he could recall seeing so many years ago in Henry Ford's eyes, back when they were building the first Model T at Highland Park. It was a look of excitement and determination, the knowledge that something great was about to happen.

On January 8, 1941, without any official approval from Washington, Edsel Ford announced that his family would begin immediately with plans to build a new type of factory. He would build the largest, fastest, most destructive, and most expensive airplane in the US military arsenal, he claimed, in numbers never before dreamed possible.

"We hope to be in production by the end of the year," he said.

All he had to prove that he could get the job done was his reputation and Sorensen's sketch, across the top of which was written "1 plane per hr, 400 per mo." The math, as Edsel and Sorensen figured it, was one plane every hour, two nine-hour shifts per day, six days a week. That added up to about four hundred bombers.

Roosevelt's Office of Production Management shot down the idea at least for the present, asking Ford to build parts and not the whole plane. The idea was simply too audacious.

One week after the initial sketch, Edsel's staff produced a new one — a more detailed drawing of a bomber factory with pencil sketches of long-winged planes moving down an assembly line like church crosses. It took nearly two months to convince the government to grant Ford a contract for complete bombers. By that time, Edsel, Sorensen, and their men were already moving at speed on the project.

When news got around — that an automaker was claiming it could turn out a four-engine bomber every hour — the aircraft manufacturers scoffed. At a meeting held at Detroit's Center Building to bring aviation and automotive minds together, North American Aviation's chief executive, James "Dutch" Kindelberger, stood before the Motor City's power elite and insisted that it couldn't be done. The automotive companies did not have the experience to build good airplanes, with their ultra-minuscule tolerances and innumerable complexities.

"You cannot expect blacksmiths to learn how to make wrist watches overnight," Kindelberger argued.

On March 3, 1941, Edsel's first bomber contract came through, not for $200 million but for $480 million — an order for 1,200 B-24 "knockdown" airframe assemblies (practically everything but the engines, delivered in pieces) and 800 complete planes, with the authorization to build a government-owned factory. Edsel agreed to spend the first $47 million out of pocket to get the factory built, with the understanding that the government would reimburse Ford in total. According to the contract, the government would cover the cost of the planes and pay Ford an 8 percent profit.*

---

* This was a standard contract under Roosevelt's war production plan. As Roos-

In Washington, many were infuriated by the news that Henry Ford — Oval Office nemesis, union enemy number one — should be granted such an enormous government contract. Henry had defied the Supreme Court by refusing to sign a deal with the auto unions. Eleanor Roosevelt told delegates that it was "a bad thing to give contracts to uncooperative people."

But Roosevelt turned a blind eye. He told Secretary of War Henry Stimson that it was time "to let bygone issues go and concentrate on getting Ford to play fair with labor in the future."

The President needed bombers.

One day after the contract was signed, the first team of Ford officials flew to San Diego to begin studying the B-24 Liberator. "We descended on the Consolidated people," remembered Roscoe Smith, who would soon play a major role in the bomber program. Some checked into the San Diego Hotel, others the El Cortez. Smith rented a floor of office space in the Spreckels Building downtown for headquarters. "Of course we were all very much awed by the size and complexity of the whole thing. I know for two weeks after I got there, I was in a daze."

"I remember we first talked of probably one plane an hour," said Logan Miller, who was among the initial wave of engineers to arrive in San Diego. "That was a dream more or less, and considered by aircraft people an impossibility. When we were told to do a thing, it was always a policy never to say no."

More men flew in from Dearborn until the crew reached two hundred — engineers, production experts, layout men, tool and die makers. Since they were moving to the West Coast with no end date on the project, Edsel personally paid for each man to take his wife with him. As the team set up on the West Coast, news came from Europe that Bulgaria and Yugoslavia had joined the Axis alliance, offering

---

evelt's secretary of war, Henry Stimson, put it to the President: "If you are going to war in a capitalist country, you have to let business make money out of the process or business won't work" (Doris Kearns Goodwin, *No Ordinary Time: Franklin and Eleanor Roosevelt: The Home Front in World War II* [New York: Simon & Schuster, 1994], p. 56). A fixed fee enabled manufacturers to do the job right without cutting corners.

more airfields, factories, and troops to the Nazi war machine. The word from Washington: speed!

The team of engineers began the job with a "breakdown" — reducing the plane to its smallest pieces, which could be studied and produced en masse. The job came to a halt on day one.

"They were supposed to have blueprints at San Diego," said Smith. "Their blueprints were not up-to-date and neither were their templates. If we wanted to know what a part actually looked like, we had to go out to the ship and see what it was like on the ship, which was entirely different from the blueprint. There was an awful lot of redesigning done. I spent about six months in San Diego. We had all we could get out of them. The rest of it was strictly up to us."

Metallurgists studied the materials so they could begin sourcing them. Eighty-five percent of the plane was made of aluminum alloy; 13 percent steel; 0.33 percent magnesium; 0.66 percent brass, copper, and bronze; and 1.01 percent rubber, glass, and plastic. Electricians dug deep into the Liberator's nervous system. There was no blueprint of the wiring. Each Consolidated plane had its own handcrafted electrical setup, designed according to the whims of the man on the job that day. The Ford men discovered that they would need over five miles of wire for each ship — of various thicknesses, cut into nearly three thousand pieces, with lengths varying from eight inches to thirty-two feet. It took four generators to run a Liberator. Each one supplied enough electricity to power an average household.

In Dearborn, an army of professional artists came on board to draw airplane parts in three dimensions so the manufacturing men could figure out how to make each one. Blueprint makers used state-of-the-art developing machines, spitting out 50,000 square feet of sensitized paper every day. By the end of four months, Edsel and Sorensen were nervously scratching their heads at over 5.9 million square feet of blueprints — all to make one plane.

All this work had to be done as fast as possible, so the tool designers could order the machines — drills, lathes, X-ray machines, jigs, cranes (there would be twenty-nine miles of cranes), and presses that would weigh hundreds of thousands of pounds, nearly all of them custom-built. A thousand men worked around the clock seven days a week for months to design machine tools — according to automotive methods. The tool-design job was by far the most difficult ever undertaken. At one point, the chief tool designing engineer, William Pioch, came to Sorensen with an idea to build one machine that could carve out massive thirty-ton center wings, each one like the one before, like carving out wooden baseball bats. He showed his design to Sorensen.

"Gee, that's going to cost a lot of money," Sorensen said.

"Yes, but here's the proposition," said Pioch. "It takes 550 man-hours to do the operations that this one machine is going to do in six man-hours." In other words, six men, one hour. That was the goal: a bomber an hour. At that rate, with labor cost savings, the machine would pay for itself in no time, Pioch argued. And unlike the B-24 center wings made at Consolidated in San Diego — each one different from the next — these wings would be alike, perfectly mass-produced. "I would like to build a good wing," said Pioch.

Sorensen gave it the okay. The machine would end up costing taxpayers $250,000. Would it work? Time would tell.

At the same time, a plant layout committee working with Detroit's most famed industrial architect, Albert Kahn, was carefully designing the floor space. This plant would have to accommodate some 1,600 machine tools, 7,000 fixtures and jigs, some of those jigs twelve times the height of Edsel Ford. Before placing any machine, the team had to figure out how many men would be working there, what the electrical requirements would be, and where to fit crane ways. A network of pipes and lines would be built into the structure like a circulatory system, moving oxygen, compressed air, paraffin, machine oil, steam, acetylene, hydrogen, oxygen, and two kinds of gasoline (73 octane for trucks and cars, 100 octane for airplanes) to different sections of the plant and the airfield hangar.

Would an operation create fumes or smoke? Special ventilation would be needed.

Would a specific job require dangerous materials such as cyanide or acid? Tanks to hold these substances would have to be situated and reinforced safely under the floor.

The Fords enlisted Major Jimmy Doolittle to help begin planning for the airfield that would border the bomber factory. Edsel aimed to build the most modern, technologically advanced airport in the world, from which his bombers would make their maiden flights.

On May 5, Roosevelt called upon the nation's industrial force for "a substantial increase" in airplane production once again, particularly the heavy bomber. "The effective defense of this country and the vital defenses of other democratic nations requires that there be a substantial increase in heavy bomber production," the President said in a letter that was published in hundreds of newspapers. "I know of no single item of our defense today that is more important than large four engine bomber capacity."

With every passing day, the pressure on Edsel Ford and Charlie Sorensen mounted. From Berlin, Hitler promised to torpedo American ships delivering munitions to Britain. Roosevelt declared an "Unlimited National Emergency." The war was moving closer to home.

11

Willow Run

Spring to Fall 1941

> The Industrial Revolution has now been fully applied to killing.
>
> — *The Economist, soon after the outbreak of World War II*

ON A COOL MARCH day in 1941, under an iron-gray sky, a train of Ford cars pulled to a stop in a vast empty field outside a village called Ypsilanti, twenty-seven miles due west of Detroit. Doors were wrenched open, and out stepped Henry Ford, Edsel, Sorensen, Harry Bennett, and Henry's physician Dr. McClure. A chilly wind swirled the hair on their heads. The brown fields were still shaking off the last of winter's frost, the grass crunching under their feet. Sorensen spread his long arms like wings and pronounced, "We'll put up a *mile* plant *right* across here!"

The plot of land — 1,450 acres, 240 of it an orchard that would require clearing — belonged to Henry. He farmed soybeans and apples here. Ironically, the property where Roosevelt's "Arsenal of Democracy" was about to grow its deepest roots was a veritable shrine to pacifism. Henry had built something called Camp Willow Run here years earlier, a place for boys whose fathers had been killed or disabled in World War I. The camp, which still drew disadvantaged boys to live in tents and farm the land in summer, was named for the gurgling creek that snaked through the fields. The boys could study their

Bible lessons in a little white wooden chapel that stood by an apple tree in the sun.

At the time, the location seemed perfect. The only problem: convincing Henry Ford to let go of the land. None of the men standing there that morning could know that they were about to make their first mistake in the Willow Run adventure — and it would be a grave one.

Staring out at his fields, Henry spoke bitterly of the project. Why would the Fords build the largest airplane factory in the world — a war factory — here in this quiet farm country outside Detroit, thousands of miles from violence he believed would never touch them? He couldn't make sense of it.

That night Edsel visited Henry at Fair Lane. He was careful (Dr. McClure's orders) not to get his father too upset. He tried to explain to Henry that this was not a matter of whether or not to build a new Ford model or design a new braking system. It was a matter of good and evil. When Edsel left Fair Lane, he called Sorensen and gave him good news: he had convinced his father to let go of the land. The next day Sorensen ordered a secretary to secure the title, and then he notified army officials.

"There was nothing to stop us from now on," he said.

Two weeks later, Edsel and his father stood watching as loggers began to clear the apple trees and Michigan sugar maples. By now the Fords were calling the bomber factory after the creek that ran through these fields: Willow Run. Henry had demanded that the creek not be disturbed; it would run beneath the factory. In days to come, laborers would see birds that had formerly lived in the trees around this creek nesting in the bomber plant's steel girders. Henry wanted the timber cleared with his antique saws. The steam-powered circular saws — six feet in diameter — sheared through the timber, the metal blades turning red-hot.

"It took me 29 years to plant, cultivate, and make that fine orchard," Henry said. "It took those tractors and bulldozers just 29 minutes to tear it all down."

In an office in Detroit, architects from the firm of Albert Kahn were laying out a map of the factory, planned big enough for 100,000 laborers. Instead of a straight assembly line, as it had appeared in

Sorensen's original sketch, the architects designed the plant in an L shape so that it would not spill out of Wayne County—which was Republican and anti-FDR. The county had gone to Hoover in the 1932 election, Landon in 1936, and Willkie in 1940. Henry's tax dollars would stay in Republican Wayne County, not Democratic Washtenaw County, which had voted for Roosevelt.

Before a stake tore into the dirt, the first news articles about the bomber-an-hour plan hit the dailies across the country. An artist made a first rendering of "Ford's Warbird Hatchery." Edsel called his plan "a revolution in aircraft production methods." The news came as a boost to Americans. As historian Douglas Brinkley later put it: "It was the first concrete news of mobilization that the average American could understand. . . . To Americans, that rate of production seemed enough to vanquish any enemy, anywhere."

The first sign that things were about to go drastically wrong came in early June. Roosevelt's Office of Production Management contacted Edsel. The OPM was sending a man up from Washington to see the bomber plant site.

"Apparently the Plant Site Board have had some reservations in their mind regarding the Willow Run site," Edsel told Sorensen on June 4, 1941. "This man is out to get information regarding the matter and report back to the board."

Muscular bulldozers had already cleared the land. Railroad tracks were being laid, a spur that connected the site to the nearby New York Central line so that raw materials could roar in day and night. When Edsel looked at these cleared fields, he saw everything moving along as planned—what would be, someday soon, the crowning achievement of his family empire and his career.

Edsel wondered: what could be wrong with this location? It was too late to turn back now.

Harry Bennett arrived at his office one morning during the early days of the Nazi pounding of London to find Charles Lindbergh waiting for him. In the basement of the Rouge, the aviator—who was now thirty-eight years old—stood as tall and slim as ever. Thus his nickname, Slim. His blond hair had begun to recede, but his pale, chiseled face still looked younger than his years. Lindbergh was ten minutes early for a scheduled meeting with Henry Ford. Promptly at 9:00 AM, Henry arrived. The men exchanged good mornings and then moved into Bennett's office, where Lindbergh made Henry a proposition.

The aviator had become the most prominent voice of an emerging political force called America First — the largest, most powerful anti-interventionist group in the nation. Since Henry Ford's stance on war was well known, Lindbergh was hoping Henry would join the cause.

Henry had befriended Lindbergh in the years since the aviator took both father and son Ford on their first flights in his *Spirit of St. Louis* in 1927. The aviator had visited the Rouge often in 1940, touring the factory with Henry and Edsel. They had spoken for hours about aviation, the various planes being used in the war, and the strengths and weaknesses of each airpower.

"I have great admiration for this man," Lindbergh said of Henry. "He has genius, understanding, fearlessness. . . . He is, and will always remain, one of the greatest men this country has produced."

Henry and Lindbergh never lacked for conversation. They were both born in Detroit. Both had become icons of modernity's defining ambition, to harness power. Unlike Edsel, Lindbergh could talk with Henry for hours about what became known at the time as "the Jewish Question." Both Henry and Lindbergh had controversial views on the Jews, and both stood accused of anti-Semitism and Nazi sympathies. Both had received the Grand Cross of the German Eagle from Hitler, and both had endured extreme public censure when they refused to give the medal back. Most importantly, they shared a disdain for the President.

"I wish I trusted him more," Lindbergh said of Roosevelt. "What has happened to America? To the character of the pioneer? To the courage of the Revolutionary Army? To the American destiny we once had?"

Henry had reservations about joining America First. Later that day, however, Bennett phoned Lindbergh and said that Henry was willing to join. A half hour later, Henry phoned Lindbergh himself. "He asked if a donation would be in order," recalled Lindbergh. "I told him that accepting membership was the most important aid he could give."

"Your stand against entry into the war has already had great influence," Lindbergh said. "And if we are able to keep out of it, I believe it will be largely due to the courage and support you have given us."

Thus, Henry Ford joined the most controversial anti-FDR group in the country, just as Edsel was building the highest-profile war production factory in the President's Arsenal of Democracy.

Three months after his meeting with Henry Ford, on January 23, 1941, Lindbergh sat down at a small table at 9:55 AM in the new House Office Building in Washington, surrounded by politicians and reporters, jammed elbow to elbow in a sweaty conference room. The aviator was set to deliver testimony before a congressional committee. It would be one of the most shocking pieces of testimony anyone in that room had ever heard.

Lindbergh was the only man in the country who could speak about the Luftwaffe with intimate knowledge. He had personally examined Germany's air force as late as 1938. He was the only American Goering allowed to fly the Luftwaffe's machines and inspect its facilities. Probably no other foreigner from any nation had seen the Luftwaffe's buildup with such immediacy, and no other figure had reported more facts back to the US government. "Nobody gave us much useful information about Hitler's air force until Lindbergh came home in 1939," said Air Corps chief Hap Arnold.

Now in Washington, as Lindbergh leaned over a table to speak into the microphone, spotlights captured a look of bitter determination on his face. The United States, Lindbergh said, should seek a "negotiated peace" in Europe, even though Hitler had invaded peaceful nations from Poland to France to Norway, committing atrocities along the way. Many took the aviator's message of appeasement as confirmation of his Nazi sympathies. Lindbergh's reasoning was even more surprising to the American public: the United States should stay out of the war because the nation was not capable of creating an air force in time that could beat the Luftwaffe. Against Hitler, America and Britain simply could not win.

"Our own air forces are in deplorable condition," Lindbergh said as cameras clicked and rolled. "Regardless of how much assistance we send [to Britain], it will not be possible for American and British aviation, concentrated in the small area of the British isles, to equal the strength of German aviation." He warned that if America joined the war, it "would be the greatest disaster the country has ever had."

It was no secret that Lindbergh was a suspected Nazi sympathizer. His testimony did not help his cause. When asked point-blank during his testimony "which side would it be to our interest to win [the war]?" he answered: "I would prefer to see neither side win."

Throughout 1941, Lindbergh toured the nation making speeches — at Chicago's Soldier Field, the Hollywood Bowl in Los Angeles, New York's Madison Square Garden. By this time, America First had swelled to 800,000 members, including future president Gerald Ford, the film producer Walt Disney, the poet E. E. Cummings, and the novelist Sinclair Lewis. Still, Henry Ford was the group's highest-profile member. And Lindbergh's politics could not have been more controversial.

"The three most important groups who have been pressing this country toward war are the British, the Jewish, and the Roosevelt Administration," he said in front of a crowd of 8,000 in Des Moines, Iowa. America was "on the verge of war," but it was "not yet too late to stay out."

Roosevelt went on the attack. "If I should die tomorrow," the President told Secretary of the Treasury Morgenthau over lunch, "I want you to know this. I am convinced Lindbergh is a Nazi." At a campaign rally for Roosevelt at Madison Square Garden, the name Henry Ford drew boos so loud that the voices shook the building's girders. The Roosevelt administration's loudest attack dog was Harold "Old Curmudgeon" Ickes, secretary of the interior, who called Lindbergh "the No. 1 United States Nazi fellow traveler."

"No one has ever heard Lindbergh utter a word of horror at, or even aversion to, the bloody career the Nazis are following," Ickes said in a statement, "nor a word of pity for the innocent men, women, and children who have been deliberately murdered by the Nazis in practically every country in Europe." Mocking the aviator for his Nazi medal, Ickes called him a "Knight of the German Eagle."

Under public attack from Washington, Lindbergh resigned from the Air Corps Reserves — a move he would soon regret. Ickes made another statement: "Mr. Lindbergh returned his commission with suspicious alacrity. But he still hangs on to the Nazi medal!"

Given the publicity, Henry Ford quietly removed his name from the roster of America First. But his loyalty to Lindbergh remained. Together they would soon find themselves fighting a far greater battle.

12

Awakening

Spring to Fall 1941

> When we are talking about America's war production job we
> are discussing the biggest job in all history.
>
> — WAR PRODUCTION BOARD CHIEF DONALD NELSON

IN THE SPRING OF 1941, American industry awoke from the long,
cold slumber of the Great Depression. In rural towns, silent factories
full of rusted-out machinery and cobwebs sprang to life, the sleepy
roads around them alive again with traffic. In the Rust Belt, smokestacks spit streams of telltale smoke. At shipyards along the coasts
and on lakes and rivers far inland, cranes swung against the sky while
the steel hulls of new ships crashed into the water. At aviation companies in Seattle, Baltimore, Buffalo, and Bethpage, New York, men
who'd been unemployed for years lined up to grab their pick of positions. Few ever dreamed they'd get to create a piece of a machine
that could fly.

In Radford, Virginia, and Sandusky, Ohio, construction crews
were quickly erecting new gunpowder factories. In Milwaukee, the
Allis-Chalmers agricultural equipment factory began tooling up to
make turbines for navy vessels, while the Cluett, Peabody, & Co. shirt
and pajama company across town started on the biggest job of its history — weaving thousands of military uniforms.

"America is like a giant boiler," British foreign secretary Lord Grey once said. "Once the fire is lighted under it there is no limit to the power it can generate."

Nowhere was that fire set to blaze like it would in Detroit and its suburbs. The Big Three auto companies were still pumping out shiny chrome-bumper cars. At the same time, the auto industry was signing the lion's share of government contracts. At hulking factories specializing in car bodies—GM's Fisher Body, the Murray Corporation, and Briggs (owned by Edwin Briggs, who also owned the Detroit Tigers)—executives were hiring men to build parts for the four-engine B-17 Flying Fortress. At the Hudson Motor Car Company, engineers were figuring out how to make frames for the B-26 "Widowmaker" Marauder, a twin-engine medium bomber designed by the Baltimore-based aviation pioneer Glenn Martin. On the assembly lines where glamorous Cadillacs were built, GM executives would soon be rolling out 16.5-ton M5 light tanks, each with a pair of V8 engines and two transmissions.

Car companies were taking on jobs that they had no experience doing, and hiring workers who had never fabricated a bicycle pedal, let alone a piece of a tank or a machine gun shell.

In the suburb of Warren, the steel skeleton of Chrysler's $20 million Detroit Tank Arsenal was in place, a factory that would soon swell to 1.25 million square feet. The company's imperturbable workaholic boss, K. T. Keller, had bulldozed some of the land himself. Even before the walls were up, production men began building twenty-eight-ton M3 Sherman tanks destined to roll over the borders of Nazi-occupied territory. Keller brought in a steam locomotive on the plant's railroad siding just to heat the place. The plan: to build more tanks in this one factory than Hitler was producing in all of Nazi Germany.

"It is the biggest thing we have ever undertaken," Keller said, referring not to tanks but to Detroit's overall war production plan. "It is so big that we cannot measure it and it gets bigger every day. We are ready to make a million of anything if they will let us know what they want."

In the vast fields outside of the city, where Henry Ford's orchard and his boys' camp had long thrived, the Willow Run bomber plant began to rise out of the ground. Workers laid the first concrete pilings on April 20, 1941. The spur from the New York Central Railroad reached the site on May 3. The first structural steel framework went up May 13. Construction workers began pouring the concrete floor on June 25. Albert Kahn's architects had designed floor space not just for the machine shop, stockrooms, and assembly line, but also for a fully equipped hospital, metallurgical and X-ray laboratories, toilets, and cafeterias capable of feeding tens of thousands of laborers at a time.

Daily Willow Run reached wider and higher into the sky — three stories up, farther from one end to the other than the eye could see. At night, construction workers toiled under Hollywood-style klieg lights. The world had come a long way in the forty years since Henry Ford worked in Detroit's Edison electric plant, powering the city's first dull streetlamps.

Adjacent to the Willow Run site, graders leveled the airfield. It took them 94 days to flatten the earth, moving 650,000 cubic yards of dirt. Engineers spent 107 days laying 16 miles of sewer and 58 miles of drain tile underground — critical to keeping the airfield dry, lest the runways crack and buckle when the earth froze in winter. The field naturally drained toward the northeast, and yet there was no outlet there, so the engineers used a complex network of drainpipes to move rainwater into the little Willow Run Creek on the other side. In the end the sewer gangs could brag that they had put in a drainage system under the airfield big enough for a thriving small city.

Before Willow Run's brick walls were complete, before the place even had a roof, Ford Motor Company began hiring workers. The first employees were put on the payroll in early November 1941, and the first production man-hours were logged on November 15. The little roads leading to the factory parking lot clogged in the early mornings with men seeking work, many having traveled hundreds of miles to get there.

The 420 acres of land bordering the construction site were home to 94 houses and 331 people. It was a rural enclave just outside the teeming Detroit metropolis. The local tavern, built in 1829, had the "atmosphere of an antique shop," according to one frequenter. The first new arrivals drew consternation from the locals — who were unaware that an estimated 100,000 workers were soon expected to be punching time cards at this bomber factory.

All the while, the conflagration overseas continued to spread. As Willow Run's concrete floors were being laid, Hitler shocked the world by attacking the Soviet Union. Operation Barbarossa sent over 3 million German troops and 600,000 motor vehicles over the border. The Soviet forces crumpled under the treads of the Panzer tanks. Hitler had proven what machines could do in the hands of a madman. Under the onslaught of Nazi troops and pilots, the Soviet dictator Joseph Stalin turned to the United States. He too needed tanks, trucks, and airplanes — equipment that would have to be built on the assembly lines of America.

When Washington inquired, Edsel Ford promised: the company's Liberator bombers would take flight in the spring of 1942, ahead of schedule.

"These are terrific stakes," a *Fortune* reporter wrote of Willow Run in 1941. "No piece of armament that we are forging is more important [than the heavy bomber]. . . . The Allied nations have desperate need for a breakthrough weapon. The heavy bomber has the range and striking power that global war demands. . . . It may save our honor, our hopes — and our necks."

One night over dinner at a fine Washington seafood restaurant in 1941, Edsel and Sorensen sat talking about the old days, when Edsel was a kid riding his bike around the Mack Avenue plant and Sorensen was a $3-a-day pattern-maker. With all these trips together, the two had cemented a deep bond. They had known each other since Edsel was old enough to take his first steps on wobbly legs. Now they were a team running an empire — Edsel making the decisions in his corner office, Sorensen in the factories, making things happen. They shared the purpose of the war between them, a chance to make a difference in a way neither ever imagined among all their lofty ambitions.

"I was devoted to him, and he knew it," Sorensen said of Edsel. "When he became President of Ford Motor Company, he never did treat me like [he was] a boss; but I always worked for him as though he was my boss. He was gentle, considerate of others, unsparing of himself—and he was a *man*."

After dinner that night, Edsel suddenly doubled over in pain. Alarmed, Sorensen helped him back to his hotel room and called for a doctor. The physician gave Edsel pain medication, and Sorensen sat by his bedside until sunrise.

"I was afraid it was his end," Sorensen later said. "It scared me to see the agony he was in at times."

What was causing this agony inside Edsel? The attacks were getting worse. For months, Edsel's doctors had been trying to get him to come in for examinations. But he was tired of the enemas and pills and probes. "There would be no indication for any tube swallowing this time," Dr. John Mateer wrote him, urging him to come in for more tests. "I realize how very busy you are at the present time."

Edsel was working grueling hours—sometimes sixteen hours a day—and enduring increasing pain in his gut due to a health condition that had doctors confounded. He appeared to have gastric ulcers, but doctors had no idea how to treat them. Perhaps ulcers were not Edsel's problem. Perhaps his suffering was caused by something more biologically sinister.

At Gaukler Pointe, his wife Eleanor begged him to slow down. "I can't spare the time," he said. A moment of respite was rare indeed. He was a busy man, and perhaps in some ways he hid behind his business, his many important obligations. He was like many people defined by those obligations, so how could he say no? Not only was he suffering the weight of war work, but he was president of the Detroit Institute of the Arts and the Ford Foundation, a trustee of the National Foundation on Matters of Business Policy and the National Foundation for Infantile Paralysis, a member of the National Advisory Committee of the American Red Cross, vice president of Henry Ford Hospital, and chairman of the board of the Detroit University School.

Meanwhile, Knudsen called Edsel again, this time asking if Ford Motor Company could mass-produce another aircraft engine critical to the defense effort. It was a big job and would require major resources and serious expertise. With Sorensen, Edsel flew to the Pratt & Whitney plant outside Hartford, Connecticut, to inspect the

Franklin Roosevelt giving a "fire-side chat" in the White House. He delivered his Arsenal of Democracy chat on December 29, 1940.

Getty / Time & Life Pictures

Henry Ford and his only child, Edsel, in an early Ford automobile in 1905. Within a few short years, Henry would become arguably the world's most famous man.

From the collections of The Henry Ford

Henry and Edsel in 1928. Edsel Ford was president of Ford Motor Company from 1919 until his death in 1943.

From the collections of The Henry Ford

"Cast Iron" Charlie Sorensen with a section of a B-24 Liberator four-engine bomber, circa January 1942. *Getty / Time & Life Pictures*

Harry Bennett commanded Ford's Service Department — "the most powerful private police force in the world," according to the *American Mercury* magazine.

Walter P. Reuther Library, Wayne State University

When it was completed in 1920, Henry Ford's the Rouge was the world's largest factory.
Corbis / SuperStock

The Battle of the Overpass outside the Rouge on May 26, 1937. Harry Bennett's "Gestapo" (left) confronts union men.

Walter P. Reuther Library, Wayne State University

"I do not know how many times I was conscious or unconscious," said union man Richard Frankensteen (center) of the Battle of the Overpass.

Walter P. Reuther Library, Wayne State University

Strikers at the Rouge in April 1941 accuse Henry Ford of Nazi sympathies.

Getty/New York Daily News

Hitler salutes a parade of Nazi tanks in the late 1930s. Fourth from right is Hermann Goering, chief of the German air force. *Corbis*

Charles Lindbergh (left) testifies before Congress in February 1941. American and British air forces could not "equal the strength of German aviation," Lindbergh said.

Corbis/Hulton-Deutsch Collection

Henry and Edsel Ford in 1940. Henry was one of the nation's most outspoken antiwar activists.

Getty/Archive Photos

Henry Ford II (right) at the Rouge in Dearborn, Michigan. Edsel Ford's oldest son left the navy in 1943 to try to take over the family empire.

Getty/Time & Life Pictures

Inside Ford's Willow Run bomber factory, hailed by the *Washington Post* as "the greatest single manufacturing plant the world has ever seen." *From the collections of The Henry Ford*

B-24 Liberators in a shakedown flight over Willow Run in 1943. Charles Lindbergh flew many of these test flights himself.

From the collections of The Henry Ford

Women workers at Ford's bomber plant. "Rosie the Riveter" was based in part on a Willow Run riveter named Rose Monroe.

Library of Congress

The "Billion Dollar Watchdog" Harry Truman (behind boy) and his Truman Committee at Willow Run. Senator Truman's 1943 report on the "bomber-an-hour" experiment was devastating.

Library of Congress

Willow Run's last Liberator, circa June 28, 1945. This bomber was later placed in downtown Detroit as a peace memorial in honor of Edsel Ford's death.

From the collections of The Henry Ford

From left, Joseph Stalin, Franklin Roosevelt, and Winston Churchill, at the Tehran Conference on December 1, 1943 — deemed the high point of Roosevelt's presidency.

Getty/Popperfoto

Liberators make low-level attack runs during Operation Tidal Wave (August 1, 1943), the bombing of Hitler's greatest source of oil — Ploesti, Romania.

U.S. Air Force

B-24s return to Ploesti to destroy the Nazis' source of fuel, six days before D-Day in 1944.

Library of Congress

R-2800 Double Wasp — a relatively new, air-cooled, 18-cylinder radial engine, introduced in 1939. General Hap Arnold, who was spearheading Washington's effort to build American airpower, met them there. He gave Edsel and Sorensen a blow-by-blow.

The Double Wasp was rugged, versatile, and easy to maintain, its 18 cylinders joined at the center like pieces in a pie. The engine put out 2,400 horsepower, and weighed 2,350 pounds — more than a horsepower per pound, an impressive achievement.

"Just think," Sorensen said, "one cylinder is bigger than a [Lincoln] Zephyr engine."

Auto men like Edsel and Sorensen were accustomed to speaking loudly, so they could be heard over the groan of engines. But on the test bed, this Double Wasp's song was deafening.

"You have seen the modern industrial miracle," Sorensen said, gazing at this engine that could throttle a human over 300 miles per hour through the sky. Sorensen begged Edsel for the job. "Give me the Rouge," he pleaded.

Edsel smiled — it was a deal. The pair moved on to the War Department in Washington to make the agreement formal on 4,000 engines and a new factory that would be built onto the Rouge. Edsel signed a letter of intent on a contract that would soon make Ford one of the world's biggest heavy-rated aircraft engine producers — on top of the bomber-an-hour job. The Fords agreed to front the $14 million to get the factory built — a "blackout building" with no windows so it could function in total darkness in case of air raids.

"It will be completely guarded by men and by barbed wire," Edsel told reporters. "Since it will have no windows, the newest type of indirect lighting and of air conditioning will be employed for maximum efficiency."

Before the official contract was signed, Edsel broke ground on the new aviation engine plant at the Rouge. He ran the construction hoe with his own hands, wearing his usual fine tailored suit and pocket square. The factory was completed in miraculous time, mere months. By the time Edsel's first Pratt & Whitney Double Wasp landed on the test bed at the Rouge, Sorensen had designed an ingenious dynamometer system. When the aircraft engines were tested, the system harvested their energy output, which was then used to power machines building new Double Wasps. In essence, the factory could partially power itself.

Edsel had another reason he could not leave his job behind: he had two important new employees working for him — his boys Henry II and Benson. As the war preparedness fever heightened the pressure at every level in the company, Edsel's sons began their careers. Henry II had known his whole life that his destiny was the Rouge. Now he was inside working full-time — but not on cars. Sorensen assigned him to the Rouge's dynamometer lab, running Double Wasp aircraft engines on the test bed. It was hard work, in the loudest room in the factory.

The sight of young Henry at the Rouge was an antidote for Edsel's stress. He had long imagined and wondered where Henry II would excel, what his favorite part of the business would be. The design department, where Edsel felt most at home? Business, the part of the company that most needed new blood? Henry II had his grandmother's well-girthed body and his mother's eyes. Edsel knew his oldest son had a hard road ahead of him, and he worried over his ability to handle it all. The young man couldn't hide his nerves; the anxiety was all over his face, from the weight of the expectations.

Unlike Edsel, his son Henry II could not remember a day when he was not filthy rich. At Yale, where the students called him "T" after his grandfather's Model T, Henry II failed engineering. "The other guys said sociology was a snap course, so I figured that was for me," he later said. "I flunked it, too." He left the university without his diploma after he was caught cheating on a final exam.

At Henry II's twenty-first birthday party, bandleader Tommy Dorsey regaled guests, along with twenty-three-year-old up-and-comer Frank Sinatra. Soon after, Henry II was married to Anne McDonnell, an attractive Catholic woman from a wealthy New York family. The society papers called it "The Wedding of the Century." Pope Pius XII sent his personal blessing. Upon the occasion of his wedding, Henry II received 25,000 shares of Ford stock, in recognition that (in his father's words) he would "join the Ford Motor Company as your future business."

Now here he was in the Rouge, his fingers raw, his face smeared with grease. Engineer Laurence Sheldrick took Henry II and his brother Benson under his wing.

"I'll give those boys all the credit in the world," Sheldrick said. "They certainly didn't pull any punches about getting their hands dirty."

Sheldrick had Henry II and Benson reporting directly to a black foreman. When Henry Ford came to see his grandsons, he had Harry Bennett by his side. Bennett saw Edsel's kids reporting to a black man. He pulled Sheldrick aside and, as the engineer later recalled, "called me everything on the map." Sheldrick went to see Edsel right away.

"Don't pay a bit of attention to him," Edsel said of Bennett. "That's good for the boys. Keep them right there."

But Sheldrick didn't keep them there. He had a more critical assignment for them. He transferred the Ford boys to the Jeep program, where they worked on the assembly of the first "blitz buggy" that Edsel was now building for the military, off the assembly lines at the Rouge. One day Sheldrick asked Edsel if he would come see a shakedown of the first Ford military Jeep.

"I'll never forget this day," Sheldrick recalled. "I told Edsel that if he would stop by Rotunda Drive on the way from lunch he could see the Jeep operating." A whole group of cars came down and parked on the road. Among his men, Edsel stood waiting. Sheldrick gave a signal, and the first Ford-built Jeep came tearing out of the woods, with Henry II and Benson in the cockpit. "This jeep just came out of nowhere up to their father. He got one hell of a kick out of that. That was one time that I saw Edsel when he was thoroughly enjoying himself. He was awfully proud of his boys."

Then the dreaded day came when Edsel saw Henry II in uniform for the first time. To avoid the uncertainty of his draft placement, Henry II enlisted in the navy. Sorensen offered to file exemption papers for the young man, but neither Henry II nor Edsel would allow it — not after what Edsel had endured during World War I. Benson was just behind his older brother, enlisting in the army.

Edsel was crushed the day Henry II left the Rouge, bound for the Great Lakes Naval Station north of Chicago. It was an emotion that could not be fathomed until experienced. Eleanor Roosevelt had expressed it best, what it felt like to see a child in uniform leave home during wartime. "I had a feeling that I might be saying goodbye for the last time," she wrote. "It was sort of precursor of what it would be like if your children were killed and never to come back. Life had to go on and you had to do what was required of you, but something inside you quietly died."

Henry Ford was infuriated by the idea of his grandson in uniform, and he tasked Harry Bennett with getting Henry II out of the military. Bennett began to meddle, making calls to high-level officials, and word got back to Edsel. He wrote his father a letter.

"Now that [Henry II] is in the Navy he is trying to do a good job," Edsel wrote, "and he can't do it with all the string-pulling and high-pressure from Bennett. . . . Henry feels his place is in the Navy. . . . We, who are after all his parents, have given the whole matter a lot of thought and believe as Henry does and it is his decision to make and he is making it. You are the only one who can do anything with Bennett and we would appreciate very much if you would call him off."

As a father, Edsel could see his own past in a new light. He had been forbidden by *his* father to fight in World War I. Henry Ford had subjected Edsel to humiliation at its apotheosis to keep him out of the trenches — to keep him safe. But the cost was the loss of Edsel's honor, a wound perhaps deeper than death. Edsel could not inflict that wound on his own son. And yet he feared the consequences. Could Henry II be asked to make the ultimate sacrifice?

13

Strike!

Spring to Winter 1941

Practically all the Ford employees are fearful of Bennett. They speak of him privately as if he were a combination of Dracula, Pearl Bergoff, and J. Edgar Hoover. They are convinced that he has as many spies in his pay as Hirohito of Japan, and they credit him with a malevolent omniscience that would do honor to the devil himself.

— *The American Mercury, May 1940*

EARLY ON THE MORNING of April 2, 1941, eight Ford workers who had been fired by Bennett's Service Men for union activity called for a strike at the Rouge, claiming that the firings had violated federal law. First a few men joined the strike. Then a few more. Then, under the astonished eyes of suit-and-tie management, workers en masse dropped their tools and made for the doors. The pounding noise of machinery in the Rouge gave way to the sound of boots clattering — thousands and then tens of thousands of men walking off the job.

There had never been a strike at the Rouge. The walkoff appeared impromptu, but in fact the United Auto Workers had planned ahead. Thousands of men, most of whom didn't work for Henry Ford but did support the auto unions, were on their way to Dearborn. Cars with license plates from states all over the Midwest thundered into the Rouge parking lot, carrying bruisers with baseball bats and iron rods.

Harry Bennett was ready for them.

The morning of the strike, union picketers barricaded the three main entrances leading in and out of the plant. Groups also block-aded tunnel-ways and railroad tracks. No one could come in or out. Inside the factory, Bennett organized a group of 2,500 black strike-breakers. They were armed with knives, hand-sharpened metal rods, and badges saying 100% FOR FORD. Bennett had promised them they would be "paid around the clock" if they refused to exit the Rouge. For months he had recruited aggressively among the black commu-nity for his Service Department. Two-thirds of the black laborers in Detroit worked for Henry Ford. Bennett sought out the largest men, armed them, and inflamed their rage against "whitey." Now he was prepared to set them loose like cats among the pigeons.

Bennett was set to play out a daring, all-or-nothing strategy. That first day of the strike — now a fully loaded racial standoff between white union men outside the Rouge and black Service Department loyalists inside — Bennett sent a wire directly to the President of the United States, informing Roosevelt that the Rouge had been seized by "communist terrorists."

"Unlawful sit-down strikes, followed by seizure of highway ap-proaches and entrances to the plant in a Communistic demonstra-tion of violence and terrorism have prevented the vast majority of our 85,000 employees from going to work at the Rouge Plant," Bennett cabled the White House. "Communist leaders are actively directing this lawlessness."

Within hours the strike turned violent. "Iron bolts and nuts flew through the air in a wholesale barrage from the factory roof," said one reporter on the scene, "while several hundred Negroes with steel bars and knives charged out of the main gate, No. 4 at the Rouge plant."

"I went out to the Ford Rouge Plant to see for myself just what is going on," said a broadcaster on Detroit's WJR radio at 6:00 PM that first day of the strike. "I found all the streets and highways leading to the gates on Miller Road in Dearborn barricaded with planks, bricks, debris, and various other obstructions. Pickets milled around by the hundreds, in groups, carrying clubs, sticks, and other articles of defense or attack. I saw a number of persons injured by bricks, clubs, and fists."

Bennett held a press conference. "The unions seized our plant like burglars," he told reporters, "and if the Fords were to condone such actions it would be like saying 'come on, take us over.' Mr. Ford is convinced that his policies are just and right."

Union officials were working their own angle. "The Ford company is attempting to sabotage the defense program because of its Nazi connections," one told the *New York Times*. "It has sought to impede defense by turning down contracts for the British. The Ford company incited violence during the strike and pitted race against race."

With the climactic battle between Bennett and the unions at hand, the little man locked down in an office with his boss. "Mr. Ford wanted to fight the thing out," Bennett later recalled. "He told me to arm everyone we had in the plant, and use tear gas if necessary."

Edsel was in Florida on a brief trip, trying to regain his health. He got word of the strike by phone and jumped on the first plane he could, bound for Detroit.

As the sun went down, the 2,500 strikebreakers locked inside the Rouge began to grow hungry and terrified for their lives. Union men were hurling stones through windows. Bennett and Henry monitored the situation from afar. An executive named Mead Bricker showed up in a panic. People were brawling outside the Rouge gates, he panted. It was black against white, and entirely out of control.

"Oh, don't worry about that," Henry said. "It isn't rotten enough yet. It will straighten itself out when it gets rotten enough."

In the White House, Roosevelt was busy handling some of the most careful political negotiations of his career. He was pushing the Lend-Lease bill through Congress, which would allow him to send munitions to the British military without violating Washington's Neutrality Acts. The controversial bill, critics pointed out, would enable the President to legally come as close to war against Hitler as he could without sending a man into battle. At the same time, his administration was posturing with the Japanese, who were moving troops deep into Indochina. Soon the President would order the seizure of all Japanese assets in the United States and, more importantly, an embargo of high-octane aviation fuel, knowing that military aggression from the Japanese was likely to come in the form of guns and horsepower mounted on wings.

Unbeknownst to Roosevelt, the Japanese already had a spy on the ground in Hawaii, scoping out the bombers and boats at Pearl Harbor.

When Harry Bennett's wire arrived, Roosevelt considered it coldly. Bennett was asking the President to send in troops. The idea of laborers walking off the job when critical defense work was under way infuriated everyone in the White House. Eleanor Roosevelt received word from civil rights leader Mary McLeod Bethune, who had inside information. The Ford Company, she said, was using black workers as "the backbone of the Ford anti-union force." Bethune worried that this strike was about to turn into "one of the bloodiest race riots in the history of the country," a riot that "would set race relations back a quarter of a century."

Roosevelt feared that if he sent in troops he would throw fuel on the flames. Instead, he sent in Walter White, head of the NAACP, and Thomas Dewey, a lawyer and future governor of New York (who would face Roosevelt as the Republican presidential candidate three years later).

As ambulances in Dearborn hauled off dozens more injured on days two and three, news came that Hitler had invaded Greece. His troops took Athens in a matter of hours. Republicans saw an opportunity to attack the Democratic president for not forcing an end to the Rouge strike with National Guard troops.

"With the help of the President of the US, Hitler has closed the Ford plant," snapped Michigan congressman George Dondero.

Democratic leaders were "assuring us that you were going to do something," Congressman Clinton Anderson of New Mexico wrote Roosevelt on day three of the strike. "Instead of that we get news that the Ford plant is compelled to close, to the tremendous joy, I am sure, of Mr. Hitler."

When Edsel arrived in Dearborn, he found his father, Bennett, and Sorensen holed up in an office. Edsel was "extremely alarmed when he learned of our plans," as Bennett remembered, "and he insisted that we give up any such ideas" of fighting it out. Edsel demanded that Ford do as the other motor companies had done: sign a contract with the unions, as federal law dictated. The Supreme Court had ruled that Ford had no choice.

"I'm not going to sign this contract!" Henry screamed. "I don't want any more of this business. Close the plant down if necessary."

Edsel begged his father to listen to reason. If Ford didn't sign with the union, the government could come in and take over.

"Well, if that happens, they will be in the motorcar business, and we won't."

By day four, the strike had left all thirty-four Ford assembly plants in the forty-eight states on lockdown, for fear of further violence. Some 130,000 workers were left idle. In Dearborn, Bennett ordered the ship *Henry Ford II* up the river to the Rouge, where it unloaded sandwiches and liquor to the men locked inside, who were now driving Jeeps all over the factory and looting the place. Around the Rouge gates, government sound trucks attempted to diffuse the standoff: "The patriotic thing to do is to keep the wheels of our defense factories humming."

The NAACP's Walter White brought in his own sound trucks to try to get the men out of the Rouge. "I walked in the picket line around the plant and attempted to talk to a Negro inside, who brandished a frightening weapon several feet in length," said White. "Across the main entrance of the River Rouge plant stood an apparently impregnable wall of human flesh."

A few miles away, on the quiet veranda of Henry Ford's Fair Lane mansion, Henry sat reading the latest news of the strike in the paper when he saw Bennett's automobile round into the driveway. Out stepped Bennett and Michigan governor Murray Van Wagoner, an emissary of the President.

"Well, you've got a plant," Henry said to the Governor. "What are you going to do with it?"

The Governor appeared overwhelmed. "Van Wagoner became very agitated," according to Bennett, "and seemed incapable of coherent speech."

For ten full days the strike wore on, until the Governor brokered a settlement. Henry agreed to discussions with the United Auto Workers — to come to the negotiating table and nothing more. "We'll bargain until hell freezes over," said Bennett. "But they won't get anything."

When the black strikebreakers left the Rouge under police protection, federal investigators headed in to survey the damage. The next morning Edsel awoke and heard on the radio that his father had caved to the UAW. Bennett had signed the contract, agreeing to all the union's demands. It was over.

Edsel was dumbfounded. He rushed to the Willow Run construction site to find Sorensen. "What in the world happened?" he asked.

"I was just about to ask you the same thing," Sorensen responded.

They sought answers from Henry, who explained that he had told his wife that he was going to close down the Rouge. Clara Ford had been in conference with Edsel. If Edsel couldn't convince his father to sign with the union, at least he could convince his mother that it was the right thing to do. "Mrs. Ford was horrified," Henry told Edsel the morning after the strike ended. If Henry and Bennett continued to fight the union, "there would be riots and bloodshed," Henry said, "and she had seen enough of that." He paused.

"Don't ever discredit the power of a woman."

In the struggle with Harry Bennett, the union contract was Edsel's greatest victory to date. Henry Ford was crestfallen. "It was perhaps the greatest disappointment he had in all his business experience," Sorensen said.

"Mr. Ford gave in to Edsel's wishes," said Bennett. The union would never have won "if it hadn't been for Edsel's attitude."

In Edsel's office in the fall of 1941, he spent innumerable late-night hours in conference with military figures in Washington, who heaped more defense jobs on his desk. Soon Ford Motor Company would be generating more military material than the entirety of Mussolini's Italy.

At Highland Park, where the Model T was born, Edsel and Sorensen were tooling up to assemble M7 anti-aircraft guns. Inside the Rouge, they were overseeing the construction of the largest magnesium foundry in the world. Because magnesium was unquenchable if it caught fire (burning at 3,300 degrees), the foundry in the Rouge required extraordinary amounts of safety precautions.

Just a year earlier, at the Lincoln plant in downtown Detroit, Edsel had rolled out the first production Lincoln Continental — a Euro-styled chariot destined to rank high on "most beautiful cars of all time" lists forever. Now the Lincoln factory was tooling up to build aircraft superchargers. Like super-lungs, they enabled military planes to breathe harder so they could travel faster, especially at high altitude where oxygen was thin.

It seemed so incongruous, this newfangled science, wild ideas matched with industrial prowess, all of it destined to play a key role in the ultimate battle between good and evil. Under all that pressure, Edsel's health continued to decline, and sixty-one-year-old Sorensen fainted twice — once while walking with his wife (his head hit a curb and he needed stitches), then again in the Rouge. Edsel himself was so on edge that he nearly came to blows on one occasion with Bennett. While in a meeting with his father and Sorensen, Bennett entered and announced that he had heard rumors of a kidnap plot aimed at Edsel's kids. Bennett wanted to send Service Men to protect them. Worn thin, Edsel uncharacteristically exploded.

"Stop this talk!" he shouted. "Leave the boys alone! I don't want protection for myself or my sons!"

Bennett tore off his coat and charged. Sorensen pushed Edsel out the door before Bennett's blows could land.

The situation was spinning out of control. "Never was any business run like the Ford empire," Sorensen wrote in his memoirs. "If a story was written as a fairy tale the public would reject it as too fantastic to believe."

Then one morning the bombs came.

14

Air Raid!

December 7, 1941

We are now in this war. We are all in it — all the way.

— FRANKLIN ROOSEVELT, *December 9, 1941*

AIR CORPS AND NAVAL personnel were still clearing the sleep crust out of their eyes when the telltale roar of engines turned their eyes to the east. The scene: Pearl Harbor, Hawaii, December 7, 1941, 7:55 AM. On the horizon, a vast storm cloud of airplanes appeared, a pack of Japanese combat planes, many of them streaking low over the ocean, which sparkled in the morning sun.

Earlier that morning, radar had picked up some mysterious signals, which were mistaken to be American planes flying from California to Hawaii. Now a fleet of Japanese attack planes was moving in — forty-nine high-altitude bombers, fifty-one dive-bombers, forty torpedo bombers, and forty-three single-engine fighters. They were headed for Battleship Row, where American ships were tied in port.

The US navy warships were on "Condition Three" alert. Peacetime, no anti-aircraft guns manned. The soldiers and sailors who happened to be near their anti-aircraft guns at that moment found their ammunition boxes locked. They did not have the keys. Aboard the ships, loudspeakers crackled out the alarm.

"Air raid! This is no shit!"

The first ship hit was the *Arizona*. An armor-piercing bomb exploded on the ship's forward deck, setting off over a million pounds of gunpowder inside. A sailor would report seeing the *Arizona* "jump at least 15 to 20 feet upward in the water and sort of break in two." The ship sank in nine minutes, with nearly 1,200 sailors aboard.

Meanwhile, more Japanese pilots were sweeping low above the mastheads and releasing their payload. "Their accuracy was uncanny," said one American officer.

Columns of steel-gray smoke and fire blistered the sky as the great iron hulls moaned and rolled over, capsizing into the muddy ocean. More waves of attack planes appeared — among them the Zeros, the Mitsubishi-powered 300-mile-per-hour fighters that would soon become legendary. The attacking planes moved in low over Pearl Harbor's airfields, Hickam and Wheeler. The American warplanes were grouped together for protection against sabotage. It was hard for the Japanese pilots to miss. Only a few American aircraft managed to scramble up into the sky before the surprise assault on Pearl Harbor was over.

Nearly 2,500 American sailors were dead, and many more wounded. The surprise attack proved the worst naval disaster in American history. It was also devastating to American airpower. Roughly three hundred planes — nearly all of the fighters and bombers stationed in the Pacific — were destroyed.

Roosevelt was sitting in his White House study with his closest aide and friend, Harry Hopkins, when his phone rang shortly after 1:30 PM Washington time.

"Mr. President," said Frank Knox, secretary of the navy, "it looks as if the Japanese have attacked Pearl Harbor."

"No!"

Roosevelt hung up the phone. It must be a mistake, said Hopkins. The President disagreed. It was no mistake. Moments later, Admiral Harold Stark phoned confirming the news.

The President wheeled quickly in his chair to the Oval Office. "His chin stuck out about two feet in front of his knees and he was the maddest Dutchman . . . anybody . . . ever saw," according to a White

House Secret Service agent. Soon the phone rang again. Hawaii governor Joseph Poindexter delivered more news from Honolulu.

"My God," Roosevelt spit, "there's another wave of Jap planes over Hawaii right this minute!"

Once again, the airplane had successfully delivered a surprise and destructive attack. If anyone needed proof of the importance of airpower in the new global playing field, Pearl Harbor was it.

In the hours to come, across America, the most shocking news since the assassination of Abraham Lincoln made its way over radio broadcasts. Crowds gathered in front of the White House on Pennsylvania Avenue, cheering on the President, not knowing what else to do. Inside in the Oval Office, congressional leaders and cabinet members horseshoed around Roosevelt's desk. He briefed them on the latest news, stopping to check the cables that were being handed to him.

"How did it happen that our warships were caught like tame ducks at Pearl Harbor?" shouted Senator Tom Connally of Texas. "How did they catch us with our pants down?"

"I don't know, Tom," Roosevelt said with his head bowed. "I just don't know. . . . The fact is that a shooting war is going on today in the Pacific. We are in it."

When Churchill called the White House from England, he said with shock, "Mr. President, what's this about Japan?"

"It's quite true," Roosevelt said. "They have attacked us at Pearl Harbor. We're all in the same boat now."

A few minutes after 5:00 PM the day of Pearl Harbor, Roosevelt called his secretary, Grace Tully, to his study. The President sat with his desk covered in piles of notes.

"Sit down, Grace," Roosevelt said. "I'm going before Congress tomorrow. I'd like to dictate my message. It will be short."

He spoke in a steady tone, more slowly than he usually dictated. "Yesterday comma December 7th comma 1941 dash a day which will live in world history. . . ."

The next day Roosevelt delivered his famous "Day of Infamy" speech.

"Powerful and resourceful gangsters have banded together to make war upon the whole human race," he said. "Their challenge has now been flung at the United States. We are now in this war. We are all in it — all the way. Every single man, woman, and child is a partner in the most tremendous undertaking of our American history."

The United States declared war on Japan on December 8. Due to the Tripartite Pact — which tied the Axis powers, Germany, Italy, and Japan, together as one military force — Hitler and Mussolini declared war on the United States. The United States declared war on the Axis powers on December 11. In the next few days, Bulgaria and Romania declared war on the United States. Britain declared war on Bulgaria. Holland declared war on Italy. Belgium declared war on Japan.

National superpowers had chosen sides. All that was left was a fight to the death.

PART III

THE BIG ONE

I was the flight engineer on the Wyatt crew [under pilot Second Lieutenant Bert Wyatt], who perished on their sixth mission while returning from a giant raid on Berlin on April 29, 1944. I survived because I was disabled on an earlier mission and was being X-rayed at the hospital when the fatal mission was flown. Our B-24 Liberator, named El Lobo, was hit over the target, lost two engines, but made it halfway home to England. At which point it was shot down by a German fighter plane near the village of Dinklage in northern Germany. In 2006 I traveled to Dinklage and participated in a small ceremony with local dignitaries and newspapers in attendance. They presented me with several fragments of the plane, which they located with metal detectors. The Germans treated me like a celebrity instead of a guy who helped bomb them to smithereens.

— JACK R. GOETZ, *Penn Valley, CA*

15

The Grim Race

Winter 1941 to Summer 1942

Orators, columnists, professors, preachers, and propagandists performed magnificently with the theme that World War II was a war between two ideologies. But whatever inflamed people's minds in warring countries, victory was on the side of the heaviest-armed battalions. The conflict became one of two systems of production.

— "CAST IRON" CHARLIE SORENSEN

ON THE MORNING OF December 8, 1941, America awoke as a nation paralyzed with fear. The skies were pregnant with hellfire, citizens across the country were told by their most trusted officials.

"This is war," one army lieutenant general announced. "Death and destruction may come from the skies at any moment." "The war will come right to our cities and residential districts," New York's Mayor Fiorello La Guardia said in a speech. He had recently put on order over 100,000 gas masks in expectation of chemical warfare in New York City. "At the present time, under the present relative position of the enemy, we may not expect long-continued sustained attacks such as the cities of Great Britain have suffered, but we will be attacked — never underestimate the strength, the cruelty of the enemy."

Across the Motor City and its suburbs the morning after Pearl

Harbor, paranoia reigned. With all the war work in Detroit, it was obvious that the city could prove a key strategic target, that it had a bull's-eye on it. Six truckloads of soldiers swarmed the streets, taking positions at bridges and tunnels. Police patrolled defense plants, with orders to guard with "special vigilance." "Detroit found itself on a war footing today," read the *Detroit News* front page, "with Federal, State, and City law enforcement agencies taking extraordinary precautions to prevent acts of sabotage against vital services and defense industries."

In his office in Dearborn, Edsel scrambled that morning to get word from Washington. A cable arrived from General George C. Kenney.

"The Under Secretary of War has directed that all necessary steps be taken immediately to increase munitions manufacture to the highest possible level STOP. To effect this end production must be placed at once on a twenty four hour day seven day a week basis STOP."

Another cable came through from Robert Lovett, the assistant secretary of war for air. "We are going to raise our sights all along the line," he cabled Edsel, pointing out "the vital part which we are counting on the Ford Motor Company to play. [Willow Run] is the keystone in the arch of the big government plants, and for that reason we are most anxious for it to get into operation at the earliest possible date."

Edsel cabled Washington a response: "We fully realize gravity of situation and importance of earliest completion and operation of our aircraft motor and bomber plants. Entire staff bending every effort to cooperate. Plant progress at present well ahead of machinery schedule."

Next, Edsel contacted Bennett, who ran the company's personnel office, and told him to start hiring more men. They needed the plants to run around the clock. "The war won't wait," Edsel said. "We have no time to waste."

When Henry Ford heard the news of Pearl Harbor, he told Edsel: "We might as well stop making cars now." So grave was the morale and so deeply rooted the purpose that Henry dictated a cable to his archenemy, President Roosevelt, wishing him "the strength and wisdom necessary for the task you have received. Our organization in all its departments is in fullest cooperation with the government's purpose. Henry Ford."

Edsel had read letters from his executives in England telling him about the bombs dropping on their factories, about how they had painted the huge rooftop of the great Dagenham plant black in an attempt to hide from the Nazi bomber pilots at night. Now he had to plan for air raids himself, and quickly. He sent a memo to Bennett, putting him in charge of "the general plan for protecting employees and property in case of air raids." If Bennett was good at one thing, it was fighting. Edsel would make use of his talents.

All communication with German Ford executives was now cut off. The last communiqué between Ford's German plant and Dearborn's high echelon of executives came a few days before Pearl Harbor.

"Please tell me is Cologne and other associated plants operating are you all well [sic]," cabled Sorensen. "All plants operating and all managers and executives are well," came the reply.

When Edsel drove out to the Ypsilanti site to gauge progress at Willow Run, he saw its red brick shell standing stark against the blue sky. The building, the airfield, the hangar — all of it was almost complete, a sprawling marvel of industrial ambition. Willow Run was shaping up to be not just the world's largest airplane factory, but also the world's largest factory of any kind under one roof. To train workers on how to build these airplanes, Edsel had started construction on a $500,000 school on the Willow Run grounds, with a capacity for 8,000 students.* The last of the runways was drying. To form the runways the company had poured enough concrete to construct a 20-foot-wide highway 115 miles long.

Thousands of men now worked in the bomber plant; the first piece of a B-24 would be completed two days after Pearl Harbor. But the cavernous factory still appeared vastly empty. Edsel had promised that the bombers would take flight in May, just five months away.

Critics in the aviation industry were still arguing that mass pro-

---

* The author's grandfather-in-law, Kenneth Wheeldon, studied as a Liberator mechanic at this school.

duction of four-engine bombers was impossible, that the entire production strategy of Willow Run was off the mark. Edsel had banked
the reputation of his family empire on the proposition that it was not.

Days after Pearl Harbor, Roosevelt gathered Washington's power
elite in the White House to discuss war production. The Nazi juggernaut seemed impregnable, and the air in the President's office was
thick with anxiety. As Roosevelt's chief speechwriter, Robert Sherwood, put it: World War II was "the first war in American history
in which the general disillusionment preceded the firing of the first
shot."

"I have been thinking about the munitions which this country
must produce in order to lick the Germans and the Japs as quickly
as possible," Roosevelt said with his trusted confidants around him.
"And by my usual rule-of-thumb method I have arrived at the following figures. I am going to make a speech before Congress in a few
days and tell them what I expect the country to produce. I am going
to state these figures publicly."

One of Roosevelt's advisers interrupted him. "Mr. President, I
doubt that we ought to mention those figures to the public. Won't
they give out too much information to the enemy?"

"These figures are high because they represent what we simply
have to produce," Roosevelt said. "I have absolute confidence that the
country can do the job, and because I believe these figures will tell our
enemies what they are up against, I want to make the figures public."

He told his staff not to fall out of their chairs. Then he listed the
numbers that he expected American industry to meet: 60,000 flying machines, 45,000 tanks, with ships, guns, and bullets in proportion — all in the year 1942, which would begin in roughly three weeks.

Washington's power brokers all agreed that the four-engine
bomber, a new weapon that could strike devastating blows at the enemy — the Consolidated B-24 Liberator and its cousin, the Boeing
B-17 Flying Fortress — would play a critical role in the war. The first
B-17s had arrived in Manila three months before Pearl Harbor. Secretary of War Henry Stimson said in a cabinet meeting that the heavy
bomber had let "American power back into the islands in a way which
it has not been able to do for twenty years." He told Roosevelt that the

four-engine bomber had brought about a "reversal of the strategy of the world."

The President agreed. He was, in the words of his closest aide Harry Hopkins, "a believer in bombing as the only means of gaining a victory."

In a sense, the war was shaping up to be a race to gain mastery of the skies by mass-producing airplanes and innovating more speed, range, efficiency, and reliability. Competition was the impetus for innovation, especially with survival hanging in the balance. The Allies and Axis were locked in a competition to build airpower. In a speech that had been recently published in the American press, the Luftwaffe's chief, Hermann Goering, had said: "If hitherto we produced hundreds of airplanes daily, we will produce many more hereafter. . . . We must produce planes in numbers and of a quality that seems unthinkable, but which is possible in Adolf Hitler's Reich."

The President could not hide from the numbers. Intelligence sources inside Nazi Germany painted a terrifying picture. Since the war started in Europe in 1939, the Nazis had continued to exponentially increase their productive capacities. Under the genius engineer Fritz Todt and, later, Professor Albert Speer, new factories in Germany, worth some 12 billion reichsmarks, were rising out of the earth and spitting out armaments on their assembly lines for Hitler's war machine. Three new factories — each of them bigger than Hitler's Volkswagen plant — had been completed in eight months' time, all of them to build the Luftwaffe's Junkers Ju 88, a versatile two-engine bomber that could near 300 miles per hour and carry over 4,000 pounds of TNT.

Speer's industrial organization had no fewer than 10,000 assistants, an army of its own devoted to organizing the war machine's factories, which were all working according to the American methods of Henry Ford. From Germany's many boat works, seventeen new U-boats were motoring into the Atlantic every month. From car factories all over Europe, rugged trucks added more horsepower to the firepower. As Speer himself would recall after the war: "Hitler's point of view was: The more I demand, the more I receive. And to my astonishment programs which industrial experts considered impossible to carry out were in the end actually surpassed."

Owing to labor shortages, the Nazis had begun to employ slave labor. As Hitler put it as early as November 9, 1941: "The area working directly for us embraces more than 250 million people. Let no one doubt that we will succeed in involving every one of these millions in the labor process."

In Washington, meanwhile, Roosevelt wanted to know: where were America's bombers?

"Preliminary figures have just come through on four-engine bombers," White House official Isador Lubin said. "They do not look so hot." By now, the federal government had signed four companies to build B-24 bombers: Consolidated (the original designer), Douglas, North American, and Ford Motor Company (the only one of the bunch that was not in fact an aviation company). Thus far, only Consolidated was actually rolling out bombers. And yet its production figures were dismal. Consolidated "fell down badly," according to Lubin. The company produced just twelve B-24 Liberators over the previous month, and production speed was actually *declining*.

On January 6, less than a month after the United States entered the war, Roosevelt's motorcade pulled up to the Capitol Building, where the President was set to deliver his 1942 State of the Union Address. The radio audience swelled into the millions, across the country and overseas. "In fulfilling my duty to report on the State of the Union," Roosevelt told Congress, "I am proud to say to you that the spirit of the American people has never been higher."

The room erupted with applause, but every politician clapping knew the statement was utterly untrue.

Roosevelt laid out his plan, asking American industry to build 60,000 airplanes. The number drew gasps.

"The superiority of the United States in munitions and ships must be overwhelming, so overwhelming that the Axis nations can never hope to catch up with it," Roosevelt told Congress. "In order to attain this overwhelming superiority, the United States must build planes and tanks and guns and ships to the utmost limit of our national capacity. We have the ability and capacity to produce arms not only for our own armed forces, but also for the armies, navies and air forces fighting on our side. As we get guns to the patriots in those lands, they too will fire shots heard around the world."

Who was going to build all this war matériel? And where? As one of Roosevelt's key production organizers, Donald Nelson, later said: "Automotive conversion was the first and biggest item on our agenda. The story of production for war . . . centers around the story of the conversion of our automotive industry — the most colossal aggregation of industrial might in history. We knew that we would have to fight a highly motorized and mechanized war — or a *losing* war."

On January 24, 1942, the 750 most powerful manufacturing men in Detroit gathered in a meeting hall downtown to confront the job ahead. Already, the Roosevelt administration had deflected some blame for the nation's lack of preparedness. Military production had been front-page news all through 1941. Now the war was on, and Detroit was still making shiny chrome-bumpered customer cars.

Representing Washington in Detroit was Ernest Kanzler — Edsel Ford's best friend, the man whom Henry Ford had unceremoniously fired from Ford Motor Company years earlier. Henry didn't bother attending the meeting; he loathed Kanzler. "Edsel and Kanzler should be bankers," Henry said of them — to his mind, the ultimate insult. Kanzler was a Harvard-educated lawyer with brilliant, probing eyes, a bald pate, and not a lick of patience. He had been sent by government officials to deliver a hostile message: the auto industry had better get moving on war production or else.

Suddenly, this aggressive and accusatory Washington emissary was on the opposite side of the table as Edsel Ford. Miffed by Kanzler's strong-arm attitude, Edsel started calling his best friend "Mr. Kanzler."

Sitting before the brain trust of Detroit, Kanzler pounded a gavel. "We must have at once," he said, "in fact we should have had it yesterday, an all-out war economy. We were all agreed upon what we want to do to Hitler and the Japs. I say to you, gentlemen, we have got to develop a new point of view."

According to government contracts, Roosevelt was depending on the auto industry to produce 75 percent of the military's new aviation engines, 80 percent of the tanks, one-third of the machine guns, and 100 percent of the cars and trucks. Oldsmobile cannon shells, Packard marine and aviation engines, Buick aviation engines, Dodge gyrocompasses and ambulances, Studebaker troop transporters, Cadillac tanks and Howitzer cannons, Dodge shortwave radar sets, Chrysler field kitchens, A. C. Spark Plug .50 caliber Browning machine guns . . .

Some of this matériel was already being delivered. The great majority had yet to see the light of day. Meanwhile, Detroit was using up raw materials for customer cars still rolling off the assembly lines. The auto industry was consuming 51 percent of the nation's malleable iron, 75 percent of the plate glass, 68 percent of the upholstery leather, 80 percent of the rubber, and 34 percent of the iron. Every molecule of that material and more was needed for war production.

Now Kanzler wanted to know: why, for example, had Willow Run yet to roll out a bomber?

Charlie Sorensen stood and faced down Kanzler, his infamous temper raging. "Blanket charges of this description, indicting a whole industry, are just as absurd as blanket indictments of a whole people," he said. As for Willow Run, Ford Motor Company had come up with the bomber-an-hour plan on its own accord, and the company had footed the money to build the bomber plant out of its own pockets. Was that not patriotism, flying its most ambitious colors?

"Mr. Edsel Ford and I went west at the request of the Army to look over a bomber with the idea of determining whether we could produce such planes in quantities," Sorensen said furiously. "Without a dollar of government money, without so much as a telegram telling us to go ahead, we made a start on Willow Run. It cost millions. But we did it. Instead of wasting time we have advanced by months the day on which we will be producing planes in great quantities. If that's failure to cooperate we don't know what the word means."

GM's new president Charles Wilson (who had replaced William Knudsen, now that Knudsen was a key dollar-a-year man in Washington) put it all in perspective: "When you convert one of our factories, you move everything out and start with a blank space. Out of a long row of intricate machines on the production line, a certain percentage can be used in the manufacture of a war product. But the production line will necessarily consist mainly of new, special purpose machines."

Where would those machines come from? It would take months

alone just to design and build them, Wilson said. And that was the case for every auto plant asked to build a war product it had never built before.

Kanzler laid down the law. The motor companies had to stop making customer cars. (Ford Motor Company would roll out the last wartime civilian automobile on February 20, 1942.) The nation was on the cusp of the most profound economic shift in history, Kanzler said, and Detroit had to take the lead. There in front of the city's most powerful auto men, he predicted: "You won't recognize this nation four months from now."

Each day in the first two months after Pearl Harbor, Edsel arrived at Willow Run to find it bigger and more crowded than it was the day before. By now, the first bomber parts were visible to the eye, though none had been pieced together yet to resemble anything like an airplane. It seemed so odd to witness men fabricating bomber parts while air raid defense and fire teams ran drills through the factory — men in heat-resistant asbestos suits and fluorescent armbands that could be seen in total darkness, running around with stretchers and fire extinguishers.

Edsel had poured all his energy into building this plant, knowing that it could someday soon be leveled in seconds under the apocalyptic rain of incendiary bombs and their unquenchable, fiery jelly. ("One spark," according to Willow Run's air raid training literature, "will eat through your skull or body.")

But then he knew that his operatives in Europe — men like Maurice Dollfus in France and Dr. Albert in Germany — worked under far more threatening circumstances.

One day in February 1942, Edsel received a strange letter from Maurice Dollfus. The letter itself was forbidden fruit. Once the United States entered the war, communication with executives in Nazi-occupied territory became strictly illegal. With the permission of the US State Department, Edsel had negotiated a line of communication into Europe. He was desperate for information from inside Nazi-occupied territory. Were his long-trusted executives safe? What would happen to the company's assets there? Ford's chief executive in France, Dollfus, was allowed to deliver correspondence via an intermediary named George Lesto, who was able to travel to Vichy, France, where he could mail documents to the United States.

"Since the state of war between the USA and Germany I am not able to correspond with you very easily," Dollfus wrote Edsel on January 28, 1942. "I have asked Lesto to go to Vichy and mail to you the following information."

According to Dollfus, the Nazis were asking for all the trucks that Ford of France could deliver. The Wehrmacht needed all that horsepower and more to carry troops and equipment. The war had actually benefited the bottom line. "It is a fact," Dollfus reported, "that [Ford's] prestige in France has increased considerably and is now greater than it was before the war." For years Ford of France had been a financial drain. Now, in 1942, profit would hit 58 million francs, all of it funds paid out by the Nazi regime. Dollfus was amazed at the shift in fortunes. He called the profits "brilliant."

"At this state I would like to outline the importance attached by [German] high officials to respect the desires and maintain the good will of 'Ford,'" Dollfus wrote Edsel. "And by 'Ford,' I mean your father, yourself and the Ford Motor Company, Dearborn. . . . Even in the case of a completely victorious German peace, the rights of the shareholders will be protected."

Of course, the happier the Nazis were with Ford of France, the safer its assets. Dollfus was quite clear that cooperating was the only way Ford of France could survive. As correspondence continued, Edsel found himself in the awkward position of thanking Dollfus for his careful work in protecting company property — in effect, for cooperating with the Nazi warlords.

"I am quite sure that this has been done under the utmost of difficulties and with much hard work," Edsel wrote Dollfus. "We are very proud of the record that you and your associates have made in building the company up to its first great position under such circumstances."

In the spring of 1942, Dollfus communicated more information through Lesto. Ford's manufacturing plant in Poissy had been hit by the British, he reported. The Royal Air Force had dropped twenty-three bombs on the Poissy plant, eight of them hitting their target. One worker was wounded, and the factory had suffered damage —

broken cranes, a smashed cafeteria, plenty of shattered glass. Edsel communicated back that he had seen the images of the bombed-out factory in the newspapers and was pleased that the papers did not mention the fact that the factory shown in the pictures was a Ford factory. Citizens of the United States might be quite miffed to find out that Ford factories in Germany and France were helping to build the arsenal of the enemy.

Soon Dollfus was writing again to deliver news of more bombings. The Poissy factory had been hit four times by the British, but Dollfus was still doing everything he could to make trucks. Edsel dictated his last letter to the Frenchman on July 17, 1942. He was pleased that Dollfus was in "good health" and "carrying on the best way possible under the circumstances."

"I have shown your [last] letter to my father and Mr. Sorensen," Edsel wrote, "and they both join me in sending best wishes for you and your staff, and hope that you will continue to carry on the good work that you are doing."

For Edsel, this was an innocent remark, meant as a thank-you to a longtime friend whose life was at risk. The remark would come back to haunt him in ways he couldn't possibly imagine.

The safety of European assets was a terrible source of anxiety for Edsel. Tax law deemed that any property held in an enemy nation "is treated as becoming worthless on the date war with such country was declared by the United States." The outcome of the war would have serious consequences for the Ford family that went beyond any sense of justice or patriotism. Edsel and Sorensen had cultivated European operations so carefully, for so many years. Now that military strategy held factories as prime targets, would any of it survive? Would Ford employees be added to the list of the war's casualties?

That spring Edsel suffered another attack of abdominal pain. Laid up at Gaukler Pointe, he struggled to regain his strength, with his wife by his side. They had grown more alone through the years. They had many acquaintances, but how many true friends? ("It was generally understood," Ford executive Roscoe Smith once said, "that it was too dangerous to get too close to Edsel.") Now their children were gone—the two older children married and in the military, the two younger at boarding school.

Despite the Edsel Fords' immeasurable wealth, there was something spiritually desolate about their lives. Like Fitzgerald's Jay Gatsby, their money and the circumstances that came with it had isolated them. And now Edsel faced his own humanity in a new way. "There is no difference between men, in intelligence or race, so profound as the difference between the sick and the well," Fitzgerald had written.

At forty-eight years old, Edsel was gaunt, his appearance that of a man many years beyond his age. Suffering acute pain and exhaustion, he checked into Henry Ford Hospital, careful to keep the news quiet so that no reporters would show up. His doctors decided that it was time to open him up and take a look. The day of the operation, Edsel's wife was a wreck. Sorensen waited through the hours with Henry, unable to work.

"This was the worst kind of news," Sorensen later wrote, "to find Edsel so ill. He took it all very bravely. We were doing nothing but war work now, and were fully controlled by the government. Slight of build, [Edsel] was thin and worried. . . . Henry Ford was worried. I spent most of the day [of Edsel's operation] with him. He sure had something to worry about."

When Edsel's doctors peered into his stomach, they saw for the first time the culprit, what was causing the man so much agony. Ulcers, they learned, were not Edsel's problem. His disease was in fact far more dangerous.

16

"Detroit's Worries Are Right Now"

Spring to Summer 1942

Throughout the land a mighty revolution is in progress. American industry is beating the ploughshares of peacetime — the autos, the electric refrigerators, the toasters and the washing machines — into the swords of total war: planes, tanks and high explosive bombs. It is a revolution to which there can be but one end: The doom of Nazidom.

— *New York Times, July 12, 1942*

EDSEL FORD AWOKE FROM surgery with half a stomach, in a world he could barely recognize.

His doctors informed him that they had found tumors inside him, removed what they could, and taken half of the organ as well. They did not know if the tumors would grow back. Edsel was severely ill, the doctors explained, and carrying on work could kill him. The medical field knew little about stomach tumors or what caused them. For Edsel, the diagnosis was not only depressing but painful.

Still, how could one feel sorry for oneself lying in a hospital bed when so many young men were overseas fighting the Nazis and Japanese, dying in the trenches?

When Sorensen visited Henry Ford Hospital, he found Edsel "better than I expected." Edsel reached out his hand, and Sorensen took it with his huge calloused fingers. The white-haired production wizard was surprised by the affection that had grown in him for Edsel over the years. It was an almost paternal sensation. Sitting by the hospital bed, he thought of all that Edsel had endured at the hands of Henry Ford and Harry Bennett. *How could anyone ever be mean to him?* he thought to himself.

Edsel wanted all the news. So Sorensen gave it to him.

Willow Run was continuing apace. The factory was all but completed, and thus far employment had hit nearly 10,000 workers. The first B-24 center wing was nearly finished. The new school on the Willow Run grounds to train bomber workers and Liberator mechanics was built, and the first students had enrolled.

But there was bigger news. The war work in Detroit, and at Willow Run specifically, had captured the imagination of millions in America and in Britain. It seemed to happen overnight. The President was making numerous speeches, including his State of the Union, about how this war would be fought and won: not just in military theaters but at home on assembly lines, where men like Edsel and Sorensen were demigods. The famous American motor companies were being called "self-contained 'Arsenals of Democracy.'" It was as if the production man was a new kind of military general, fighting an engineer's war. And now the press had swarmed Detroit, after the biggest home-front news story so far.

The *Washington Post:* "What may not be generally known is the amazing story of how Detroit is rapidly being transformed from a center of peacetime production into the greatest war production area to be found anywhere on the globe."

Fortune: "A terrible burden has fallen upon the city, for Detroit must now become the main plant in the Arsenal of Democracy."

Look magazine: "The scale of Detroit's war boom stuns the imagination."

Of all the figures in the Motor City, the press zeroed in on Henry Ford as the main character in this narrative. Of course, Edsel understood the irony. Henry had had little to do with Ford Motor Company's war work; he was, in fact, a virulent pacifist who had to be convinced ad nauseam of the importance of military preparedness. And he was getting lauded as the industrialist making the greatest contribution. Such were the whims of iconography.

Henry made the cover of *Time* with an inscription that read, "Mass Producer: Out of Enormous Rooms, Armies Will Roll and Fleets Will Fly." "Even the American people do not appreciate the miracle [of Detroit's war production], because it is too big for the eye to see," the magazine stated. "There is no better sample than Henry Ford. If Armageddon is to be decided in Detroit, Armageddon is won." *Life* magazine pronounced that "Henry Ford is still the greatest man in Detroit." Also weighing in was the *New York Times:* "Once old Henry Ford gets his teeth into the Germans it will be all over but the signing of the armistice."

Willow Run had taken center stage. The length of its assembly lines was "more than three times the height of the Empire State Building," noted the *Christian Science Monitor,* "and four times that of the Eiffel Tower." According to a *Washington Post* report, Willow Run was "the greatest single manufacturing plant the world had ever seen." "All 16 major league baseball teams could play eight simultaneous games before crowds of 30,000 each [inside Willow Run]," the *Post* reported. "And there would still be room enough left over for a full-sized football game before an additional 30,000 spectators." The *Wall Street Journal* called the bomber plant "the production miracle of the war."

"It is a promise of revenge for Pearl Harbor," the *Detroit Free Press* gushed. "You know when you see Willow Run that in the end we will give it to them good."

When Britain's Royal Air Force flew over German cities dropping thousands of propaganda leaflets, Ford's Liberator factory was offered to the enemy as a symbol of American might. "In one American factory alone," the leaflet read, "the new Ford plant at Willow Run, Detroit, they are already turning out one four-engined bomber able to carry four tons of bombs to any part of the Reich every two hours."

Lying in bed recuperating from surgery, Edsel found all this publicity unnerving. Roosevelt and Churchill were clamoring for airplanes now. *Willow Run had yet to produce a single one.*

• • •

When Edsel returned to his Dearborn office in Ford's Administration Building, he appeared unsteady on his feet. The first thing he did was seek out his father and kiss him on the cheek. Edsel's secretary A. J. Lepine had everything perfectly organized for him. Get-well letters filed into Dearborn by the bushel, including one from President Roosevelt's appointments secretary, Marvin McIntyre, who added on a thank-you for the Ford car with a hand-operated throttle that Edsel had delivered to the President for his use at his country estate in Hyde Park, New York.

"I guess the pressure got too high at Dearborn," Edsel wrote back in longhand, addressing the President's secretary as "Mac." "I had to go into the hospital. I am feeling fine again and anxious to get back on the job."

More than ever, Edsel needed his sons by his side. "He wanted them near him," Sorensen recalled. "We talked about it every time we had a few moments together." Edsel wanted to be assured that if anything happened to him, his son Henry II was ready — to take on Bennett, to become president of Ford Motor Company, to help realize the dream of Willow Run. But Henry II insisted on staying in the military. Edsel kept the severity of his condition a secret from his children. Meanwhile, he could sense the anxiety in his son's letters.

"This man's navy is plenty tough," Henry II wrote his father from Chicago's Great Lakes Naval Station. "This afternoon they gave us drill for over an hour and I was in charge of one of the battalions. Of course I don't know how to lead this sort of thing, so I made plenty of mistakes and the thing turned out to be one terrible mess."

When Edsel drove out to Willow Run, the building appeared along the roadway, with a pair of water towers standing tall behind it. He limped slowly through the main entrance. On one side: the Personnel Building, which included the executive offices, the lobby, and Plant Protection headquarters, with its own locker room, gunsmith, and radio dispatcher's office. On the other side: the Visitors' Lobby, where all visitors, potential employees, and vendors had to produce identification and proof of citizenship. Along with American flags, government signs caught Edsel's eye:

REMEMBER PEARL HARBOR

AMERICA NEVER LOST A WAR

GOVERNMENT PROPERTY

He entered the main plant, with its interior skeleton of steel gird-ers, tiled floor, and no windows or natural light. Ford executives had taken to calling this space "the most enormous room in the history of man." Some 156,000 40-watt Sylvania fluorescent bulbs gave the scene an eerie glow, especially when workers looked at their watches and saw that it was midnight. This was the largest lighting installa-tion ever created.

Edsel saw thousands of laborers on the job, but no completed bombers. Not even close. The majority of the plant stood on the ground floor, which was ringed by a second-floor mezzanine of of-fices. In one corner on the second floor, the Plant Hospital was set up behind large doors with red crosses on them. When Edsel inspected the hospital, he saw the most modern medical facility ever built into a factory, with antiseptic white ceramic-tiled walls, soundproof ceil-ings, six physicians, forty nurses, a sanitary engineer, a staff of den-tists, X-ray machines, separate wards for men and women, and oper-ating rooms. Every new employee received a physical here. Over the next three years this hospital would also see its share of amputations due to injuries inside the plant — ninety-six in total.

The bomber construction area was divided into two sections: manufacturing and assembly. Raw materials came into manufac-turing via the New York Central railroad spur, the entry bays ser-viced by four 30,000-pound cranes. In the metal shop, welders and blacksmiths would soon be molding up to ten tons of sheet metal into 3,000 different bomber parts each week. Next to the shop stood five parallel rows of iron-gray hydraulic presses, some weighing as much as 700,000 pounds. They stamped out bomber parts — the sound of each stamping as sharp and loud as a car smacking into a tree. The presses were continuously lubricated by 1,500 gallons of oil each day, the tanks located underneath the floor.

Willow Run was designed to build Liberators in five subassem-blies — the center wing, the nose and cockpit, the aft fuselage, the tail, and the outer wing — then bring them together for the final product. The interchangeable parts made their way around the plant on a system of twenty-nine miles of conveyors on the ceiling, like upside-down railroads, some rated to carry five tons, some fifteen. The metallurgical laboratory was situated in the southwest area of manufacturing; here bomber parts were heat-treated, chemical-tested, plated, and painted. Alloys were mixed like ingredients in a bakery. Foundry workers melted aluminum and stirred it with precise amounts of copper, chromium, molybdenum, tungsten, vanadium, and most commonly carbon.

Technicians used the most powerful X-ray machines on earth — General Electric models operating at 240 kilovolts — to check metal castings that could cause a plane to crash if they failed. Every critical casting would pass through these X-ray machines, keeping them humming around the clock.

The various parts came together in the assembly area — all of which converged into a single assembly line. Soon this row would stretch with bombers, one after the other, each exactly alike, just like Model Ts. Or so Edsel hoped. He knew the effort to beat the Nazis and the Japanese depended on these bombers. He had to get them off the ground by his deadline.

May was three months away.

In the fields outside the bomber factory, Edsel saw a disturbing sight. He could recall standing in these fields with his father and staring at the horizon a year earlier, the view before them like a bucolic painting full of trees, birds, and a broad sky. Now trailer parks stretched out across the fields, a sea of muddy dwellings in the shadow cast by Willow Run. Shantytowns had emerged on the lawns of local farms and on the edges of the trailer parks. It was as if someone had lifted a city the size of Ann Arbor, with its state university, and plopped that population here where there was no infrastructure, no real sewage system, and few sources of potable water. Every day there were more arrivals, and there was nowhere for them to go.

When Edsel chose this site and convinced his father to give up the land, he had figured that the local towns and the city of Detroit — twenty-seven miles away — could supply the huge labor needs. However, once Washington's Office of Price Administration set up its rationing system and distributed its "War Ration Book Number One" (nicknamed the "Sugar Book"), workers were no longer allowed to drive the twenty-seven miles from Detroit to Willow Run, owing to restrictions on gas and rubber tires. If people wanted a paycheck working at the bomber factory, they had to live in its direct vicinity or they would spend upward of three hours each day trying to get to work and back on buses that were overcrowded, unreliable, and, at forty cents a day, expensive to ride ("an unreasonable burden upon the wage earner," as one Washington investigator put it).

The government had started work on a new highway to connect Willow Run to downtown Detroit. (Today this highway, the Edsel Ford Expressway, is part of I-94.) But it would take time to complete, and what good what it do if people were forbidden by law from driving on it?

All over the country, infrastructure struggled under the weight of the most sudden and profound mass migration the United States had ever experienced. Seventeen million Americans would leave their homes for a job in a war factory between 1940 and 1945. In a nation suffering its twelfth year of depression, a steady paycheck was worth the move. Few urban centers would see a larger in-migration than the four counties in the Detroit–Willow Run area, into which 212,457 would arrive between 1940 and 1944, according to census figures.

One couple, Mr. and Mrs. John Castle, closed up their beauty parlor in central Michigan and drove their five-year-old car and trailer to Willow Run in the early days of the war. "Arrived here about eight o'clock this morning in the rain!" Mrs. Castle wrote in her diary. "Drove miles, it seemed, to find a park. Every place had more trailers than the law allows, and every private yard either had its quota or else 'didn't want any.'"

The couple found a vacancy at a government-owned trailer park. At the bomber plant, Mr. Castle signed on as a parts inspector and his wife as a file clerk. "It was still dark when we left the trailer," she said of their first day. "What a sight the Bomber Plant was all lighted up! It is such a *huge* place! And the never-ending traffic pouring through its gates!"

It was all very "romantic," in her words. But life in the trailer park

quickly grew sour. There were two washing machines for sixty families, often with OUT OF ORDER signs on them. The trailer park's under-
sized sewer lines clogged and froze. "This means all our waste water
will have to run out on the ground," Mrs. Castle recalled. "Our line
is not the only one that's frozen." The faucet where sixty families got
their drinking water froze too. "I inquired at the office where to get
our drinking water and was told to get it in the laundry room. There
has been a sign in the laundry room over the faucet reading, 'This water is *not* safe for drinking purposes.' But tonight, the word *not* was
crossed out!"

Others recorded similar concerns. A Mrs. Sam Gordon arrived at a
Willow Run trailer park with a baby recovering from kidney surgery.
She found the place filthy — garments on clotheslines freezing even in
April, little kids roaming free and covered in ringworm. Cold medi-
cines and aspirin were as rare and valuable as blocks of gold. "If there
were any better place to go we'd certainly pull out," she wrote in her
diary, "but I don't think you can find anything much different within
driving distance of the plant."

Edsel realized that the housing crisis could throw a wrench into
the bomber production process. If workers could not find an adequate place to live, or if they could not get to work, the bombers
wouldn't roll. He reached out to his contacts in Washington, pleading
for help. His pleadings quickly reached the White House.

The President imagined a government-financed "Bomber City"
alongside Willow Run, an entire city freshly built with government
money. It would be "a city of homes well planned and designed,"
Roosevelt described it, "and owned by defense workers, as a symbol
of the America we are defending and the America we are rebuilding
for the future."

However, where would the materials come from? And with what
man-hours would such a city be built? All that aluminum and steel
and labor was needed to build the Arsenal of Democracy, the tanks
and airplanes and guns. And how long would Bomber City take to
construct? As one war worker put it: "Detroit isn't worrying about
tomorrow, mister. The boys in the Pacific are yelling for help today.
Detroit's worries are right now."

Roosevelt delegated the Bomber City job to his uncle, Frederic

Delano, chairman of the National Resources Planning Board. "I have been asked by the President," Delano wrote Edsel, "to do all I can to expedite the provision of adequate housing, transportation and other facilities for the workers who will be employed at the Willow Run Bomber Plant."

Delano's agency picked a piece of property near the plant for Roosevelt's $35 million Bomber City. Henry Ford protested. He wrote the President directly. The agency had "picked a site for this purpose which includes land owned by me," Henry wrote Roosevelt, "which I have been using as an agricultural training school for young men. May I solicit your assistance in stopping this project until a more suitable site is selected." Besides, Henry argued, a Bomber City would "concentrate people where they might be bombed."

Henry's real concern: what would happen to Bomber City when the war was over? It would become a rusted-out eyesore on his land. When the President's Federal Public Housing Authority set up stakes in fields to build Bomber City, Harry Bennett sent his men to tear them out.

Edsel could never have foreseen the rationing rules, including the rule that people would be forbidden from commuting between Willow Run and Detroit. He realized for the first time that his choice for the bomber plant location had been a massive, irrevocable mistake. He had a health crisis brewing, and there seemed no way to stop it.

17

Will It Run?

Spring to Fall 1942

> I have seen the science I worshiped, and the aircraft I loved, destroying the civilization I expected them to serve.
>
> — CHARLES LINDBERGH

AT 12:30 PM ON March 24, 1942, a train screeched into Michigan Central Station in Detroit, bound from Boston. From a Pullman car, Charles Lindbergh stepped onto the siding with a suitcase in his hand. The platform appeared crowded. All over the country, urban train stations were symbolic microcosms of America in wartime — everyone in a hurry to get somewhere, teeming crowds, a great migration, most notably fresh-faced boy-men in military uniform. Increasingly, there would be more Americans on crutches in train stations, in wheelchairs, or in coffins making their final journey home.

A phone call from Harry Bennett had summoned Lindbergh to Detroit. The aviator had found himself in a position that bordered on the bizarre. With a critical shortage in labor across the country, in a nation desperate for airpower and trained pilots, the world's most famous aviator was unemployed and seemingly unemployable.

Lindbergh couldn't find a job.

Edsel was laid up ill at the time. Henry, Bennett, and Sorensen welcomed Lindbergh in Dearborn. Over lunch, Lindbergh shared pieces of his story. As Henry Ford knew, of course, the aviator had done everything he could to keep America out of the war, resigning from the Air Corps Reserves and deeply alienating the President in the process. "Now that we are at war," he said, "I want to contribute as best I can to my country's war effort. . . . I *must* take some part in it, whatever that may be."

He had asked officials in Washington to be reinstated in the Air Corps so he could fight overseas. As the ardent antiwar activist would later learn, he was strangely non-averse to killing in military engagement, as long as he was sure he was shooting at enemy soldiers and not civilians. But for now, the military didn't want him. The Roosevelt administration wanted nothing to do with him.

"He is a ruthless and conscious fascist," Secretary of the Interior Harold Ickes told the President, "motivated by a hatred for you personally and a contempt for democracy." Ickes went on to say that it would be "a tragic disservice to American democracy" to allow "this loyal friend of Hitler's . . . a chance to gain a military record."

"What you say about Lindbergh," Roosevelt had responded, "and the potential danger of the man, I agree with wholeheartedly."

When Lindbergh went seeking a way to participate in the war effort on the home front, he was blackballed. The only man unafraid to hire him was Henry Ford. Thus the aviator's arrival in Dearborn.

Had any public figure ever been more misunderstood? Lindbergh was no Nazi, nor was he a pacifist. His politics were esoteric and even dangerous, but he considered himself an American patriot. Now he believed that his phones were being tapped by the FBI, and he was being called a traitor.

After lunch, Henry, Lindbergh, Sorensen, and Bennett headed down the road to Willow Run. Inside, the clattering of the machines assaulted the eardrums. To Lindbergh, it seemed a cacophony without parallel. They moved slowly so Henry Ford could keep up, the old man's eyes vacant, as if he were lost. "The plant has progressed greatly since I was last there," Lindbergh wrote in his journal that night. "Runways all in, most of the building finished, much of the machinery installed." Like anyone else who visited Willow Run, Lucky

Lindy was awed by the sheer ambition of it. He saw "acres upon acres of machinery and jigs and tarred wood floors and busy workmen . . . a sort of Grand Canyon of a mechanized world."

Almost exactly a year had passed since Henry and Edsel stood on this plot of land watching the giant saws clear the sugar maples and apple trees. And now? "The Ford schedule calls for the first bomber to be produced in May," Lindbergh wrote in his diary. "From the appearance of the factory it seems to me it will be very difficult to meet this program. It will be little short of a miracle if the actual production of four-engine bombers is under way in April."

While in Washington attempting to get his Air Corps commission back, Lindbergh had heard firsthand how desperate the army was for four-engine bombers. And how the hubris of Ford's bomber-an-hour plan had offended the aviation industry's top figures. No one believed the Fords could pull it off. As Lindbergh remembered Assistant Secretary of War Robert Lovett saying: "The rest of the industry was very much opposed to the Ford company entering aviation, and hoped the production program would *not* be met." Lindbergh had personally argued with officials over the subject.

"There is no question of the Ford Motor Company's ability to place the large bomber on mass production," he told officials in Washington, "provided that sufficient raw material, government furnished equipment, and outside purchased parts are available under reasonably normal conditions."

Now in Dearborn, Lindbergh could see for himself how far off track the job seemed to be.

He checked into the Dearborn Inn, taking a room on the second floor ($10.50 a night). He agreed to a salary of $666.66 per month (the equivalent of what he would have earned if he were in the Air Corps). Sorensen offered Lindbergh more, but the aviator refused. On his first day, like all other new employees, he walked through Willow Run's front doors into the Personnel Building, where his identification was checked. He was fingerprinted not once but twice.

And so Lindbergh and Henry Ford — the nation's two highest-profile anti-interventionist activists, both of them enemies of the President, both accused Nazi sympathizers and accused anti-Semites, both decorated with swastika-emblazoned medals by Hitler himself—joined hands in the campaign to build the most destructive weapon in the Arsenal of Democracy.

Lindbergh wasn't the only celebrity working at Ford Motor Company during the war. Gray-haired Jim Thorpe, the 1912 Olympic gold medalist and pro football hero, took a job at the offices of the Rouge. So did Jesse Owens, described by Ford's in-house publication as "the man who first put the blitz on Berlin" by winning Olympic golds in 1936 before the enraged blue eyes of Hitler himself. Unlike those men, however, Lindbergh was a lightning rod.

Some workers at the Rouge protested against the controversial aviator's appointment. Newspapers ran editorials denouncing Lindbergh as a troublemaker, moving Ford's chief legal counsel, I. A. Capizzi, to fire off threatening letters. Bags of mail arrived in Dearborn from concerned citizens who thought Lindbergh was a Nazi. "I am so anti-Hun and anti-Jap," read one, "the damn dirty rats, that I don't want to see anyone take any chances with such a type of a man as Lindbergh."

Henry and Edsel paid these attacks no mind. Aviation engineers were "as scarce as hen's teeth," in the words of General Oliver Echols of the Air Corps. Finally, at the most ambitious venture in aviation history, someone had arrived who knew all there was to know about airplanes.

Bennett set Lindbergh up in an office on the side of Willow Run farthest from the airfield. He gave him a 1942 Mercury with a radio transmitter in it so that Lindbergh could stay connected to the executives at all times within ten miles of the bomber plant. Lindbergh quickly became fascinated with the inner workings of this Machiavellian empire.

"These relationships between the officers of the Ford Company are becoming of great interest to me," he wrote in his journal. "Every one of these men has a strong character, and loyalties and conflicts weave in and out through every move they make."

"Sorensen has the reputation of being the best production engineer in the United States," Lindbergh wrote, "of imposing and 'bull-ing through' sweeping ideas quickly formed, of being ruthless in his dealings with men. . . . 'Cast Iron Charlie,' they call him; men's eyes drop to their work as he passes along the aisles of the shops; no man wishes to cross him, and no man can cross him and hold his job. . . . His heart is so filled with his love of the machine that it has somewhat crowded out his love of the man who must run it. He is certainly one of the men who has built this nation into whatever it is today."

As for Edsel, there were rumors. Soon after Lindbergh started work at Willow Run, he got a phone call from Bennett, who said in confidence that Edsel had cancer of the stomach and that doctors were giving him a year or two to live. These rumors were incredible. Edsel's two older sons were in the military. His father was now seventy-nine years old, the sharp edges of Henry Ford's brilliant imagination blown dull by the years. Who would lead the great Ford empire if Edsel perished?

Lindbergh wanted to get to work, to serve his country, but he found the inner workings of this empire so strange that he advised the company's executives that he was having trouble fitting in. "I came here in hope that I might offer suggestions and advice," he told Sorensen. "I find, however, that the company's policies and methods are so different from the others I have followed in the past that, until I learn to understand them better, I must consider myself more a student than an advisor."

As March yielded to April, with Edsel's promises to deliver bombers to the military in May, Lindbergh began to hear more grumblings from his contacts in Washington. The news from overseas was getting grimmer by the day. It had now been five months since the United States had entered the war. Not one yard of enemy territory had been taken. Not one successful campaign had been launched. Hitler's U-boats, the rattlesnakes of the sea, were wreaking havoc in the Battle of the Atlantic, sinking ship after Allied ship. In the Pacific, the Japanese had taken Java, parts of the Solomon Islands, and the Philippines. Burma, a critical strategic outpost, was about to fall. General Joseph Stilwell reported from the Far East: the Allies needed airplanes! The Japanese were attacking with waves of fighters. "We couldn't retaliate," General Stilwell reported, "because we didn't even have an anti-aircraft gun."

The President wanted to know: where were the Liberators?

"They don't give me anything to eat," Edsel confided in a friend that spring. He was living on a diet of painkillers. "They just feed me pills!"

"You can't go far on pills."

"No," Edsel said. "I get hungry once in a while."

In his corner office, Edsel felt like he was trapped in a bad dream. The bomber-an-hour project was spinning out of control, and his every minute was a frenzy of problem-solving. All the social and production pitfalls sparked by the new wartime economy had come to fester at Willow Run as if in a petri dish — only a petri dish the size of the largest factory under one roof that had ever been built.

Bomb threats caused work stoppages almost daily. "Caution and paranoia were part of the daily routine at Willow Run," remembered Wally Pipp, who worked in plant security. (Pipp was a former first baseman for the New York Yankees, replaced in 1925 by Lou Gehrig.) "It was quite an experience. We had to check everything — look in the garbage cans and everywhere."

Engineers at Willow Run were complaining that deliveries of raw materials were failing to show up. Edsel had to fly to Washington to beg for rubber, copper, and especially aluminum. With all the industrial production in the United States — ships and tanks and guns and airplanes — there weren't nearly enough raw materials to go around. Ford Motor Company was given top priority by the Roosevelt administration: "A-1-A." However, as the ambitious shipbuilder Henry Kaiser put it: "A priority is something which gives you an option to ask for something which you know you're not going to get anyhow."

Wildcat strikes occurred with regularity, owing to constant intimidation by Bennett's Service Department. Army inspectors came to Willow Run and were bewildered by Bennett's labor policy. As Lindbergh put it: "Bennett is certainly a colorful character. . . . But I sometimes wonder whether Bennett does not try to handle the Ford workmen with a little too much of the mailed fist."

Soldiers headed for hellholes were outraged by the idea of labor strikes in war factories. ("I'd just as soon shoot down one of those strikers as shoot down Japs," said one Air Corps pilot. "They're doing just as much to lose the war for us.") But this was America, land of the free. Citizens could not be forced to work — the way they were in Hitler's Germany.

Bennett wouldn't back down. At one point, he got in an argument with Willow Run's day-to-day superintendent, Roscoe Smith, over the placement of soda machines. In an office with Sorensen present, Bennett slugged Smith with a sharp right hook, sending him tumbling to the ground. Smith got up and felt a wound bulging on his head. He walked off and never returned to Willow Run.

"You were trying to do a job for your country and for the company and trying to do a job for yourself," he later said. "I was really relieved to get out."

Every day Edsel and Sorensen were given updates on how many laborers punched in the day before. The numbers didn't add up; people were simply not showing up for work. So Edsel commissioned a study to find out why. For starters, the military was draining the labor force. As soon as a man was trained to build an airplane part, at great expense, he might be called to duty — here today, gone tomorrow. And it was only getting worse. The armed forces were going to drain several million men from the ranks of factory workers by the end of 1942. Other workers left their jobs at Willow Run because tire and gas rationing prevented them from getting to work, or they couldn't stand the living conditions around the factory. Or they simply found a better job elsewhere.

Desperate for able bodies, Bennett dispatched recruiters to sweep through the southern states passing out flyers to strangers: "Willow Run, the Largest Bomber Plant in the World, Located in Detroit Area, NEEDS: MEN AND WOMEN." Mobs of new faces gathered in the bomber plant's Personnel Building. A good portion of them were rural Southern blacks who had never traveled out of the farmland where they were raised, who had come by bus hundreds of miles with tickets provided by Ford Motor Company. They wore rags and spoke strange backwoods dialects. One man showed up without shoes. "They didn't know whether to send him into the plant or not without shoes, but they finally did," remembered Ford engineer Anthony Harff. "The fellow said he never wore shoes in his life."

The influx of new black labor heightened racial tension in the factory and caused more wildcat strikes. As one laborer put it: "I'd rather see Hitler or Hirohito win the war than work beside a nigger on an assembly line."

For many Americans, no sight symbolized the nation's effort on the home front more than women working in war factories. As early as 1941, the federal government had campaigned to place women on assembly lines. The War Department asked Edsel to hire 15,000 female workers at Willow Run. He was happy to oblige. The first woman employed at the bomber plant was Agnes Menzies — a nurse in the First Aid Department. Another woman named Rose Monroe started at Willow Run soon after Pearl Harbor. An attractive tomboy-type brunette, Rose had driven in an old Ford from Kentucky with two young girls in tow. She worked jackhammers and rivet guns at Willow Run.

One day Rose Monroe caught the eye of a government man who had come looking for the right woman to serve as a promotional figure, an example that could get more women out of the home and into the factories. Here was Rose Monroe — attractive, tough, determined. Rose Monroe became "Rosie the Riveter," a symbol of American strength and teamwork, promoted in government newsreels and posters, painted by Norman Rockwell, mythologized in a big band tune.*

> *All the day long,*
> *Whether rain or shine*
> *She's part of the assembly line.*
> *She's making history,*
> *Working for victory*
> *Rosie the Riveter.*

---

* Rose Monroe was not the only woman upon whom the Rosie the Riveter legend is based. The story of Rosie would take a book of its own to fully unravel.

As at other war factories, women were hired at salaries slightly less than what men made. (At Willow Run, unskilled male laborers started at 85 cents an hour, for nine-hour shifts, five days a week.) Management put up signs inside the bomber plant: GENTLEMEN WATCH YOUR LANGUAGE. THERE ARE WOMEN PRESENT. Within weeks, foremen put up their own signs: WOMEN WATCH YOUR LANGUAGE. THERE ARE GENTLEMEN AROUND HERE. ("Some of these women had words I never even heard of," remembered one foreman.) Edsel's wife, fearing that children would be left alone to fend for themselves without their mothers, arranged to have posters put up in the female bathrooms urging women workers to utilize government-operated day care facilities.

All the while, the housing debacle outside Willow Run worsened. By this time, over 30,000 people had moved into this rural backwater on the outskirts of Detroit. Nearly 2,000 were living in makeshift tarpaper shacks and chicken coops. In one instance, a nun entered a shack and found a newborn baby inside with her mother. The baby was wrapped in newspapers to keep her warm. In another, health authorities tested local wells by dropping purple dye into some local toilets. They later pumped purple water out of nearby wells that were being used by families for drinking water. Officials feared what a typhoid epidemic in Detroit could do to the war effort. Photographs of kids living in squalor around Willow Run appeared in newspapers across the country. It looked like a scene out of the Third World, but it was right there in Ypsilanti outside Detroit, where a year earlier the biggest local news might have been a cat stuck in a tree.

In Washington, Senator Harry Truman and his Truman Committee investigating defense production organized a hearing to discuss the Bomber City that Roosevelt wanted built beside Willow Run. The city would cost $125 million in materials that the government didn't have, and $125,000 in labor that the government didn't have either. And where would the construction workers live while Bomber City was being built? What about police and fire departments? Schools and a hospital? Edsel was estimating a peak employment of 60,000 at Willow Run, down from the original estimate of 100,000. That still required thousands of dwellings and all manner of infrastructure.

The government pushed ahead on Bomber City, the construction set to start in the fall of 1942 — promising more traffic jams and shortages of just about everything. Bomber City was projected to open early in 1943. Judging from the news from abroad, the war could be lost by that point.

Meanwhile, there sat Edsel Ford in his corner office, living on painkillers, the weight of it all on his shoulders, wondering when the first Ford B-24 Liberator would take flight. Wondering, perhaps, if he would live to see it happen at all.

18

Bomber Ship 01

May 1942

> Over all, we feel the intangible dominating presence of rules, rules, policies, social controls, all holding thousands of divergent personalities firmly in the intermeshing action patterns of giant mass production.
>
> — WILLOW RUN ASSEMBLY-LINE WORKER

ONE DAY A THIRTY-NINE-YEAR-OLD man named James Edson Stermer arrived at Willow Run's personnel office for his first day of work. He was not much different from the other thousands who came to work at the bomber plant that day — a Detroit Institute of Technology professor who was taking on a job to contribute to the war effort. But his story illustrates what it was like to walk through those factory gates in the middle of World War II.

Stermer was pointed to the Plant Hospital for his physical. Height: 5′10″. Weight: 189 pounds. Blood pressure: 144. Two nurses X-rayed his chest to rule out tuberculosis, handling him "as impersonally as freight-handlers on the Michigan Central," he remembered. He moved to a private cubicle and was told to strip off his clothes.

"Operations?" a nurse asked.

"Yes — appendix out."

"Hold out your hands.... Turn them over.... Up! ... Out! ... Touch the floor! ... Stoop! ... Okay, wait as you are for the doctor."

After a quick consultation with a physician, Stermer was sent back to the personnel office, where he was fingerprinted three times (once for company records, once for the Michigan State Police, and once for the FBI). He had his picture snapped for his ID badge, was given a locker for his personal things, then was sent inside the factory, where, after a stint as a stock handler at 85 cents an hour, he enrolled in riveting school.

"It is impossible in words to convey the feel and smell and tension of Willow Run under full headway," Stermer wrote in his journal. "The roar of the machinery; the special din of the rivet guns, absolutely deafening nearby; the throbbing crash of giant metal presses; busy little service trucks rushing down endless aisles under the blue-white fluorescent lights; the strange far-reaching line of half-born skyships growing wings under swarms of workers meeting deadlines."

The place teemed with workers — black, white, young, old, men, and women. About one-third of the assembly-line workers were female, spanning the social spectrum from the wives of successful businessmen to ex-prostitutes. The sections of the plant were marked with a grid, so Stermer could find his way. Letters ran north and south, and numbers east and west, like the street grid of a city.

The riveting theory teacher — a big, gray-haired fellow named Mr. Farley, who had worked for years at the Rouge — gave Stermer a lecture intended (in the new employee's words) "to orientate trainees to the airplane industry, to the relation of the airplane industry to the war effort, and to the war effort in relation to the preservation of the American way of life." Then it was time to start firing rivet guns.

Nothing could seem simpler to the uninitiated. But Stermer was about to find out: riveting was anything but simple. He was assigned a workbench, clamps, a hammer, a punch, goggles, and drills of various sizes. On his first day, his boss told him, "It costs about $250 to train a first class riveter. To understand rivets, one has to know how to measure them. Therefore, you will have to learn how to use a measuring scale."

Each bomber required 360,000 rivets (all made on the premises), some one-sixteenth of an inch long and weighing 0.00005 pounds, others fifty times that length and weighing 0.05 pounds. Some were nickel-steel, some pure aluminum, some stainless steel, others aluminum-steel alloy, and all were carefully engineered to perform their job not just on the ground but 20,000 feet up, where temperatures dropped to 40 below and the atmospheric pressure plunged. Rivets were kept in iceboxes at negative 20 degrees Fahrenheit until they were used — part of the heat-treating process to make them as strong as possible.

"Riveting is a social operation," Stermer remembered. "It involves two persons interacting, one to direct the rivet gun, the other to oppose the hammer at the other end of the rivet with the bucking bar." At one point, he drove in thirty rivets only to find that he had jammed half of them. His foreman "got red in the face."

The nine-hour shift moved slowly. In the cafeteria, Stermer paid 38 cents for lunch: a meat sandwich, an apple, a piece of pie, soup in a paper carton, and a pint of milk. The size of the cafeteria itself was overwhelming. Each day cooks served 1,500 pork chops, 550 pounds of trimmed beef, 700 pounds of potatoes, and nearly 10,000 rolls. Rationing limited each worker to consumption of 1.53 "meat points" per day.

After lunch Stermer returned to riveting. He spent a week studying riveting theory before he was handed over to a foreman on the assembly line. The more hours he put in on the job the more overwhelmed he became. "One thing that impressed me again today was the importance of ear plugs," Stermer wrote in his journal. "The din without them is absolutely deafening. Yet nothing was said about them during orientation or theory school. So many little adjustments in this place could be made so much easier if somebody would just give them a little thought — and pass the results of the thinking along!"

To Stermer, it was clear that the scope of this industrial adventure and the speed at which the factory had been built had caused a rift between the imaginations that had dreamed up Willow Run and the man who held the rivet gun in his hand. It was the imagineer's job to concoct this giant mechanism and to envision it from its totality down to the rivet. But Willow Run was so vast, and dreamed up and built so quickly, that it was functioning like a timepiece in which all the little parts did not fit together properly.

The first of May arrived, the month when the military chiefs were scheduled to take delivery of the first Ford bomber. But there was no bomber. The war overseas was being lost and the bomber-an-hour goal was not yet remotely in sight. Months earlier, Willow Run was the celebration of the Allied war movement on the home front. Now the plant was becoming an embarrassment in front of the whole nation. One federal official called Ford's bomber-an-hour experiment "the worst mess in the whole United States." Others had begun to call Willow Run "Will It Run?"

"The powers that control the plant and its environment are unable to grasp the fact that *we are at war*," stated the *Detroit News*. "And to realize that the great, basic purpose of the plant is to help *win* — perhaps even decide the issue of the war."

When it seemed like things couldn't get worse, Edsel got word of a special visitor who would soon be arriving at Willow Run. The identity of this visitor was top-secret, but Edsel figured it out quickly when Secret Service agents showed up asking to snoop around. The President himself was going to visit the bomber plant, and the clock was ticking. The pressure to get Willow Run fully in production would heighten with every hour until Franklin Roosevelt arrived.

From his dock on Lake St. Clair at Gaukler Pointe, Edsel boarded a Grumman amphibious airplane on the morning of May 15, 1942. He had taken possession of a government-issue plane to commute from Grosse Pointe to Willow Run, flying in a fraction of the time it took him to travel the forty-five miles by car.

The plane motored along the glistening lake and took flight, banking into a turn that revealed through a window an aerial postcard picture of downtown Motor City, its iconic edifices poking through the spring haze. There was the luxurious Book-Cadillac Hotel (the tallest hotel in the world when it was completed in 1924),* General

---

* The Book-Cadillac Hotel was famous for being the place where Yankee first baseman Lou Gehrig collapsed three years earlier, causing him to miss a game

Motors' magnificent headquarters along the river, and the Guardian Building, which local authorities had turned into a kind of command center for the city's war production effort.

Minutes later, Edsel stepped off the plane on the runway at Willow Run, in front of the control tower and the airfield's hangar. He had a spring in his step on this morning. The first Ford-built B-24 — Bomber Ship 01 — was set to roll off the assembly line. It was an "educational" airplane built with parts fabricated by Ford and others supplied by Consolidated Aircraft in San Diego.

At the door of Willow Run that led onto the airfield, the bomber stood on its huge rubber tires. It was not only a weapon but a symbol of American strength in a new kind of war. "The B-24 has guts," said the army air force's pilot instruction manual. "It can take it and dish it out. It can carry a bigger bomb load farther and faster, day in and day out, than any airplane that has passed the flaming test of combat."

The bomber's skin was made of aluminum stamped so thin that you could stab through it with a knife. Inside were 4,000 feet of rubber and metal tubing; like arteries and veins, these tubes moved fuel, oil, oxygen, de-icing fluid, and hydraulic fluid throughout the machine. The cockpit, the airplane's brain center, was a cramped cavern with cast-iron seats for the pilot and copilot, specifically built to protect these men from flak and gunfire coming from below.

Eighteen rubber fuel cells were mounted inside the wings (twelve in the center wing, three more each in the outer wings, for even weight distribution). These tanks held 16,320 pounds of 100-octane gasoline (2,720 gallons), and the bladders were self-sealing. In the event a bullet shot through one, it instantly sealed itself to prevent fire. In the belly of the plane, the bomb bay was constructed to hold 8,000 pounds of payload in three different ways: four 2,000-pound bombs, eight 1,000-pound bombs, or twelve 500-pound and twenty 100-pound bombs.

On the assembly line's final stage, workers on elevator systems had guided spray-paint guns over every outer inch of the ship. Bomber Ship 01 was a shade of army green dull enough so that the metal did

---

against the Detroit Tigers, ending his streak of 2,130 consecutive games played. Gehrig would later be diagnosed with "Lou Gehrig's disease."

not reflect the sun. Workers had also mounted all the government-issue equipment, such as gauges, life rafts, and the bombsight. And there were those big engines — a quartet of Pratt & Whitney power plants built by other companies, notably the Buick division of General Motors. (Ford's Pratt & Whitney engines built in the Rouge were used on other planes, not the B-24.)

By the time Bomber Ship 01 made its way out the doors under the beating sun, Edsel, Sorensen, and a sprawling crowd of laborers, engineers, military officials, and representatives from Washington had gathered on the airfield. On a dais in front of the bomber, Edsel stood by an American flag flicking in the wind, enjoying a round of applause, the sweat beading on his brow. Southern Michigan was in the thick of a spring heat wave that afternoon — over 90 degrees.

"The plant itself needs no praise," Edsel said, his voice loud and tinny through the microphone. "It speaks for itself. It is a fine plant, splendidly equipped, and eloquent of what can be accomplished by cooperation between government and industry, management and labor, army officers and production engineers, civilians and military men. Unfortunately this plant has been the subject of some premature and inaccurate publicity. That, perhaps, was natural. For Willow Run has become a symbol of the United States in the air. . . . Every employee and every manager here pledges all out cooperation until the V of velocity in production, and valor in combat, becomes the V of final victory."

Although Lindbergh was very likely on hand, Ford's chief test pilot, Harold Henning, did the honors on this day. Inside the bomber's cockpit, with a copilot beside him, Henning powered up the Liberator's radial engines at 3:15 PM. The crowd watched from a distance as the plane taxied to the top of a runway, in awe of the Liberator's size and its thunderous song. As one pilot who flew a B-24 said upon first seeing it: "It was HUGE. I was completely amazed by its monstrous size, its four mighty engines."

When Henning had the Liberator's engines up to temperature, he pointed Bomber Ship 01 down the runway and gunned the throttles. The ship shuddered for a moment, the throbbing engines straining to collect those tens of thousands of pounds and thrust them forward with all the power of a herd of 4,800 thoroughbred horses. Edsel stood amid the crowd as if alone, watching this airplane gather speed and lift itself off the tarmac, climbing in altitude as its exhaust note began to slowly fade.

It had been a bitter battle to get this first ship built, and there was still a long war ahead. But for a moment, watching that flying machine arc into a smooth bend, Edsel allowed himself some quiet satisfaction, as if the plane's takeoff had lifted an unbearable weight from his shoulders. He could not help but smile.

He was back in the airplane business again.

19

Roosevelt Visits Willow Run

September 1942

My feelings against Americanism are feelings of hatred and deep repugnance. . . . Everything about the behavior of American society reveals that it's half Judaized and the other half Negrified. How can one expect a State like that to hold together — a country where everything is built on the dollar?

— ADOLF HITLER

SHORTLY BEFORE MIDNIGHT ON September 17, 1942, the President slipped quietly out of Washington with a retinue of officials from the military and the White House. His private train left the nation's capital under the cover of night. The train had a stocked bar, Secret Service operatives manning all the doors, and a special car configured to carry the President's limousine, like a garage on steel wheels. He had scheduled a trip across the country and back, over 8,750 miles, to see for himself what the country had become — a full inspection of this new America, of which he was the chief architect.

Roosevelt's first stop: Detroit.

Thus far, in the Oval Office, the story of the war's first eight months had unfolded like a montage of crushing news — "the winter of disaster," as the President's top speechwriter put it. "The awful realization was slowly coming over the country," said War Production Board chief Donald Nelson, "that America was losing a war, the greatest in history, one upon which our national existence depended."

Cables and phone calls had crisscrossed the Atlantic between the President and Prime Minister Churchill, in a morbid game of discursive ping-pong. "The news is going to get worse and worse before it begins to get better," Roosevelt told Churchill.

On the home front, production numbers were falling far behind quotas. The most serious issue was the failure of industry to launch airpower. Through Roosevelt's Lend-Lease program, the United States was scheduled to deliver 1,709 planes to the Soviet Union, 3,305 to Britain, and 340 to other Allied nations. Many of those airplanes could not be delivered because they had not yet been built. The planes that foreign governments wanted most were the hardest to build: four-engine bombers. The need for bombers had become an obsession.

"I have been deeply concerned at the slow expansion of the production of heavy and medium bombers," Churchill had said. "Other long-term projects must give way to the overriding need for more bomber aircraft." On another occasion: "We must aim at nothing less than having an Air Force twice as strong as the German Air Force by the end of 1942. It is the very least that can be contemplated, since no other way of winning the war has yet been proposed."

On August 8, 1942, Roosevelt had received a memo from White House statistician Isador Lubin. "The airplane production situation appears to be getting progressively worse," Lubin wrote. "Not only have we failed to meet your directive as announced in January [a schedule of 60,000 planes for 1942], but we have failed even to realize the schedules that had been laid out before we entered the war."

Infuriated, Roosevelt fired off a memo that landed on half the desks in Washington. "I am concerned by the figures on production of combat planes," he wrote. "The bomber deficit in July seems to be the most serious. . . . I think you should hold a clinic on this patient. Then you can let me know what disease he is suffering from and how he can be cured!"

Of all the wartime production centers, Detroit had become the most important — and thus far, the most disappointing. Crowded, hot, teeming with exhausted laborers who were far from their homes and suit-and-tie engineers working themselves to exhaustion, the city had become a seething hotbed of potential violence. With the constant flow of poor Southern African Americans into the city, it was only a matter of time before it erupted in full-blown race riots, according to local authorities. The age-old murderous Southern race conflict was being transplanted into an overheated, overcrowded industrial megalopolis.

Morale had shifted significantly in three months. One confidential government report circulating around the nation's capital, called "All's Not Well in Detroit," detailed how the auto industry was 60 percent behind military production quotas. In an issue of *Life* that hit newsstands just days before the President's train screeched north from Washington to see the auto industry's progress, the magazine summed up the situation with a cover story called "Detroit Is Dynamite."

"The news from Detroit is bad this summer," the story began. "Few people across the country realize how bad it is. Wildcat strikes and sit-downs, material shortages and poor planning at the top have cut into Detroit's production of war weapons. The result is a morale situation which is perhaps the worst in the US. Detroit can either blow up Hitler or blow up the US."

On September 18, the President's train roared into Detroit. That afternoon, Edsel Ford, his father, Charlie Sorensen, and Harry Bennett stood fidgeting at the northwest corner of Willow Run, where the rail tracks swept against the concrete siding. Secret Service, State Police, and US troops surrounded them. Lindbergh made sure not to show up for work on this day, wanting nothing to do with his archenemy, President Roosevelt. At 3:40 PM, the President's special train pulled up to the bomber factory, right on schedule.

When the door to Roosevelt's train car opened, a special ramp with railings flopped down on the siding. With no use of his legs, Roosevelt grabbed ahold of the railings to support himself as he made his way down the ramp on his own power, his face showing the strain as the muscles in his arms flexed. Photographers were gentlemen back then. None would consider snapping the President in a moment of weakness.

"I was astonished to find him so helpless," Sorensen remembered. "He was in agony."

Roosevelt's bulletproof Lincoln phaeton limousine was ready — top down, ample chrome sparkling in the Michigan sun. It was a beautiful car, born on the assembly line at Edsel's Lincoln factory in Detroit. Roosevelt wore a light gray suit with a black tie and his usual wire-rim spectacles. At the car door, a large muscular guard lifted him into the air as if he were a child and placed him in a seat in back.

Standing by, Henry Ford scowled in the presence of his nemesis. How awkward it was to have Roosevelt here on his property. But then Henry had to be reminded: this was not his property. Willow Run was government property.

Edsel, meanwhile, smiled nervously at his friend Roosevelt. Edsel felt as many Americans did: boundless respect for this man who had overcome so much to contribute as much as he had. And yet, on this occasion, as Edsel shook the President's hand, he could not hide from the facts: his aviation venture had cost the taxpayers hundreds of millions, and his promise of a bomber an hour had gone woefully unfulfilled.

Ford Motor Company had thus far rolled out but a single Liberator — Bomber Ship 01. They were four months and counting behind schedule.

Secret Service men placed Henry in the back of the Lincoln phaeton between the President and his wife. Edsel and Sorensen sat in front next to the driver. With military and bureaucrats in tow, the car pulled toward the bomber plant's gaping doors. Willow Run swallowed them up.

Bennett had organized the proceedings. The route the phaeton was to travel was marked with flags, guiding the driver through the factory. The President and First Lady were all smiles, chatting amiably. As the limousine moved into the manufacturing area, Edsel explained the machinery to Mrs. Roosevelt while Sorensen did the same with the President. In the backseat, sandwiched between Roosevelt and his wife, seventy-nine-year-old Henry sat in silence, staring off with glazed-over eyes.

"It was evident to me that he was not enjoying the company," Sorensen remembered. "The President and Mrs. Roosevelt were indifferent to him."

Roosevelt had never been inside an airplane factory. Edsel had the place pasted with American flags. Secret Service men eyed the laborers suspiciously. Any worker who had a lunch pail was told to set it on the ground a few feet away, for fear that it could be concealing a weapon. The 35,000 working at Willow Run at the time knew a visitor was on the way, but the visitor in question was but a rumor until he arrived. All around the President, workers stopped and applauded.

"We're with you, Frank!" yelled one.

"How do you like it, Mr. President?" yelled another.

The President waved and smiled, feeding off the enthusiasm. In the front seat, Edsel studied him with glances over his shoulder. Roosevelt's face had a way of expressing amazement and confusion simultaneously, revealing everything and nothing at the same time. His political skills were uncanny, this ability to keep everyone on their toes, always guessing as to what he was thinking.

"Charlie, what is that?" Roosevelt asked Sorensen, pointing to a machine that cut a piece of a wing and then bent it into shape. Sorensen couldn't help but sound like a PR man as he explained how the company had set up the factory to build bombers according to automobile manufacturing methods, something that had never been done.

The First Lady raised one of her favorite causes, women workers. She was pleased to see so many females with sleeves rolled up — terrific fodder for her next newspaper column. Even before Pearl Harbor, she had championed the cause of women workers for the Arsenal of Democracy. Edsel explained that Willow Run was now employing thousands of women and the number was rising by the week.

"Franklin, look over here," Eleanor Roosevelt said.

The President turned and blinked his eyes to make sure he knew what he was seeing: dwarfs toiling inside a hole in a bomber. Edsel explained. The dwarfs had been hired to climb inside a section of the center wing, where normal-sized people could not fit. They worked in there firing rivet guns — more proof of the almost Rube Goldberg-esque ambition of this operation. Roosevelt swung the door to the phaeton open, and two dwarfs approached. They shook hands and talked with the President while official photographers captured the moment for the newspapers.

Moving along, Edsel showed the President the giant seventy-five-foot-long super-truck that Ford Motor Company was using to move "knockdown" assemblies (bombers without engines, in pieces) from Willow Run down to Douglas Aviation's plant in Tulsa, Oklahoma, for assembly. The huge eighteen-wheelers were powered by two Ford V8 engines and drove with US Army escort trucks protecting them. They were the biggest trucks ever to hurtle down an American road. Roosevelt asked if these were the trucks that motorists were complaining about, causing traffic problems. Before Edsel could answer, the phaeton moved to the ell in the factory, the spot where Willow Run cornered abruptly at the Washtenaw County line.

"And so this is the city line!" Roosevelt exclaimed loud enough for all to hear. Yes, the *Democratic* president had heard about the plant layout, how Henry Ford had demanded that Willow Run be built L-shaped so that it stayed within the confines of a *Republican* county that voted against Roosevelt in three straight elections. Sitting between the President and First Lady, Henry Ford squirmed.

The group moved to the most impressive machine inside Willow Run: the center-wing mechanism. Here was the $250,000 apparatus that cut days of work into a six-hour job creating the Liberator's fifty-foot-long center-wing section. Sorensen and Edsel explained in detail how every center wing that this machine spat out was exactly like the one before.

At the end of the assembly line, the group could see a row of partially built B-24s slowly taking shape, in various forms of undress. By the time the party drove out of the plant onto the airfield apron, the afternoon sun had ducked toward the western horizon. On the runway lay the finale. The Air Corps had organized a gathering of American military airplanes all in a row, to showcase the rise of the nation's airpower. Here stood the B-24 Liberator, its sister plane the Boeing B-17 Flying Fortress, several Martin B-26 Marauders (medium bombers powered by 2,000-horsepower R-2800 Double Wasp engines built by Ford at the Rouge), the famed Republic P-47 Thunderbolt fighter (also powered by a Ford engine), the North American B-25 bomber, the Lockheed P-38 Lightning, a Bell P-39 Airacobra, a bunch of Curtiss P-40 Warhawks, and some training Vultees and Cessnas.

Next to those, Edsel had organized a showcase of his war work, all the military equipment that the Rouge, Highland Park, and Lincoln factories were producing. The Ford medium tank, the Ford V8 tank engine, the T-17 armored car, the T-22 light armored car, the one-and-a-half-ton army truck, the amphibious reconnaissance car, the 75-millimeter cannon mount, the Jeep, two kinds of anti-aircraft gun directors, and the Pratt & Whitney Double Wasp aviation engine — which the Rouge was now pumping out at a rate of more than 600 a month, the equivalent of 720,000 horsepower every thirty days.

From his limousine, the President sat quietly admiring all that machinery, a rare moment of silence for this loquacious man. He completed his visit with a twenty-minute conference alone with Henry and Edsel. What they discussed will remain forever between them. But it was clear that Willow Run was behind schedule. And that it had better get up to speed. When the party left, Roosevelt held a small model of a Ford-built B-24 Liberator in his hand — a gift from Edsel.

Two weeks later, the President arrived back at the White House. The nation he had seen was still in the early part of a long journey. And yet, every part of life was affected by the war, for everyone. He was astonished by what he had seen. This was a country that had rolled up its sleeves. Nearly 3.5 million Americans had left their homes, their schools, and their jobs to serve in the military in 1941 and 1942. Innumerable businesses that didn't serve the war effort had vanished. In the first two months of the war alone, about 300,000 retailers had closed their doors in what *BusinessWeek* called "the most severe contraction in the business population that we have ever experienced."

Because of rationing, a cup of coffee was a luxury. Canned beer was hard to come by because tin was needed for munitions. Harder still to find was whiskey — alcohol was needed for torpedo fuel and for medicinal purposes. Finding a steak was like winning the lottery — unless you got it from "Mr. Black" (the thriving black market). Americans were now buying horse meat and even muskrat meat for their tables. Housewives were ordered to retain cooking fats in their kitchens and return them to butcher shops. One pound of cooked animal fat contained enough glycerin, they were told, to produce gunpowder for fifty .30 caliber bullets.

Rationing changed the way people dressed and bathed. Wartime forced the issue of racial and gender integration as never before. Because labor was in such demand, jobs that blacks could never attain before were now open to them. As one African American woman famously put it: "Hitler was the one that got us out of the white folks' kitchen."

The President was happy with what he saw — this new America slowly coming into its own. In his post-trip press conference, surrounded by the White House press corps, he had little to say about Willow Run, except this: like the war itself, Ford's bomber experiment was not going exactly as planned. Willow Run was "not yet in production."

20

A Dying Man

Fall 1942 to Winter 1943

This hour I rode the sky like a god, but after it was over, how glad I would be to go back to earth and live among men, to feel the soil under my feet and to be smaller than the mountains and trees.

— CHARLES LINDBERGH

CIRCLING THE SKIES OVER Willow Run in the flight deck of a B-24, Charles Lindbergh worked through a series of maneuvers with a copilot beside him. He had probably piloted a wider array of flying machines than any American. But he'd never flown an airplane as uncomfortable — nor any that required as much pure arm strength — as a B-24 Liberator. It was like flying "a 1930s Mack truck," as one aviation historian put it.

The wheel in the cockpit connected to a system of cables mounted on pulleys within the body of the airplane that activated the flight controls (ailerons, rudders, and elevators). It was all operated marionette-like by the pilot's arms and feet. The wheel (or the "yoke") controlled the ailerons on the wings; turn left for a left turn, right for a right turn. Two foot pedals could also turn the plane left and right, while the wheel also controlled the vertical stabilizers; push the wheel forward to aim the nose into a descent, or pull back to raise the nose further into the sky.

After an hour or two, the muscles in Lindbergh's arms ached from exhaustion. Meanwhile, the rest of the crew tested out their equipment. Bombardiers opened and closed the bomb bay doors, then dropped dummy bombs into Lake St. Clair, while radiomen and engineers worked over their gauges and electronics.

Up at 20,000 feet, with no pressurized cabin, the temperature could sink below –40 degrees Fahrenheit, the icy wind blowing right through the cockpit. Having worked up a sweat on takeoff, the pilot's face could freeze onto the rubber oxygen mask. There were no windshield wipers. If it was raining, the pilot had to stick his head out the window to see the runway upon landing. There was also no real bathroom — not a big deal during a two-and-a-half-hour shakedown flight. But on a ten-hour bombing mission, all an airman aboard a Liberator had access to was a tube for urination (which often froze and clogged) and a bag for defecation.

As Lindbergh began his descent, the bomber rattled and banged. Gas fumes filled the cockpit. When the rubber wheels touched down, his hands were cramped and shaky. He headed for the showers. Later, he arrived in a conference room for a debriefing with Henry Ford, Edsel, Bennett, Sorensen, and several other engineers.

The date was October 26, 1942. By this time — a month after the President's visit to Willow Run — bombers had begun to trickle out of the factory, and Lindbergh's job was to size them up. He found the airplane "unnecessarily awkward" and the instruments "more complicated than the keyboard of a pipe organ."

"I found the controls to be the stiffest and heaviest I have ever handled," he said. The closer he looked at these airplanes, the more he was alarmed. The Ford-built B-24 was "the worst piece of metal aircraft construction I have ever seen," Lindbergh concluded. He added:

Rivets missing, rivets badly put in, rivet holes started and forgotten, whole lines of rivets left entirely out, wrong-sized rivets, lopsided rivets, badly formed skin, corner cuts improperly made, cracks already started, soft metal used where hard metal is essential, control holes left out, pilot's escape hatch incredibly badly constructed.

The army was now taking possession of Willow Run's first bombers, and the company was getting a reputation for turning out poor-quality workmanship. The arrogance of Ford's bomber-an-hour plan had infuriated the other airplane manufacturers. Aviation men were hoping that Ford would fail, and so far it had. Lindbergh was hearing more grumblings from Washington. The government was ready to come in and take over Willow Run.

It was true, Edsel confirmed. He had gotten word that Missouri senator Harry Truman was arranging a trip to Willow Run for a full congressional investigation into the plant's failure. Senator Truman would be arriving in a matter of weeks. The Truman Committee had grown very powerful in the first year of the war. The press was bound to be horrible.

"You'd better be prepared," Lindbergh said, "and see if you can't do something about it."

Grimacing, Edsel argued to bring on more workers at once. They needed more bodies! The original projections had called for more than 65,000 more workers than were on the payroll at Willow Run at that time.

But new workers had to be trained, Lindbergh reminded everyone. "We have more than 30,000 employees at Willow Run now," he said, "and less than 400 of them had experience in aircraft manufacture before they came here."

Sorensen stepped out of character and admitted guilt. "We knew it was a tough problem, but we didn't know it was quite so tough," he said.

Edsel fired back with exasperation: "But a lot of people told us it was." The company "had made all kinds of production promises for months and listened to none of the warnings," he said.

Henry spoke up: "What are we going to do about this place?"

No one had yet come up with the answer.

In Washington, on July 11, 1942, a strange letter appeared on the desk of Secretary of State Cordell Hull, arriving via airmail from the office of Felix Cole, the American consul general in Algiers, Algeria. The memo's title: "A New Ford Motor Company for Africa." The letter explained that Ford's French division—which was then building trucks for the Nazis — had established a new company in Algiers, that at least one person involved in the new arrangement was said to be "unscrupulous" and "100 percent pro-German," and that the local commercial circles were "pointing an accusing finger" at the new African Ford company, questioning where its loyalties lay — with America or with Germany.

The news of the new company, Ford-Afrique, made it to Secretary of the Treasury Henry Morgenthau's office. Morgenthau was an upstate New York Jewish gentleman farmer turned diplomat who mistrusted major corporations and their executives, whose judgment was easily clouded, the Treasury secretary believed, by a lust for profit. He had been quietly crusading to expose corruption and war profiteering over the past year. During the war, his office, along with others in Washington, would conduct either formal or informal investigations into major American powerhouses with financial ties to Nazi Germany, such as Standard Oil and Chase National Bank.

Henry Ford was already on Morgenthau's radar — ever since Henry refused in 1941 to build Merlin aircraft engines for the British. Now there was this suspicious new Ford company incorporating in northern Africa. Soon Morgenthau's agents were looking deeper into the situation. Could this company in Africa be used to support Hitler's war effort? What did Ford executives in Dearborn know about it?

On December 7, 1942, Edsel Ford was in his office when he got the shock of a lifetime. An investigator named J. John Lawler showed up with a warrant to search the premises. The warrant was on a US Treasury Department letterhead, signed by Mr. Lawler and one J. W. Pehle, an assistant to Secretary of the Treasury Henry Morgenthau. "You are hereby instructed and required," the warrant began, "pursuant to the provisions of Section 5(b) of the Trading with the Enemy Act . . . to produce upon presentation of this instruction . . . any and all books of account, contracts, letters, notes."

Edsel was baffled and frightened. Why would the Treasury Department want to search his papers? The investigator, Lawler, found Edsel and his assistant, R. I. Roberge, "extremely curious as to the reason for this investigation." They were "not at all certain of what the Treasury's interest was."

For an hour and a half, Edsel answered questions, which centered on his correspondence with Ford's top man in France, Maurice Dollfus, who was known to be serving the Nazi warlords. Apparently, Dollfus had started this new Ford company in Algiers. The African Ford company had come up in Dollfus's correspondence with Edsel, so Edsel had some rudimentary knowledge of it. But he knew almost nothing of the details.

When the Treasury investigator left Dearborn for Washington, he carried with him piles of Ford Motor Company contracts and letters, which Edsel shared freely, including his correspondence with the eloquent if not mysterious Dollfus. What, Edsel wondered, could he have done to violate the Trading with the Enemy Act? Was this all some kind of mistake?

One cold morning that winter Edsel awoke at Gaukler Pointe with a severe fever and a flare of agony in his gut. With his wife Eleanor's help, he got himself in a car, and a driver motored him to Henry Ford Hospital. Eleanor Ford asked the doctors to summon the best abdominal specialist in the world. Soon Dr. Roscoe Graham was en route from Toronto to perform surgery. He opened Edsel up and found tumors that had taken root so deep in the stomach that there was no way to get them out. After the surgery, the physician approached Edsel's wife gravely.

"I'm sorry," he said, "but I can do nothing to help Mr. Ford."

Edsel was dying.

He stayed in the hospital for another week until his fever retreated. Then he headed home to Gaukler Pointe. The mansion's vast sitting rooms and warrens were devastatingly quiet. Mail poured in from friends who had heard of his hospital stay.

"I do hope you are not suffering from any serious illness and that you will soon be back on the job," wrote J. Edgar Hoover.

"Dear Edgar," Edsel wrote back, "I am sorry to say that I was laid up for a couple of weeks. I seem to have the thing under control at the present," he lied.

Eleven days after his surgery, Edsel was back at Willow Run. "Looks bad," Sorensen wrote in his diary. "Something wrong with him. . . . Stress and strain is the worst thing for that ailment." In retrospect, Sorensen looked back on these days bitterly, believing that Edsel's life could still have been saved. "If Edsel could have dropped out of sight for a while at this time and gone in for a cure, he would have recovered." Another Ford executive put it this way: "What he should have done . . . is to have taken his dough out of the company and quit."

Eleanor begged her husband to leave the job behind, but Edsel refused. What was his life but a struggle for integrity and meaning? To prove he was no prodigal son, to fill the roomy shoes of his famous father? Why give up now when his greatest battle could still be won? Why surrender?

Unaware of the severity of the illness, Henry had no sympathy, blaming his son's condition on his taste for a drink and a smoke. "If there is anything the matter with Edsel's health," he told Sorensen, "he can correct it himself."

Edsel's children were unaware that the illness was terminal, but they knew something was terribly wrong. Benson, Edsel's second-oldest, was driving with Sorensen one day on military leave. He unleashed his rage at Henry Ford.

"Grandfather is responsible for Father's sickness," he shouted, "and I'm through with him!" Sorensen tried to calm Benson down, but it was impossible. The young man was hysterical over the condition of his father.

The cruel Detroit winter set in, and Edsel soldiered on — battling production problems and nervously awaiting word from Washington about the Treasury Department's strange investigation of his files. "I had no idea," said his secretary A. J. Lepine, "seeing him almost every day at the office that he was seriously ill."

Edsel tried to find pleasure in his children. His daughter Josephine moved her wedding date up so that he could attend, though she perhaps did not entirely understand why. The proud father of the bride-to-be received a letter from Mr. Condé Nast asking if Josephine would pose for a photograph for *Vogue* magazine. (Edsel approved, but the photograph was never taken.) When Edsel walked his daughter down the aisle on January 2, 1943 — less than a month after the Treasury investigator had raided his office — he looked dapper and sophisticated as always, though the wedding guests whispered that something appeared wrong about him.

Josephine married Walter Buhl Ford (no relation), and Edsel took delight in calling the newlywed couple the Ford-Fords. He hosted the reception at Gaukler Pointe, where family and friends clinked champagne glasses inside the beautiful mansion, with its gaping Gothic fireplace and dramatic chandeliers.

As for Edsel's oldest son, Henry II was still stationed at the Great Lakes Naval Base outside Chicago. Edsel realized that this internecine drama was about to fall right in Henry II's lap. Young Henry would need all his strength and nerve in the coming months ahead. In Chicago, Henry II and his wife Anne gave birth to their second daughter that January of 1943. Edsel and Eleanor took a train to the Windy City and checked into its finest hotel, the Drake. Edsel stood by his son as the grandchild was baptized in a nearby church.

Dutifully, Edsel tried to get along with his father. "The baby is a beauty and didn't make a murmur during the ceremony," he wrote Henry from Chicago. It seemed like such a short time ago that Edsel was trotting along beside Henry through the long aisles of Highland Park, looking up at his father like he was a god. Henry and Edsel had clashed on many occasions through the years, but Edsel had always looked up to his father. Being a loyal son was an intrinsic part of his definition of success. "I think Edsel Ford was infinitely more than a loyal son," one high-level Ford man, A. M. Wibel, said of his boss. "I just think he adored his dad and what he stood for."

In the end, if Edsel was going to be remembered, his legacy would be Willow Run. And so he put all his strength into it. "I spent all day yesterday at Willow Run," he wrote his father in the winter of 1943, not long after being diagnosed as terminal. "Talking manpower, work incentives, trying to make plans to reduce absenteeism, now over 10% per day."

The plant was getting close, Edsel knew, to realizing its ambition. He could feel it. The bomber-an-hour goal was not out of reach. The war was slipping away, and so was his own personal battle, a fight for integrity he had waged his entire adult life. It was not too late to turn everything around — but Edsel was running out of time.

PART IV

—————

THE RISE OF AMERICAN
AIRPOWER

It was this feeling of the unknown. What were we going to face?
What was a mission going to be like? We were very green, not
really prepared for it. There were ten of us: pilot, copilot, navigator, bombardier, engineer, radio man, second radio man, second engineer, and two gunners. I was a rear gunner. Our first
mission was over Aschersleben — I'll never forget it — in the
heart of Germany. It was an airfield. I was a nineteen-year-
old kid. I remember planes flying, and I remember the cold.
At 30,000 feet, to see so many planes and fighter planes and
bombers, it was just awesome. Let me put it like that: awesome.
It was just surreal.

— Benjamin Napolitano, *Stamford, CT*

21

Unconditional Surrender

Winter 1943

We will make Germany a desert. Yes, a desert.

— WINSTON CHURCHILL

AT MIDNIGHT ON JANUARY 11, 1943, a pair of Pan American clippers sat ready to taxi on an airfield runway in Miami, surrounded by the most crack security team anywhere on earth. Aboard one of the planes, the President of the United States sat with his seat belt on, feeling the rumble of the engines in his bones. He had taken a private train south from Washington along with a group of the most exalted minds in the US military, some two dozen in total. With the party strapped into the belly of the two planes, the pilots squeezed the throttles. They lifted off, bound across the Atlantic Ocean for Africa.

No American president had ever flown overseas — a testament to the infancy of aviation. (Only one had ever flown at all: Roosevelt's cousin Theodore enjoyed a four-minute jaunt aboard a plane built by the Wright Brothers in 1910.) Roosevelt was also about to become the first American president since Abraham Lincoln to travel into an active theater of war. At that same moment, Winston Churchill sat aboard an airplane with his team of top military and political thinkers, headed from the United Kingdom to the same destination — Casablanca. For his private aircraft, Churchill had chosen an American-made B-24 Liberator with passenger seating built in place of the bomb racks.

Because of heavy winds, the President's clipper flew low over the Atlantic, not much more than 1,000 feet over the water, cruising at a speed of 105 miles per hour. Locked in steel boxes with detonators attached (in case of emergency) were the secret papers that were the focus of what would soon be known as "the Casablanca Conference." These papers held the answer to the question of how the war would be won, if it would be won.

Roosevelt had plenty to think about over the long haul. Though his war plans were top-secret, his overall strategy was far from it. Anyone who'd read a newspaper in recent months knew that in order to win the war, the Allies were desperate for mastery of the skies.

In numerous polls, Americans had chosen the heavy bomber as their favorite weapon. *Fortune* magazine: "The people are sold on peace through air power." The entire American public had gone bomber-crazy. Films like *Dive Bomber* (1941, with Errol Flynn) and *Flying Tigers* (1942, John Wayne) thrilled movie audiences. "Our heavy bomber is our greatest weapon," John Steinbeck wrote in his book *Bombs Away* (1942), after spending a month flying with a crew. Aviation pioneer Alexander de Seversky's literary polemic *Victory Through Airpower* (1942) made #1 on the *New York Times* bestseller list.

Still, production of aircraft in the United States had a long way to go to secure victory.

"Despite all the talk about reorganizing the flow of raw materials," Harry Hopkins told the President, "and despite the fact that the aircraft construction program was the subject of conversation through the entire months of September and October, it appears that not a Goddamn thing was done to overcome production difficulties."

The head of the Air Corps, General Hap Arnold, also agreed, singling out the failure of one particular company. "There has been some delay in new producers getting started," according to Arnold, "such as Ford." Arnold reminded the President of "manpower complications, such as in Detroit."

As for the overall narrative of the war at this point, finally the Allied leaders could celebrate good news. Two months earlier General

Dwight Eisenhower had landed his troops in the North African the-ater, beating back Nazi general Erwin Rommel and his Afrika Korps. Operation Torch was the Allies' first major, successful land, sea, and air campaign against Hitler.

As news of these battles along the northern coast of Africa thrilled Americans at home, the first headlines announcing genocide at the hands of the Nazis also appeared in the American and British press. What many in high levels of government had long suspected was now becoming a matter of revealed truth.

"One is almost stunned into silence by some of the information reaching London," Edward R. Murrow reported over CBS radio. "Some of it is months old, but it's eye-witness stuff supported by a wealth of detail and vouched for by responsible governments. What is happening is this: Millions of human beings, most of them Jews, are being gathered up with ruthless efficiency and murdered. When you piece it all together . . . you have a picture of mass murder and moral depravity unequaled in the history of the world."

In Casablanca, twenty miles from the Atlantic coastline in French Morocco, the President's plane touched down and taxied to a stop at 6:20 PM local time. All around the airfield, the earth was scarred by fighting that had been staged there just weeks earlier. The President's motorcade arrived at the Anfa Hotel outside the city at 7:00 PM on January 14, 1943. Roosevelt wheeled his chair inside a villa called Dar Es Saada (Arabic for "House of Happiness"). The decor was so opulent that the President whistled and joked, "Now all we need is the Madame of the house!"

Security was hyper-alert. The American and British politicians and officers were warned not to drink anything but bottled water, for fear of poisoning. Secret Service men burned all trash in the ho-tel rooms, lest the slightest detail of the conversations in Casablanca reach the wrong ears. Barbed-wire fences surrounded the area, and a bomb shelter was built into a swimming pool.

A knock on the President's door at Dar Es Saada signaled the ar-rival of Winston Churchill. The two protagonists remained that night in conference until 3:00 AM. The historic Casablanca Conference had begun.

• • •

In the compound of villas in Casablanca, elite British and American commanders worked through a series of conferences picking apart every theater of war and outlining the progress of factory production at home. Roosevelt and Churchill agreed: the defeat of Nazi Germany would get priority over the war with the Japanese. Among the many decisions made, they outlined a plan to combine the American and British air forces in an effort to pummel Nazi Germany into submission.

Daring missions in the skies over Germany would require huge fleets of bombers. Massive casualties were expected. When the machines were shot down, more machines would have to appear in the skies behind them. To ensure victory, the assault would have to be brutal and relentless.

There remained one difference of opinion among the British and American leaders: how to utilize the heavy bomber, which was a controversial annihilation device. Churchill was a proponent of bombing cities by night. In darkness, bomber crews were less likely to get hit by anti-aircraft flak. The dapper, Bentley-driving British air marshal, Arthur Harris — nicknamed "Butch" for "Butcher" — had come under attack for his embrace of area bombing, the destruction of cities, which was after all a form of terrorism. The Prime Minister's science adviser, Lord Cherwell, called this tactic "de-housing the workers," destroying civilian homes and thus the morale of the men and women working in Axis war factories. This kind of bombing ensured casualties among civilians.

American strategy was to bomb precision targets by day — military installations, oil refineries, boat works, and airplane factories. Anything to cripple the Nazi war machine. Even if the bombers missed their targets and hit civilian homes (which they invariably would with great frequency), the cause seemed morally dignified. And the Air Corps bombers were built to attack by daylight. The downside to precision bombing: to hit a target, even with the latest bombsight and radar equipment, a pilot had to attack in broad daylight and in the direct path of anti-aircraft gunners. Which meant higher casualty rates among bomber crews and more destruction of airplanes.

The debate grew fierce. Unlike the Americans, the British civilian population had been brutally attacked by the Luftwaffe, with innumerable casualties among women and children. Churchill and "Butch" Harris had a different sense of high moral ground than their counterparts across the Atlantic. At Casablanca, the two parties came to an agreement. The Americans would bomb strategically by day, while the British would commence area bombing by night. These officials named their top-secret plan "The Combined Bomber Offensive."

On January 24, Roosevelt sat down in the Casablanca compound in front of nearly forty members of the British and American press who had been flown in on government airplanes. The President sat comfortably in a tan suit, with Churchill to his left in a black suit and bow tie, bowler hat in his lap. Those reporters got the scoop of a lifetime: the Allied leaders had gathered in the heart of the African war zone. The message was clear.

The turning point of the war had come.

"I think it can be said that the studies during the past week or ten days are unprecedented in history," Roosevelt began. "Some of you Britishers know the old story. We had a General called U. S. Grant. His name was Ulysses Simpson Grant but in my and the Prime Minister's early days, he was called 'Unconditional Surrender' Grant. The elimination of German, Japanese, and Italian war power means the unconditional surrender of Germany, Italy, and Japan. That means a reasonable assurance of future world peace. It does not mean the destruction of the population of Germany, Italy, or Japan, but it does mean the destruction of the philosophies in those countries which are based on conquest and the subjugation of other people.

"This meeting," the President concluded, "is called the 'unconditional surrender' meeting."

Before the Allied leaders headed for home, the American military commanders conceived a plan for the US Army Air Corps' most critical onslaught within Nazi-occupied Europe. They would hit Ploesti, the Romanian city with its sprawling ring of oil refineries, which were within the long range of the B-24 Liberators. In an engineer's war, which pit highly mechanized military forces against one another, this one strike could destroy the source of one-third of Hitler's oil production. Ploesti was "the taproot of German might," as Churchill put it. The American Joint Statistical Survey, a think tank of military minds, had called Ploesti "by far the most decisive objective of the war." A precision strike could stagger the enemy, plug the flow of oil to the Nazis, and stop Hitler's motorized forces in their tracks.

Ploesti was also the most heavily armed oil installation on earth, surrounded by radar warning systems and innumerable batteries of Germany's now-famous 88 anti-aircraft cannons, which were developed by the German powerhouse Krupp. The plan would require a long-distance strike by a massive fleet of bombers that would take off from Benghazi in the Libyan desert, flying a round trip of some 2,400 miles.

Only the B-24 had the range and firepower to accomplish such a mission. It would require many dozens of them, the largest American air armada ever assembled up to that time, like a city of planes in the sky moving at well over 200 miles per hour. Military brass eventually named the mission Operation Tidal Wave and scheduled the strike for August.

"The Billion Dollar Watchdog," Harry S. Truman, arrived at Willow Run with the Truman Committee – officially known as the Senate Committee to Investigate the National Defense Program – less than three weeks after the Casablanca Conference, on the morning of February 19, 1943. Truman wore a dark double-breasted suit, a fedora, and a no-nonsense stare that made him look like he was peering off a postage stamp. Edsel Ford greeted the committee's seven senators (five Democrats, two Republicans, most of them freshmen). Gaunt and weary, he led Truman and his entourage into the bomber plant.

Fifty-eight-year-old Senator Truman of Missouri was one of the most intimidating figures in America. Not that he was a bully. He was on a personal crusade to protect the American taxpayer during the transformation from peacetime to a war economy. He had come a long way since the war began. Three years earlier, Truman couldn't get the President's secretaries to return his calls. He was considered a front for the real power out of Missouri and called "an errand runner for Kansas City politicos"— namely, "Boss Tom" Pendergast, head of Missouri's Democratic Party, who had recently been convicted of tax evasion and sent to Leavenworth.

Not long before Pearl Harbor, Truman had offered his services to fight waste and corruption in the national defense effort. Only after he promised not to criticize the President — after he swore he was "100 percent behind the administration"— did Roosevelt establish the Truman Committee on March 1, 1941, authorizing the senator to make a full investigation of "the operation of the program for procurement and construction of supplies, materials, vehicles, aircraft, vessels, plants, camps, and other articles and facilities in connection with the national defense."

With his team of handpicked Washington operatives, Truman went on a rampage. He drove 10,000 miles in his own car to visit military bases and other government construction sites, exposing contractors who were wasting time and money, seeking out morally ambiguous profiteers, and saving millions of government dollars. Truman's hearings in Room 449 in the Senate Building and the meetings in his private office sitting room known as "the Dog House" had become a major story of the war effort. His work was deemed so vital that the senator who couldn't get the President's secretary to return his calls a year earlier landed on the cover of *Time* magazine. He was so ambitious, it was as if this Missouri politician had his sights on the Oval Office.

Before arriving at Willow Run to conduct his investigation into the delays, "Give 'em Hell Harry" promised reporters: "We will get all the facts."

Edsel sat down over doughnuts and coffee with the senators that morning and made his appeal. He had a keen political mind and saw Truman's visit not as an attack but as an opportunity to plead for Washington's help. Thus far, twenty-three months after construction crews broke ground at Willow Run, the company had yet to fly off its one-hundredth airplane— a far cry from a-bomber-an-hour production. Edsel methodically explained the problems that were causing delays.

For starters, he was having trouble getting people to show up for work. He begged the senators "to exert influence on the War Manpower Commission to improve the labor situation at Willow Run." The bomber plant had the highest absentee rate of any war plant in the country. Edsel broke out a chart and showed it to the committee. The month before alone, 2,060 workers had left Willow Run. As of that very week, Willow Run training programs had taken in 20,177 trainees, and 11,094 of them had quit before the program was over — more than half. The reasons varied.

Drafted into the military: 1,737
Enlistments: 1,472
Found another job: 843
No place to live: 314
Needed at home: 334

Next Edsel led the senators into a conference room where a stack of blueprints three feet high sat on a table. The blueprints showed changes that the army wanted made to the bomber. The Liberator had been designed by Consolidated Aircraft in 1938, the first prototype was in flight a year later, and the bomber was then put into production. It had all happened so fast. Now wanting to improve the design, the army was sending over dozens of changes every week.

Nothing threw a wrench into the mass-production process like changes to the product that the manufacturer was trying to produce. Ford Motor Company was using hard-steel dies at Willow Run, according to automaking methods — a controversial move, aviation experts were quick to point out early on. Steel dies could not be altered. If the airplane part changed, the steel die that crafted that part became garbage and needed replacing. A new one had to be created from scratch.

The army's latest request was for a new machine gun turret built into the nose of the Liberator below the cockpit. Bomber crews flying the Liberators overseas had asked for this change, to help defend against attacking enemy fighters coming at them straight on. When Edsel ventured to Washington to beg General Arnold to stop the requests for changes to the airplane, the General replied: "I'd feel as if I had blood on my hands if I ignored those boys' suggestions."

So now Edsel's men had three months to begin delivering bombers with this new nose turret — a huge job.

Edsel introduced the Truman Committee to Willow Run's new daily superintendent, an engineer named Mead Bricker who'd practically grown up in the Rouge. "Now, look," said Bricker, and he began to explain what happened when the government asked for a change to the bomber. "We'll show what it means in delay, what it means in equipment, what it means in jigs and fixtures and the whole conglomeration of things that goes into that kind of engineering process." Bricker then led the senators onto the Willow Run assembly line, where the deafening noise made them cringe in their suits. Bricker pointed to a specific machine that made a piece of an airplane wing. And if that airplane piece was altered?

"You affect this whole line of procedure," he screamed over the assembly-line roar. He went through all the steps that were needed to make the part and detailed how it all had to change. "That has all got to be designed and blueprinted and put in operation."

"Now you may not be familiar with all these things," Bricker continued, "but this is what happens every time we get a new bale of changes that have to do with this plane. Until you find out, gentlemen, what kind of plane you're going to build, and until you perfect the design, we can't guarantee to meet any schedule."

"Well," Truman spoke up, "I certainly can see how changes jimmy up your fellow's program."

At lunch in a conference room, the committee hurled questions at Ford engineers as Truman walked slowly around looking at pictures of airplanes on the walls. The senators were concerned about this expensive machine that made center wings. Why did this one center-wing machine cost taxpayers $250,000? They wanted to know about the hard dies that Ford was using, according to automobile manufacturing methods. Why did Ford use hard dies when the aviation firms used soft ones that were more flexible in the production process?

Truman himself didn't say a word. As one engineer present bitterly said: "Maybe we should have had a piano there or something. He could have played 'The Missouri Waltz.'"

Before the committee left, the senators posed for a ceremonial photo out on the airfield with a B-24 bomber towering over them, like a beast standing over its prey. Truman stood in the center holding his hat, and with the camera aimed, he finally allowed himself a smile. When the committee released its report, neither Edsel nor Sorensen could do the same.

Ford "had not produced at Willow Run a plane which was capable of use at the front," the Truman Committee found. One line in the report cut Sorensen's and Edsel's souls as if with a jagged knife. "The production line was set up similar to an automobile assembly line," it read. "This was probably a mistake."

22

Taking Flight

Spring 1943

Show me a hero and I'll write you a tragedy.

— F. Scott Fitzgerald

The spring of 1943 was Edsel Ford's last season on earth. He spent it under relentless duress. Chasing the bomber-an-hour goal, he summoned all his strength, hoping his last lungful could breathe life into Willow Run.

In March, he stood next to Colonel Thomas Drake on a stage in front of a crowd gathered outside the Rouge. At that moment, the R-2800 Double Wasp aircraft engines built at the Rouge were throttling airmen into battle all over the globe, in the B-26 Marauder medium bomber, the P-47 Thunderbolt fighter, the F6F Hellcat aircraft carrier fighter (which would destroy 5,163 enemy airplanes during the war, at a cost of 270 of their own), and the Curtiss C-46 Commando troop transporter (otherwise known as "the Whale"). On behalf of the Rouge workers, Edsel accepted the Army-Navy "E" Award for Excellence, a ceremonial nod from Washington. The Colonel passed Edsel a red-white-and-blue flag with a large white "E" stitched across it as a crowd applauded and whistled.

Edsel had always wanted to turn his family empire into a modern aviation powerhouse. Now this boyhood dream had come true, under the oddest of circumstances. Holding the Army-Navy Excellence flag, he began a bittersweet speech.

"The presentation of this flag does not indicate that we have reached the top of our stride," Edsel said. "The engine we worked on this morning will be carrying American airmen over some distant theater of war a few weeks from now. Let us make it a good engine for the safety of our airmen and let us produce it promptly that it may reach them in time and in ever increasing numbers."

On the stage, Edsel appeared exhausted, as if each word he muttered taxed him. Nearby his father stood watching him with concern.

At Willow Run, bombers were filling the two hangars at the airfield and circling the skies in ever-increasing numbers. Each of the problems that Edsel had detailed for the Truman Committee, he and Sorensen were now tackling one by one.

Edsel had the idea of subcontracting bomber parts to other plants to quicken production. The Rouge was now producing stabilizers, radio operator doors, and side gunner doors. Edsel's Lincoln plant was making engine cowlings and air ducts. The Gibson Refrigerator Company of Belding, Michigan, signed on to produce center-wing flaps. The Metal Molding Company of Detroit agreed to make bomb racks.

All through the winter, recruiters had swept through the rural South, signing on workers to stem Willow Run's labor shortage. By March 1, 1943, the bomber plant employed 6,491 from Kentucky, 1,971 from Tennessee, 714 from Texas, 450 from West Virginia, 397 from Arkansas, and 314 from Missouri. There were also men and women from Egypt, Iceland, New Zealand, Panama, Turkey, Chile, and Cuba. In his war factories, Edsel employed 4,390 blind or deaf laborers, 111 deaf-mutes, 3 armless men, and 10 legless men. Willow Run had, about that time, reached peak employment: 42,331 workers, a number equivalent to the population of a small city.

Workers in the bomber plant began noticing men and women watching them with stopwatches in hand. Edsel had created what he called the Time Study Department — an attempt to perfectly integrate man and machine on the assembly line, to bridge that gap that separated the imagineer's big-picture perspective from the worker with the rivet gun in his hand. The team of statisticians consisted of forty-one men and twenty-two women. If the factory was meant to be as finely integrated and tuned as a watch, their job was to make it run on time. They whittled the bomber job down to as many singular tasks as possible, then studied the length of time it took for each. They factored in "unavoidable delays" for each worker (thirty minutes every nine-hour shift for bathroom visits, for example, including the trip back and forth). Then they swarmed the bomber plant timing spray-painters and oilers and jig operators with their stopwatches.

The Time Study Department created a chart for each foreman. At the end of a shift, production figures could be measured against this chart. If the two did not match up, the foreman had to answer to Charlie Sorensen. In all, executives estimated that the Time Study Department was saving the company $100,000 with every ship delivered to the army.

By now, requests from the Air Corps for changes to the airplane had begun to fall off. The engineers at Willow Run could focus on building bombers, rather than altering their assembly line to accommodate changes to the bomber. The B-24 was no longer a moving target. Daily, Willow Run grew more precise, fluid, and intelligent, and faster in its every task.

In April, Edsel had a chart sent off to the White House, a page splattered with numbers, the most important of which showed production figures at the bomber plant. The chart looked like it was plotting an airplane in takeoff, building in altitude. Willow Run produced 75 planes in February 1943, 104 in March, and 150 in April. One of the President's secretaries, Marvin McIntyre, placed the production card on the Oval Office desk with a note that read, "You will probably understand this. I don't but I am going to have somebody explain it to me." (The President wrote back: "You don't have to understand it. FDR.")

And still Edsel was continuing to sign new defense contracts: amphibious vehicles, armored cars, jettison gas tanks, and squad tents. The Rouge assembly lines were spitting out not one but two different kinds of tanks (the M-4 and the M-10). From its lumber mill in Kingsford, north of Detroit, Ford Motor Company had begun to construct Waco CG-4A gliders — engineless aircraft that were towed up into the sky and then released, so they could fly quietly behind enemy lines. Painted army green, the wooden glider measured 83.6 feet by wingspan and 48 feet in length. It could carry fourteen soldiers plus a pilot, and it could also carry a Jeep and a Howitzer into battle. The glider was a novel contribution to American airpower. "Never before in history had any nation produced aviators whose duty it was to deliberately crash land," one army general later said of these gliders.

That spring, Edsel wrote William Knudsen in Washington. "Our war jobs are coming along fine," he noted, "and we will be making a lot of stuff by August. All told, our employment will total 220,000 people, against 120,000 [during peacetime] on automobiles." The numbers were astounding. The war had forced the company to build incredibly complex machinery that it had never built before—at a volume and speed considerably greater than it had ever achieved churning out automobiles. Since the war had started, Ford Motor Company had stopped making cars and had grown considerably.

In March 1943, the first part of Bomber City opened its doors. Called Willow Lodge, it was an entire neighborhood built in open fields, completed four months after groundbreaking. The first of thousands of men, women, and children arrived with their old cars and worn-out rationed tires, their suitcases, and their hopes for an easier life. Bomber City appeared as Roosevelt had originally imagined it: "a city of homes well planned and designed . . . a symbol of the America we are defending and the America we are rebuilding for the future."

That didn't mean it was an easy place to live.

Willow Lodge was a sprawling, campuslike community bordering Michigan Avenue, the main local road that traveled straight into the heart of Detroit twenty-seven miles away. The homes were one- or two-bedroom, dormitory-style apartments made of semipermanent materials, attached in fifteen long rows (some two-story, some one-story), with flat roofs and hastily constructed windows. Willow Village—the rest of Bomber City—would soon follow nearby, with homes for 2,500 families and a shopping center.

Bomber City was characterized by a clash of cultures, with blacks and whites, Northerners and Southerners, day-shift and night-shift laborers—all migrants—living in tight quarters. If America was a melting pot, this was its perfect microcosm. The quarter-inch-thick walls were far from soundproof. People got to know each other quickly, even if they never shared any interpersonal communication.

James Edson Stermer, the thirty-nine-year-old Detroit Institute of Technology professor who had come to work as a riveter at the bomber plant, moved into Willow Lodge's B Dormitory soon after it opened. He paid $5 per week for a single room at Willow Lodge, his lease signed with the US government. "I wander upstairs through over-heated halls to No. 160," he recalled of the day he moved in, "a clean, bare cubicle in brown beaverboard, approximately eight by ten [feet], equipped with an open clothes-nook without hangers, a four-drawer bureau, a wall mirror, one chair, one single bed, one wastebasket, and an outside view through the lone window of the bare 'campus.'"

With babies crying and night-shift workers coming and going, sleep came in fits and starts. "Practically every night I have been awakened two or three times by other roomers," Stermer remembered, "men coming in noisy-drunk, men shouting to their friends along the length of the corridor, alarm clocks going off in nearby rooms. If a man doesn't impair his hearing in the deafening clamor of the rivet guns on the job, he stands a good chance of wearing his nerves down trying to sleep under a barrage of hillbilly sociability in the Lodge between 2 a.m. and 4 a.m.!"

A haze hung above Bomber City, thickening in the cold months. The homes were heated with soft coal, which was dispensed one ton at a time in wooden bins along the streets. The temperature in the dorms was kept above 80 degrees.

For entertainment, which the government considered important for morale, Willow Lodge featured a bowling alley and a movie theater that showed films three nights a week. There were dances and communal picnic tables. There was also plenty of vice, for anyone looking for it. "Professional gamblers and fast women quickly moved in for a cleanup," a *Detroit News* reporter wrote of Willow Lodge. Once Federal Housing Commission officials got word of illicit activity, they sent the police in with instructions to clear out suspicious characters.

Each morning Stermer took the "Cattle Car"—a crowded Greyhound bus—to the bomber plant, and every evening he came home to Willow Lodge the same way. The bus came about every eight minutes, and the trip was one mile long. With seats for forty, the Cattle Car often fit more than double that number, the aisles filled with standing passengers. On each ride, Stermer saw the blank faces and bloodshot eyes of the tired, the sometimes sick, and the sometimes injured from their long hours amid the booming machinery. By one historian's estimate, compared to soldiers overseas, twenty times more workers died or were injured in war-related industries on the home front in 1942 and 1943.

They were a grim army of foot soldiers, fighting the Battle of Production. But at least now the men and women at Willow Run could show up for work and collect a check with regularity, with a pillow a reasonable distance away.

While far from luxury living, Bomber City, now that it had begun to open, finally started to solve the absentee problem that had plagued Edsel and Sorensen for months. In the executive offices of Ford Motor Company in the spring of 1943, Edsel began to see a shift in morale, even as he himself grew weaker and closer to death. Banner headlines told the stories of battles won overseas. The tide was turning, and the rising production figures at Willow Run seemed to mirror the overall war effort.

In April, Edsel permitted a rare one-on-one interview with a reporter, something he loathed doing. Agnes Meyer of the *Washington Post* met with him in his office. Pictures of his kids and of B-24s in flight adorned the walls. The reporter found Edsel "very old and very young, very sure of himself and very diffident, a man of brilliant mind who has preserved his integrity, elasticity and independence against heavy odds." As for the bomber plant? "In terms of engineering," Meyer wrote, "Willow Run is considered by those who know most about such things to be the supreme achievement of American Industry."

So, she wanted to know, what took so long for Willow Run to begin to realize its promise?

Edsel went through the whole program, reliving the last harrowing two years of his life. When the bomber-an-hour plan was first hatched in San Diego, he explained, "the automobile was still in general use. There was no restriction on gas and rubber. We therefore expected no housing problem, nor a transportation problem." The employment of women on the assembly lines required unexpected new responsibilities, he explained. Nearly one-third of the workers at Willow Run were now female.

The changes in the industry were all a part of a new America being born, Edsel said. Soon, he predicted, "there will be so many new developments in the mechanical field, television, airplanes, streamlined transportation and other things that will make new kinds of employment. The new era that lies before us is largely a question of planning, but the planning must come from people who have had the time and have given the thought to fitting the pieces together." With the important contributions of major industrialists, a postwar future was bright, explained the man who knew he would not live to see it. "We businessmen," Edsel said, "will have enough to do."

Forty-one thousand feet up over Willow Run, deep into the stratosphere, the airfield's mile-long runways appeared no larger than pencils that one could snap in the fingers. Charles Lindbergh sat strapped in the single-seat cockpit of a Republic P-47 Thunderbolt fighter-bomber — nicknamed "Jug" for juggernaut. Motoring through the ether at speed, he was about 12,000 feet higher than the summit of Mount Everest. Lindbergh was eight miles high.

Only a handful of pilots had ever flown at such altitudes. Under one wing, he could see the city of Detroit with its tight collection of buildings perched on the river, peaceful under a gauze of vapor cloud. Under the other wing was Toledo, Ohio, in the distance. Lindbergh set the trim tabs and adjusted the engine's turbocharger for the oxygen-deprived air, enabling the engine to breathe. Though he wore his oxygen mask, he panted for air. He engaged his radio, sucking in a gasp before each word:

"Willow ... Run ... tower ... from ... army ... six ... zero ... three ... eight ... over."

A reply came from the airfield control room, but Lindbergh couldn't make out the words. He was flying too high; the radio couldn't function.

Suddenly, he felt a jolt of dizziness — a sensation he had experienced before. He was about to faint from lack of oxygen, and he was alone in the cockpit with the engine roaring. His senses opened up, grasping for consciousness. Was something wrong with the oxygen mask? He knew from experience in an altitude chamber that he had about fifteen seconds to solve the problem, or he would likely lose consciousness and control of the airplane. If he descended rapidly, he could level off in air with more oxygen, at an altitude where he could breathe. So he shoved the yoke forward. The Thunderbolt plunged into a howling dive.

Thirty-five thousand feet.

Thirty-four thousand.

Thirty-three thousand.

Lindbergh's eyes struggled to read the dials on the instrument panel. Then everything went black. He lost his eyesight. He could still hear the roar of the engine, but he had gone blind. He shoved the yoke harder, fighting the machine for his life.

Thirty-three thousand feet.

Thirty-two thousand.

The instrument panel came back into focus, his eyesight returning. Instinctively, he pulled back on the stick and leveled off. He had made it.

When he landed the Thunderbolt, he stepped onto the concrete runway in his army-issue flight suit: drab green head to toe, heavy leather boots, helmet and goggles, parachute strapped to his back. His senses tingled with alertness. After a consultation with a mechanic, he learned that his oxygen gauge was slightly off. Though the gauge said he had more oxygen, he had run out. His life had nearly been extinguished by a quarter-inch error of a tiny instrument needle.

For Lindbergh, it was just another day on the job.

As he drove from the airfield to his office inside Willow Run, he struggled with philosophical questions. *Returning from the border of death always makes one more aware of life,* he thought to himself. And so he gazed on the bomber plant with new eyes. As a young man, Lindbergh had found in the science of aviation an epistemology, a science he believed would open the universe to humanity and bring nations together. This was what it had now become: a ruthless weapon.

"Now, it seemed a terrible giant's womb," he wrote of this moment, staring at Willow Run.

Growling, clanging, giving birth to robots which were killing people by the thousands each day as they destroyed the culture of Europe. Inside, crawling over jigs and wings like ants, were thousands of men and women, sacrificing sunlit hours, home and family, shop and farm, to serve this hellish monster. This was the temple of the god of science at which we moderns worshipped.... Here I watched a steel door lift and an airplane roll outside; while, in reality, the walls of a cathedral fell and children died.

With hundreds of bombers rolling out of Willow Run each month now, Lindbergh had found himself quite busy. The airfield would see over 7,000 Liberator takeoffs in 1943 alone. Each bomber required a two-and-a-half-hour shakedown flight and a pass on hundreds of checkoffs before it could be delivered to the army. Lindbergh spent hours each day in-flight and in the airfield hangars, mixing with other test pilots in the instrument laboratory, the engine shop, the parachute loft, and the exercise rooms.

At the request of the army, Lindbergh began a series of high-altitude flying experiments, motoring higher and higher into the stratosphere over Willow Run, using his own body as a test dummy. Army intelligence had received word that the Nazis were conducting their own altitude experiments. If a bomber could drop its payload from 40,000 feet up, it could do so at little risk of anti-aircraft gunfire. The Nazis could employ this kind of bombing as a terrorist tactic, dropping TNT indiscriminately on London or even New York. (Hitler had a deep desire to tear down Manhattan's world-famous skyline. After the war, the Allies would uncover a secret Nazi map of New York with German writing and a bull's-eye on Midtown.)

In Germany, Heinrich Himmler — head of the SS and co-architect of the "Final Solution," the holocaust that was at that time unfolding — had arranged to move a compression chamber to the Dachau concentration camp, where a research doctor named Rascher used 200 prisoners, mostly Jews, to conduct experiments. The prisoners were thrust into the chamber and exposed to high-altitude conditions. Nearly half died from lack of oxygen, perishing in a panic under the watchful eye of Dr. Rascher. The rest were executed afterward so that news of these experiments could be kept secret. Still, Allied intelligence got word of them. Churchill told his advisers that "the enemy will very likely start high-altitude bombing."

At Willow Run, Lindbergh conducted experiments in a new $125,000 altitude chamber built by Ford engineer Emil Zoerlein. The chamber was the most cutting-edge of its kind. It resembled a chunk of an airplane fuselage, big enough for fourteen men, with five circular windows cut into the side. The apparatus was so large that the chamber was built on one floor at Willow Run while the machinery that controlled it was installed on the floor directly below. A control panel stood next to the chamber so that the man running it could see inside.

Unlike other chambers, which could only simulate altitude (like the one at the Mayo Clinic in Minnesota, where Lindbergh also conducted tests), Willow Run's could affect altitude and temperature conditions, taking a man up to 60,000 feet and 70 degrees below zero. Freezing temperatures at such altitudes could damage equipment, and so such testing was deemed critical. The chamber was also built to test the ability of humans to endure high-altitude conditions and to handle emergencies that could arise in such situations.

Lindbergh made his maiden voyage in the altitude chamber in 1943. He wore a special thick leather suit, which made him sweat uncontrollably upon entry. An attending physician attached an oximeter to the lobes of the aviator's ears to observe the oxygen levels in his blood. The airlock door was closed, and Lindbergh gave the thumbs-up. A 500-horsepower gasoline car engine pumped up the pressure, and slowly Lindbergh ascended into a phantom stratosphere.

The aviator had flown 43,000 feet up in a P-47 Thunderbolt. "Forty-three thousand feet is obviously close to the maximum altitude where one can remain for long without a pressure mask," he wrote in his diary. And yet, soon after, he made a "flight" of 49,000 feet without a pressure mask in the altitude chamber in Willow Run. Only three men had ever flown higher in actual airplanes.

Lindbergh wondered: Just how high could a person go before vapor formed in the bloodstream, before he touched the ceiling of human endurance and consciousness? Could he fly higher than any man ever had, while keeping his feet on the ground inside Willow Run? He was, in his own words, "anxious to find out."

23

"The Arsenal of Democracy Is Making Good"

Winter to Summer 1943

> The criminal, corrupt Fascist regime in Italy is going to pieces.
> The pirate philosophy of the Fascists and Nazis cannot stand
> adversity.
>
> — FRANKLIN ROOSEVELT, *1943*

DURING HIS State of the Union Address in January 1943, the President stood at his podium engulfed by microphones. Behind him, Vice President Henry Wallace and House Speaker Sam Rayburn were as still as statues. Spread out around the House chamber, the nation's elected officials awaited the message, divided as usual in policy but all behind the President in his campaign to protect the nation and win the war.

Now ten years in office — longer than any other president — Roosevelt was a veteran of these speeches. This one — which would be translated into twenty-six languages — would be remembered for what the *Washington Post* called its "glorious goals." The United States would "bomb [the Japanese] constantly from the air," Roosevelt declared. As for the Nazis, "we are going to strike, and strike hard." In the end, however, the speech's main focus would be not just on the war abroad, but also on the Battle of Production at home.

"In 1942, we produced 56,000 combat vehicles, such as tanks and self-propelled artillery," the President said. "We produced 21,000 anti-tank guns, six times greater than our 1941 production. We produced ten and a quarter billion rounds of small arms ammunition, five times greater than our 1941 production and three times greater than our total production in the first World War. . . . Few Americans realize the amazing growth of our air strength."

Roosevelt concluded, "I think the Arsenal of Democracy is making good."

Since he had first delivered his "Arsenal of Democracy" speech on December 29, 1940, the President's message had never veered. In speech after speech, he had continued to define and redefine this term. The phrase had been uttered by others before, but now it was attributed to Roosevelt, who had come to define it in a new way. The arsenal concept's underlying goal was to inspire American men and women, whether they worked in a factory or on a farm or in a laboratory studying the fragility of a uranium-235 atom. Every worker of every shade made a difference. Every time an alarm went off and an American got out of bed to go to work, that made a difference.

Only now, early in 1943, did many Americans begin to fully grasp the arsenal concept's meaning and its genius. As historian Jorg Friedrich put it: "Military strength was no longer based on the military abilities and skills of officers and rank and file but on the capacity of industry to supply the front with more and better weapons. The war of the future would be decided not at the theater of war but far behind the lines, in the factories and dwellings of the workers."

Now, in the spring of 1943, Roosevelt spent hours sitting alone in the Oval Office with his mountain of memos and confidential war progress reports. It was in these top-secret reports, to a large degree, that he consumed the overall narrative of the war. It was in these reports that the President could see his arsenal coming into its own. The war progress reports brimmed with heroic stories of battles not just overseas but in office buildings and factories in America.

General Electric, the nation's largest electrical equipment outfit and its fourth-largest corporation, was on its way to producing $3.3 billion worth of war equipment, most notably 30,000-horsepower naval turbines.

Westinghouse Electric of Jersey City, New Jersey, was building bombsights, radar equipment, and other machinery worth nearly $1.5 billion.

The Kleenex Tissue Company was building .50 caliber machine gun mounts.

An orange-squeezer maker was producing bullet molds, a casket builder was producing airplane parts, and a pinball-machine maker was turning out deadly armor-piercing shells.

Dow Chemical had invented a plastic sheeting substance with which to wrap and seal munitions headed for overseas, coating tanks, airplanes, and machine guns to protect them from moisture and salt from the sea. This new substance would be called Saran Wrap.

For some, the defining production story of the war would be that of Henry Kaiser, the upstate New York–born industrialist whose company had played a major role in building the Hoover Dam and was now churning out Liberty ships from his shipyards with miraculous speed.

Even the US pharmaceutical industry was playing a critical role — pumping out rivers of a new wonder drug called penicillin.

Economists had long postulated what a full-on war economy could do for the Great Depression. The year before the war began, unemployment in the United States hit 17.2 percent. In the spring of 1943, the rate fell to 4.7 percent. "The war has finally accomplished most of what the New Deal set out to do," *Washington Post* columnist Raymond Clapper wrote in 1943. (Clapper would be killed a year after penning these words, while reporting on the war in Europe.) "The war has given every workman a job at high wages, and removed him from dependence on charity."

Perhaps the best news of all on the home front: Detroit was finally showing its muscle. In 1943 Secretary of War Henry Stimson put a military plane at William Knudsen's disposal to tour the nation for a full report on war production. The former General Motors president was now a lieutenant general in the US Army — the first and only civilian to this day to receive such a commission. He visited 1,200 factories, flying a quarter of a million miles. When he delivered his report to Stimson, it told a story in which Detroit's auto industry played the starring role in the Battle of Production.

The state of Michigan received 10 percent of the billions of dollars' worth of war production contracts, more than any state except New York, which had more than double the population of Michigan. And the great majority of those contracts in Michigan were being executed in one city, Detroit, and its suburbs.

Chrysler's Detroit Tank Arsenal — a factory that didn't exist three years earlier — had now succeeded in building roughly as many tanks as all the factories in Nazi Germany combined. On the first floor of an abandoned department store at 1525 Woodward Avenue in Detroit, the motor company had set up a makeshift laboratory for its "X-100" program. With the FBI working as security, Chrysler engineers were developing diffusers for a government project so secret that none of those engineers had any idea what the diffusers were for. Only after the war would they find out: they were helping to build the atomic bomb.

All ninety-four of General Motors' plants stateside were throbbing with efficiency. GM was building Allison aircraft engines and Avenger and Wildcat fighter planes. American soldiers were motoring into battle in GM tank destroyers, amphibious "DUCK" trucks, and two-and-a-half-ton troop transporters, and they were firing GM-built submachine guns, bullets, and mortar shells at the enemy.

The city of Detroit had grown so rapidly in the past two years that its population was threatening to surpass Philadelphia's to make it the third-largest city in America. General Motors of Detroit had become the number one military contractor in the United States, ahead of the aviation powerhouse Curtiss-Wright in second place and Ford Motor Company in third. According to a public poll in 1943, however, Americans believed that no single Detroit industrialist was contributing more to the war effort than Henry Ford.

In July 1943, Roosevelt made a short getaway to the property he liked to call Shangri-La, the woody presidential retreat seventy miles northwest of the White House, now known as Camp David. He was preparing a talk with his speechwriters. The day before the speech, he held his regular press conference. Winged by reporters, he smiled with his cigarette holder dangling from his mouth. There had been some rioting recently in the United States, and the papers had criticized the President for his handling of the home front. A reporter asked what his upcoming speech was going to be about.

"It's going to be about the war," Roosevelt said straight-faced.

"Abroad or at home, sir?"

"You know," Roosevelt said, a little miffed, "I hoped you would ask that question just that way. There are too many people in this country . . . who are not mature enough to realize that you can't take a piece of paper and draw a line down the middle of it and put the war abroad on one side and put the home front on the other, because after all it all ties in together.

"When we send an expedition to Sicily," Roosevelt continued, speaking of Operation Husky, the Allied invasion of Sicily that began July 9, "where does it begin? Well it begins at two places practically. It begins on the farms of this country, and in the mines of this country. And then the next step in getting that army into Sicily is the processing of the food, and the processing of the raw material into steel, then the munitions plants that turn the steel into tanks and planes. . . . Then it's put on ships that are made in this country."

The invasion of Sicily, the President pointed out, was a perfect example of his arsenal concept. It required 14,000 Jeeps and trucks, 600 tanks, and any number of airplanes — equipment that was built on assembly lines by civilians, who were pouring out more trucks and tanks and airplanes with each passing day. The plan was working. As the President famously said in 1943: "Yes, the Nazis and Fascists have asked for it. And they are going to get it."

Edsel Ford was at his desk one day when he received a shocking letter. The missive was addressed to Edsel's secretary Lepine, and it was signed by a lower-level Ford executive.

"Last night at five o'clock I took a call from a person who refused to give his name," the letter read, "who said that defense material valued at $8,000 to $12,000 was being taken out of the Rouge Plant in trucks every day, the material being sold on the outside by a ring of men. He accused Mr. Harry Bennett as leader."

Edsel had long suspected that Bennett's tentacles were woven deep into the underworld, and that this underworld thrived right under the Ford family's noses, here in Dearborn. For months there'd been rumors of thefts in the plants. Others had accused Bennett before—but they learned their lesson quickly. "If anybody made a complaint about any stealing around the plant," said Ford production engineer Mead Bricker, "usually Bennett had them beaten up."

Was Bennett running an inside job? For a man who didn't get paid piles of money, he lived a high life, with properties and boats and horses. "I don't have any idea how much he pilfered," Edsel's son Henry II later said of Bennett, "but I'm positive—although I don't have any proof—that he could not have lived the way he did on the salary he had. . . . He stole the place blind either through the dealers or some other fashion. I don't know how the hell he did it, but he did it."

Edsel was determined to solve this case. If he could prove Bennett's guilt, he could get rid of him once and for all. Edsel had an ace up his sleeve—his dear friend in Washington, J. Edgar Hoover, head of the FBI. The pair dined together in the nation's capital regularly. Edsel gave Hoover a call. Soon the FBI's Detroit bureau chief, John Bugas, arrived in Dearborn. The thirty-five-year-old lawyer and G-man from tiny Wamsutter, Wyoming, had a lanky basketball player's body, a curiously canine face, and the cowboy mentality he had honed during his years working as a national park ranger.

Bugas spent the better part of a Saturday with Edsel, talking over the security of Ford's war plants and the accusations of theft on company and government property. They toured Willow Run and the Rouge, examining locations where trucks could move government property out the doors under the cover of night. Neither Bugas nor Edsel knew at the time of their first meeting that it would be one of the most important of both of their lives.

It turned out that Bugas knew Harry Bennett well. Through the late 1930s and into the 1940s, Bennett was probably the FBI's most valuable informant in the Detroit area. "On numerous occasions when serious crimes occurred in Detroit and elsewhere in the state," Bugas wrote in an FBI report dated March 30, 1939, "[Bennett] has personally entered activities of the investigation and been of considerable assistance." Bugas called Bennett "a very valuable friend of this office."

Still, Bennett's service to the Bureau did not warrant immunity.

212 · THE ARSENAL OF DEMOCRACY

He may have been above the law within Henry Ford's empire. But he was not above the law in the eyes of J. Edgar Hoover.

John Bugas first joined the nation's most elite police force in 1935, the year its name changed from the Bureau of Investigation (BOI) to the Federal Bureau of Investigation (FBI). He was a fearless, inventive investigator, adept at the art of fisticuffs while wearing a suit. As a special agent in Alaska and Alabama, Bugas rose quickly through the ranks. "Guns, tough situations and ornery men were . . . second nature to him," as his daughter would later say. Hoover assigned Bugas to head up the Detroit bureau in 1938, more than doubling his pay to $6,500 a year.

The Motor City was no stroll in the park. It was a tangled nexus of opposing forces: labor versus management, black versus white, rich versus poor. During Prohibition, given its close proximity to Canada, it became the home of a thriving underground economy that continued to bubble up after the "Noble Experiment" ended and the bars restocked their liquor shelves. As the *Detroit News* stated in 1939: "In no city was there such an unholy alliance among hired gunmen, high-level executives, government officials, and police agents as openly existed in Detroit."

Since the start of the war, Detroit had morphed from a hard city into what *Time* magazine called "the biggest wartime boomtown of all," with a surging population full of out-of-towners. Bugas was the man in charge of policing its underworld.

After Pearl Harbor, frightened citizens turned up at his offices at all hours to report "suspicious Japs" and suspected Nazi spies. The phones rang off the hook. Within two days after the United States entered the war, Bugas had taken into custodial detention forty "dangerous aliens"— thirty-eight Germans and two Italians, including an economics professor at the University of Detroit. Sleepless and overworked, Bugas drank paranoia from his coffee cup. He'd spent enough time snooping around certain German restaurants downtown to see men furtively handing each other Nazi propaganda, whispering to each other with German accents.

There were Nazis in America, right in Detroit. The question was: how dangerous were they?

Even before the United States entered the war, Bugas had already made several high-profile busts of spies and potential foreign terrorists. In 1940 he uncovered a plot to blow up the Dodge factory downtown, taking into evidence a tin containing forty dynamite caps and a mysterious note: "This is all I can get. I'll have the other soon by the time you are ready for it. Watch Mike. Don't let him know too much. I must see you on the weekend. Things is shakey."

In another foiled plot, the G-man used an apartment with one-way mirrors to gather information on an attractive German countess and Nazi spy named Grace Buchanan-Dineen. It was "a bizarre plot," in his words. "It will sound like a storybook reading, it is so fantastic." She led him to five other Nazi operatives working in the Detroit area, feeding facts on American aviation production back to the German government.

These agents were not working alone. The Nazis' thirst for knowledge about America's bomber program was insatiable. Bugas's Detroit detective work had uncovered spying equipment as well as Nazi flags, rifles, and handguns. With his help, the FBI had cracked the largest espionage case in US history days before Pearl Harbor. A double agent named William Sebold brought down the Duquesne Spy Ring; thirty-three suspected Nazi spies were taken into custody, one of them in Detroit.

Bugas was also surveiling certain auto executives, under suspicion for Nazi sympathies. Among them: Ernest Liebold, Henry Ford's longtime secretary, who had power of attorney over Henry's bank accounts. Liebold had close ties to one of the Nazi spies busted in the Duquesne Spy Ring; Bugas had caught them communicating on various occasions in 1940 and 1941, recording the encounters on 16-millimeter film. According to informants, Liebold had proclaimed the night the Nazis attacked Poland that Germany would "blow the hell out of London in three weeks and teach the damn Jew bankers a lesson." Informants also told the FBI that Liebold called President Roosevelt "a Jew" and that the Ford secretary's wife had once remarked, "When Hitler comes here you will be glad you knew us." Liebold had even allegedly bragged that he had access to the blueprints of the Willow Run bomber plant.

Bugas's investigation ultimately found Liebold to be harmless. It is highly likely that Harry Bennett had something to do with these findings.

Like everyone who spent time with Edsel Ford, Bugas found him eminently respectable. After their first meeting, Bugas sent in his operatives to question various members of Bennett's Service Department. Did they know anything about these reported thefts? What was the status of Ford security? Bennett was reputed to know everything that went on within the Ford empire. But he claimed no knowledge of thievery.

Bennett grew tired of the FBI's questions. In an office, he had it out with Edsel. He was "sick and tired of having my men called in by Bugas."

"We've got to do something," Edsel responded. The allegations claimed that crooks were walking off with thousands of dollars' worth of government property every day. "They're carrying the goddamn plant away!"

Bugas and J. Edgar Hoover together produced a dense twelve-page report for Edsel. It focused on the protection of war plants against sabotage (background checks on all employees and security around specific areas of danger, such as large tanks of gasoline or chlorine gas "of sufficient volume to cause considerable danger in the event it should be suddenly released"). The report also focused on protecting the factories from theft.

Even after this report was filed, however, Bugas continued to show his face around the Rouge and Willow Run. Edsel had put the G-man and Bennett on a crash course.

24

Death in Dearborn

Spring to Summer 1943

I do miss him so terribly that at times it seems impossible to go on, and yet I feel so very close to him that that gives me comfort. I brought down so many pictures so that everywhere I look I can see him.

— MRS. EDSEL FORD, *August 1943*

EDSEL WAS IN HIS office in early April 1943 when the company's head of purchasing, A. M. Wibel, came to see him. Harry Bennett had made deals with suppliers for some materials, Wibel said, and these suppliers seemed a little dubious. As head of purchasing, and a longtime respected Ford executive, Wibel had to deal with the Washington accountants. The war plants were government property. Anything fishy and the accountants would invade the place. Now Wibel came to Edsel, raising a red flag.

"There were people that we were asked to put on the payroll for no apparent reason except to pay a debt of some kind," Wibel said. "They were people that had to be paid for something they never did."

Fed up, and with nothing to lose, Edsel went looking for Harry Bennett, unleashing his fury. Bennett was stunned. He went to Henry Ford — who by now, nearing eighty years old and suffering significant signs of dementia, was an easy target for a master manipulator.

"You know Edsel is sick," Bennett said, "and here's Wibel, making him upset! You make up your mind whether you are going to lose Edsel or get rid of Wibel."

Soon Wibel was told that his days at Ford — over thirty years — were over. He was sent home for good. Since Edsel was nineteen years old, he had known A. M. Wibel. "Wibel was one of the Ford greats," Sorensen later said. "From then on," he remembered sadly, "events moved with the inevitability of a Greek tragedy."

On April 15, 1943, Edsel arrived at work late and in pain. "Looks like a sick man to me," Sorensen wrote in his journal. "I am worried about him." That night, at home, Sorensen's phone rang. It was Henry Ford. He told Sorensen to meet with Edsel and make him "change his attitude on everything." Henry went on a rant — about Edsel's Grosse Pointe friends like Ernie Kanzler (whom Edsel's kids called "Uncle Kanzler") and their society cocktail parties, and about Harry Bennett. Sorensen grabbed a pencil and took notes, cataloging Henry's complaints about Edsel:

Discord over handling labor unions.
Bennett in full accord with Henry Ford. Henry Ford will support
     Bennett against every obstacle.
Change relations with Bennett.
Kanzler relationship — wants it broken up.
Regain health by cooperating with Henry Ford.

The father-and-son relationship had come to an impasse. The next morning, Sorensen went to Edsel's corner office and showed him his notes. Edsel fell to pieces.

"I feel I can be helpful," Sorensen said, "but if you wish, I will go no further. It's evident where Mr. Ford is getting these ideas. But to me that is not so distressing as would be a break between you and your father."

In tears, Edsel sat slumped on a couch. "The best thing for me to do is resign," he said. "My health won't permit me to go on. Charlie, I want you to know I appreciate very much what you are trying to do. It is a kindly thing to do and I respect your help."

"If you go," Sorensen said, "I go too."

For the next two hours, they discussed their obligations. The President needed them. Their country needed them. Willow Run was almost in full production. The bomber-an-hour goal had yet to be achieved, but it was in their sights. Sorensen asked Edsel to do one thing: it was time for Henry Ford II to leave the military and join his father at Willow Run and the Rouge. Edsel needed his oldest son now. Perhaps it was clear to Sorensen in that moment: for Edsel, there was no tomorrow. Henry II was going to have to take on his father's battles, and the sooner he got started the better.

The next day Sorensen told Edsel and Henry Ford that he had to get away. He couldn't take the pressure anymore. He took a brief trip to his vacation home in Miami. The day after he left, Edsel came to work and took a long, slow walk alone through Willow Run. He let the pounding machinery assault his ears and breathed in the myriad of smells — oil, metal dust, antiseptic floor cleaner, paint from the spray guns. He could see the bombers lined along the assembly line, one after another. His two-hundredth Liberator was on that day nearing the end of the assembly line. On the airfield, the bombers taxied for takeoff, test pilots feathering engines and motoring into the ether.

When he got tired, Edsel left Willow Run and returned home, his driver charioting him through the estate's security gates onto the sprawling property. His wife was waiting for him there. Edsel never left Gaukler Pointe again.

In a makeshift infirmary in his mansion, Edsel lay on his deathbed. His doctors took readings on a thermometer and saw the mercury rising. In addition to his stomach pain — which the physicians believed to be incurable cancer — Edsel was suffering from undulant fever. He had apparently picked up the illness from drinking milk from his father's farm. When he felt strong enough, he took short doctor-escorted walks along the lakefront in his backyard, so he could see the sunshine and hear the sound of the water lapping against the stones on the shoreline.

"He didn't complain and he wasn't morose," one of his doctors later remembered. "He knew that the end was near and that he couldn't do anything about it."

Edsel's best friend Kanzler called often to cheer him up. But Kanzler talked too much, exhausting Edsel. "Kanzler doesn't know what a telephone is for," Edsel said. His soft-spoken wife was a fixture, but other than Eleanor, Edsel was alone much of the time. All his life, his wealth and his position had isolated him, even in the end.

Henry had no idea how sick Edsel was. When he visited Gaukler Pointe and saw his son, he still believed that Edsel could be saved. He wanted to know when Edsel would be back at work. On May 18, in a meeting with the family physician, Dr. McClure, Harry Bennett, and Charlie Sorensen, the doctor informed Henry that Edsel was not coming back to work.

At first, Henry thought rationally. The company's chief lawyer, I. A. Capizzi, appeared to discuss the handling of Edsel's estate. But soon after, Henry unleashed his rage. He insisted to his doctors that they restore Edsel's health. "I expect you to keep my family well," Henry barked at Dr. McClure. "That's what you and the others are there for."

The doctor took the criticism calmly. Henry was old and ill. "We must expect Henry Ford to do unusual things," Dr. McClure told Sorensen. "He should not be around the plant or having anything to do with the business."

Facing eternity, Edsel had one last chance to set some plans in motion, one last shot to influence the future. Not long before his final illness, he contacted the FBI's John Bugas and pleaded with him to continue the Bureau's investigation of thefts at Ford properties.

Could Bugas bring down Harry Bennett?

Second, Edsel spoke to his best friend Ernie Kanzler about getting Henry II out of the military and back to Dearborn. Kanzler had high-level contacts throughout Washington. Surely he could convince the government that Henry II's presence in Dearborn was critical. Without Henry II to watch after Edsel's interests, there was no telling what would happen. It was time for Edsel's eldest son to return home to fight for his birthright.

In late May, three of Edsel's children — Henry II, Benson, and Josephine — returned home to be by his side. The youngest, William, was graduating from Hotchkiss, an East Coast boarding school. Edsel didn't want William to miss the graduation ceremony. Luckily, the date was moved up because so many students were enlisting in the military. William Clay Ford (who would go on to be a longtime owner of the NFL's Detroit Lions before his death in 2014) made it home to see his father just in time. "I didn't even know how bad it was until about three days before the graduation when I got a letter from him saying how sorry he was he wouldn't be there," William later remembered. "I was disappointed. I was not only getting a diploma but a trophy for being the school tennis champion and I wanted him there."

By Edsel's deathbed, William showed his father his trophy. "I think he willed himself alive until the day I got home," he said. "He was very coherent and we had a fine conversation."

Edsel's life was a plot that ended before its climactic moment. He knew that his eldest son, Henry II, sitting then by his side, would be the one to see this plot through to the end. Edsel told young Henry to go see Bob Gregorie in Ford's Design Department. He would find in Bob Gregorie an ally, a man Edsel trusted, to help him get started.

There was nothing left to do but rally around Edsel and await his last breath. It came at 1:10 AM on May 26, 1943. He was forty-nine years old.

The next morning workers arrived at Willow Run and the Rouge to find flags at half-mast. Ford design chief Bob Gregorie, one of Edsel's closest confidants, remembered that morning: "As we drove through the gate — we were four in a car, sharing rides in those war days — we saw the flag at half-staff. We knew it was Edsel. We had lost our man. We all started crying." Sorensen arrived at his office at 9:15 AM, and Henry Ford called an hour later. Sorensen found the old man "very well composed." As for himself, "I cracked up," Sorensen recalled.

Condolence letters streamed in from all corners of the globe — England, Egypt, Australia, Finland, South America. The President penned his note to Mrs. Edsel Ford the day Edsel passed. "My dear Mrs. Ford," Roosevelt wrote, "in the passing of your devoted husband in the full tide of his career, a powerful force has been lost to the war effort. He had devoted his superb abilities wholeheartedly to the defeat of the Axis powers and his passing in this critical time in our history is a grievous loss to his country's effort and to the cause of the United Nations. My heart goes out to you and to all of the family in deepest sympathy." The President wired another condolence directly to Henry, expressing his "heartfelt sympathy in which Mrs. Roosevelt joins."

Edsel's family arranged for his coffin to lie in state in a funeral home in Detroit so that anyone who wished could pay their respects. They were shocked when they saw the lines form outside. Over a thousand people showed up to say good-bye to Edsel, who had given his life to the city and its defining industry. Laborers, foremen, engineers, executives, politicians. Men arrived in dirty work clothes from assembly-line shifts to wait on line, while next to them stood other Detroiters in fine-tailored suits who had come by chauffeur-driven limousine. The United Auto Workers Local 600 sent a slew of gardenias. Even the union leaders adored Edsel.

The day of his funeral, flags all over Detroit hung at half-mast. At Ford plants in Allied nations all over the world, during Edsel's funeral service, the machines stopped and the lights went out for five minutes. The clanging presses and jigs of Willow Run and the Rouge fell silent. Workers were left in the dark to stare at their toes.

"When the plant shut down for Edsel's observance," remembered one Ford worker, "the motors of the machine tools stopped, the pounding of the massive metal presses quit, and the piercing rhythm ceased. The silence was deafening. As all of us stood there, an Irish tenor began singing the Lord's Prayer, his tender voice echoing throughout the plant. We all broke down. It was terribly moving."

At the service at Christ Church in Grosse Pointe, Edsel's best friend Kanzler fell to pieces and had to be helped from the room. Bennett did not come to the funeral, knowing he would not be wanted there. The church pews filled to capacity with near and distant family members and the auto industry's most famed engineers, men like Lieutenant General William Knudsen, Chrysler's K. T. Keller, and General Motors' Charles Wilson. Henry Ford sat stonelike in a pew with his wife Clara. Nearby, Sorensen held his head low. "That last year he lived was strenuous far beyond his endurance," Sorensen said of Edsel. "He was responsible for the good name the Company had established all over the world."

Sorensen could recall a day two years earlier when Henry mysteriously slipped him a card with a prose poem he had written. The poem was about fathers and sons. It struck Sorensen so deeply that he saved it. And it struck him, in that moment at Edsel's funeral, how much father and son adored each other, and how painful to both their interpersonal struggles became. The poem was called "What Is a Boy?"

What Is a Boy? He is a person who is going to carry on what you have started. He is to sit where you are sitting and attend when you are gone to those things that you think are so important. . . . He will assume control of your cities, states, and nation. All your work is going to be judged and praised, or condemned, by him. Your reputation and your future are in his hands. All your work is for him, and the fate of the nation and of humanity is in his hands.

Sitting next to his mother in a church pew, Henry Ford II's piercing blue eyes clouded with grief and worry. In his navy uniform, now twenty-five years old, he appeared bewildered. One person present said he looked "totally at sea." His father was gone. His mother was so distraught that a suicide attempt was not out of the realm of possibility. (In fact, she would talk often about it in the days to come.) All his life, Henry II had traveled a road that led to his father's corner office, where he expected to assume Edsel's responsibilities as president of Ford Motor Company. And now? He appeared lost.

Edsel was buried at the Woodlawn Cemetery in Detroit, the gray marble edifice etched with a simple marking: EDSEL BRYANT FORD, 1893–1943. His wife, who never married again, would join him there thirty-three years later. The remains of one of Detroit's most misunderstood and tragic figures rests at Woodlawn to this day.

In Washington, meanwhile, Edsel's name began to come up in secret conversations, for reasons outside his death. On the very day Edsel died, at 5:07 PM, a Secret Service agent arrived at the White House bearing a memo that read "Strictly Confidential" and "For Attention: Miss Tully," President Roosevelt's secretary. Grace Tully placed the envelope on Roosevelt's desk. Inside was a letter from the Treasury secretary, Henry Morgenthau. It regarded the investigation into the new Ford-Afrique company, and the correspondence between Edsel Ford and the head of his French division, Maurice Dollfus, that

a Treasury agent had confiscated from Edsel's office five months earlier.

"My dear Mr. President," Morgenthau's note read, "I am sending you herewith a one page memorandum and a brief summary of
amazing and shocking correspondence between Edsel Ford and Mr.
Dollfus, Managing Director of the Ford interests in France. As late as
July 17, 1942, after the French company had been bombed on June 6,
1942, Mr. Edsel Ford wrote as follows to Mr. Dollfus: 'I have shown
your letter to my father and Mr. Sorensen and they both join me in
sending best wishes for you and your staff, and hope that you will
continue to carry on with the good work that you are doing.'" The
Treasury report explained how Dollfus was protecting Ford property
in France by cooperating with the Nazis, delivering Ford trucks to
Hitler's Wehrmacht. The entire investigation seemed to hinge on this
one statement from Edsel: "the good work that you are doing."

Was Edsel applauding Dollfus for profiting by cooperating with
the Nazis? Or was he thanking Dollfus for his efforts to protect the
Ford empire's assets inside Nazi Germany—for his efforts to simply survive as a company executive and a human being? Either way,
French Ford was thriving, thanks to Nazi investment. "There would
seem to be at least a tacit acceptance by Mr. Edsel Ford" of some cul-
pability for the "receipt of favors from the German Reich," the lead
investigator J. John Lawler wrote in his report.

The Treasury Department's investigation remained open.

"Probably the loss of no other corporation head in the United States,"
noted the *Wall Street Journal*, "would have the same import and create as many problems as does the passing of Edsel Ford."

Edsel's death left the empire adrift. For almost exactly half of his
life—twenty-four years—he had served as president of Ford Motor Company. Because of the death tax on Edsel's 42 percent share
of the company, the family had to mobilize its lawyers and accountants. And who would run Ford now? Who could adequately assume
control of the nation's third-largest defense contractor leading up to
World War II's climactic battles?

A believer in reincarnation, Henry said that he and Edsel would
soon be together again, working hard, communicating through ma-

chines, as they always had. "Well, Harry," Henry said to Bennett, "you know my belief—Edsel isn't dead." Henry would talk about reincarnation, then drop it. "Now, we aren't going to talk about it anymore." Then he would bring up Edsel again, unable to stop, as if uttering those two syllables could somehow ease his pain.

"I just can't get over it," Henry said. "I've got a lump right here in my throat. Clara sits down and cries and gets over it, feels a little better. I just cannot do it. I have a lump here and there's nothing I can do about it."

"Harry," Henry said at one point, "do you honestly think I was ever cruel to Edsel?"

"Well," Bennett answered, "if that had been me you'd treated that way, it wouldn't have been cruelty."

"Why don't you give me an honest answer?"

"Well, cruel, no; but unfair, yes. If it had been me, I'd have got mad."

"That's what I wanted him to do. Get mad."

One night soon after Edsel's death, the telephone rang in Charlie Sorensen's home. When he picked up, he heard Henry Ford's voice on the line. Sorensen nearly dropped the phone when Henry delivered his news: Henry himself intended to assume the responsibilities of president of Ford Motor Company.

By his own admission, Henry was completely out of it. "I never know where I'm going in the morning," he told one friend around this time. "I just get up and go out in the car and just drive around someplace. . . . I wouldn't know where I was going next but I would just drive along until I got an idea that I should go to some other office or drop in and see somebody else."

At times, Henry had asked to see certain Ford executives who hadn't been working at the company for years. At other times, he would appear childlike, somehow reverting back to the simple Henry who had existed before any cars had ever hurtled down Detroit's Woodward Avenue. Now he was intent on leading one of the largest corporations in the world.

Impossible, Sorensen thought to himself.

Six days after Edsel's death, Ford Motor Company's board of directors met in a Dearborn office. Mrs. Edsel Ford attended in her late husband's place. With Harry Bennett and Sorensen standing by, Henry announced that he would once again become president of Ford Motor Company, a position he had not held since 1919. Edsel's wife Eleanor was furious. It was tasteless to hold such a meeting so soon after Edsel's death, she said.

"You, Mr. Ford," she is alleged to have said. "You're the one who killed your son!"

"Most of us," said Sorensen, "were stunned."

On the way out of the conference room, Sorensen pulled Henry aside. "You've got a job now," he said bitterly. "Now *you* run it!"

Henry said, "Charlie, everything is going to be the same with you and me, just as it always has been."

"You've taken a job," Sorensen said. "I know you don't realize what that means, but this time you've got to. Edsel did. I can work with anyone who understands his responsibilities. But you don't." Sorensen pleaded to bring in Edsel's kids to run the company. They needed Henry II desperately. "As things stand now," Sorensen said, "we're slipping. These boys will be some foundation for the future. Better give some thought to that."

Not long after Edsel's funeral, Ernie Kanzler ventured to Washington, as Edsel had asked him to do before his death. When military officials heard Kanzler's plea — to release Henry II from the military — they saw the wisdom in it. Roosevelt was expressing deep concern about Ford Motor Company. How could Henry, at his age, effectively run a company that vast? With a mission so vital to national security?

Roosevelt discussed plans of placing the company under the stewardship of Studebaker executives. In the end, Secretary of the Navy Frank Knox decided to release Henry Ford II from the military so that he could go back to Dearborn and take control — not realizing in Washington just what that would entail.

Within a few short days, at the Great Lakes Naval Station outside Chicago, Henry II received a letter from Secretary Knox himself, regarding his discharge from the service. "My Dear Mr. Ford," it read, "the services you will render as a private individual will surpass any work you could possibly do in your present situation. I wish you all kinds of good luck. Yours sincerely. . . ."

Young Henry was going home. He had Secretary Knox's letter

framed. It would hang on the wall in his private quarters for the rest of his life.

Henry II packed his bags, gathered his wife and two young children (his third, Edsel II, had not yet been born), and boarded a train headed east to Detroit. The job ahead of him seemed impossible: to wrestle this industrial giant out of the claws of Henry and Bennett, in the name of his father. On the train, Henry II sat in a daze with his family around him, wearing not a military uniform but his civilian clothes. As the train plunged eastward, he ran into an old friend of Edsel's. They talked about the sad news of Edsel's death, and young Henry suddenly burst into tears.

"He was a saint, just a saint!" Henry II shouted. "He didn't have to die. They killed him!"

PART V

———

D-DAY AND THE
BATTLE OF DEARBORN

The whole Ploesti episode began on a high note as far as I was concerned. After six months of combat operations in very cold and hostile winter skies over Europe, we were shifted, without explanation, to low-level formation practice over the green fields of England. We were told that for the time being, at least, there would be no combat — and it was springtime. There were new crews and new B-24s to replace those that had been lost, and losses had been severe for our group. We didn't understand then that this relatively pleasant interval was preparation for an exceptional mission.

— COLONEL WILLIAM R. CAMERON, *Pilot, Operation Tidal Wave*

25

Operation Tidal Wave

August 1, 1943

We flew through sheets of flame, and airplanes were everywhere, some of them on fire and others exploding. It's indescribable to anyone who wasn't there.

— COLONEL LEON JOHNSON, *Commander of the 44th Bomb Group*

THE DAY BEGAN AT 2:00 AM at the American airbase in Benghazi,
Libya. Bomber crews were awoken from their tents by alarms and
shouting voices. "Get up! Get up, you guys! Roll out of those sacks.
This is the day!" They were fed a big breakfast of eggs and coffee,
though many were too nervous to eat. Before sunrise, the crews were
riding Jeeps through the desert to their bombers to go through their
preflight checkouts.

There were 1,763 of them, army airmen from every state of the
American union. All were volunteers, and a large number were under
twenty years old, having come of age during the Great Depression.
Spread out over five airfields across four miles, a force of 178 B-24
Liberators — commanded by Brigadier General Uzal Ent — stood on
their tricycle landing gears, fueled up and ready to fly. It got so hot in
those planes in the desert, even at sunrise, the airmen joked that they
could bake bread in the cockpits. Minutes before 6:00 AM, the first

Liberator sparked an engine. Soon the desert was alive with roaring thunder, 712 engines spewing acrid smoke, blowing up clouds of desert sand that hadn't seen a raindrop in months.

Operation Tidal Wave — first conceived among the Allied military brass at the Casablanca Conference — targeted Ploesti, Romania, home of Hitler's greatest wellspring of oil. Ploesti was an oil boomtown north of Bucharest in the Transylvanian Alps. Nine vital refineries ringed the city, huge tanks full of highly explosive liquid, along with their pipes, stacks, generators, and machinery of all kinds. To ensure maximum target precision and avoid enemy radar, Tidal Wave was planned with an unprecedented low-altitude approach. The bombers would make their attack runs at treetop level at nearly 250 miles per hour.

Each Liberator was loaded to 64,000 pounds, greater than the proscribed takeoff weights, with extra fuel tanks built into the bomb bays to make the 2,400-mile, thirteen-hour round trip. They carried aboard "more killing power than two Gettysburgs," as one Air Corps journalist put it — 1.25 million rounds of shells, 622,000 pounds of bombs, plus boxes upon boxes of smaller flammable-jelly-encased incendiaries that the airmen would throw out the windows.

The first plane to take off was the *Wingo-Wango*, piloted by one Brian Woolley Flavelle of Augusta, Georgia. Others followed in two-minute intervals. The crews aboard could communicate with one another by intercom, but to avoid enemy radio detection they had orders for strict radio silence. Without communication, Tidal Wave would require perfect execution of the mission plans.

Bomber pilot John R. "Killer" Kane remembered sitting in the cockpit of the *Hail Columbia* with engines throbbing that morning, staring down an open runway that led to hell. "I looked around in the peculiar reddish glare and saw billowing clouds of dust swirling into the sky to color the sun a bloody red," he later wrote in his diary. "At 0710 sharp, we began our roll down the runway, on our way to Ploesti."

For weeks, these men had lived in the Libyan desert training for Tidal Wave — not just the airmen, but an army of mechanics, engineers, mess tent operators, and commanders. It was hard living in the rat-infested desert airbase. The daylight heat sometimes hit 125 degrees.

They had little drinking water, and none for bathing or washing their clothes. The only way to escape the heat was to hitch a ride a few miles to the African coast, where they could dive into the Mediterranean.

Even before they had arrived, the airmen had lived through ordeals more difficult than they ever could have imagined. When they had volunteered for the Air Corps, the government did not yet have the facilities to train them all. They had been shipped from base to base all over the United States, most having left home for the first time. The pilots had been subjected to rigorous psychological workups, as well as stringent physical exams. The eye tests weeded out the biggest number of them. Flight training itself — for the pilots, navigators, bombardiers, engineers, and gunners — was terribly dangerous. Thousands died in crashes before they ever reached overseas. The men who made it to active duty had accomplished 360 hours of flight training time, more than three times that of German airmen.

Even still, nothing could prepare them for Tidal Wave. It was Colonel Jacob Smart of Ridgeland, South Carolina, who had come up with the plan to attack Ploesti's oil refineries at treetop level. Smart was adamant that surprise was key to this top-secret mission and that the low-level approach could avoid radar. So positive was Smart that the mission would work that he had asked to fly it himself. (He was pulled from it at the last minute by his superiors.)

Military brass agreed that only the B-24 Liberator had the power, range, and striking capacity for Tidal Wave. It would be the ultimate test for the airplane, which was at that time being built by four companies in the United States, most notably at Willow Run.

Training required hours of low-altitude formation flying in Liberators. "For days," Killer Kane wrote in his diary, "you could look around almost anywhere on the desert and see formations of B-24s skimming along the ground, just missing what few palm trees there still were. . . . The sheep herders on the desert really had a rough time!" At such low altitude, the sensation of speed could be overwhelming. "When you go 200 miles per hour, at an altitude of eight feet, you really know you're going 200 miles per hour," remembered Tidal Wave pilot Captain Philip Ardery.

The crews were given "the most complete and detailed briefing of any air raid in history," Kane remembered. A Connecticut architect named Gerald Geerlings was brought in to build a small-scale model of Ploesti, using photographs of Romania he found in a library in Cambridge, England. British intelligence summoned the public to donate postcards and pictures of vacations in Europe (no specific location could be mentioned, for it was top-secret). Office jockeys spent interminable hours hunting through these pictures for any shot of Ploesti. Having never been to the Romanian city, Geerlings was able to build a model of Ploesti to such detail that an Allied officer who had once lived there could find his old apartment building.

A British aristocrat named Lord Forbes and a New York newspaperman named "Tex" McCrary teamed up to create a forty-five-minute film with sound that instructed the crews on how to find Ploesti and where the strategic targets were located. The military had never made a training film like this before. The filmmakers placed an 8-millimeter camera on a child's tricycle, which panned around the three-dimensional model of Ploesti that Geerlings had built. To make sure the film got everyone's attention, it started out with a shot of a smiling, fully naked female.

"Now the object of this operation," the film's narrator said as the airmen sat listening, "is to choke off that flow of Romanian oil to the Nazis. . . . You men have been selected to do this job."

Outside of the Ploesti model, the attacking crews had no idea what they were about to fly into. Aerial reconnaissance flights, the brass figured, would give away the target. So none were flown.

Luftwaffe chief Hermann Goering understood the strategic importance of Ploesti. He assigned the Nazis' military attaché in Bucharest, forty-eight-year-old Alfred Gerstenberg, to defend it. A highly intelligent and refined patriot, Gerstenberg had worked for months to turn Ploesti into the most heavily armed anti-aircraft fortress on the planet. As one of his staff officers recalled: "[Gerstenberg] was a dedicated man. To better fulfill his duties he learned to speak Polish, Russian, and Romanian. He worked 16 hours a day with one goal in mind: to make Ploesti too costly for the enemy to attack."

Church towers, ridges, bridges, rooftops of all kinds, even hay bales in fields were armed with the now-famous German 88-millimeter anti-aircraft gun. Gerstenberg had over 100 barrage balloons armed with bombs attached to the refineries. At the moment of alarm, his men would winch these balloons attached to cables into the sky so that the cables would entangle attacking planes, setting off the balloons' explosives. Fleets of Messerschmitt fighters were parked at airfields in the surrounding areas, ready to take flight. Gerstenberg even built a special train he called *Die Raupe* — the Caterpillar — that would run along tracks through the Ploesti Valley with 88s sticking out of each rail car so that the train could move in pursuit of warplanes.

For Gerstenberg, it wasn't a matter of whether Ploesti would be targeted; it was a matter of *when*.

The night before Tidal Wave, at the Benghazi airbase, the American flight crews sat writing letters to their families. They were told by their superiors to write these farewell letters; if they didn't return, the army would send the letters for them. The crewmen knew they were flying a highly dangerous mission. It was no secret among the ranks that the highest levels of command had worked out, in General Dwight Eisenhower's words, "mathematical probabilities in great detail" as to the number of expected casualties compared to the amount of destruction the mission would inflict.

"We dreaded this mission," Killer Kane wrote in his diary. "Tension was building up in the entire group. It was getting to where I couldn't sleep [and] the knowledge that the mission might turn out to be a suicidal one with disastrous results turned my sleeping moments into nightmares."

The final briefing, delivered by Major General Lewis Brereton, failed to lift the mood among the bomber crews.

"If you do your job right it is worth it," Brereton said, "even if you lose every plane. You should consider yourself lucky to be on this mission."

At 6:00 AM on Sunday, August 1, the Liberators took flight. The armada made its way across the Mediterranean in blue skies at 2,000 feet, flying in V-formations of three planes each, interlocking so that the planes spread out across five miles in the sky, their wings just twenty-five feet apart. Never before had the United States launched an armada of bombers bigger than this one.

Unbeknownst to the Allies, the Luftwaffe had launched a crack signal interception group in Athens. This crew picked up signals of the bombers in flight. The B-24s also tripped over radar in Yugoslavia. A chain of communication began. General Gerstenberg's phone rang, alerting him of the armada flying fast, due north.

"It is unclear what is developing," a Nazi commander told him. "But we think the objective might be Ploesti."

Gerstenberg soon confirmed the bombers' target. The Germans knew the Liberators were coming.

In the cockpits, the Liberator pilots saw the first sign that things were about to go horribly wrong hours before they reached Ploesti.

The armada was moving around 175 miles per hour in formation. Pilots and copilots were trading off on the controls. The engineers managed the ships' awkward fuel system, eyeing the four glass tubes filled with liquid mounted behind the pilot. Each tube measured fuel in one of the main tanks, which had to be filled carefully from the other tanks (eighteen in all) while in flight. Machine gunners sat in the turrets, which were as tight as coffins when the airmen were wearing their flight suits and parachutes, or waited nearby for word of attack. The rattle inside the airplanes was deafening, and the vibration was a slow assault on the nerves.

Then it appeared: a virtual wall of cloud cover. The Liberators had ascended to 11,000 feet to clear the tops of northern Greece's Pindus Mountains, but above those peaks the cloud cover reached thousands of feet higher. Pilot Edwin Baker remembered seeing that white wall: "A cold chill went down my spine. . . . It was obvious we were going to have to fly through there."

In the clouds, with strict orders for radio silence, the bombardment groups lost each other. By the time they climbed out of it, they were spread out over sixty miles, out of sight from each other.

Meanwhile, at his headquarters in Ploesti, General Gerstenberg ordered all fighter planes into the air. At the oil refineries, men were slowly winching up cables, raising bomb-stacked barrage balloons into the sky. Gunners manned the 88s, ears open to the guttural tune of the big American engines.

The Liberators began to descend as they crossed the border over Romania, traveling now in random packs. Then disaster struck again. A lead plane in one of the bombardment groups made a wrong turn over a town called Targoviste. The Liberators behind that pilot followed him. Aboard a B-24 called *Brewery Wagon*, the navigator phoned the pilot over the intercom.

"If this is the correct turn, I'm lost. This heading is all wrong!"

But it was too late. The group continued for miles before they realized their mistake. The carefully synchronized attack approaches were now completely in disarray.

Aboard *Hail Columbia*, Killer Kane marveled over the beauty of the Romanian countryside, with its brightly painted homes and verdant summer fields. Behind him flew his group and another pilot's group in formation, forty-five Liberators, nine planes wide and five rows deep. These pilots had no idea where the rest of the bombardment groups were located. Through the windshield, the target came into focus.

"In the distance toward Ploesti," Kane remembered, "the sky was the ominous black of a threatening thunderstorm. It would be our luck to arrive there during a heavy rainstorm so that we could not see ahead of us. I tried to fit the steel helmet over my radio headphones but could not get it on. As I was looking toward Ploesti, I saw all hell break loose, the whole area just burst into flames. With that view of the target, a cold hand seemed to reach inside my breast and grip my heart."

Kane realized that another bombardment group had already begun to hit its targets. He could see those huge birds swirling over the flames of the refineries, curling through the mushroom clouds of black smoke. The weird barrage balloons and concrete gunner towers made the scene appear otherworldly. Kane gunned the engines, his speed climbing to well over 200 miles per hour. As he descended to 200 feet, "everything but the kitchen sink began to rise from the ground at us."

The deafening flak from the German 88s blew holes in planes, clipped off wings, sheered tails from the fuselages. The refineries of Ploesti had now erupted in balls of fire, with the long-winged Liberators shrieking in random arcs, diving in for attack runs at 245 miles per hour, some just twenty feet off the ground. Pilot Philip Ardery remembered "a bedlam of bombers flying in all directions, some on fire, many with smoking engines, some with gaping holes or huge chunks of wing or rudder gone; many so riddled their insides must have been stark pictures of the dead and dying or grievously wounded men who would bleed to death before they could be brought to land."

Kane and his group approached their targets. They thundered over a rail track when the pilots saw a train moving under them. It appeared like a normal train with a locomotive pulling cars. Then the doors opened and out of every one of those cars gunners opened up, sending tracer bullets and flak across the sky like sheets of metal rain. It was General Gerstenberg's *Die Raupe* — the Caterpillar.

The gunners in the Liberators let loose with everything they had. Aboard the *Hail Columbia,* Kane had a pair of .50 caliber machine guns that he aimed out the window of the cockpit. "We had to shoot our way in," he remembered. He fired 2,500 rounds in a minute and a half. "On our right [the] flak train moved full speed down the track with guns belching black puffs at us. They were shooting 88s like shotguns, with shells set to go off immediately after they left the gun barrels. A sprinkle of light rain spread a film of rain water over the windshield."

A gunner named Kozak remembered seeing a Liberator take a punch from an 88. He could see the pilot, a friend named Gooden, in the cockpit. "I could see Gooden working the controls," remembered Kozak, "and power his plane into a refinery to shorten the war. The building, the plane and the crew exploded together."

Aboard a Liberator called *Euroclydon,* a navigator named Warner felt the impact of the 88s. "Another shell exploded behind me," he later remembered, "which shattered my shoulder blade and put shrapnel into my head. The concussion blasted me back through the [airplane] into the flames. My feet were in the fire and one of my arms was hanging out the open nose-wheel door. I was lying there kicking and screaming with my feet in the fire and my arms in the slipstream."

One B-24 nosedived into a Ploesti street. A musician standing nearby remembered feeling the earth shake with the impact. "The bomber crashed into a three-story brick building," he recalled. It was a women's prison. "Flaming petrol flowed through the cell blocks and down the stairs," the musician remembered. The petrol caught fire and spread through the building. Locked in cells, prisoners slowly died one by one. Their screaming could be heard outside the burning building for hours.

When the Liberators dropped the last of their bombs, the pilots still flying turned and headed for home. It was a grim scene – many hours of flight with the dead and dying aboard. Though the mission would take roughly thirteen hours total, the entire attack lasted twenty-seven minutes from the first bomb to the last. Gerstenberg's Messerschmitt fighters chased the Liberators due south, picking off airplanes along the way. The bomber crews would get accustomed to these grim airborne hunting grounds. Remembered one airman: "Planes fell in flames, men fell in parachutes, some candlesticked [when their parachutes failed to open]. Pieces of men dropped through the hole."

Flying over the Mediterranean hours later, pilots manning broken ships saw red flares firing into the sky in the distance, the Benghazi airbase beckoning them home. The sound of the rubber wheels touching down was one that none would ever forget. All night, Tidal Wave survivors went in search of their friends, to find out who had made it and who had not. One intelligence officer approached a pilot named Reginald Phillips, who was resting in a shack in the desert.

"What was your overall impression of the mission?" the officer asked.

Phillips was so exhausted that he could barely move his jaw. "We . . . were . . . dragged through the mouth . . . of hell."

To this day, Operation Tidal Wave is the most highly decorated mission in US military history. In the official tallies of Operation Tidal Wave, 446 American airmen were killed or missing. Of the 178 bombers that had taken part, 88 returned to Benghazi, and few of those were undamaged. The casualty rate was so high that military leaders began to call August 1 "Black Sunday." For this effort, the mission had knocked out less than half of the refinery operations. Soon they would be running at nearly 100 percent again, pumping out fuel for Hitler's tanks and airplanes.

Days after Black Sunday, President Roosevelt spoke to Congress about Operation Tidal Wave. Like so many things in the war so far, this mission had confronted unforeseen obstacles. The casualty rate was unacceptable, he admitted, "but I am certain that the German or Japanese High Commands would cheerfully sacrifice tens of thousands of men to do the same amount of damage to us, if they could."

Already in Washington, plans had begun to germinate. The Allies would go back to Ploesti with more Liberators, a more deadly force, and a more strategic attacking plan. Next time they would hit it harder.

26

The Detroit Race Riot of 1943

Summer 1943

> 23 Dead in Detroit Rioting; Federal Troops Enter City on the
> Orders of Roosevelt.
>
> *— NEW YORK TIMES, front page, June 22, 1943*

THE DAY AFTER Edsel Ford's funeral, Henry Ford II and his "Uncle" Ernie Kanzler opened the private safe in the basement of Ford's Administration Building. Together they looked through a pile of dusty official documents hunting for anything that could be used in a court of law to wrestle the empire away from Harry Bennett, who now stood as the most likely candidate to become the next president of Ford Motor Company after Henry Ford.

They found nothing.

Young Henry was almost twenty-six. He had his grandmother's chubby body, a nervous high-pitched voice, and no business experience to speak of. He had grown up in this empire; it was not just his birthright, but his identity too. Outside of his brief stint in the military, it was all he'd ever known. But he had never fought in the trenches of office warfare, certainly not against foes like Harry Bennett, in a business as hotly competitive as the auto game, at a company with some 230,000 domestic employees who did not know him as their boss.

Even as a schoolchild, Henry II's name had defined him. "The whole school—boys as well as teachers—was always, somehow, in awe of him," as one childhood friend put it. "People might pretend otherwise, for the best of reasons, and they might try to treat him normally. But no one could ever quite forget that he was Henry Ford II."

Growing up, he had an idealistic relationship with his grandfather. Henry Ford had a special affection for young children; they seemed to strip him of his dark side and bring out the affectionate paternalism of his younger years. When his grandkids were young, Henry built a working farm on his land for them so they could learn to grow crops. He built a winter Christmas cottage for them, filled with toys, surrounded by real reindeer. Among Henry II's earliest memories, he could recall playing in the inner sanctums of the Rouge with Henry Ford. "We . . . were allowed the run of the whole damn company," Henry II remembered. "We could run railroads. We could get up in the engines and run them around the Rouge." Henry II could remember learning to drive as a twelve-year-old on the streets of Detroit, grinding through gears as his famous grandfather sat beside him in the passenger seat, both smiling ear to ear.

Now Henry II was a man, fatherless in a world where his father had been all but crucified, in the midst of a world war so out of control it seemed like the spinning globe was set ablaze. Henry II had no particular job at Ford Motor Company, no title or formal duties. His first day, he went to the Design Department to find Bob Gregorie, as Edsel had suggested.

"Father told me to start here," Henry II said.

"That's amazing," recalled Gregorie, "when you think about it. Here Edsel was on his deathbed, and one of the things he wanted to impress upon his son was the importance of the Design Department to the future of the company."

Gregorie had known Henry II since he was a little boy. However, soon after Henry II's return to Dearborn, Bob Gregorie was fired. "The whole place was a nuthouse," he said of Ford Motor Company at the end of 1943.

Henry II spent anxiety-ridden hours wandering the grounds of Willow Run and the Rouge, not knowing what else to do. Rather than address him as "Mr. Ford," as others did, Bennett called him "the fat young man walking around with a pad in his hand."

"I am green," Henry II told anyone who would listen, "and I am looking for answers."

The spotlight was on him. Everywhere he went, people pointed and whispered. *That's the new Henry Ford. He sure doesn't look like Henry Ford. He failed engineering in school! Can he save the company?*

"All these people, they are determined to compare me to my grandfather," Henry II told reporters when they came for a scoop. "I am no more like my grandfather than the man in the moon. I am like my mother."

Henry II didn't get any help from Henry I. When the young man visited his grandfather, he got a chilly reception. Henry Ford seemed irritated by the presence of Edsel's sons. At one point, he asked Sorensen to send Henry II off to California, as he had asked Sorensen to tell Edsel so many years before during the heated battles over the Model T in the mid-1920s. History was repeating itself.

Young Henry did the best he could to please his grandfather — who, after all, was now president of the company.

"I hope that somehow and in some way I can be of some value to you," Henry II told Henry I, "and possibly relieve you of some few things and maybe in some small way do a few things daddy used to do," he said, referring to his deceased father as he always had done when he was alive, as "Daddy."

Eventually, Henry II gathered the courage to move some personal belongings into his father's corner office. He hung a picture of Edsel on the wall, so that the father was looking over the son's shoulder. Then he set out to win a war of his own. For weeks he read through his father's files, trying to understand what he should be doing, looking for answers. One observer found him studying Edsel's papers "like a cryptographer looking for a clue."

Sorensen was thrilled to see young Henry. "Nothing pleased me so much in a long while like Henry II's decision to come back again," he wrote in his journal. He advised Henry II to get around the plant, let the workers see him. Sorensen promised that the whole atmosphere would change just by the young man's presence. Said another Ford engineer, Anthony Harff: "When Mr. Henry Ford II came into the picture, why, we felt our prayers over a great number of years had been answered. We actually prayed for something like this to happen."

"Something had to be done to save the company," Sorensen remembered. "I was hearing rumblings from Washington." His fears were confirmed when he heard Drew Pearson, the powerful journalist who wrote the syndicated column "Washington Merry Go Round," talking on the radio about how Henry Ford was too old to run his company and Roosevelt was ready to take the place over at any moment.

And what of the Treasury investigation? Ford executives who knew about this investigation* understood that whatever the findings regarding Dearborn's relationship with its French division during the war and the Trading with the Enemy Act, Washington lawyers would be able to twist the evidence enough so that it could be used to pry the company from the family's hands.

Under Sorensen's iron fist, war production had continued to impress Washington. The skies over Willow Run filled with bombers from morning to night. Lindbergh's test flights saw a constant improvement in the quality of the Liberators, which were being delivered to the army at a quickening pace. Ship number four hundred rolled out of Willow Run on June 17, with another one hundred right behind.

But what of the future? Without top leadership, Ford Motor Company was left rudderless.

All signs pointed to disaster. Edsel had left behind a monster of war productivity: tanks, tank engines, bombers, airplane engines, superchargers, trucks, Jeeps, amphibious Jeeps, gliders, generators, gun mounts, a menu of spare airplane and tank parts, and a smelter pumping out 110,000 pounds of dangerously flammable magnesium per month. Racial tensions in the factories were high. All communication with factories in Axis territories had long since been cut off.

---

* Today little is known about who at Ford Motor Company knew about the Treasury's investigation. Nothing about it is stated in Charles Sorensen's memoirs. It's quite possible that Henry Ford II knew nothing about it.

With no job duties per se, Henry II focused on his task ahead — unseating Harry Bennett. As Henry II later said: "Harry Bennett is the dirtiest, lousiest, son-of-a-bitch I ever met in my life."

There was only one way to handle a man like that, and that was to look him in the eye, show no fear, and employ the same Machiavellian tactics that Bennett had mastered himself. One day, soon after his discharge from the navy, Henry II went to see Harry Bennett in his office. Bennett controlled the Ford empire from behind his locked door, outside of which a heavily muscled secretary sat leaning over an instrument panel covered in signal lights and switches — telephonics that connected Bennett to all his underlings, his tentacles reaching the empire's darkest corners. The secretary buzzed Henry II in, and he pulled a seat up next to Harry Bennett's desk.

The two men sat and chatted amiably, Bennett in his trademark bow tie, Henry II in a fine-tailored suit, as his father had always worn. Both men chuckled nervously, folding their hands on Bennett's desk, the eye contact awkward and side-glancing. Bennett knew exactly what young Henry was up to. He had come to take over, to fill his father's shoes — to exact revenge.

This thing killed my father, Henry II thought to himself. *I'll be damned if I'm going to let it kill me.*

During those first weeks after Edsel's death, Henry II saw top engineers flee the company. Without Edsel, there was no protection from Bennett and the Ford Terror. All the old Edsel loyalists now stood to pay a price.

At one point, Henry II got word that a top Willow Run engineer — William Pioch — was going to quit. Pioch had headed up tool design in the bomber-an-hour project and had himself designed the $250,000 machine that churned out bomber wings like baseball bats. Young Henry called for Pioch, who showed up in his corner office.

"What do you want to quit us for?" Henry II asked.

"Well, I don't like this setup you've got."

"What do you mean, you don't like it? What don't you like about it?"

"You've got a stinkin' setup here," Pioch said. "It's rotten. The people that are trying to run this place, I hate to tell you this, but I don't trust them. I don't like the man that is running this place. He has a bunch of guys out there that I can't work with." Henry II knew exactly who this *he* was. "They don't take any orders from me," Pioch continued. "They don't listen to me. They don't report anything to me, and they are people that are supposed to be working for me. I'm not getting anyplace."

"Would you stay if you worked for me?" Henry II asked.

"I certainly would."

Pioch agreed to give it more time.

Still, the exodus of Edsel-loyalists continued. Famed Detroit auto men like Laurence Sheldrick and Joe Galamb, whose contributions to Henry Ford's empire through the years were immeasurable, walked away forever. In place of these departing figures, Harry Bennett installed his own men. The power struggle at Ford became the talk of the town.

"In Detroit today, a casual passing mention of the Ford name will elicit tales and elaborations of tales about portentous goings-on inside the Ford empire," read a long story in *Fortune* magazine. "A visitor to Detroit encounters them everywhere. They all say that Henry Ford, who will be eighty-one on July 30, is dominated by Harry Bennett, the man who has run Ford's private police for more than 20 years, and that all Ford executives who would not bend the knee to Bennett have 'resigned.'"

The bloodletting grew so severe that even Sorensen himself saw the writing on the wall: "I decided that I had had enough. The picture was very clear now; the team was breaking up. The captain was a sick man. . . . The line coaches were gone. If anyone made a brilliant play, he was called out. As for me, there was only one thing for me to do, see that Henry II stayed on."

As Henry II struggled to get his feet under him in the summer of 1943, a heat wave took hold of Detroit. The factories sweltered. Local authorities made contact over growing rumors that violence was about to break out in Ford's factories. The racial strife had simmered for months. Now it appeared ready to boil over.

Remembered Harry Bennett: "Everyone's nerves were stretched to the breaking point. As a final complaint, we were soon faced with a situation of extreme racial tension in the Detroit area. We got a tip that if race tensions broke into violence, as seemed likely, it was going to begin at the Rouge or at Willow Run."

On the hot morning of June 20, 1943, foremen at Willow Run and the Rouge stopped work. Complaining of poor conditions and intimidation by Harry Bennett's Service Men, they walked off the job. The machines ground to a halt. Local and state police came whistling to the factory grounds, fearing the worst. All day police carefully managed the standoff, trying to keep the peace.

As the sun dipped into the west, however, word came that a fight had broken out in downtown Detroit, a brawl between blacks and whites. The violence was spreading out of control. Cars full of men left the Rouge and Willow Run, headed downtown along Michigan Avenue. When they reached the inner city, they found it on fire. Detroit was dynamite, and someone had lit the fuse.

A heat wave had the city on edge that afternoon of June 20, 1943. The mercury spiked over 90 degrees, a thick humid heat that got under the skin. At Belle Isle Park, situated on an island in the Detroit River a short bridge from downtown, a thousand people — mostly black — were taking refuge in the breeze skimming off the water.

As car and foot traffic headed back over the bridge at the end of the day, some black teenagers bumped into a white sailor and his girlfriend. The sailor didn't take it kindly. A scuffle broke out. A white man came to the sailor's aid — then another. A black man stepped in — then another. A white girl punched a black girl, who fell to the ground; she got up and bloodied the white girl's nose. In a minute's time, the violence began to spill from the bridge into the city — black against white.

At the Forest Club — a famed jazz bar on Hastings Street in the heart of Paradise Valley, Detroit's Harlem — black revelers were drinking and dancing to a jazz band when a man in a suit stopped the music. He grabbed a microphone and announced that a fight had broken out at Belle Isle Park, that some white men had thrown a Negro woman and her baby into the river, killing the child. For months, rage had mounted among the black community — rage against a government that would not let them fight in the war as soldiers next to their fellow white citizens, rage against white suppressors who confined them to overcrowded, vermin-infested neighborhoods and paid them less for the same assembly-line jobs. Now this bar full of black men emptied, all of them headed for the Belle Isle Bridge.

At a navy hangout down the street from Belle Isle, a group of two hundred white sailors were killing time over card tables. A man out of breath came bursting through the door. Blacks were beating up some white men and women on the bridge, the guy shouted. They had to do something! Two hundred Caucasian sailors charged outside, boots clattering down the pavement.

By sunset, brawls had broken out all over downtown Detroit. There were so many Southern black "hillbillies" and white "hoodlums" fighting in the streets that the police were outnumbered and helpless. Once the law lost control, there was no stemming the violence. Now the sun had set. It was dark, and the nation's fourth-largest city was in the hands of enraged rioters.

Mobs of white men — many of them members of the Ku Klux Klan — swarmed the slums, armed with baseball bats and knives. Blacks amassed by the hundreds on Woodward Avenue, stoning innocent people's cars and terrorizing storefront clerks. Teenage Mexican pachucos in zoot suits joined the rioting. When crowds emerged from the Roxy Theater into the hot night, white men pulled bewildered blacks out and beat them senseless in front of their wives and girlfriends.

In city and state buildings, government officials sat in their offices, frightened for their lives. Surely the police would regain control. In the mayor's office on the corner of Jefferson and Woodward Avenues, Mayor Edward Jeffries was stunned to learn that members of his police department were locking themselves inside their squad cars for their own safety. For months, Jeffries had witnessed what he called "the rising tide" of racial aggression in the city. He had argued for a policy of maintaining "racial characteristics of neighborhoods," believing that the best way to avoid violence was to keep blacks and whites apart. One police sergeant had said of the surging antagonism: "It will either blow up or blow over."

It was now clear which would be the case.

The first death was reported at 6:15 AM Monday morning, fourteen hours after the riot began. Mayor Jeffries phoned Governor Harry Kelly. It was time to declare martial law.

At sunrise on June 21 — "Bloody Monday" — the streets of Detroit had taken on a post-apocalyptic glow. Fires blazed in cars and in storefronts, with no engine siren signaling that help was on the way. Instead, air raid whistles howled. Mayor Jeffries ordered all schools and businesses closed. Governor Kelly canceled the Indians-Tigers game and the day's horse races. The war factories in the city and surrounding villages locked down. Citizens were advised to stay in their homes and lock their doors. There were mobs hunting the streets, and no one to stop them.

Four white boys drove in their car shouting, "Let's go out and kill a nigger!" They spotted fifty-eight-year-old Moses Kisko waiting for a streetcar that would never come. The sound of a gunshot was the last thing Kisko ever heard.

Another white mob roamed hunting for "fresh meat," as garbage and busted glass crunched on the pavement beneath their feet. One rioter later said: "Jesus, but it was a show! We dragged niggers from cars, beat the hell out of them, and lit the sons of bitches' autos. I'm glad I was in it! Those black bastards damn well deserved it." Said another white man: "There were about 200 of us in cars. We killed eight of them. I saw knives being stuck through their throats and heads being shot through. They were turning over cars with niggers in them. You should have seen it. It was really some riot."

As hospital emergency rooms filled with casualties suffering gunshot and knife wounds, the completely white state and city police force turned on Detroit's black population. Walter White, head of the NAACP, rushed to the Motor City and what he saw stunned him: "Not even in the South had I ever seen so total a breakdown of law enforcement." Caucasian police officers were beating and shooting black men in Paradise Valley.

When the sun set, police hunting for murder suspects set up searchlights in front of the Vernor Apartments on Cabot Street, inside which innocent black families huddled. The officers opened fire, shooting bullets and tear-gas canisters through windows. Black snipers climbed up on the roof and returned gunfire.

"Word got around pretty fast," said one black man. "Those police are *murderers*. They were just waiting for a chance to get us. We didn't stand a chance. *I hate 'em. Oh God, how I hate 'em.* The fellows who had guns were ready to go. They were saying, 'If it gets tight, get two whites before you go.'"

Roosevelt was enjoying a post-dinner cocktail with the First Lady and Queen Wilhelmina of the Netherlands at his home in Hyde Park, New York, when the call came through, at 9:45 PM on Monday, June 21. Michigan governor Harry Kelly was on the line, pleading for federal troops. Detroit was on fire.

The news was no surprise. For months, authorities had warned the White House about racial tension on the home front, especially in Detroit. America before World War II was still largely a Jim Crow nation. The war had forced the issue of integration like nothing ever had before. Decades of progress had been shoehorned into two short years, but not everyone was ready for it. That very day, Eleanor Roosevelt had written a newspaper column about race in America. "The domestic scene is anything but encouraging," she wrote. "And one would like not to think about it, because it gives one a feeling that, as a whole, we are not really prepared for democracy."

At midnight on June 21, the President signed a proclamation mobilizing federal troops. His statement ordered rioters to "disperse and retire peaceably to their respective abodes."

"It shall be lawful for the President of the United States . . . to call forth the militia. . . ."

Within the hour, the 701st Military Police battalion came sweeping across Detroit's ravaged streets in Jeeps and trucks with machine guns at the ready — about thirty vehicles and 3,800 men. By sunrise, the cooled streets had fallen quiet.

Three days of violence claimed thirty-four lives. The Detroit Race Riot of 1943 was the bloodiest racial standoff in America in over twenty years. An estimated seventeen of the dead were killed by police, and all but nine were black. Some $2 million worth of property was destroyed. As for man-hours lost in the war plants, they numbered in the many millions.

The NAACP's Walter White wandered the streets in the aftermath, amazed at what he saw. "Not long afterward," he said, "I was destined to see bombed-out victims of Nazi terror in Europe. In Detroit I found the same bewilderment at senseless human cruelty on the faces of Negro victims of the same foul hate which Hitler had spewed upon Europe and the world."

All week Detroit's race riot was front-page news. The nation was horrified that hatred so murderous could rear its head on the home front among citizens who were supposed to share the common goal of winning the war and proving that democracy was superior to fascism. Who was at fault? Many pointed at Nazi saboteurs.

"We have no definite knowledge that any axis agents or propaganda inspired this trouble," Mayor Jeffries said. "If we did those agents would be in jail. But if I were an axis agent I would be rubbing my hands in glee over this." Others in the national press attacked the First Lady, who had argued for some time to use the war as an impetus for integration. "It is blood on your hands, Mrs. Roosevelt," Mississippi's *Jackson Daily News* declared.

As the city returned to work on Thursday morning, many feared that the rioting was no climax but a foreshadowing of something more catastrophic on the horizon. At Willow Run and the Rouge, several thousand black assembly-line workers filed through the gates beside their fellow white citizens for the morning shift on June 23. In Ford's Administration Building offices, executives feared the worst. Sure, they were a few miles from downtown Detroit, where the rioting occurred. But the sweltering factories could erupt in violence at any moment. Henry II seemed as rattled as ever, and Harry Bennett had his men at the ready. "This rioting was a frightful experience for everybody," Sorensen remembered. "They brought in tanks and ran them through the streets in the danger zones."

Said one Detroiter: "When the army leaves, who knows what will happen?"

27

"The United States Is the Country of Machines"

Fall 1943

> We'll not capitulate. Never. We can go down. But we'll take a
> world with us.
>
> — ADOLF HITLER, *December 1944*

"I'M NEARLY DEAD," Roosevelt told his secretary of labor, Frances Perkins. He was sitting in the White House on September 1, 1943, complaining of exhaustion. The Prime Minister was visiting from Britain, and he always kept the President up late. Churchill was an impulsive and indefatigable houseguest. "I have to talk to the PM all night," Roosevelt told Perkins, "and he gets bright ideas in the middle of the night and comes pattering down the hall to my bedroom in his bare feet.

"I have to have my sleep," Roosevelt said.

The war was taking its toll on everyone in Roosevelt's administration. The President's closest aide, Harry Hopkins, who had come to stay a night in the White House three years earlier and had never left, had to be confined to his bed after he collapsed. Hopkins slept in a second-floor bedroom with his new wife, the former Paris editor of *Harper's Bazaar*. He had lost his eighteen-year-old son Stephen in the war. Churchill had a cold flare up and was attempting to douse it with sherry. A close friend of Roosevelt's described the sixty-one-year-old president as "tired, with dark rings under his eyes." He was also suffering from hypertension and serious heart problems. His doctor described his condition as "God-awful."

Still, Roosevelt and Churchill could be found in their makeshift White House map room gazing at the world at all hours. The President had converted the ladies' cloak room in the basement into his top-secret map room, with maps filling the walls detailing every theater of combat. The two Allied leaders plotted deep into the night. And each morning Roosevelt's valet, Irvin McDuffie—a Southern black man who suffered from his own form of exhaustion (he was an alcoholic)—came to lift the weary president from his bed and help him dress.

When he was not entertaining visitors or traveling, Roosevelt spent hours alone in the Oval Office, working through his mountains of memos. His cabinet members and confidants were amazed at the President's ability to consume information and instantly commit facts to memory. Among those many memos was one he received around the time of Churchill's September visit—a classified report from Donald Nelson, chairman of the War Production Board, on the progress of production on the home front. Nelson had been the subject of some argument recently. There were those who questioned his ability to do his job. He was a nice guy—and that was no compliment in Washington. In this memo, however, the President liked what he was seeing.

After Pearl Harbor, Nelson wrote,

a flexible productive system, geared to the needs of total war, had to be improvised almost overnight. . . . I need not tell you that we have met with some disappointments and have made some errors in achieving the results. But the record certainly makes it clear that the American industrial system can be justifiably proud of an astonishing display of economic muscle. Today, we are turning out nearly as much material for war, measured in dollar value, as we ever produced for our peacetime needs. The essence of the report is that, in the main, the productive achievement of the American war economy in 1942 met the requirements of our war strategy; and that the prospects for 1943 are for a quantity and quality of production that will realize to the full the tremendous potential of American industry.

The President turned the page and studied the report. Shipyards were turning out eight aircraft carriers every month. Before the war, America's shipbuilding industry was minuscule. Now it was the biggest in the world. At the time of Pearl Harbor, Britain's military was larger than America's. Now the US fighting force was twice as large as the British empire's and was making four times as many munitions. Production of raw materials was tremendous. Chromite – up by almost 700 percent. Aluminum – up 77 percent. Magnesium – up 220 percent. Molybdenum, tungsten, vanadium – these were the raw ingredients of modern warfare. Production of each was skyrocketing.

Roosevelt was so pleased with Nelson's production figures that he told Nelson to give them to the newspapers. So Nelson did. The news went global, reaching across the ocean, where Nazi leaders consumed these production figures with disbelief.

"Donald Nelson has issued a report about American armament production," Joseph Goebbels wrote in his diary. "It exceeds all previous American exaggerations. We simply must do something to offset this American munitions propaganda."

Of all the figures moving across the Oval Office desk, few must have pleased Roosevelt more in the fall of 1943 than the memos showing airplane production. A year and a half had passed since he had called on the nation to produce 60,000 airplanes. During those eighteen months, the President had on many occasions expressed his fury over deplorable production numbers. "The only answer I want to hear is that it is under way," he'd told his military leaders. "Get the planes off with a bang next week." Now a new flying machine was being born in the United States *every five minutes.*

According to a top-secret document from Donald Nelson's office, four-engine bomber production – B-24 Liberators and B-17 Flying Fortresses – rose from 5,376 total in the fourth quarter of 1942 to 8,321 in the first quarter of 1943, to 11,928 in the second quarter of 1943. Medium bomber production spiked similarly, from 7,603 to 15,213, during the same period.

Air Corps chief Hap Arnold had slaved so doggedly to organize the Air Corps and launch American airpower that by the fall of 1943 he had survived the first of four heart attacks he would suffer during the war. Before World War II, the US Air Corps consisted of about 20,000 men. Now it numbered 2.4 million personnel in all ranks.

One amazing story that illustrated the ingenuity of the Air Corps took place on the tiny Mediterranean island of Gozo, off Malta. The isle was covered with trees and hills, and yet it was situated in a prime striking zone from which to launch aircraft on missions over Axis territory. An American engineer told Britain's air marshal, Keith Park, that he could clear the terrain and build an airfield in ten days' time. Park thought this notion preposterous, but asked, "When can you start?"

"As soon as my equipment can get here."

Soon ships landed, delivering bulldozers and trucks and mechanical shovels. Thirteen days after that equipment arrived, airplanes were taking off from runways on Gozo.

The Air Corps was also experimenting with faster, bigger, more destructive weapons. The summer of 1943 saw the first missions of the new P-51 Mustang, soon to be universally regarded as the best single-engine fighter developed during the war by any nation. ("It's the best handling pursuit plane I've ever flown," Lindbergh wrote in his journal after his first test flight at Willow Run.) Finally, the Allies had a fighter escort with the agility and speed to outmatch the Nazi Messerschmitt Bf 109s and Japan's Mitsubishi Zeros, as well as the range to accompany heavy bombers on their long missions. The majority of the P-51 Mustangs were powered by Merlin engines built by Packard in downtown Detroit.

At the same time, the army's new "superbomber," the four-engine Boeing B-29, was readying for its first missions. The B-29 was even larger than the B-24, with better range and a bigger payload. With its pressurized cabin, it could climb safely to higher altitudes, and it featured remote-controlled machine gun turrets. Hap Arnold had big plans for the B-29.

Things in the White House map room were looking better by the day. Armed with good news from the war theaters and Nelson's production figures, Roosevelt and Churchill began to plan another key summit meeting. They would gather with Joseph Stalin in person for the first time, on some safe middle ground. Soon the meeting was set — for Tehran in November.

In September 1943, Albert Speer, Hitler's minister of armaments, gathered Nazi leaders at Germany's Air Force Experimental Center in Rechlin am Müritzsee to discuss the latest intelligence on American aircraft production. There, his top technical assistants showed charts that mapped the numbers of B-24 Liberators and B-17 Flying Fortresses rolling off American assembly lines compared with the number of bombers rolling off the Nazis' own lines. For the Nazis, the charts told an unnerving story.

"What alarmed us most were the figures on the future increase in four-motored daylight bombers," Speer recalled.

When Speer asked Hitler to consider these production numbers, the Fuehrer brushed them off.

"Don't let them fool you," Hitler said. "Those are all planted stories. Naturally those defeatists in the Air Ministry fall for them."

The Air Corps' four-engine bombers were now, however, hitting targets in Nazi Germany. As the destruction mounted, it became impossible for Hitler to ignore. The American heavies came in swarms, and their destructive capacities were unprecedented, hitting a submarine factory in Wilhelmshaven, the Focke-Wulf airplane factory in Bremen, and a ball bearing factory in Schweinfurt (where the Air Corps was hit with heavy anti-aircraft resistance and casualties). Each mission aimed to level a strategic target, to cripple Hitler's war machine. But invariably, bombs destroyed civilian homes and buildings nearby.

"The day raids by American bombers are creating extraordinary difficulties," Joseph Goebbels wrote in his diary. "Industrial and munitions plants have been hit very hard. . . . Some eighty to one hundred thousand inhabitants without shelter. . . . The people in the West are gradually beginning to lose courage. Hell like that is hard to bear."

Throughout 1943, the Allies' Combined Bomber Offensive moved deeper into Nazi-occupied territory, the British striking cities by night and the Americans hitting strategic targets by day. Hamburg, nearly incinerated in a firestorm by Operation Gomorrah, had taken the worst of it, with 40,000 killed. By this time, Hitler's health had begun to seriously decline. His hair was graying, he slumped and limped, and his left hand trembled uncontrollably. Those closest to him recognized a shell of a man, one who seemed as though he might shatter to pieces on the floor if tapped on the shoulder.

It became increasingly undeniable that the Nazis were losing the race to roll airplanes off of assembly lines. With this failure, Goering was cast off by the Fuehrer, left to his drug-induced lethargy on the political sidelines.

The closer the air raids moved toward the heart of Berlin, the more Hitler saw morale around him plummet. When the Americans sent a bomber mission over the city of Aachen, inside Germany near the Belgian border, the engagement left an American fighter plane in pieces in the city. When a Nazi official reported the news to Goering, he refused to believe a fighter plane could penetrate that deep into Nazi-occupied territory. Pacing the halls of the Air Ministry, Goering unleashed his fury.

"Don't let them fool you," Goering said. "Those are all planted stories. . . . What's the idea of telling the Fuehrer that American fighters have penetrated into the territory of the Reich?"

Goering's junior officer explained that anti-aircraft gunners had shot a plane down. It was still there, an American fighter plane, in pieces on the ground, in Aachen — proof that the fighters had penetrated.

"I officially assert that the American fighter planes did not reach Aachen."

"But, sir, they were there! Herr Reich Marshal, they will soon be flying even deeper."

"I hereby give you an official order that they weren't there!" Goering screamed. "Do you understand? The American fighters were not there! Get that! I intend to report that to the Fuehrer!"

In November 1943, Roosevelt sat aboard a US Army plane flying low over the pyramids in Egypt. He was en route to Tehran for what would be one of the twentieth century's most memorable political events—the Tehran Conference. Over Egypt, he asked the pilot to circle the pyramids, so that he could witness their magnificence from above.

"Man's desire to be remembered is colossal," he said aloud.

Soon Roosevelt, Churchill, and Stalin were in the Russian embassy in Tehran discussing military strategy. It was the first time the three Allied leaders had gathered in one place, and the first time Roosevelt had met Stalin in person. The American president wore a suit and tie, while the two other leaders came in military uniform. Spirits were high, and glasses were raised.

From every theater of war, the Allied leaders heard good news. In the Battle of the Atlantic, a police force of Very Long Range Liberators (B-24s rigged with extra fuel capacity for extreme range) had fanned out over U-boat hunting grounds, destroying Nazi subs, clearing the shipping routes for American munitions to reach Europe. Stalin's Red Army had defeated the Germans at Stalingrad in one of the most brutally fought battles of modern times. American forces had seized Guadalcanal in the first major offensive victory over the Japanese. The Allies had launched Operation Husky—the invasion of Sicily, commanded by the military's rising star, General Dwight D. Eisenhower. Sixteen days after the first paratrooper landings, Italian dictator Benito Mussolini had been removed from office and had gone into hiding. His execution was imminent.

It was time for the Allied leaders to begin serious discussions on Operation Overlord—the invasion of Europe, the climactic battle of World War II. But Roosevelt, Churchill, and Stalin also had some celebrating to do. On November 30, the three gathered for a dinner to honor Churchill's sixty-ninth birthday, with top-ranking military officials from all three nations present. Never had so much brass gathered at a single dinner table before, and never had modern history concocted such a strange alliance as this one—specifically Stalin, who as the supreme dictator of the Soviet Union had allegedly ordered the execution of hundreds of thousands of his own citizens. He was hardly a friend of democracy.

"I think about a hundred toasts and speeches must have been given," General Hap Arnold recalled. "Stalin went around the table and clicked glasses with all the military men. He drank his liquor out of his own bottle — it was rumored there was nothing but water in it." When it was Stalin's turn to speak, the Soviet leader rose and put World War II into perspective. Curiously, his toast sounded like something that Henry Ford might have said, if Henry had ever put on a military uniform. Or William Knudsen, Charlie Sorensen, or Edsel Ford.

"I want to tell you," Stalin said, "from the Russian point of view, what the President and the United States have done to win the war. The most important things in this war are machines. The United States has proven that it can turn out from 8,000 to 10,000 airplanes per month. Russia can only turn out, at most, 3,000 a month. England turns out 3,000 to 3,500. . . . The United States, therefore, is the country of machines. Without the use of these machines, through Lend-Lease, we would lose the war."

The proceedings made Roosevelt swell with pride. "If there was any supreme peak in Roosevelt's career," the President's chief speechwriter Robert Sherwood said, "I believe it might well be fixed at this moment, at the end of the Tehran Conference."

When it ended, the leaders and their military officials returned to their command centers and steeled themselves for the D-Day invasion. But first, as agreed upon at the Casablanca Conference nearly a year earlier, they needed to gain full mastery of the skies — total air supremacy over Europe. The Combined Bomber Offensive would gather all its four-engine bombers and let them loose over Nazi territory, in the most striking display of airpower ever executed. General Arnold gave the order to his top-ranking Air Corps officers on January 1, 1944.

"This is my personal directive to you: DESTROY THE ENEMY AIR FORCES, IN ITS FACTORIES ON THE GROUND AND IN THE AIR."

28

Ford War Production
Exceeds Dreams

Winter 1943 to Spring 1944

Detroit, where they stand in line for a glass of beer, where you can't get a good steak even from Mr. Black, where more dames wear slacks than in Hollywood, where somebody made a mistake and a race riot resulted, where there are more hillbillies than in Arkansas, and where everybody has two sawbucks to rub against each other. Detroit, the hottest town in America. . . . If the backwoods improves after the war, Detroit can take a major share of the credit, for there are over 400,000 people here who previously lived in whistle stops, four corners, and fur pieces down the road.

— *DAILY VARIETY, October 29, 1943*

IN THE MOTOR CITY, news of the Tehran conference hit the front pages on the morning of December 6, 1943. For Detroiters, the "Big Three" meant the world's biggest car companies — General Motors, Chrysler, and Ford. Now the *Detroit News* offered a new definition with a historic photo of Roosevelt flanked by Stalin and Churchill. Papers across the country ran the full text of the "Declaration by 3 Allied Powers."

"We have concerted our plans for the destruction of the German forces," the Tehran statement read. "We have reached complete agreement as to the scope and timing of operations, which will be undertaken from the east, west, and south. . . . No power on earth can prevent our destroying the German armies by land, their U-boats by sea, and their war plants from the air. Our attacks will be relentless and increasing."

By this time, Detroit's production frenzy had reached its crescendo, and the men, women, and children hustling along its frozen streets took pride in seeing that photo of the Big Three, knowing that their city had become the most important locus of wartime production in the world. From the fourth-largest city in America, some 30 percent of the nation's war matériel was pouring forth onto ships and through the skies to overseas bases.

For years, the motor industry icons had battled against each other in ruthless capitalist warfare, the all-consuming clamor for automobile market share. Now they worked together as a team. "Ford is making all-important units for General Motors," wrote one journalist in *Collier's* magazine, "and the latter is loud in its praise of the lean, dry genius whom it used to pretend to ignore. It's just as if the Brooklyn Dodgers took a few days off and won a few games for the Phillies."

General Motors was about to deliver its 854,000th military truck. GM's Oldsmobile division had already delivered nearly 40 million artillery rounds. Pontiac had reduced the cost of its complex Oerliken anti-aircraft gun by 23 percent. Chrysler's Dodge division was moving shortwave radar systems out at $9,386 apiece; engineers had figured out how to make them at 57 percent less cost than eighteen months earlier. The company's gyrocompasses, each weighing 1,300 pounds, were costing 55 percent of the original fee, saving the government over $19 million on that one contract alone.

Readers flipping through popular magazines (a common pastime before TV sets appeared en masse in households) saw pages upon pages of automobile company advertisements with no pictures of automobiles:

The Toughest Fords Ever Built . . . Hard-hitting M-4 Tanks and
  M-10 Tank Destroyers

Horsepower Wins Wars . . . Chrysler Division of Chrysler
    Corporation
Pontiac: Building Fast and Building Well . . . For Liberty

Even as the labor market more than doubled in the Detroit region, the auto men running war factories had taken drastic measures to fill them with workers. Cadillac's general manager, Nicholas Dreystadt, had been tasked with building top-secret bombsights on assembly lines where two years earlier workers were crafting luxury automobiles with the first-ever automatic transmissions ("Announcing the New Cadillac-Engineered Hydra-Matic Drive"). Desperate for hands to run machines, Dreystadt recruited 2,000 black prostitutes off the streets of Detroit — and their madams.

"They know how to manage the women," he said.

Dreystadt made training films on how to build gyroscopes and put these women to work building these complicated objects. The unions protested, calling the Cadillac manager "nigger lover" and "whore monger."

"These women are my fellow workers," Dreystadt argued. "Whatever their past, they are entitled to the same respect as any one of our associates. For the first time in their lives, these poor wretches are paid decently, work in decent conditions, and have some rights."

Soon these "red light district" women were surpassing quotas, and the bombsights they built were helping airmen to hit their strategic targets aboard bombers over enemy territory.

At Willow Run, Henry Ford and Harry Bennett turned up each morning to watch bombers roll out of the factory's gaping jaws and onto the airfield runways. Striding through Willow Run among the half-built bombers, Henry appeared an anachronism, as skinny as an insect and barely alert. He famously said around this time: "I invented the modern age." But the war had accelerated all the nuances of modernity. History was being made at an exponentially faster pace than Henry Ford could fathom, and there were few better examples than the destructive devices that surrounded him and flew overhead.

How the world had changed before Henry Ford's eyes, since the day he unleashed his Quadricycle upon the streets of Detroit in June 1896, with its four horsepower and its doorbell for a horn.

All through the winter, the bomber plant's speed quickened, its operations more finely tuned and perfectly integrated with each shift on the assembly line. Willow Run produced 125 Liberators in September 1943, 150 in November, 165 in December, and 210 in January. By November 1943, Willow Run had birthed its first 1,000 bombers — and the second thousand were quickly on the way.

Only a year earlier, "Will It Run" was an embarrassment, held as an example in the national spotlight of all that could go wrong in the conversion to wartime. Now company public relations men began inviting back all those reporters and public officials who had brutally maligned it.

"Long lines of huge B-24 heavy bombers standing along the edge of the airport at Willow Run give visual evidence at what is being done at the world's largest airplane factory," wrote one journalist. "The whole operation is so vast, so sensational, that it conveys the impression of a sort of Niagara Falls of industry. The wonder is that anyone could get such a vast plant into production in less than two years."

The *Hartford Courant:* "Willow Run Performing Brilliantly." The *Christian Science Monitor:* "Ford War Production Exceeds Dreams."

Visitors turned up daily to eye the industrial marvel. Walt Disney came to see it, as did William Randolph Hearst, Navy chaplain William McGuire (famous for the phrase "Praise the Lord and pass the ammunition"), and a certain European female sniper who had personally killed 309 Nazis. ("She was a strange, rather good-looking girl," said Sorensen. "Hard to believe that she could be a killer.")

By the end of winter, even the hypercritical Charles Lindbergh had to admit that the factory was humming. "We have been ahead of schedule for several months now," he wrote in his journal on March 27, 1944.

"Bring the Germans and Japs to see it," Sorensen said of Willow Run. "Hell, they'll blow their brains out!"

Around the time of Roosevelt's Tehran Conference, the government asked a team of engineers from the aviation firm Curtiss-

Wright to fly in for a quality control report on Ford's Liberators. The engineers swarmed the factory and the airfield.

"That Ford is producing high-grade planes is obvious," read their assessment. "For all operations from pre-flight to delivery there are only 30–40 crabs [problems that needed fixing] written on each ship. From our point of view, this was phenomenal. However, this wasn't always so, for until a comparatively short time ago, the number of crabs ran as high as 800."

Still, the ultimate goal — a bomber an hour — eluded Willow Run. The job was not done yet, not at home or abroad.

One morning during the winter after Edsel's death, a beat-up old car pulled into the parking lot at Ford's Administration Building, and out stepped tall and lanky John Bugas. He was no longer with the FBI. Starting on this day, he was an employee of Ford Motor Company. Bennett had hired Bugas. He had grown so tired of the G-man and his boys crawling all over the Rouge that he decided to poach Bugas from the Bureau and install him as his top assistant.

"John's the smartest man they've got," Bennett told his Service Department thugs. "I'm going to hire him. I can give him twice what he's getting with the FBI, and he's worth it. He can be a big shot in the company, and that's what he likes. He doesn't have to cater to any of the big shots we got. He'll work for me."

Bugas wasn't expecting any job offer. He wrote his boss J. Edgar Hoover in Washington, as if embarrassed by the situation: "The offer came as a complete surprise, and without any solicitation whatsoever at any time from myself."

Twice the pay? Bugas took the job.

That first day, he returned to the parking lot to find that his car had been stolen. After some investigating, he learned that Bennett had taken his old clunker and replaced it with a brand-new Lincoln, with a big engine and plenty of shiny chrome. A new car during the war? According to the rationing rules, this was highly illegal — unless Bennett had submitted all the special paperwork, which was doubtful. "I had a terrible time getting my old car back from him," Bugas remembered.

As the company's new head of industrial relations, Bugas found himself at Bennett's side day and night. They had known each other since Bugas had first arrived to head up the FBI's Detroit office five years earlier. All through those years, Bennett had served as one of Bugas's top FBI informants. Now Bugas was taking his wife Maggie to Bennett's "Castle" for parties and riding Bennett's horses. Bugas was an athletic type with picaresque stories of busting spies and bare-knuckle gallantry — just the kind of guy who could fit into Bennett's crowd, if he so desired. Maggie Bugas liked to tell the story of the time that she and her husband were on a train when a man started verbally abusing a girlfriend. Bugas stepped in to stop it, and when the man swung at him, Bugas grabbed him by the neck and let him have it.

At first, Bugas made Henry II nervous. The new executive struck young Henry as yet another hurdle, another one of Bennett's pawns — and a crafty one at that. "At first," recalled Henry II of Bugas, "I didn't know how to play him."

But soon Henry II figured out where Bugas's real allegiances lay: with Edsel Ford. Edsel had forged a friendship with Bugas before his death. Bugas had developed a keen sense of the difference between good and evil during his time with the FBI — including which side he belonged on. As one Ford biographer wrote, "The FBI man was actually a sort of time bomb Edsel had left ticking in Bennett's vicinity."

Sorensen and a handful of military officials stood one afternoon at the Willow Run airfield watching a tow-plane pull a Ford-built Waco CG-4A glider skyward. Before his death, Edsel had signed contracts to build the gliders from the family's lumber mill in Kingsford, north of Detroit (today famous for its Kingsford brand of charcoal). Now officials from Washington had flown in to see the Ford glider in action, a sort of informal christening. The Allies were planning on using the gliders in massive numbers to land the first wave of troops behind the beaches on D-Day.

As Sorensen watched from below, the glider disengaged from the tow-plane and its pilot steered into a series of graceful maneuvers, diving into arcing bends, then straightening into a hover, the glider silent as it made its approach back to the ground.

The sound of an engine disrupted the scene. Sorensen turned and saw an automobile screech to a halt in front of him. One of Bennett's Service Men jumped out, his face contorted with anger.

"Nobody invited Mr. Bennett!" he shouted.

Sorensen and the military officials looked at the man, amazed.

"Nobody invited Mr. Bennett!" he screamed again.

The group remained speechless. So the man jumped back in his car and tore out of there, leaving Sorensen chuckling to himself.

Still, Sorensen knew he had angered Bennett, who would certainly retaliate in some backhanded political machination. People were whispering about Sorensen — and he knew it. He was exhausted and slipping, and as the most powerful of all the Edsel supporters, he knew he was a prime target. Sorensen was also hearing a new wave of rumors that the President was going to sweep in and take over Ford Motor Company. A friend in Washington's Office of Price Administration had personally called Sorensen on the phone to tell him that Roosevelt was adamant: Henry Ford had to be removed as president of the nation's third-largest defense contractor. Roosevelt was about to place his own operative in charge.

Sorensen had one last fight in him. He prepared to take Henry II on an important political mission. They would go to Washington, New York, everywhere they could get a meeting with the power elite of government, finance, and industry. After a train ride to New York City, Sorensen presented the new Henry Ford to the heads of the big banks. The pair flew together to Washington, where Henry II shook hands with General Arnold and General George Marshall, America's highest-ranking military figure.

In his office in the recently completed Pentagon, General Arnold showed Henry II and Sorensen aerial surveillance photos of damage to a factory in Regensburg, Germany, which had been bombed by Allied planes — some very likely built at Willow Run. Arnold was able to enlarge one photo so they could look through the smashed roof into the Nazi factory.

Henry II must have thought of his dad, looking at the work Edsel had done in a new light. Sorensen saw his work in a new light too — direct evidence of what American bombers were doing to the enemy. "That is the way to win the war," he said. "We will get all their essential plants."

Exactly, General Arnold agreed. That was the strategy of the US Air Corps — to stop Hitler by stopping his war machine.

Henry II left Washington thrilled and empowered. He was rubbing elbows with the nation's elite. Back in Dearborn, Sorensen was driving with Henry Ford I one day when the old man asked how Henry II was getting along.

"He's doing fine," Sorensen said. "I feel like a father toward him now. I'm going to help him every way I possibly can."

Henry II was under fire. At every turn, he suffered the ignominy of Harry Bennett's tactics. One day Henry II was meeting in his office with Sorensen when Bennett phoned. Young Henry picked up and got an earful. He couldn't get a word in. Bennett was furious about something and letting Henry II have it. Sorensen left the room so that Henry II could endure the embarrassment in privacy. When Sorensen walked back in, he found Henry II utterly composed. Young Henry said nothing about the phone call and continued calmly with Sorensen where he had left off.

Sorensen smiled. Henry II was tough all right. He had a rugged outer shell, something Edsel never possessed. *The boy can take it,* Sorensen thought to himself. *Everything will work out all right.*

Henry II amassed a small group of loyalists around him. There was the legendary Ford sales chief Jack Davis and the engineer Mead Bricker — a disciple of Sorensen's who was now the superintendent of Willow Run. And then there was John Bugas, the former G-man. In a private dining room at the Detroit Athletic Club, Henry II and his allies held meetings early in 1944 and plotted a scheme to sink Harry Bennett.

Bugas came up with a good piece of advice. If they were going to challenge Bennett, they needed protection. "First," Bugas told Henry II, "get your grandfather to sign a piece of paper saying that nobody can get fired around here without your permission."

Harry Bennett had hired Bugas, but he soon figured out which side the former FBI man was on. Bugas was an Edsel loyalist, and Bennett grew wary. "He seemed to sit around most of the day," Bennett recalled, "his jacket off and his gun jutting from the shoulder holster beneath his arm." As for Bugas, "I was as isolated as a tuberculosis germ." One day Bugas showed up for work to find that his desk had been moved into a bathroom, separated from a toilet by a partition.

The war in Dearborn was on.

Early in 1944, Henry Ford's two most famous employees left him.

Charles Lindbergh got a call from Washington. He was given paperwork that allowed him to fly to the Far East, where he could put his aviation skills to work in the assault on Japanese-held islands. Each atoll was critical, as these tiny tropical isles gave the Allies opportunity to build airfields closer and closer to their ultimate targets in that hemisphere: Tokyo, Osaka, Kumamoto, Hiroshima.

Lindbergh lunched at Willow Run with Harry Bennett on March 29. Henry Ford and Henry II came to wish the aviator the best of luck. On the 31st, he took a train out of Detroit bound for Hartford, Connecticut, with a stopover in New York. The next morning, he arrived in a hospital room where a nurse laid out six humongous inoculation syringes.

"Is someone else taking this, too?" Lindbergh asked nervously.

"No," said the nurse, "these are all for you."

Schick test, typhoid, typhus, cholera, tetanus, smallpox. Lucky Lindy was headed for the jungle, where the expertise and agility he demonstrated in his flights over Willow Run would pay off. (As for his altitude experiments, Lindbergh's highest flight above Willow Run was 43,020 feet, a rare accomplishment at that time for a pilot in a nonpressurized airplane.) The aviator bought himself a Brooks Brothers military uniform — he was to go on "technician status," meaning he could wear a navy uniform without a rank insignia — and an Abercrombie & Fitch waterproof flashlight.

In two months' time, he was piloting a TBF Avenger over the remote Japanese island of Rabaul, strafing a home in the jungle from which enemy tracer fire was blasting. "I hope there was no one in that building except soldiers — no women, no children," he wrote after this mission. "I will never know. There is no time to think about it. Tree tops are 20 feet below, passing at 400 miles per hour."

As for Cast Iron Charlie Sorensen, his departure after thirty-nine years at the company was tainted by political bickering — no surprise.

On March 4, 1944, the newspapers carried a headline that was a shocker for those in the auto business: "Henry Ford Fires Sorensen."

But the story was not as simple as it appeared.

At sixty-three, Sorensen could not bring himself to face another year. Any day now, Willow Run would reach its ultimate goal of a bomber an hour. Sorensen had lived through the hardest three years of his life and had said good-bye to his dear friend and boss Edsel in the process. He informed Henry Ford's secretary, Frank Campsall, that he was going to retire. He spent his last days introducing Henry II to anyone and everyone he could and saying warm good-byes to the men he had managed with ferocious intimidation for decades.

Not long before his final day, which came in January 1944, Sorensen attended a ceremony that moved him deeply. It was not a ceremony for his retirement. He was too impatient to endure such formalities. The ceremony was for Edsel. Sorensen accompanied Henry II to a small gathering at Henry Ford's museum of antique machinery, where Henry had amassed all the original tools in the workshop where he had taught Edsel some basic skills, back when Edsel was a boy. This was the reconstructed workshop where Edsel first ran a band saw and swung a hammer, where he learned to respect the power of machinery after slicing a finger painfully.

At the ceremony, Sorensen stood with Henry Ford for a photograph. It was the last picture they shared together.

On January 15, 1944, Sorensen showed up for his final day of work. The towering white-haired Dane was on his way to his car when Henry Ford pulled up in his own chauffeur-driven ride. Sorensen said he was leaving in the morning for his place in Miami. He wanted to sail his boat into a sunset. He was never coming back. The two men stared awkwardly into each other's tired eyes, wondering how the years had flown by so quickly.

Henry said, "I guess there's something in life besides work."

Sorensen nodded. Henry followed him to his car. They shook hands, and Sorensen pulled away. The two men never saw each other again.

About six weeks after Sorensen's last day, the headlines appeared, saying not that he had retired but that he had been fired. It was likely

Bennett's last cheap shot. And with Sorensen gone, Bennett was one step closer to the ultimate prize, the presidency of Ford Motor Company. The news of Sorensen's departure moved the Shakespearean power struggle into its final act.

"For months the world-straddling empire of Henry Ford has quivered and groaned like a leviathan with acute indigestion," commented *Time* magazine. "Cause of the upheavals has been the rival ambitions of the empire's two powerful princes: tough Director Harry Bennett and smooth Production Boss Charles E. Sorensen. Last week, the empire had its biggest convulsion of all."

Sorensen moved down to his vacation home in Miami, where he tried to find meaning in the sound, not of roaring bomber engines, but of wind whistling through palm fronds. And the Motor City seemed to motor on without him. "He was a hard-boiled, hard-fisted fighter and probably would prefer to be known as such," a Willow Run worker said of Sorensen upon his departure. One day in his mailbox, Sorensen found a letter from Henry Ford II.

"For myself," young Henry wrote, "I have always felt that every time I had some opportunity to be with you in the shop I would learn something that would be of value to me, at some later date. The various trips we made to Pratt & Whitney, Consolidated, and other places, will always be something that I want to remember. In closing, I should like to say that I know all the rest of the family feel as I do, and I am sure my father would also if he were alive today. I should like to feel that you would call on me if I can ever be of any help in any way in the future."

Sorensen folded the letter and placed it in a safe place with his most important documents. Then he slipped his exhausted body into a hammock. He was done with Detroit, he said to his wife. Done with the rubber shortages and the boiling hot metal and the Motor City politics. He couldn't take one more day! Then the phone rang. It seemed there was a job open back in the auto business. The Jeep manufacturer Willys-Overland needed a chief executive. Was Sorensen interested?

He smiled. Damn right, he was.

29

D-Day

Winter to Spring 1944

In this poignant hour, I ask you to join with me in prayer. Almighty God. Our sons, pride of our Nation, this day have set upon a mighty endeavor . . . to set free a suffering humanity.

— ROOSEVELT'S D-DAY PRAYER, June 6, 1944

ON FEBRUARY 20, 1944, the US Air Corps unleashed its full bombing force upon Nazi-occupied Europe. Operation Argument — or "the Big Week," as the press called it — dispatched an average of 722 heavy bombers with 768 fighter escorts daily from the Eighth and Fifteenth Air Forces, for six straight days. As one German historian put it: "Nothing in war history up to that time was even remotely comparable to the annihilating capacity of those hordes in the sky."

Secret military documents listed the American bombers' targets for the President in the White House: eleven fighter plane factories, fifteen bomber factories, seventeen airplane engine plants, twenty submarine yards, thirty-eight locomotive building shops, thirty-seven electric plants, fourteen aluminum plants, two synthetic rubber plants, and twenty-three oil plants.

When the American bombers flew their first mission to strike hard at the heart of Berlin, on March 6, the city crumbled and burned.

"The picture that greeted my eye on the Wilhelmplatz was one of utter desolation," Goebbels wrote in his diary. At the beginning of the war, Goebbels had this to say: "What can the USA do faced with our arms capacity? They can do us no harm." And now? "Blazing fires everywhere," he wrote. "Meanwhile I learn that my mother and my mother-in-law were bombed out completely in Moabit. Their homes have simply vanished."

To report on the state of Berlin for CBS radio, Edward R. Murrow flew over Germany's capital in an Air Corps bomber. "Berlin was a kind of orchestrated hell, a terrible symphony of light and flame," he said in one report. "The job isn't pleasant; it's terribly tiring. Men die in the sky while others are roasted alive in their cellars. . . . This is a calculated, remorseless campaign of destruction."

Following the Big Week, nearly every day in March 1944 bombers with fighter escorts — fleets of some 1,500 warplanes per day — struck at Nazi targets. In April the bombers returned to Ploesti in Romania to destroy Hitler's most important source of oil. The first mission flew on April 5; nine groups of B-24s and four groups of B-17s dropped nearly 1.2 million pounds of TNT on Ploesti on this single mission alone. The TNT reduced the oil refineries to towering columns of smoke that could be seen from tens of miles away.

"We really clobbered them that day," recalled Bill Harvey, a bombardier aboard a Liberator named *Maiden USA*. "Flames shot high in the air and we could see secondary explosions in the refinery and loading areas."

For the next month, bombers continued to rain explosives over Ploesti's refineries, culminating in a May 31 pounding by 428 Liberators.

Inside Germany, Nazi leaders struggled to comprehend the images of Berlin that surrounded them. "Along the Kaiserdamm everything is still on fire," Goebbels wrote in his diary. "Groups of people scamper across the streets like veritable ghosts. . . . The misery that meets my eyes is indescribable. My heart is convulsed at the sights. But we grit our teeth. Sometimes I have the impression that the Berliners are almost in a religious trance."

The bombings assaulted Hitler's nerves so intensely that he had trouble writing his own name. With his hands shaking violently, he found it difficult to sign the forms that crossed his desk day and night. Goering had all but disappeared from the scene; Hitler refused to see him, calling Goering's once-"invincible" Luftwaffe an "absolute failure." By this time, two of Goering's top deputies, Ernst Udet and Hans Jeschonnek, had committed suicide. And each day the American bombers returned, roaring over cities and villages. As Hitler's production chief, Albert Speer, later wrote in his memoirs: "I could see the omens of the war's end almost every day in the blue southern sky when the bombers of the American 15th Air Force crossed the Alps from their Italian bases to attack German industrial targets."

With Ploesti in ruins, Hitler's Panzer tanks stopped in their tracks, robbed of their lifeblood. The Luftwaffe also all but ran out of gas. Speer informed Hitler that "the enemy has succeeded in increasing our losses of aviation gasoline up to 90%."

Crew who flew aboard the Liberators on these missions saw fewer attacking pursuit planes as the spring weeks passed. The Liberators sailed in ever-increasing numbers over Germany, with painted pinups on the fuselages, exotic names ("Strawberry Bitch," "Shady Lady"), and bomb markings indicating the number that each plane had dropped on Nazi-occupied territory. The Liberator airmen called their bomber the "Flying Box Car," "Spam Can in the Sky," and "Old Agony Wagon." Among those who flew aboard B-24s over Germany in these missions were Hollywood leading men Jimmy Stewart and Clark Gable, journalists Walter Cronkite and Andy Rooney, and future presidential candidate George McGovern, among thousands of others.

When Allied military leaders honed in on France's network of railroads, a fierce debate broke out. Bombing the rails would paralyze the Nazis' ability to move munitions about France, upon whose coast the D-Day invasion was about to land. However, it would be impossible to bomb the railroads without killing scores of innocent French citizens who lived nearby.

"Postwar France must be our friend," Churchill pleaded. "It is not alone a question of humanitarianism. It is also a question of high state policy."

In the end, the Free French leaders agreed with General Eisenhower that the plan had to go ahead. French citizens were told by radio and leaflet to evacuate any area near a railroad. In the days before D-Day, Allied heavy bombers dropped seventy-six kilotons of TNT on France's railroad system — about five times the explosive power of the atomic bomb that would soon be dropped on Hiroshima.

On May 4, 1944, a month before the D-Day invasion, the machines at Willow Run shut down momentarily so that workers could gather outside the east end of the assembly building at 2:15 PM. It was a beautiful spring day in southern Michigan, thousands of miles from the combat in Europe and the Far East. On a stage, the American Legion Edsel B. Ford Post Band played, the tubas honking out "America the Beautiful." Harry Wismer — one of the first big sportscasters, who had called the play-by-play for the Detroit Lions on the radio before the war had started — grabbed a microphone as master of ceremonies. The crowd had gathered for the presentation of the Army-Navy "E" Excellence Award for the Willow Run bomber plant.

Willow Run had continued to accelerate production all spring long, speeding toward its goal of a bomber an hour, 400 a month. In March, Ford built 324 Liberators. In April, 325. In May, 350. Soon, there was no doubt, it would hit its mark. The presentation of the Army-Navy Excellence flag signified the approval of Washington — and confirmation that the experiment at Willow Run had fulfilled its promise, that Edsel Ford and Charlie Sorensen had proven all the naysayers wrong.

Onstage, Henry Ford II accepted the "E" flag from the navy's Captain Robert Velz and lifted it triumphantly so that it rippled in a light breeze as the crowd whistled and applauded. The band played "The Star-Spangled Banner" while navy men raised the E flag and the American flag on either side of the stage. Then Henry II took his place in front of the microphone and prepared to give his first speech as a representative of the Ford family. It was fitting that his first major official duty was to honor Willow Run. Henry II was standing in for his father, in what would have been Edsel's most triumphant moment.

He appeared different from a year earlier. His eyes were harder, less forgiving. His face had hardened too. In the months since he had left the navy, under the careful tutelage of Charlie Sorensen, Henry

II had grown into himself and acquired confidence that he would not end up a footnote in the history of the Motor City. He'd begun to exhibit the fearlessness that would define him in later years, when he would become one of the most powerful businessmen in the world. The Ford scion sipped in a breath and began.

"It is certainly with mixed emotions that we meet here today," he said. "Four years ago this spring there was no Willow Run. This land — 1,800 acres of it, covered today by a gigantic monument to industrial might — was producing agricultural products. But war was upon the world and our country's participation was nearing. Mass production of the B-24 Liberator bomber, the largest, fastest and hardest-hitting of them all, was handed to us as our job."

Henry II spoke of the engineering miracle, of the Truman investigation, of the overwhelming social problems that accompanied this industrial adventure. How everything had gone so wrong, and how, through sheer determination and patriotism, the men and women who ran this factory and worked inside it had turned it around. Now everything was going right.

"It is just another proof that in America we can do the impossible," he said. "And that the impossible always proves the nemesis of those enemies of peace and progress who attempt every so often to upset our relentless struggle upward toward a better world for all men everywhere."

In the White House, the President was studying top-secret documents in preparation for D-Day. A military force of staggering size and complexity had already begun to amass in Britain, a force that would swell until it reached 175,000 men, 50,000 vehicles of all types, well over 5,000 ships, and over 11,000 airplanes, plus guns, bullets, medicine, food, and cartons upon cartons of cigarettes from the tobacco fields in the American South, all scheduled to land on French soil in the space of twenty-four hours. This was the Arsenal of Democracy at its height, built not just by the United States but with fantastic contributions from Britain and Canada.

In the Battle of Production, the Nazis were proving an extraordinary foe. Suffering the brutal ravage of the Allied bombers, their production of war munitions continued, the factories filled with slave labor. So ingenious were Hitler's engineers, so nimble and intelligent was his top production man, Albert Speer, that Germany had managed to move machine tools out of bombed-out factories and into underground caves. Airplane engines were being constructed inside mountains. Church bells were melted so that the metal could be used for munitions. One company alone, Krupp, was producing U-boats, 88 anti-aircraft cannons, tanks, guns, and armor of all kinds.

Still, the confidential reports regarding production in America that crossed Roosevelt's desk in the spring of 1944 were nothing short of miraculous — specifically when it came to four-engine bombers. According to a March 1944 top-secret report to the President: "Heavy bomber production was again outstanding with 1,508 acceptances of B-17s and B-24s." The month before the D-Day invasion, a confidential war progress report stated: "May was a great month for planes . . . with heavy bombers making a brilliant showing." Simultaneously, the President received secret wires to his map room telling of the Allies' mastery of the skies in Europe. On May 8, 1944: "Operations of our Air Forces during the past four months have definitely resulted in marked depletion of German Air Power."

In the final hours before D-Day, Roosevelt received another confidential production report. A chart showed "The 'Big Ten' of the Invasion," listing the number of aircraft mass-produced between 1940 and 1944. Number one on the list: the B-24 Liberator. Over 10,000 of them had taken flight. Nearly half of those built so far had rolled out of Willow Run, and in the coming months Ford's production would increase until it was making 70 percent of the nation's Liberators. At the time of the invasion, the Liberator had already become America's most mass-produced airplane of any kind, ever.

By June 5, twenty-four hours before D-Day, the tension in the White House had grown unbearable. Looking at the President, Eleanor Roosevelt saw that her husband had become elderly. Now in his fourth term in the White House and his third year of the war, he had given all he had to his country. According to one presidential secretary, "every movement of his face and hands reflected the tightly contained state of his nerves." On that very day, Rome fell to the Allies. Roosevelt wrote to Churchill: "We have just heard of the fall of Rome and I am about to drink a mint julep to your very good health." But no one could celebrate in the White House.

Operation Overlord – the D-Day invasion – was the largest, most hazardous military enterprise ever to be undertaken. The President had called on his nation to build the Arsenal of Democracy, and his nation had come through for him. All he could do now was sit and wait for news from Europe.

Under the cover of night in the early hours of June 6, 1944, the largest air armada in history banked downward over the beaches of Normandy, flying just 500 feet over the breaking waves. The decibels were immeasurable. "As dawn broke," recalled one captain standing on the beach, "we could observe one of the most impressive sights of any wartime action. Wave after wave of medium and light bombers could be seen sweeping down the invasion beaches to drop their bombs."

"Rosie the Riveter back home had been very busy," said another American who witnessed this scene.

For CBS radio, Murrow was reporting from London, watching the bombers take off on their D-Day missions. "Early this morning we heard the bombers going out," he announced. "It was the sound of a giant factory in the sky."

The first planes to bomb the beaches were B-26 Marauders, built by the Glenn L. Martin Company outside Baltimore. They were powered by Pratt & Whitney Double Wasp engines, a huge number of them built at the Rouge factory in Dearborn, Michigan, under the supervision of Charlie Sorensen and Edsel Ford.

At the same time, 1,200 American heavy bombers swung low over the beaches and over the oil refineries of Ploesti, Romania. Over those oil refineries, 407 B-24s made their attack runs on D-Day, delivering knockout blows.

Flocks of Waco wooden invasion gliders, carrying equipment and airborne troops, whistled engineless over the Normandy beaches, nearly 1,500 aircraft strong. The Wacos had been built by many companies, such as Michigan's Gibson Refrigerator and Arkansas's Ward Furniture Company. But no outfit had built more of those gliders than Ford Motor Company. The predawn landings came in two waves: one named Chicago, the other Detroit.

The Allied forces rolled out their tanks and equipment and guns. Over 1,000 landing craft unloaded men, tanks, Jeeps, and trucks. In the first fifteen hours, American forces pushed 1,700 vehicles onto Utah Beach alone (there were five landing beaches in all).

By the time Overlord's supreme commander, General Eisenhower, set foot on the sand, it was littered with broken vehicles, torn apart by enemy gun and cannon fire. "There was no sight in the war that so impressed me with the industrial might of America as the wreckage on the landing beaches," Eisenhower recalled. "To any other nation the disaster would have been almost decisive. But so great was America's productive capacity that the great storm occasioned little more than a ripple in the development of our build-up."

From day one of World War II, the airplane had revolutionized combat. In the war's climactic battle, it remained a key weapon. On the D-Day beaches, Eisenhower was joined by his son John, who had just graduated from West Point. Above them, Allied planes of all kinds flew over at low altitude, the furious exhaust notes of the engines driving through the percussion of gunfire.

"You'd never get away with this if you didn't have air supremacy," John said to his father.

"If I didn't have air supremacy," General Eisenhower answered, "I wouldn't be here."

The morning of D-Day, the moment clocks hit 10:00 AM in Detroit, citizens all over the city heard a strange orchestra of factory whistles and church bells. The deafening machinery in the myriad war factories was silenced. Workers put down their tools. Schoolchildren dropped their books and pencils on their desks. Buses and streetcars slowed to a stop. Pedestrians with newspapers tucked under their arms — which already had their D-Day headlines because of the time zone difference with Europe — stopped and hung their heads in prayer.

Then, after those few minutes of tribute, the streetcars and autos and buses and factories gunned their engines again. There was a job to do, and the soldiers in the Battle of Production were going to work.

In the offices at Ford Motor Company — as in offices in every city in America — men in suits stood, steadying their nerves, listening over the radio to the speech General Eisenhower gave to his troops upon sending them into battle on D-Day morning. Many would describe a sensation of terrific fragility while listening to Eisenhower's voice. The speech came over the radio again and again, all day long.

> Soldiers, sailors and airmen of the Allied Expeditionary Force. You are about to embark upon a great crusade, toward which we have striven these many months. The eyes of the world are upon you. The hopes and prayers of liberty loving people everywhere march with you. In company with our brave Allies and brothers in arms on other fronts, you will bring about the destruction of the German war machine, the elimination of Nazi tyranny over the oppressed peoples of Europe, and security for ourselves in a free world. . . . Our air offensive has seriously reduced their strength in the air and their capacity to wage war on the ground. Our home fronts have given us an overwhelming superiority in weapons and munitions of war. . . . The tide has turned! The free men of the world are marching together to victory!

One month after D-Day, Willow Run met its goal of a bomber an hour, 400 per month, and then exceeded it. Newspapers across the nation heralded the achievement of Edsel Ford and Charlie Sorensen's bomber factory. Willow Run produced 415 Liberators in July 1944. A month later, that number hit 432.

For the rest of 1944 and deep into 1945, Allied airpower rained terror on the Nazis. It became clear that the war was going to be won, and soon. In his father's corner office, Henry II could see in the newspaper and radio reports what the rest of America was seeing. Under the relentless pounding of heavy bombers and under the conquering treads of Sherman tanks, the Third Reich was crumbling. Good would defeat evil in the end.

But in Dearborn, there was one battle left to fight.

30

The Final Battle

Spring to Fall 1945

Don't make the mistake of pulling the trigger, because I'll kill you. I won't miss. I'll put one right through your heart, Harry.

— JOHN BUGAS

A RUMOR SPREAD THROUGH the Ford offices in 1945 like some kind of bad odor. Henry Ford had created a codicil to his will, it was whispered, and the codicil stipulated that no one could be named president of Ford Motor Company for the present time and for ten years after his death. When Henry passed away, according to these rumors, the board of directors would run the corporation's day-to-day affairs, with Harry Bennett as secretary.

Now eighty-one, Henry's grip on reality had continued to slip away. He was succumbing to time. "There was a great change in his physical appearance," remembered longtime Ford man Charles Voorhess. "He had lost his contented nervous energy and drive." Henry would begin sentences and forget what he was saying. He would ask to see employees who had not worked for him for years or, in some cases, decades. When Henry II visited his grandfather at Fair Lane, he was unable to get through to the old man. It was as if he were talking to a replica of the real Henry Ford.

THE FINAL BATTLE • 279

Young Henry took the news of the codicil gravely. He told the few trusted colleagues he had that he was considering leaving it all behind, that he had just about had enough. He faced the same decision his father had faced so many years before. Edsel could have walked away as a young man and lived a quiet life of luxury, putting his family over his job duties. Instead, he took on the challenge of running the empire. It was probably the hardest decision Edsel ever made, and the one that earned him the most respect in his life.

Henry II pressed on. He agreed with his confidant John Bugas that the only way to handle this situation was to confront Bennett about the codicil. So Bugas went to see Bennett in his office in the basement of the Rouge. Bennett's secretary buzzed him through the door. Bugas found Bennett agreeable.

"You come in here tomorrow," Bennett said, "and we'll straighten the whole thing out."

When Bugas arrived the next day, Bennett produced the document. In a bitter display, he dropped the codicil on the floor, lit a match, and set fire to it. When the document was reduced to a pile of ashes, Bennett swept them up, dumped them in an envelope, and handed it to Bugas.

"Take this back to Henry," he said.

("It wasn't any good anyway," Bennett later said of the document, when questioned by the company's chief legal counsel, I. A. Capizzi. "Mr. Ford had carried the instrument around in his pocket for a long time and had made a lot of scribblings on it, including verses from the Bible.")

Next, Henry II paid a visit to Fair Lane. He made sure that his grandmother Clara was present, as well as Henry.

"I think it's about time we did something to clean this place up," Henry II told his ailing grandfather.

Clara Ford spoke up, trying to get through to her husband. "Henry, I think young Henry should take over."

Henry II left Fair Lane without getting the answer he wanted. But he returned. He refused to give up.

"Look, you're not well," Clara Ford told Henry. "And it's about time somebody got in there."

Henry II said, "There are things going on that shouldn't be going on, and I think we've really got to stand up and do some things. I think that *I've* got to do some things, and I just can't get to you often enough to discuss all the details with you."

As the legend of Ford Motor Company goes, it was Eleanor Ford — Edsel's widow — who came to her son's aid. It was Eleanor who ultimately played a chess move that could not be defended. "He killed my husband," she allegedly said of Henry Ford. "And he's not going to kill my son." She demanded that Henry Ford II become president of Ford Motor Company. "If this is not done," she told the family, "I shall sell my stock."

Her demand sent a shock wave through Dearborn. If Eleanor Ford sold her stock, a large portion of the company would go to the highest bidders on Wall Street. Not in over two decades had anyone owned a crumb of Ford Motor Company outside of the Ford family.

The threat worked. Days later, Henry Ford called his grandson to Fair Lane. Henry I offered Henry II the company's presidency. "Okay, Henry," the old man said, "you take over. You call the board meeting and I'll write my letter of resignation."

Already, Henry II had begun to evolve into the legendary chief executive he was about to become. A year and a half had passed since he had left the navy and returned to Dearborn. In the name of his father, he had fought for the reins of one of the biggest companies in the world — and now he had won. Facing his grandfather's offer of the presidency, Henry II's answer set the tone for the company's next forty years.

"I'll take it only if I have completely free hand to make any change I want to make."

In April 1945, the Allies closed in on Berlin. On the 12th, with American troops less than 100 miles from the Nazi capital, Roosevelt was visiting his retreat in Warm Springs, Georgia, where he had a special pool for polio victims that was built through a charitable donation by Edsel Ford. It was a Thursday. The President was sitting for a portrait by the artist Elizabeth Shoumatoff. As his staff set a lunch table, he told them the portrait would soon be done, to wait just a bit to bring the food.

"We have just fifteen minutes more," he said.

He raised his right hand to his forehead "in a jerky way," as Shoumatoff recalled. After a pause, he put his left hand to the back of his head and muttered his final words: "I have a terrific pain in the back of my head."

His eyes closed and he lost consciousness. Franklin Roosevelt was dead. The President was sixty-two years old, the victim of a cerebral hemorrhage. Today Shoumatoff's painting—*Unfinished Portrait*—hangs in the Little White House Historic Site in Warm Springs.

With American troops closing in, Adolf Hitler remained locked in a secret Berlin bunker with his wife Eva Braun (they had married in a private ceremony on April 29) and his dog Blondi. Also present was Hitler's propaganda chief Joseph Goebbels, with his wife and six kids. They danced, enjoyed champagne, all the while readying themselves for suicide. There was no more use fighting off the American air offensive. "Hitler said it was no good to bomb American airplanes because more of them would come like bees," Goering later recalled.

"Believe me," Hitler said of these final hours, "it will be easy to end my life. A brief moment, and I am freed from everything, released from this miserable existence."

The dog was the first to go, poisoned with prussic acid. Eva Braun was next, also taking the poison. When she had sucked in her last breath, Hitler sat to the right of her slumped figure and whiffed the almond stink of the acid she had swallowed. He lifted his 7.65-millimeter Walther, aimed at his right temple, and pulled the trigger. The date was April 30, ten days after his fifty-sixth birthday. Goebbels followed, taking his wife and all six of his young children with him in the act of suicide.

Berlin fell two days later.

On May 7, 1945, Nazi Germany offered the unconditional surrender that Franklin Roosevelt and Winston Churchill had called for at the Casablanca Conference. In Detroit that morning, the streets crowded with revelers who stood ankle-deep in confetti hurled out the windows of the tall buildings downtown. Fearing the worst, the State Liquor Control Commission ordered all liquor stores closed and locked for twenty-four hours. Thousands huddled around radios to listen to the official announcement of V-E Day from the new president, Harry Truman, whose ambitious work with the Truman Committee throughout the war had vaulted the Missouri senator all the way to the vice presidency and now, with the death of Roosevelt, the office of the nation's chief executive.

On August 6, under orders from President Truman, the Allies' new superbomber, the Boeing B-29 Superfortress, dropped the "Little Boy" bomb on Hiroshima in Japan. Three days after "Little Boy," the second atomic bomb, "Fat Man," landed on Nagasaki.

Japan surrendered on August 14. On that morning, the *Detroit News* banner headline read: "Truman's Proclamation – War Ends!"

The month that Hitler died, signs appeared all over Willow Run.

"To the Employees of The Ford Willow Run Plant: Changing war needs and the rapid collapse of the German Luftwaffe have reduced requirements by the Army Air Forces for the B-24 Bomber. Consequently, production will be scaled down progressively and will cease not later than August 1, 1945."

So swift was the fall of the Third Reich, however, that production ended sooner, at the end of June. When the last of the bombers rolled out of Willow Run – the 8,685th ship – Henry Ford II was there to host a ceremony. The ship was named the *Henry Ford,* though Henry I asked that his name be removed so that the workers who had built the bomber could sign their names before the army took possession.

Already by this time, the first newsreels from the liberated Nazi concentration camps had reached the masses in the United States. In these camps, the principles of American-style mass production had been applied to murder by Hitler's chief henchmen, Heinrich Himmler (who died of suicide on May 23, 1945) and Adolf Eichmann (who escaped to South America before his capture and execution in 1962), among others. When Henry Ford saw these images on newsreels, he suffered an attack of anxiety and ran out of the room. Even for Henry, the great pacifist, the images of the concentration camps redefined the work of Willow Run. It had been the work not of war but of justice.

On September 21, five weeks after Japan's surrender, the board of directors of Ford Motor Company gathered in an office in Dearborn. Henry II arrived. His mother Eleanor stood beside him. There in the conference room, a picture of Edsel hung on the wall. Harry Bennett arrived in his usual bow tie, quite aware of what was about to unfold. Henry II's younger brother Benson refused to attend, having sworn never to be in the same room with Bennett.

Henry Ford's secretary Frank Campsall read Henry's letter of resignation. Halfway through, Bennett stood and headed for the door, but Campsall stopped reading. All present asked Bennett to remain until the end out of respect for the board of directors, which he did.

Henry Ford II was named president of Ford Motor Company.

After the meeting, Bennett marched to Henry II's corner office. "You're taking over a billion-dollar organization here that you haven't contributed a thing to," he said.

Henry II responded by informing Bennett that he was fired.

"I was frightened to death it would not stick," Henry II later remembered. "I was physically scared and mentally scared."

The job fell to John Bugas to make sure it *did* stick. Later that day, the former G-man wiggled a .38 into his belt and headed for Bennett's office in the basement of the Rouge. When he pushed open the door, he saw a pair of rabid eyes aimed his way.

"You son of a bitch!" Bennett wailed.

He pulled his .45 automatic.

Bugas aimed his .38.

And for a moment, the rivaling factions that had torn America's most famous company apart for over two decades faced each other in the vessels of two men in suits, aiming gun barrels at each other across a mahogany desk.

"Don't make the mistake of pulling the trigger," Bugas said, "because I'll kill you. I won't miss. I'll put one right through your heart, Harry."

Bennett stared down the .38's barrel. Bugas's hand was steady. Bennett eased his .45 downward and offered his crooked smile. It was over.

For the rest of the day, smoke spewed from behind Bennett's office door as he burned all his papers. And for the next few weeks, Henry II took great pleasure in firing all of Bennett's cronies, over 1,000 men, personally.

Harry Bennett moved out of his "Castle." He gave a statement to the press, trying to save face; the appointment of John Bugas in his place was "just as I planned it," Bennett said. "I brought him into the company and expected him some day to fill my shoes." Bennett then disappeared forever into obscurity.

Facing retirement and his eighty-second birthday, Henry Ford complained bitterly over the disappearance of his aide-de-camp. On several occasions, he tried to reach Bennett by phone. But Bennett did not bother to answer. Then one day, after more than twenty years of seeing Bennett daily, the old man got used to not having him around.

"Well," Henry Ford said, "I guess Harry is back where he started from."

Epilogue

I flew thirty-five missions as a copilot on B-24s with the 392nd
Bomb Group. It's almost certain that anyone who flew a B-24
in training or overseas would have flown a Ford B-24 at some
point in time. When they reached the peak production at Willow Run, they were building one every fifty-eight minutes or
something like that. It's amazing. It's a big airplane and it's
complicated, and there are many, many parts. Years after the
war, I toured the Willow Run plant. I think General Motors was
building transmissions there at the time. In my imagination,
I could see the B-24s being built. It made me feel with wonder that such a thing could take place in such a short time. It's
an indication of how the entire country came together after the
Japanese bombed Pearl Harbor. It was a time that will not be
experienced again. It's difficult to describe exactly how it happened and why it happened. But it did.

— Oak Mackey, *Mesa, Arizona*

As DWIGHT EISENHOWER WROTE of World War II, "America's record in production, as well as on the battle line, is one that will fill our
histories forever." "The American war production job," wrote Donald Nelson, head of the War Production Board, "was probably the
greatest collective achievement of all time. It makes the 'seven won-
ders' of the ancient world look like the doodling of a small boy." Or as
Roosevelt himself said before his death, "The production necessary
to equip and maintain our vast forces of fighting men on global bat-

tlefronts is without parallel. I need not repeat the figures. The facts speak for themselves."

The United States produced 324,750 airplanes during World War II, more than Great Britain and the Soviet Union (the numbers two and three aircraft producers during the war) combined. To this day, the B-24 Liberator remains the most mass-produced American military aircraft ever. "The number of people involved in making it, in servicing it, and in flying the B-24 outnumbered those involved with any other airplane, in any country, in any time," wrote Stephen Ambrose in *The Wild Blue*. "It would be an exaggeration to say that the B-24 won the war for the Allies. But don't ask how they could have won the war without it."

Of the total 18,482 Liberators built during the war, 8,685 of them rolled out of Willow Run. A total of 80,774 workers (61 percent men, 39 percent women) staffed the bomber plant, with a peak employment of 42,331. The cost to make each Liberator dropped from $238,000 per ship at the beginning of production to $137,000 at the end. Under the guidance of Edsel Ford and Charlie Sorensen, Ford Motor Company also built 57,851 aviation engines at the Rouge, plus 277,896 Jeeps, 93,217 trucks, 26,954 tank engines, 2,718 tanks, 87,390 aircraft generators, 52,281 aircraft superchargers, 10,877 squad tents, 12,314 armored cars, and 2,401 jet bomb engines (which powered the new JB-2 Loon, the American copy of Hitler's V1 and V2 flying bombs, the first-ever pilotless missiles). From its Kingsford lumber mill, the company built 4,291 invasion gliders. The total dollar figure of war matériel that came off the company's assembly lines was $4,966,314,000 (in 1945 dollars).

After V-J Day, Detroit held a jubilee, with William Knudsen – the sixty-six-year-old former president of General Motors and now lieutenant general in the US Army – as its master of ceremonies. The streets crowded with revelers, blacks celebrating side by side with whites the achievement of the Motor City. It was without a doubt the greatest collective achievement of any American city, in any time, and one that could never be replicated again, under any circumstance.

For its role in World War II, Detroit still today enjoys the nickname "The Arsenal of Democracy."

• • •

In Washington, armies of office workers began the arduous job of cataloging all the government documents that, in their own way, tell the story of World War II. Among these millions upon millions of documents were the numerous reports on Treasury Department and other government agency investigations into the activities of American corporations in Nazi-occupied territory during the war.

In the case of Edsel Ford, his relationship to Maurice Dollfus, and the mysterious 1943 African Ford company, no clear evidence presented itself that Edsel knowingly profited by helping to build Hitler's arsenal after the war started. On the contrary, the Treasury investigation appeared to hinge on a misunderstanding of a single sentence, written by Edsel to Dollfus: "I have shown your letter to my father and Mr. Sorensen and they both join me in sending best wishes for you and your staff, and hope that you will continue to carry on with the good work you are doing."

Edsel was one among many American executives who got caught in Hitler's web and who found himself in the position to fight for the survival of his family's empire in Europe as a result. His father's controversial stance against the war and his antipathy to the Roosevelt administration certainly did not help Edsel's cause.

Today the Treasury investigation report on Edsel Ford can be found in the National Archives in College Park, Maryland, where journalists and authors are free to interpret it as they see fit.

American military investigators swarmed Nazi Germany when it was all over to see for themselves what the bombers had accomplished. They brought trunks full of camera equipment and interviewed survivors. "People think they are wandering in an absurd dream," remembered one German survivor. "The population seems to have melted down to a third or a quarter of what it was in one blow." Said another: "The end of the world certainly can't be worse."

Days after the Nazis surrendered, Charles Lindbergh ventured into Germany as a guest of some military officers. Lindbergh stood in awe of what he saw.

"When you looked at the cities, you felt it would take a century for the Germans to rebuild and reorganize," he wrote in his journal. Lindbergh visited Hitler's office, or what was left of it, and stood in the chamber where Hitler had thrown "the human world into the greatest convulsion it has ever known and from which it will be recuperating for generations," as the aviator put it. Lindbergh also visited the Dora-Mittelbau concentration camp, where thousands of prisoners were worked to death building V-2 missiles for the Nazis in factories located in underground tunnels. "Here was a place where men and life and death had reached the lowest form of degradation," he wrote.

The detailed US Army investigation into the Combined Bomber Offensive's relentless campaign against Nazi Germany unearthed the following facts:

> In the attack by Allied air power, almost 2,700,000 tons of bombs were dropped, more than 1,440,000 bomber sorties and 2,680,000 fighter sorties were flown. In the wake of these attacks there are great paths of destruction. In Germany, 3,600,000 dwelling units, approximately 20% of the total, were destroyed or heavily damaged. Survey estimates show some 300,000 civilians killed and 780,000 wounded. The number made homeless aggregates 7,500,000. The principal German cities have been largely reduced to hollow walls and piles of rubble. These are the scars across the face of the enemy, the preface to the victory that followed.

It was a costly victory. Of the 416,800 American battle deaths in World War II, 79,265 were airmen.

The Allied personnel marching through Nazi Germany in the spring and summer of 1945 found a surprise waiting for them. They discovered innumerable German military trucks, and later airplane parts, built by the German divisions of Detroit motor companies. Trucks built in Nazi-occupied territory by Ford-Werke AG and GM-owned Opel had mobilized Wehrmacht soldiers throughout the war. Little of this was reported in the press at the time. It was a small story that would grow bigger through the years, inconvenient for everyone involved.

Among the many investigators working in Germany from the US

Army's Financial Branch, a Brooklyn-born thirty-five-year-old attorney named Henry Schneider was dispatched to look into the affairs of Ford Motor Company's German division. When Schneider arrived at Ford's Cologne factory, he found that much of the machinery had been dispersed to other locations, given that Cologne had taken a beating from the bombings. The factory itself, however, was largely intact, save for broken glass from shelling during the fall of the city to the Allies.

Schneider found one Robert Schmidt in charge; Schmidt had been appointed by Hitler's chief war production man, Albert Speer, to place all of Ford's factories in Nazi-occupied territory in the service of the German war machine. Dr. Heinrich Albert — the man who had convinced Edsel Ford and Charlie Sorensen to agree to build trucks for the Nazis before the war — had been imprisoned for six months; he was suspected to have taken a part in the attempted assassination of Hitler on July 20, 1944.

At the Cologne factory, Schneider found in-house publications signed by Robert Schmidt swearing allegiance to the Nazis. ("We too are soldiers of the Fuehrer," Schmidt had written.) In Schneider's interviews with Schmidt, the German revealed the whole story: Before the war, and under pressure from the Nazi high command, he and Dr. Albert had convinced Ford of Dearborn to build trucks for the German government and had also bullied Ford of Dearborn into exporting critical raw materials like rubber and pig iron into Germany. He admitted that the German executives seized all of Ford's assets in occupied territory (most notably in France and in Germany) from their American bosses when the war began.

"Until 1939," the Schneider report reads, "all important matters of policy were settled from America, but after the outbreak of war American influence decreased and ceased altogether in 1941."

According to the official report, "after the outbreak of the war the Cologne works became the most important supplier of trucks to the German armed forces concentrating on the 3-ton type. The number of employees increased from about 3,500 in 1937 to over 8,000 in 1944." Schneider also learned that, as in most other Nazi war factories, Ford's had utilized vast numbers of forced laborers. At the time of D-Day, the Cologne factory had 870 forced workers from Russia and Eastern Europe, 497 Italian POW workers—nearly 2,000 total workers from outside Germany helping to build Hitler's arsenal.

On the very day the Nazis announced their unconditional surrender, the first postwar truck rolled out of Ford-Werke in Cologne. Soon more trucks rolled out, by the hundreds. Among other things, these trucks were used to begin carrying slave laborers back to their homes.

In 1998 a woman named Elsa Iwanowa filed a lawsuit against Ford Motor Company in the United States. She said she was abducted from her town in Russia and forced to work at Ford-Werke in Cologne. "The conditions were terrible. They put us in barracks, on three-tier bunks," she said in an interview with the *Washington Post*. "It was very cold; they did not pay us at all and scarcely fed us. The only reason that we survived was that we were young and fit."

Iwanowa's case was dismissed because the court lacked jurisdiction over the matter. However, following the lawsuit, Ford Motor Company launched a three-and-a-half-year research project with over forty-five archivists and historians to uncover exactly what happened at Ford-Werke during World War II. That study, *Research Findings About Ford-Werke Under the Nazi Regime,* can be found in various libraries. At no point, it concluded, did Edsel Ford, Charlie Sorensen, or any other American Ford executive play any role of aiding or approving of Nazi conduct during the war.

Henry Ford said during World War II that when it was over, he would use Willow Run to begin producing a Ford cargo plane. Those plans, however, were scrapped. Employees spent weeks at the bomber plant picking apart the B-24s flown back home from theaters of war. The Liberators were pocked with bullet holes, torn up by the legendary German 88 anti-aircraft cannons, and stained with the blood of the men who flew aboard them. Government equipment (bombs, machine guns, bombsights) was removed and confiscated. Laborers oiled the planes for storage, and hundreds were shipped to a desert facility in New Mexico, where they were left to rot.

The Liberator's time had come and gone. It was already technologically obsolete. Today there are but a few left, mostly in the hands of aviation museums. The last of the Liberators built at Willow Run —

Bomber Ship 8685, which held the signatures of Willow Run employees on its silver fuselage—was moved to downtown Detroit in 1945 and enshrined as a peace memorial for Edsel Ford. There it sat, beaten by the sun in summer and frozen by the Detroit winds in winter. Soon, it too rusted out and was taken away for scrap.

On April 7, 1947, Henry Ford died peacefully in his home at the age of eighty-three. He rests today at Ford Cemetery in Detroit. Not long before his death, he admitted his fears for the future, for what technology and machinery could do to our planet: "We have progressed so rapidly in developing machinery for killing people that humanity could not survive another war."

In Edsel Ford's corner office, Henry Ford II took control of his family's empire. He presented the first postwar Ford automobile as a gift to the new president, Harry Truman. In the following years, Henry II put in place many of the plans his father Edsel had tried to implement: a new corporate flow chart, a team of college-educated executives, nuance of every kind. Having entered the war far behind Chrysler Corporation as the number three automaker in the nation, Ford Motor Company was soon battling once again for the title of America's car brand. In honor of his father Edsel, Henry II engineered the greatest corporate comeback ever at the time. Among his most important executives was John Bugas, who made company vice president in 1959 and continued to work for Ford until his retirement in 1968.

When Henry II died in 1987, Ford Motor Company was the biggest and most technologically advanced automaker in the world.

Willow Run was sold to General Motors in 1953. GM built over 82 million transmissions in the factory until 2010, when the giant plant closed its doors for good. As of press time for this book, the factory is scheduled to be demolished. History's wrecking ball will reduce the plant to dust. But the story of the bomber-an-hour adventure—a true tale that "rivals the weirdest of fiction and the wildest imaginings of the comic books," in Cast Iron Charlie Sorensen's words—will live on.

A Note on the Text and Acknowledgments

I USED INNUMERABLE SOURCES to synthesize this narrative and its dialogue, and yet no two sources ever tell the same story. In some cases, points of view vary wildly — both those of people who were present during the events depicted in this book and those who have examined them through history's looking glass. What I tried to do was to see these events unfolding through as many points of view as possible, so that I could mold all the sources and opinions and emotions that I came across in my years of research into a narrative that I feel is honorable, while taking the form of a book that can be consumed with clarity.

The dialogue was reconstituted using innumerable sources; I did not make up a word of it myself. In rare instances, I pulled characters' descriptions of events and used their own words as dialogue. For example, in a scene in the White House on May 10, 1940, Franklin Roosevelt sat with his trusted confidants around him, discussing the shocking news of Hitler's attack on Belgium, Holland, Luxembourg, and parts of France. I have him saying: "But the new element — air navigation — steps up the speed of possible attack to 200, to 300 miles an hour." Various sources confirm the subject matter of the conversation that morning in the White House. Roosevelt uttered these specific words two days later in a speech. I re-created the scene in the White House by putting his exact words in his mouth. In these rare instances where a piece of dialogue was moved from one moment in time to another, I was careful to preserve the context in which the words were uttered so that their meaning did not change in any way.

In the end, my moral compass took the form of a question: would the people I am writing about find truth in my portrayal of them?

This book gives my name on the cover, but it is the effort of many people. I would like to express my extreme indebtedness to my superb editor, Susan Canavan, and my agent Scott Waxman for believing in this project. Their faith and their many hours of hard work on my behalf have quite frankly changed the trajectory of my future, and for that I am forever grateful. It's always best to do business with the best and brightest, and I have been blessed in this regard with both of you. I would like to thank everyone at Houghton Mifflin Harcourt and at the Waxman Leavell Literary Agency for their efforts as well.

My enduring gratitude goes out to various archivists and librarians at the Benson Ford Research Center in Dearborn, Michigan; the FDR Library in Hyde Park, New York; the National Archives in College Park, Maryland; the National Automotive History Collection at the Detroit Public Library; the Lindbergh Papers at the Yale University Library in New Haven, Connecticut; and the Chicago Public Library. Special thanks go to Greg Bradsher at the National Archives for his work on my behalf and for his great company during the days I spent in College Park.

My wife Michelle offered her valuable criticisms of this book. If I had not met her on July 19, 2000, I'd still be on page 1—not of this book but of everything in my life. How do you say thank you for something like that?

My mother Denise and my father David read every draft of this manuscript. Both would have made terrific editors. Thank you, Mom and Dad; I hope this book makes up for some of what I put you through when I was a teenager.

I want to thank the following people for sharing their thoughts and memories of World War II and of Willow Run: Carol Lemons, Robert Todd, my wonderful grandfather-in-law Kenneth Wheeldon, Benjamin Napolitano (and his brilliant son Chris), Jack Goetz, Marvin Graham, and Les Hadley. Thank you to Henry Dominguez, author of the book *Edsel: The Story of Henry Ford's Forgotten Son,* for helping me to set up some of these interviews. I would like to add a special appreciation for Oak Mackey, Liberator pilot, who shared not only his memories with me but also his technical knowledge of how the airplane functioned.

More special thanks go to Ken Gross—the most universally respected journalist I have ever met. Thank you, Ken, for your close reads of this manuscript.

I wish to express my immeasurable gratitude to Justin Manask, Lucas Foster, and Alex Young in Los Angeles for more than I could possibly put here in the space of a paragraph.

Also, I could not have put together the photo insert for this book without the help of the master of all imagery researchers, Matthew Steigbigel.

I would like to thank my family, whom I can never repay for all their love and support through the years: my sister Abby, my stepmother Susan Baime, my Aunt Karen and Uncle Ken Segal (who have always treated me like I was one of their own), my "outlaws" Connie and the late Bill Burdick, Jack and Margo Ezell, and Ken and Edna Wheeldon, my many cousins and nieces and nephews of the amazing Crystal/Sabel/Segal clan, and Oliver, Peter, and the late Ellen Segal. More special thanks go to Jimmy Jellinek and all the editors at *Playboy* magazine for their support through the years, and to Sam Walker, Darren Everson, Adam Thompson, and Leslie Yazel at the *Wall Street Journal*.

The following books proved most valuable in my research: *The Fords: An American Epic* by Peter Collier and David Horowitz, *Wheels for the World* by Douglas Brinkley, and *My Forty Years with Ford* by Charles Sorensen. Doris Kearns Goodwin's *No Ordinary Time: Franklin and Eleanor Roosevelt: The Home Front in World War II* and Jon Meacham's *Franklin and Winston: An Intimate Portrait of an Epic Friendship* are both must-reads. From an aviation perspective, *The Wartime Diaries of Charles Lindbergh*, Stephen E. Ambrose's *The Wild Blue: The Men and Boys Who Flew the B-24s over Germany, 1944–1945*, and Michael Sherry's *The Rise of American Airpower* were most helpful. The following two books proved a great foundation for beginning research on the home front: *A Democracy at War: America's Fight at Home and Abroad in World War II* by William O'Neill and *Don't You Know There's a War On?: The American Home Front, 1941–1945* by Richard Lingeman.

Finally, this book is dedicated to my family—Michelle, Clayton, Audrey, and yes, even you, Carl Carlson. I remain the luckiest bastard on earth.

Notes

page

v "Every single man, woman": "A New American Creed," *Detroit News*, December 10, 1941, p. 1. See also Robert Dallek, *Franklin D. Roosevelt and American Foreign Policy, 1932–1945* (New York: Oxford University Press, 1995), p. 317.

"I refuse to recognize": Douglas Brinkley, *Wheels of the World* (New York: Penguin, 2003), p. xv.

vii (Cover image) B-24 Liberator bombers in flight: Statistics for the B-24 are from National Museum of the United States Air Force, "Consolidated B-24D Liberator," February 4, 2011, available at: http://www.nationalmuseum.af.mil/factsheets/factsheet.asp?id=494 (accessed January 8, 2014).

Introduction

xi "the biggest wartime boomtown": Nelson Lichtenstein, *The Most Dangerous Man in Detroit: Walter Reuther and the Fate of American Labor* (New York: Basic Books, 1995), p. 176.

xii "amazing and shocking": Morgenthau, memo to FDR, May 25, 1943, "Ford Motor Company, Foreign Funds Control," box 636, FDR Library, Hyde Park, NY.

"Here was the power": Charles Lindbergh, *Of Flight and Life* (New York: Scribner's, 1948), p. 9.

"city forging thunderbolts": "A City That Forges Thunderbolts," *New York Times*, January 10, 1943, p. SM13.

Prologue

xiii On the night of December 29, 1940: Robert E. Sherwood, *Roosevelt and Hopkins: An Intimate History* (New York: Harper and Brothers, 1948), pp. 216–18; Kenneth S. Davis, *FDR: The War President, 1940–1943* (New York: Random House, 2000), pp. 81–82; Doris Kearns Goodwin, *No Ordinary Time: Franklin and Eleanor Roosevelt: The*

Home Front in World War II (New York: Simon & Schuster, 1994), pp. 194–96.

"Grace! How many times": Sherwood, *Roosevelt and Hopkins*, p. 217.

xiv "My friends, this is not": The text of FDR's "Great Arsenal of Democracy" speech was published in hundreds of newspapers. See "Franklin Delano Roosevelt: The Great Arsenal of Democracy," American Rhetoric: Top 100 Speeches, available at: www.americanrhetoric.com/speeches/fdrarsenalofdemocracy.html (accessed September 30, 2013).

xv "The Fuehrer is not just": William Stephenson, *A Man Called Intrepid: The Secret War* (New York: Ballantine Books, 1976), p. 97.

"If one makes a toy": Nevile Henderson, *Failure of a Mission: Berlin, 1937–1939* (New York: Putnam, 1940), p. 100.

"I am putting on the uniform": "Nazis Attack Poles by Land and Air," *Detroit News*, September 1, 1939, p. 1.

xvi "walls of sand that": Goodwin, *No Ordinary Time*, p. 41.

"The London that we knew": Ibid., p. 151.

"There are no words": Edward R. Murrow, *In Search of Light: The Broadcasts of Edward R. Murrow, 1938–1961* (New York: Alfred A. Knopf, 1967), p. 37.

"like criminals behind": Goodwin, *No Ordinary Time*, p. 175.

"The whole industrial strength": Donald M. Nelson, *Arsenal of Democracy: The Story of American War Production* (New York: Harcourt Brace & Co., 1946), pp. 130, 167.

xvii "The Nazi masters": FDR, the "Great Arsenal of Democracy" speech. "When I visited the still-burning": Goodwin, *No Ordinary Time*, p. 197.

xviii "What can the USA do": Ibid., p. 240.

1. Henry

3 "With his Model T": Norman Beasley, *Knudsen: A Biography* (Whittlesey House, 1947), p. 34.

4 "Mr. Bishop had his bicycle": Peter Collier and David Horowitz, *The Fords: An American Epic* (San Francisco: Encounter, 2002), pp. 1–2.

"Every clock in the Ford": Richard Snow, *I Invented the Modern Age: The Rise of Henry Ford* (New York: Scribner's, 2013), p. 16.

"I've been on the wrong": Collier and Horowitz, *The Fords*, p. 17.

5 "Mrs. Ford didn't give": Henry Dominguez, *Edsel: The Story of Henry Ford's Forgotten Son* (Detroit: Society of Automotive Engineers, 2002), p. 10.

"You can see he's smart": Ibid.

6 "Here comes that crazy": Collier and Horowitz, *The Fords*, p. 21.

"Crazy like a fox": Don Mitchell, *Driven: A Photobiography of Henry Ford* (Washington, DC: National Geographic, 2010), p. 16.

"Thrilling Trip on the First": Douglas Brinkley, *Wheels for the World* (New York: Penguin, 2003), p. 33.

7 living with Henry's: Ford R. Bryan, *Clara: Mrs. Henry Ford* (Dearborn, MI: Ford Books, 2001), p. 62 (the home is pictured).

"You'll never make a go": Collier and Horowitz, *The Fords*, p. 25.

he managed to gather: Brinkley, *Wheels for the World*, pp. 61–62.

"Let's run it!": Ibid., p. 70.

2. The Machine Is the New Messiah

9 "There is in manufacturing": Vincent Curcio, *Chrysler: The Life and Times of an Automotive Genius* (New York: Oxford University Press, 2000), p. 118.

10 "Excitement was in the air": George W. Stark, *City of Destiny: The Story of Detroit* (Detroit: Arnold-Powers, 1943), p. 501.

"Detroit in those days": Norman Beasley, *Knudsen: A Biography* (New York: Whittlesey House, 1947), p. 59.

11 "Come with me, Charlie": Charles E. Sorensen, with Samuel T. Williamson, *My Forty Years with Ford* (Detroit: Wayne State University Press, 2006), p. 96.

"I'd like to have a room": Ibid.

"I will build a motorcar": Henry Ford, with Samuel Crowther, *My Life and Work* (Whitefish, MT: Kessinger, 2004), p. 73.

12 "The man who places a part": Ibid., p. 83.

"When Henry Ford took me": Douglas Brinkley, *Wheels for the World* (New York: Penguin, 2003), p. 137.

"Fancy a jungle of wheels": Julian Street and Wallace Morgan, *Abroad at Home* (New York: The Century Company, 1914), p. 93.

"The Ford Motor Company": Brinkley, *Wheels for the World*, p. 162.

14 "He's crazy, isn't he?": Collier and Horowitz, *The Fords*, p. 49.

"Biblical principles": Ibid.

"see to it that he's": Robert Lacey, *Ford: The Men and the Machine* (Boston: Little, Brown, 1986), pp. 222–23.

"Five dollars a day was": Brinkley, *Wheels for the World*, p. 171.

"We are going to make it": Beasley, *Knudsen*, p. 71.

15 "the Zeus of American mythology": Reynold M. Wik, *Henry Ford and Grass Roots America* (Ann Arbor: University of Michigan Press, 1972), p. 6.

ranked Henry Ford third: Charles Higham, *Trading with the Enemy* (Lincoln, NE: Authors Guild Backinprint.com, 2007), p. 154.

"The machine is the new messiah": Henry Ford, "Machinery, the New Messiah," *The Forum* 79, March 1928, pp. 363–64.

"Machinery is accomplishing": Henry Ford and Ray Leone Faurote, *My Philosophy of Industry* (New York: Coward-McCann, 1929), pp. 18–19.

3. Edsel

16 "There is not a scrap": Henry Dominguez, *Edsel: The Story of Henry Ford's Forgotten Son* (Detroit: Society of Automotive Engineers, 2002), p. 4.
"I don't remember": Ibid., p. 13.
17 "Snowed all day": Richard Bak, *Henry and Edsel: The Creation of the Ford Empire* (New York: Wiley, 2003), p. 40.
"Dear Santa Claus, I haven't": Peter Collier and David Horowitz, *The Fords: An American Epic* (San Francisco: Encounter, 2002), p. 28.
"all the family talked about": Ibid., p. 44.
18 "Have you seen Ed?": Collier and Horowitz, *The Fords*, p. 44.
"I told Edsel": Dominguez, *Edsel*, p. 28.
"Father put me through": Ibid.
"the artist in the family": Irving Bacon, oral history, pp. 7 and 18, Benson Ford Research Center, Dearborn, MI.
"handsome enough to charm": Collier and Horowitz, *The Fords*, p. 88.
"Bad headache": Edsel Ford's diary, reprinted in Ford R. Bryan, *Clara: Mrs. Henry Ford* (Dearborn, MI: Ford Books, 2001), p. 352.
"sex dancing": Collier and Horowitz, *The Fords*, p. 86.
19 "Bill, I have a million dollars": Bak, *Henry and Edsel*, pp. 76–77.
OMNIUM RERUM VICISSITUDO: Ibid., p. 133.
"I don't think": Lacey, *Ford*, p. 155.
"I don't envy": Collier and Horowitz, *The Fords*, p. 62.
"Yes, I have a fine son": Ibid., p. 44.
"You wouldn't know": Dominguez, *Edsel*, p. 56.
21 "Men sitting around": Collier and Horowitz, *The Fords*, p. 55.
"Tomorrow at ten": Ibid.
"War is murder": Neil Baldwin, *Henry Ford and the Jews* (New York: PublicAffairs, 2003), p. 52.
"The word 'murderer'": Brinkley, *Wheels for the World*, p. 193.
"I will devote": Baldwin, *Henry Ford and the Jews*, p. 52.
22 "God's fool": Ibid., p. 63.
"a loon ship": Keith Sward, *The Legend of Henry Ford* (New York: Atheneum, 1972), p. 88.
"Young Ford should": Bak, *Henry and Edsel*, p. 98.
"ready to pay": *Owosso Argus-Press*, October 28, 1928, p. 6.
"I want no stay-at-home": "Edsel Ford Dies at 49; Headed Auto Empire 24 Years," *Washington Evening Star*, May 26, 1943, p. 1; see also Richard Snow, *I Invented the Modern Age: The Rise of Henry Ford* (New York: Scribner's, 2013), p. 286.
"All his life he will be": Sward, *The Legend of Henry Ford*, p. 95.

4. Learning to Fly

23   "More than electric lights": Stephen E. Ambrose, *The Wild Blue: The Men and Boys Who Flew B-24s over Germany 1944–1945* (New York: Simon & Schuster, 2001), p. 28.

His first move: "$6 Minimum Ford Wage," *Washington Post*, January 2, 1919, p. 13.

"Well, if Edsel has bought": Douglas Brinkley, *Wheels for the World* (New York: Penguin, 2003), p. 242.

24   "clapping his hands": Robert Lacey, *Ford: The Men and the Machine* (Boston: Little, Brown, 1986), p. 177.

"The fun of playing": Ibid.

25   "could lay claim to": "By Their Works Ye Shall Know Them," *Vanity Fair*, February 1928, p. 62.

By 1927, Henry and Edsel's fortune: William C. Richards, *The Last Billionaire* (New York: Charles Scribner's Sons, 1948), p. 352.

"Well, I'm just flabbergasted": Peter Collier and David Horowitz, *The Fords: An American Epic* (San Francisco: Encounter, 2002), p. 88.

"A Ford can take you": Quoted in, among hundreds of other sources, Robert Palestini, *Going Back to the Future: A Leadership Journey for Educators* (Lanham, MD: Rowman & Littlefield, 2011), p. 85.

26   "My father is a great man": Collier and Horowitz, *The Fords*, p. 45.

"I have not worked out": "Edsel Is the Boss," *Hartford Courant*, April 16, 1939, p. SM5. Edsel is known to have made this statement, with some variations, on more than one occasion.

27   "Great Britain is no longer": Peter FitzSimons, *Charles Kingsford and Those Magnificent Men* (Sidney: HarperCollins Publishers Australia, 2009), unpaginated.

"The thing did leave": Henry Dominguez, *Edsel: The Story of Henry Ford's Forgotten Son* (Detroit: Society of Automotive Engineers, 2002), p. 155.

28   "They were pioneering": William Mayo, oral history, pp. 40–41, Benson Ford Research Center, Dearborn, MI.

"This letter is to wish": Dominguez, *Edsel*, p. 163.

"The Highways of the Sky": Timothy J. O'Callaghan, *The Aviation Legacy of Henry and Edsel Ford* (Detroit: Proctor Publications, 2000), p. 189.

"There are sound economic": Dominguez, *Edsel*, p. 166.

29   "nearest approach to intensity": O'Callaghan, *The Aviation Legacy of Henry and Edsel Ford*, p. 28.

"The news just saturated": Ambrose, *The Wild Blue*, p. 29.

30   "This was the finest ride": "Ford's First Flight Is with Lindbergh," *New York Times*, August 12, 1927, p. 1.

"the godlike power man": A. Scott Berg, *Lindbergh* (New York: Berkley Books, 1999), p. 81.

"I believe that 1928": Dominguez, *Edsel*, p. 166.

5. Father vs. Son

31 "For all their ambition": Charles E. Sorensen, with Samuel T. Williamson, *My Forty Years with Ford* (Detroit: Wayne State University Press, 2006), p. 302.

"Father, I believe": Peter Collier and David Horowitz, *The Fords: An American Epic* (San Francisco: Encounter, 2002), p. 98.

32 "Edsel, you shut up": Douglas Brinkley, *Wheels for the World* (New York: Penguin, 2003), p. 400.

"Mr. Ford didn't go along": Collier and Horowitz, *The Fords*, p. 118.

"What's going on there?": Ibid., p. 92; see also Robert Lacey, *Ford: The Men and the Machine* (Boston: Little, Brown, 1986), p. 264.

"Edsel, if you really need": Lacey, *Ford*, p. 264.

"The next big development": "Edsel Ford: Eager for Rear Engines," *Washington Post*, September 8, 1935, p. B2.

33 "He attained a kind": Roger Burlingame, *Henry Ford: The Greatest Success Story in the History of Industry* (New York: Signet, 1956), p. 114.

"put Jesus Christ in my factory": Samuel S. Marquis, *Henry Ford: An Interpretation* (Detroit: Wayne State University Press, 2007), p. 10.

"There rages in him": Burlingame, *Henry Ford*, p. 120; see also Lacey, *Ford*, p. 178.

"Jewish Jazz—Moron Music": See Lacey, *Ford*, p. 1 of photo insert, for a photograph of the newspaper.

"Does Jewish Power": *The International Jew: The World's Foremost Problem* (Eastford, CT: Martino Publishing, 2010), p. 125.

34 "Mr. Ford's wishes in carrying:" Neil Baldwin, *Henry Ford and the Jews* (New York: PublicAffairs, 2003), p. 103.

"I wish I could send some": Brinkley, *Wheels for the World*, p. 263; see also Baldwin, *Henry Ford and the Jews*, p. 185.

35 "No one can charge that": Baldwin, *Henry Ford and the Jews*, p. 235.

36 "I have responsibility but": Collier and Horowitz, *The Fords*, p. 91.

"I can't even face people": Ibid., p. 98.

"Why doesn't Mr. Ford take": Lacey, *Ford*, p. 292.

"Well, by this time": Collier and Horowitz, *The Fords*, p. 96.

37 "Please be advised": Dominguez, *Edsel*, p. 2.

"It's his business": Carol Gelderman, *Henry Ford: The Wayward Capitalist* (Beard Books, 1981), p. 209.

"The next time you see": Collier and Horowitz, *The Fords*, p. 119.

"Make it a long stay": Sorensen, with Williamson, *My Forty Years with Ford*, p. 309.

38 "You know, gentlemen": William C. Richards, *The Last Billionaire: Henry Ford* (New York: Scribner's, 1948), p. 160.

6. The Ford Terror

39 "During the thirty years": Harry Bennett, as told to Paul Marcus, *Ford: We Never Called Him Henry* (New York: Tom Doherty Associates, 1987), p. 1.

"I could use a man": Ibid., p. 6.

"a pretty tough lot": Ibid.

40 "There may be a lot": Ibid., p. 15.

"Mr. Ford was a dead shot": Ibid., p. 74.

"I am Mr. Ford's": John McCarten, "The Little Man in Henry Ford's Basement," *The American Mercury*, May 1940, p. 7.

"If Mr. Ford told me": Robert Lacey, *Ford: The Men and the Machine* (Boston: Little, Brown, 1986), p. 363.

"peanuts for a salary": Bennett, *Ford: We Never Called Him Henry*, p. 110.

The Casting Director: Peter Collier and David Horowitz, *The Fords: An American Epic* (San Francisco: Encounter, 2002), p. 132.

"The Castle": Bennett, *Ford: We Never Called Him Henry*, p. 143.

41 "They're a lot of tough bastards": McCarten, "The Little Man in Henry Ford's Basement," p. 10.

"You couldn't get": Laurence Sheldrick, oral history, pp. 36–37, Benson Ford Research Center, Dearborn, MI.

"I can replace factories": Collier and Horowitz, *The Fords*, p. 123.

"Later on, the guy": Ibid.

42 "Let them fail": Carol Gelderman, *Henry Ford: The Wayward Capitalist* (Washington, DC: Beard Books, 1981), p. 313.

"Henry Ford is the only American name": Anne O'Hare McCormick, "The Future of the Ford Idea," *New York Times*, May 22, 1932, p. SM1.

"the Mussolini of Detroit": Keith Sward, *The Legend of Henry Ford* (New York: Atheneum, 1972), p. 369.

"whose particular genius": Allan Nevins and Frank Ernest Hill, *Ford: Decline and Rebirth, 1933–1962* (New York: Scribner's, 1963), p. 17.

43 "If Henry Ford would": "Edsel Ford," file 680, Franklin Roosevelt Papers, "President's Personal File," FDR Library, Hyde Park, NY.

"Well, he took up": William C. Richards, *The Last Billionaire: Henry Ford* (New York: Scribner's, 1948), p. 382.

"Ford Motor Company employees": "Ford Raises Wages $19,500,000 a Year," *New York Times*, December 4, 1929, p. A1.

"That's no good": Collier and Horowitz, *The Fords*, p. 91.

"Edsel Ford is more": Lacey, *Ford*, p. 334.

44 "the most powerful": McCarten, "The Little Man in Henry Ford's Basement," p. 9.

"There are about eight hundred": Nevins and Hill, *Ford: Decline and Rebirth*, p. 150.

"I think it was just fear": Roscoe Smith, oral history, p. 75, Benson Ford Research Center, Dearborn, MI.

"*Go like hell*": Gelderman, *Henry Ford*, p. 319.

"Henry had a way": Richard Bak, *Henry and Edsel: The Creation of the Ford Empire* (New York: Wiley, 2003), p. 161.

45 "the dirty little secret": Collier and Horowitz, *The Fords*, p. 111.

"all right": "Edsel Ford Stricken Ill on Maine Train," *Daily Boston Globe*, September 15, 1931, p. 4.

"Who is this man Bennett": Charles E. Sorensen, with Samuel T. Williamson, *My Forty Years with Ford* (Detroit: Wayne State University Press, 2006), p. 256.

46 "I don't want you to go": Nevins and Hill, *Ford: Decline and Rebirth*, p. 140.

"This is Ford property": Sward, *The Legend of Henry Ford*, p. 391.

General Motors paid $1 million: Ed Cray, *Chrome Colossus: General Motors and Its Times* (New York: McGraw-Hill, 1980), p. 288.

47 "Labor unions are the worst": Roger Burlingame, *Henry Ford: The Greatest Success Story in the History of Industry* (New York: Signet, 1956), p. 101; see also Brinkley, *Wheels for the World*, p. 145.

"a strong, aggressive man": Sorensen, with Williamson, *My Forty Years with Ford*, p. 259.

"If you want to fight": Henry Dominguez, *Edsel: The Story of Henry Ford's Forgotten Son* (Detroit: Society of Automotive Engineers, 2002), p. 278.

"If it takes bloodshed": Lacey, *Ford*, p. 370.

"They picked up my feet": Victor G. Reuther, *The Brothers Reuther and the Story of the UAW* (Boston: Houghton Mifflin, 1976), p. 202.

"My head was like": Bak, *Henry and Edsel*, p. 225.

"I do not know how many times": Gelderman, *Henry Ford*, p. 330.

"Oh my God, he looked": Reuther, *The Brothers Reuther and the Story of the UAW*, p. 202.

48 "The end of my spine": Lacey, *Ford*, p. 356.

"There is a cameraman": Sward, *The Legend of Henry Ford*, p. 394.

"His soul bled": Lacey, *Ford*, p. 379.

49 "It was like a family": Collier and Horowitz, *The Fords*, p. 96.

7. Danger in Nazi Germany

50   "The German Air Force is": "Goering Flaunts Air Force Threat," *New York Times*, March 2, 1938, p. 10.

51   "Is there going to be": Normal Beasley, *Knudsen: A Biography* (New York: McGraw-Hill, 1947), p. 189.

       "Nobody could afford it": Ibid., p. 90.

       Earlier in the 1930s, Opel had: Simon Reich, *The Fruits of Fascism: Postwar Prosperity in Historical Perspective* (Ithaca, NY: Cornell University Press, 1990), p. 111; see also Reinhold Billstein, Karola Fings, Anita Kugler, and Nicholas Levis, *Working for the Enemy: Ford, General Motors, and Forced Labor in Germany During World War II* (New York: Berghahn Books, 2000), p. 1; Edwin Black, "Hitler's Carmaker: How General Motors Helped Jump-start the Third Reich's Military Machine," *The Jewish Journal*, November 30, 2006; Allan Nevins and Frank Ernest Hill, *Ford: Decline and Rebirth* (New York: Scribner's, 1963), p. 99.

       "scared stiff": Beasley, *Knudsen*, p. 164.

       "Airplanes! Airplanes!": Ibid.

52   "Where is Goering?": Ibid., p. 192.

53   "It would be difficult": Sumner Welles, *The Time for Decision* (New York: Harper and Brothers, 1944), p. 119.

       "Not that I know of": Beasley, *Knudsen*, pp. 193–95.

54   35,000 planes per year: Ibid., p. 195.

       That Goering knows: Ibid.

55   "as big a loss as": "Frank Burke Dies; Famous Spy-Catcher in First World War; Seized Dr. Albert's Brief Case," newspaper clipping, box 1032, stack 270, row 69, compartment 69, shelf 6, "Foreign (Occupied) Area Reports" (entry 368B), Records of the Operations Branch of the Administrative Services Division of the Adjutant General's Office (record group 407), National Archives, College Park, MD.

       "rigged with microphones": V. Y. Tallberg, oral history, p. 87, Benson Ford Research Center, Dearborn, MI.

       "According to the official": Schneider report, p. 31, box 1032, stack 270, row 69, compartment 69, shelf 6, "Foreign (Occupied) Area Reports" (entry 368B), Records of the Operations Branch of the Administrative Services Division of the Adjutant General's Office (record group 407), National Archives, College Park, MD (hereafter "Schneider report").

       "How do you feel about": V. Y. Tallberg, oral history, pp. 84–85, Benson Ford Research Center, Dearborn, MI.

56   "[Dr. Albert] said that if": Ibid., p. 84.

       "There's going to be a war": Ibid., p. 101.

"Government orders do not": Schneider report, p. 27.

57 "I am a great admirer": Mira Wilkins and Frank Ernest Hill, *American Business Abroad: Ford on Six Continents* (Detroit: Wayne State University Press, 1964), p. 270; see also Allan Nevins and Frank Ernest Hill, *Ford: Decline and Rebirth, 1933–1962* (New York: Scribner's, 1963), p. 95.

"The Government of the Reich": Wilkins and Hill, *American Business Abroad*, p. 272.

Sales of cars, trucks, and: *Research Findings About Ford-Werke Under the Nazi Regime*, numerous authors (Dearborn, MI: Ford Motor Co., 2001), p. 18.

58 A number of American companies: Ibid., appendix A.

"No one who is in the public": Wilkins and Hill, *American Business Abroad*, p. 277.

"the Reich was able to extort": Schneider report, p. 4.

59 "We had not only one visit": V. Y. Tallberg, oral history, p. 50, Benson Ford Research Center, Dearborn, MI.

gave Hitler a gift: Schneider report, p. 1; see also "Ford and GM Scrutinized for Alleged Nazi Collaboration," *Washington Post*, November 30, 1998, p. A01.

"What kind of building": V. Y. Tallberg, oral history, p. 91, Benson Ford Research Center, Dearborn, MI.

"They were machining parts": Ibid., p. 92.

Henry's seventy-fifth birthday: "Ford Is Given Nazi Medal on 75th Birthday," *Washington Post*, July 31, 1938.

60 "humanitarian ideals": Max Wallace, *The American Axis: Henry Ford, Charles Lindbergh, and the Rise of the Third Reich* (New York: St. Martin's Press, 2003), p. 146.

"I question the Americanism": "Nazi Honor to Ford Stirs Cantor's Ire," *New York Times*, August 4, 1938, p. 13.

"no sympathy on my part": "Ford for US as Refugee Haven; Denies Sympathy with Nazism," *New York Times*, December 1, 1938, p. 12.

"Do you really want to get": Harry Bennett, as told to Paul Marcus, *Ford: We Never Called Him Henry* (New York: Tom Doherty Associates, 1987), p. 1.

Charlie Sorensen agreed to: Schneider report, p. 6.

Gallup poll taken in 1939: Richard Breitman and Allan J. Lichtman, *FDR and the Jews* (Cambridge, MA: Belknap Press of Harvard University Press, 2013), p. 146.

61 "Whatever the political": Johannes Reiling, *Deutschland, Safe for Democracy?* (Erlangen: Nuremberg University Press, 1997), pp. 400–401.

"should not be considered the business": "Ford and GM Scrutinized for Alleged Nazi Collaboration," *Washington Post*, November 30, 1998, p. A01.

62 "Our enemies should take note": "The Meaning of 'Blitzkrieg,'" *New York Times*, April 5, 1940, p. 19.
    "That is what will happen": Albert Speer, *Inside the Third Reich* (New York: Avon, 1970), p. 303.

8. Fifty Thousand Airplanes: Spring 1940

65 "If Roosevelt took this": Charles Lindbergh, *The Wartime Journals of Charles A. Lindbergh* (New York: Harcourt Brace Jovanovich, 1970), p. 437.
66 "I have seen war on land": Jon Meacham, *Franklin and Winston: An Intimate Portrait of an Epic Friendship* (New York: Random House, 2004), p. 7.
67 "We Americans treat our Army": Robert E. Sherwood, *Roosevelt and Hopkins: An Intimate History* (New York: Harper and Brothers, 1948), p. 76.
    "It was born of the belief": Ibid., p. 123.
    "But the new element": "Text of President Roosevelt's Message on National Defense Expansion," *Chicago Daily Tribune*, May 17, 1940, p. 7.
    "Well, to be realistic": H. H. Arnold, *Global Mission* (Military Classics, 1949), p. 165.
    "I remember the dismay": Sumner Welles, *The Time for Decision* (New York: Harper & Brothers, 1944), p. 149.
68 "You know, you and I": Meacham, *Franklin and Winston*, p. 27.
    "Good morning": Doris Kearns Goodwin, *No Ordinary Time: Franklin and Eleanor Roosevelt: The Home Front in World War II* (New York: Simon & Schuster, 1994), p. 26.
    "Who among us, except": Donald M. Nelson, *Arsenal of Democracy: The Story of American War Production* (New York: Harcourt Brace & Co., 1946), p. 85.
69 "Every Cabinet member present": "Grave Congress Hears Roosevelt's Arms Plea," *Washington Post*, May 17, 1940, p. 4.
    "These are ominous days": "Text of President Roosevelt's Message on National Defense Expansion," *Chicago Daily Tribune*, May 17, 1940, p. 7.
70 "The President came straight": Michael Sherry, *The Rise of American Airpower: The Creation of Armageddon* (New Haven, CT: Yale University Press, 1987), p. 80.
    "The President was sure": Henry H. Arnold, *American Airpower Comes of Age: General Henry H. "Hap" Arnold's World War II Diaries* (Honolulu: University Press of the Pacific, 2004), p. 71.
    "Pounding away at Germany": Sherry, *The Rise of American Airpower*, pp. 78–79.

"The United States must build": Arnold, *Global Mission,* p. 265.

71 "You'd have the Germans": Mira Wilkins and Frank Ernest Hill, *American Business Abroad: Ford on Six Continents* (Detroit: Wayne State University Press, 1964), p. 316.

"clouds of airplanes": Nelson, *Arsenal of Democracy,* p. 74.

"We hear now that the Army": "Defense Plans of President Disclosed," *Los Angeles Times,* May 16, 1940, p. 1.

"hysterical chatter": "Lindbergh Sees No Dangers," *Christian Science Monitor,* May 20, 1940, p. 6.

"What is America but beauty": Arthur Herman, *Freedom's Forge: How American Business Produced Victory in World War II* (New York: Random House, 2012), p. 13.

72 "They are unanimous": "Roosevelt Talk Fails to Reply on NRA, AAA," *Chicago Daily Tribune,* November 1, 1936, p. 1.

"First, Knudsen. Second, Knudsen": Norman Beasley, *Knudsen: A Biography* (New York: Whittlesey House, 1947), p. 230.

"Mr. Knudsen, the President": Ibid., p. 234.

"This country has been good": Michael W. R. Davis, *Detroit's Wartime Industry: Arsenal of Democracy* (Mount Pleasant, SC: Arcadia, 2007), p. 8.

"They'll make a monkey out": Beasley, *Knudsen,* p. 235.

73 "Can you build those fifty thousand": "Profiles: Production Man-1," *The New Yorker,* March 8, 1941; see also Ed Cray, *Chrome Colossus: General Motors and Its Times* (New York: McGraw-Hill, 1980), p. 316.

"tanks, airplanes, engines": Beasley, *Knudsen,* p. 236.

"The effective defense of this country": Herman S. Wolk, *Cataclysm: General Hap Arnold and the Defeat of Japan* (Denton: University of North Texas Press, 2010), p. 36.

"Your responsibility and my responsibility": Beasley, *Knudsen,* p. 242.

"speed, speed, and more speed": "Knudsen Asks Auto Makers to Step Up Defense Work," *Pittsburgh Press,* December 7, 1940, p. 1.

74 "Our immediate problem": Beasley, *Knudsen,* p. 254.

"nothing was ever impossible": Nelson, *Arsenal of Democracy,* p. 80.

9. *"Gentlemen, We Must Outbuild Hitler": Spring to Fall 1940*

75 "England's battles, it used:" Victor G. Reuther, *The Brothers Reuther and the Story of the UAW* (Boston: Houghton Mifflin, 1976), p. 228.

"obsessed with the European": Charles Sorensen, personal account, p. 733, acc 65, box 69, Benson Ford Research Center, Dearborn, MI.

"dimmed the power behind": Doris Kearns Goodwin, *No Ordinary*

Time: Franklin and Eleanor Roosevelt: The Home Front in World War II (New York: Simon & Schuster, 1994), p. 229.

76 "The people are looking": "'People's Leader' Criticized by Ford," *New York Times,* April 29, 1938, p. 14.

"They don't dare have a war": "Ford Says It's All a Bluff," *New York Times,* August 29, 1939.

"to safeguard your interests": Allan Nevins and Frank Ernest Hill, *Ford: Decline and Rebirth* (New York: Scribner's, 1963), p. 277.

"You realize, of course": Dr. Heinrich Albert, letter to Edsel Ford, July 11, 1940, acc 6, box 248, "1940: FMC Subsidiary, Cologne," Benson Ford Research Center, Dearborn, MI.

"Of course those trucks": V. Y. Tallberg, oral history, p. 96, Benson Ford Research Center, Dearborn, MI.

"under the restrictions": Dr. Heinrich Albert, letter to Edsel Ford, July 11, 1940.

77 "four Belgian employees were": Secretary of State Cordell Hull, cable to the office of Edsel Ford, May 14, 1940, Edsel B. Ford Office Papers, acc 6, box 152, "General Correspondence, 1940," Benson Ford Research Center, Dearborn, MI.

"pyrotechnic eloquence": Mira Wilkins and Frank Ernest Hill, *American Business Abroad: Ford on Six Continents* (Detroit: Wayne State University Press, 1964), p. 2.

"very often not *all* the truth": Treasury Department investigation files, p. 26, "Foreign Funds Control," box 135, record group 131, Office of Alien Property, National Archives, College Park, MD.

"Our trucks are in very large demand": Ibid., p. 26.

"In order to safeguard": Ibid., p. 27.

"Glad you are safe": Ibid., p. 20.

"I also appreciate your great effort": Ibid., p. 30.

78 "The history of our company": Maurice Dollfus to Edsel Ford, August 15, 1942, photostat in Treasury Department investigation files, "Foreign Funds Control," box 135, record group 131, Office of Alien Property, National Archives, College Park, MD.

Edsel arrived at Treasury: Henry Morgenthau diaries, microfilm roll 73, FDR Library, Hyde Park, NY.

"The enemy have a marked": Jon Meacham, *Franklin and Winston: An Intimate Portrait of an Epic Friendship* (New York: Random House, 2004), p. 48.

79 "Sure, we can do it": Donald M. Nelson, *Arsenal of Democracy: The Story of American War Production* (New York: Harcourt Brace & Co., 1946), p. 80.

"We will make all the studies": "Ford Now Developing New Airplane Engine," *Montreal Gazette,* June 11, 1940, p. 22.

"for patriotic reasons": "Knudsen to Direct Defense Tooling," *New York Times,* June 4, 1940, p. 12.

"I was concerned about Edsel": Sorensen, personal account, p. 731.

80   "I am surprised": Ibid., p. 736.

"They want war!": Ibid., p. 740.

"We wouldn't have made": David Lanier Lewis, *The Public Image of Henry Ford* (Detroit: Wayne State University Press, 1987), p. 272.

"Bill, we can't make those motors": Norman Beasley, *Knudsen: A Biography* (New York: Whittlesey House, 1947), pp. 264–65.

81   "You are mixed up with": Sorensen, personal account, p. 740.

"We won't build the engine": Lewis, *The Public Image of Henry Ford*, p. 272.

"Edsel said that his father": Transcript of conversation in Henry Morgenthau's diaries, microfilm roll 75, FDR Library, Hyde Park, NY.

"for an hour and a half: Treasury Department investigation files, p. 4, "Foreign Funds Control," box 135, record group 131, National Archives, College Park, MD.

"Edsel definitely gave": Transcript of conversation in Henry Morgenthau's diaries, microfilm roll 75, FDR Library, Hyde Park, NY.

82   "a menace to democracy": "At 78 Henry Ford Takes a New Lease of Life," *The Mail* (Adelaide), July 4, 1942; see also "The Battle of Detroit," *Time*, March 23, 1942.

"The 'Dementi' of Mr. Henry Ford": Ken Silverstein, "Ford and the Fuhrer," *The Nation*, January 24, 2000, p. 13.

"Mankind is Frankenstein": Michael Sherry, *The Rise of American Airpower: The Creation of Armageddon* (New Haven, CT: Yale University Press, 1987), p. 46.

83   "We could feel the shock": Wilkins and Hill, *American Business Abroad*, p. 326.

"There had been fighting": Meacham, *Franklin and Winston*, p. 7.

"We saw our soldiers fighting": William Stephenson, *A Man Called Intrepid: The Secret War* (New York: Ballantine Books, 1976), pp. 79–80.

"We shall need the greatest": Winston Churchill, *Their Finest Hour* (Boston: Houghton Mifflin, 1949), pp. 499–500.

84   "Mr. President, with great": Meacham, *Franklin and Winston*, p. 71.

"As a report on the state": Magazine clipping, William Knudsen Papers, box 2, National Automotive History Collection, Detroit Public Library.

"Fifty thousand airplanes": Ibid.

85   "We need more bombers": *Freedom's Arsenal* (Detroit: Automobile Manufacturers Association, 1950), pp. 2ff.

"The first half of 1941": Magazine clipping, William Knudsen Papers, box 2, National Automotive History Collection, Detroit Public Library.

"Gentlemen, we must outbuild": "Profiles: Production Man – II," *The New Yorker*, March 15, 1941, p. 26.

10. The Liberator: Fall 1940 to Spring 1941

86   "I think it well for": Tom Vanderbilt, *Survival City: Adventures Among the Ruins of Atomic America* (Princeton, NJ: Princeton Architectural Press, 2002), p. 57.
      "K.T., this is Knudsen": Norman Beasley, *Knudsen: A Biography* (New York: Whittlesey House, 1947), pp. 283–84.
87   "I believe the greatest": "Meet Attacks from Within, Sloan Advises," *Chicago Daily Tribune,* October 16, 1940, p. 33.
      "We haven't got enough": Ed Cray, *Chrome Colossus: General Motors and Its Times* (New York: McGraw-Hill, 1980), pp. 316–17.
88   "The President could take over": "Mrs. Roosevelt's View: Ford Seizure Simple," *Christian Science Monitor,* January 28, 1941, p. 9.
      "Those planes will never": Charles E. Sorensen, with Samuel T. Williamson, *My Forty Years with Ford* (Detroit: Wayne State University Press, 2006), p. 279.
      "I was over the barrel": Ibid., p. 278.
      "for the defense of the United States": "Henry Ford Reveals Company Will Make Aviation Engines for US Government," *Flint Journal,* August 17, 1940.
      "Our organization moved fast": Sorensen, *My Forty Years with Ford,* p. 276.
89   "They've had enough school": Charles Sorensen, personal account, p. 750, acc 65, box 69, Benson Ford Research Center, Dearborn, MI.
      "We are dealing with a 50,000": "Ford Plant May Build Air Battleships," *Los Angeles Times,* January 9, 1941, p. 1.
90   "We chose the name Liberator": Stephen E. Ambrose, *The Wild Blue* (New York: Simon & Schuster, 2001), p. 22.
91   "How would you do it?": Sorensen, *My Forty Years with Ford,* p. 281.
92   "the greatest industrial adventure": Ibid., p. 3.
      "To compare a Ford V-8": Ibid., p. 281.
      "the biggest challenge": Ibid., p. 282.
93   "Get serious": Douglas Brinkley, *Wheels for the World* (New York: Penguin, 2003), p. 459.
      "Why not make units for us": Sorensen, *My Forty Years with Ford,* p. 283.
      "We are not interested": Ibid., p. 284.
94   "We hope to be in production": "100 Army Bombers a Month Objective of New Ford Plant," *Boston Globe,* March 5, 1941.
      "1 plane per hr": Original sketch, acc 435, box 51, "Ford–Willow Run Bomber Plant," vol. 1, Benson Ford Research Center, Dearborn, MI.
      "You cannot expect blacksmiths": Logan Miller, oral history, p. 46, Benson Ford Research Center, Dearborn, MI.
95   "a bad thing to give contracts": Goodwin, *No Ordinary Time,* p. 227.
      "to let bygone issues go": Ibid.

"We descended": Roscoe Smith, oral history, p. 57, Benson Ford Research Center, Dearborn, MI.

"Of course we were all": Ibid., p. 58.

"I remember we first talked": Logan Miller, oral history, p. 46, Benson Ford Research Center, Dearborn, MI.

Edsel personally paid for: Ibid., p. 56.

96   "They were supposed to have": Smith, oral history, p. 57, Benson Ford Research Center, Dearborn, MI.

Eighty-five percent of the plane: "The Metallurgical Laboratories," acc 435, box 51, "Ford–Willow Run Bomber Plant," Benson Ford Research Center, Dearborn, MI.

Blueprint makers used: "Making of Blueprints," acc 435, box 52, "Ford–Willow Run Bomber Plant," vol. 18, Benson Ford Research Center, Dearborn, MI.

97   "Gee, that's going to cost": William Pioch, oral history, pp. 65–68, Benson Ford Research Center, Dearborn, MI.

98   "a substantial increase": Herman S. Wolk, *Cataclysm: General Hap Arnold and the Defeat of Japan* (Denton: University of North Texas Press, 2010), p. 36.

11. Willow Run: Spring to Fall 1941

99   "The Industrial Revolution has": David Edgerton, *Britain's War Machine: Weapons, Resources, and Experts in the Second World War* (New York: Oxford University Press, 2011), pp. 11–12.

"We'll put up a *mile*": Douglas Brinkley, *Wheels for the World* (New York: Penguin, 2003), p. 460.

100 "There was nothing to stop": Charles Sorensen, personal account, p. 774, acc 65, box 69, Benson Ford Research Center, Dearborn, MI.

"It took me 29 years": Richard Lingeman, *Don't You Know There's a War On? The American Home Front 1941–1945* (New York: Thunder's Mouth Press, 2003), p. 74.

101 "Ford's Warbird Hatchery": Brinkley, *Wheels for the World*, p. 460.

"a revolution in aircraft: "Ford's War Production Exceeds Dreams," *Christian Science Monitor*, May 21, 1942, p. 13.

"It was the first concrete": Brinkley, *Wheels for the World*, p. 460.

"Apparently the Plant Site Board": Edsel Ford, "Departmental Communication" memo to Charles Sorensen, June 4, 1941, acc 435, box 51, "Ford–Willow Run Bomber Plant," Benson Ford Research Center, Dearborn, MI.

102 "I have great admiration": Charles Lindbergh, *The Wartime Journals of Charles A. Lindbergh* (New York: Harcourt Brace Jovanovich, 1970), p. 363.

"I wish I trusted him": A. Scott Berg, *Lindbergh* (New York: Berkley Books, 1999), p. 394.

"What has happened to": Lindbergh, *The Wartime Journals*, p. 360.

"He asked if a donation": Ibid., p. 389.

103 "Your stand against entry": Allan Nevins and Frank Ernest Hill, *Ford: Decline and Rebirth* (New York: Scribner's, 1963), p. 181.

"Nobody gave us much": H. H. Arnold, *Global Mission* (Military Classics, 1949), p. 169.

"negotiated peace": "Lindbergh Hits Hysteria and Invasion Fears," *Chicago Daily Tribune*, January 24, 1941, p. 1.

"Our own air forces are": "Text of Col. Lindbergh's Statement Opposing Aid Bill," *Los Angeles Times*, February 7, 1941, p. 7.

104 "would be the greatest": "Lindbergh Hits Hysteria and Invasion Fears," *Chicago Daily Tribune*, January 24, 1941, p. 1.

"which side would it be": Ibid.

"The three most important": Jon Meacham, *Franklin and Winston: An Intimate Portrait of an Epic Friendship* (New York: Random House, 2004), p. 127.

"If I should die tomorrow": Doris Kearns Goodwin, *No Ordinary Time: Franklin and Eleanor Roosevelt: The Home Front in World War II* (New York: Simon & Schuster, 1994), p. 48.

"the No. 1 United States": Berg, *Lindbergh*, p. 418.

"No one has ever heard": Ibid., p. 423.

"Knight of the German": Harold Ickes, *The Secret Diary of Harold Ickes*, vol. 3 (New York: Simon & Schuster, 1955), p. 581.

105 "Mr. Lindbergh returned his": Ibid., p. 424.

12. Awakening: Spring to Fall 1941

106 "When we are talking": Donald M. Nelson, *Arsenal of Democracy: The Story of American War Production* (New York: Harcourt Brace & Co., 1946), p. 309.

107 "America is like": Arthur Herman, *Freedom's Forge: How American Business Produced Victory in World War II* (New York: Random House, 2012), p. 85.

"It is the biggest thing": "War Plant Would Make Big Stadium," *Washington Post*, June 11, 1942, p. 33.

108 94 days to flatten the earth: "Building of Airport," acc 435, box 51, "Ford–Willow Run Bomber Plant," vol. 1, Benson Ford Research Center, Dearborn, MI.

"atmosphere of an antique": Lowell Juilliard Carr and James Edson Stermer, *Willow Run* (New York: Arno Press, 1977), p. 19.

109 "These are terrific stakes": "Sorensen of the Rouge," *Fortune*, April 1942, p. 79.

"I was devoted to him": Charles E. Sorensen, with Samuel T. Williamson, *My Forty Years with Ford* (Detroit: Wayne State University Press, 2006), p. 304.

110 "I was afraid it was": Charles Sorensen, personal account, p. 790, acc 65, box 69, Benson Ford Research Center, Dearborn, MI.

"There would be no": Dr. John G. Mateer, letter to Edsel Ford, November 15, 1940, acc 6, box 247, Benson Ford Research Center, Dearborn, MI.

"I can't spare the time": "Edsel Ford Dies at 49; Headed Auto Empire 24 Years," *Evening Star* (Washington, DC), May 26, 1943, p. 1.

111 "Just think, one cylinder": Laurence Sheldrick, oral history, p. 321, Benson Ford Research Center, Dearborn, MI.

"You have seen the modern": "Sorensen of the Rouge," *Fortune*, April 1942, p. 114A.

"Give me the Rouge": Ibid.

"It will be completely": "Ford Starts Building," *Detroit Times*, September 17, 1940.

112 "The other guys said": David Lanier Lewis, *The Public Image of Henry Ford* (Detroit: Wayne State University Press, 1987), p. 398.

"The Wedding of the Century": Ford R. Bryan, *Clara: Mrs. Henry Ford* (Dearborn, MI: Ford Books, 2001), p. 272.

"join the Ford Motor": Allan Nevins and Frank Ernest Hill, *Ford: Decline and Rebirth* (New York: Scribner's, 1963), p. 184.

113 "I'll give those boys": Sheldrick, oral history, p. 303, Benson Ford Research Center, Dearborn, MI.

"called me everything": Ibid., p. 304.

"Don't pay a bit of attention": Ibid.

"I'll never forget this": Ibid.

"This jeep just came": Ibid., p. 305.

114 "I had a feeling that": Jon Meacham, *Franklin and Winston: An Intimate Portrait of an Epic Friendship* (New York: Random House, 2004), p. 219.

"Now that [Henry II]": Walter Hayes, *Henry: A Life of Henry Ford II* (New York: Grove Weidenfeld, 1990), p. 11.

13. Strike!: Spring to Winter 1941

115 "Practically all the Ford": John McCarten, "The Little Man in Henry Ford's Basement," *The American Mercury*, May 1940, p. 8.

116 license plates from states: Ford chief legal counsel I. A. Capizzi, letter to Senator Arthur H. Vandenberg, May 2, 1941, acc 6, box 160, "Gen. Correspondence, 1941," Benson Ford Research Center, Dearborn, MI.

and badges saying: Keith Sward, *The Legend of Henry Ford* (New York: Atheneum, 1972), p. 410.

"paid around the clock": Walter White, *A Man Called White* (Athens: University of Georgia Press, 1995), p. 213.

"Unlawful sit-down strikes": Roger Burlingame, *Henry Ford: The Greatest Success Story in the History of Industry* (New York: Signet, 1956), p. 104.

"Iron bolts and nuts": August Meier and Elliott Rudwick, *Black Detroit and the Rise of the UAW* (Ann Arbor: University of Michigan Press, 2007), p. 88.

"I went out to the Ford": "Excerpt from Jimmie Stevenson's News Broadcast," acc 38, box 95, "Subject Files: 1942, Strikes and Labor," Benson Ford Research Center, Dearborn, MI.

117   "The unions seized our": "Allis Strike Must End, Roosevelt Tells Nation," *Christian Science Monitor*, April 4, 1941, p. 1.

"The Ford company is attempting": "River Rouge Strikers Wrecked Airplane Tools, Company States," *New York Times*, April 5, 1941, p. 1.

"Mr. Ford wanted to fight": Harry Bennett, as told to Paul Marcus, *Ford: We Never Called Him Henry* (New York: Tom Doherty Associates, 1987), p. 235.

"Oh, don't worry about": Mead Bricker, oral history, p. 56, Benson Ford Research Center, Dearborn, MI.

118   "the backbone of the Ford": Doris Kearns Goodwin, *No Ordinary Time: Franklin and Eleanor Roosevelt: The Home Front in World War II* (New York: Simon & Schuster, 1994), p. 228.

"With the help of the President": Ibid.

"assuring us that you": Congressman Clinton P. Anderson, letter to Franklin Roosevelt, April 5, 1941, file 680, Franklin Roosevelt Papers, "President's Personal File," FDR Library, Hyde Park, NY.

"extremely alarmed when": Bennett, *Ford: We Never Called Him Henry*, p. 236.

119   "I'm not going to sign": Charles E. Sorensen, with Samuel T. Williamson, *My Forty Years with Ford* (Wayne State University Press, 2006), p. 269.

"The patriotic thing": Meier and Rudwick, *Black Detroit and the Rise of the UAW*, p. 94.

"I walked in the picket": White, *A Man Called White*, p. 214.

"Well, you've got a plant": Bennett, *Ford: We Never Called Him Henry*, p. 237.

120   "We'll bargain until": Burlingame, *Henry Ford*, p. 104.

"What in the world": Sorensen, *My Forty Years with Ford*, p. 269.

"Mrs. Ford was horrified": Ibid., p. 271.

"It was perhaps the greatest": Goodwin, *No Ordinary Time*, p. 230.

"Mr. Ford gave in": Allan Nevins and Frank Ernest Hill, *Ford: Decline and Rebirth* (New York: Scribner's, 1963), p. 164.

121 "Stop this talk!": Richard Bak, *Henry and Edsel: The Creation of the Ford Empire* (New York: Wiley, 2003), p. 255.

"Never was any business": Charles Sorensen, personal account, p. 912, acc 65, box 69, Benson Ford Research Center, Dearborn, MI.

14. Air Raid!: December 7, 1941

122 "We are now in": "A New American Creed," *Detroit News*, December 10, 1941, p. 1; see also Robert Dallek, *Franklin D. Roosevelt and American Foreign Policy, 1932–1945* (New York: Oxford University Press, 1995), p. 317.

123 *"Air raid!":* William O'Neill, *A Democracy at War: America's Fight at Home and Abroad in World War II* (Cambridge, MA: Harvard University Press, 1995), p. 1.

"jump at least 15 to 20 feet": Michael Slackman, *Target: Pearl Harbor* (Honolulu: University of Hawaii Press, 1990), p.114.

"Their accuracy was uncanny": O'Neill, *A Democracy at War,* p. 3.

"Mr. President, it looks": William Doyle, *Inside the Oval Office: The White House Tapes from FDR to Clinton* (New York: Kodansha International, 1999), p. 35.

"His chin stuck out": Ibid.

124 "My God, there's": Jon Meacham, *Franklin and Winston: An Intimate Portrait of an Epic Friendship* (New York: Random House, 2004), p. 131.

"How did it happen": Doyle, *Inside the Oval Office*, p. 39.

"Mr. President, what's": Meacham, *Franklin and Winston*, p. 131.

"Sit down, Grace": Doris Kearns Goodwin, *No Ordinary Time: Franklin and Eleanor Roosevelt: The Home Front in World War II* (New York: Simon & Schuster, 1994), p. 291.

"Powerful and resourceful": "A New American Creed," *Detroit News*, December 10, 1941, p. 1.

15. The Grim Race: Winter 1941 to Summer 1942

129 "Orators, columnists": Charles E. Sorensen, with Samuel T. Williamson, *My Forty Years with Ford* (Detroit: Wayne State University Press, 2006), p. 273.

"This is war": "In Air Raid Drills: San Francisco Blackout, New Warnings in New York," *Lawrence Journal World*, December 10, 1941, p. 4.

"The war will come": "The Enduring Legacy to a Generation," *Washington Times,* June 1, 2004.

130 "special vigilance": "City on War Basis; Plants Under Guard," *Detroit News*, December 8, 1941, p. 1.

"The Under Secretary of War": Cable to Dearborn, December 10, 1941, 8:46 AM, acc 6, box 254, "1941: Defense," Benson Ford Research Center, Dearborn, MI.

"We are going to raise": Robert Lovett, letter to Edsel Ford, January 22, 1942, acc 6, box 264, "1942: War Dept.," Benson Ford Research Center, Dearborn, MI.

"We fully realize": Edsel Ford, telegram to Jesse H. Jones, December 9, 1941, acc 6, box 185, "Telegrams, 1941," Benson Ford Research Center, Dearborn, MI.

"The war won't wait": David Lanier Lewis, *The Public Image of Henry Ford* (Detroit: Wayne State University Press, 1987), p. 365.

"We might as well": "Battle of Detroit," *Time*, March 23, 1942.

"the strength and wisdom": Henry Ford, cable to Franklin Roosevelt, January 30, 1942, 12:01 PM, file 680, Franklin Roosevelt Papers, "President's Personal File: Henry Ford," FDR Library, Hyde Park, NY.

131 "the general plan": Edsel Ford, "Departmental Communication" to Harry Bennett, December 3, 1942, acc 435, box 52, "Willow Run Bomber Plant," Benson Ford Research Center, Dearborn, MI.

"Please tell me is": Photograph of this cable in the author's possession; see also *Research Findings About Ford-Werke Under the Nazi Regime*, numerous authors (Dearborn, MI: Ford Motor Co., 2001), p. 87.

132 "the first war in American": Richard Lingeman, *Don't You Know There's a War On? The American Home Front, 1941–1945* (New York: Thunder's Mouth Press, 2003), p. 24.

"I have been thinking about": Donald M. Nelson, *Arsenal of Democracy: The Story of American War Production* (New York: Harcourt Brace & Co., 1946), p. 186.

"American power back into the islands": Michael Sherry, *The Rise of American Airpower: The Creation of Armageddon* (New Haven, CT: Yale University Press, 1987), p. 106.

133 "a believer in bombing": Ibid., p. 97.

"If hitherto we": "Summary of Marshal Goering's Speech to the Reich Munitions Workers," *New York Times*, September 10, 1939, p. 46.

"Hitler's point of view": Albert Speer, *Inside the Third Reich* (New York: Avon, 1970), p. 312.

134 "The area working directly": Ibid., p. 293.

"Preliminary figures have": Isador Lubin, memo to Harry Hopkins, February 2, 1942, container 125, Harry L. Hopkins Papers, FDR Library, Hyde Park, NY.

"In fulfilling my duty": "Text of Roosevelt's Message to Congress," *Boston Globe*, January 7, 1942, p. 10.

"The superiority of the United States": Donald M. Nelson, *Arsenal of Democracy: The Story of American War Production* (New York: Harcourt Brace & Co., 1946), p. 186.

135 "Automotive conversion was": Ibid., pp. 184, 212.

"Edsel and Kanzler should": Ford R. Bryan, *Henry's Lieutenants* (Detroit: Wayne State University Press, 1993), p. 147.

"Mr. Kanzler": In various pieces of correspondence in Edsel's files from this time, located at the Benson Ford Research Center, he addressed his best friend as "Mr. Kanzler."

"We must have at once": "Auto Men Pledge 'All Out' for War," *New York Times*, January 25, 1942, p. 3.

136 51 percent of the nation's: Nelson, *Arsenal of Democracy*, p. 216.

"Blanket charges of this description": "Auto Men Answer Truman Charges," January 17, 1942, p. 9.

"When you convert one": Nelson, *Arsenal of Democracy*, p. 218.

137 Ford Motor Company would roll out: Lingeman, *Don't You Know There's a War On?*, p. 66.

"You won't recognize": "Auto Work Seen Requiring 'Lot of Women,'" *Christian Science Monitor*, January 30, 1942, p. 17.

air raid defense and: "Air Raid Precautions," acc 435, box 4, "Ford–Engine Aircraft Manufacturing: Record of War Effort," vol. 5, Benson Ford Research Center, Dearborn, MI.

"One spark will eat": "E-Pound Thermite Bomb," memo, December 16, 1941, acc 435, box 4, Benson Ford Research Center, Dearborn, MI.

138 "Since the state of war": Maurice Dollfus, letter to Edsel Ford, January 28, 1942, Treasury Department investigation files, "Foreign Funds Control," box 135, record group 131, Office of Alien Property, exhibit 15, National Archives, College Park, MD.

"It is a fact": Ibid., p. 35.

"brilliant": Ibid., p. 23.

"At this state I would": Ibid., p. 34.

"I am quite sure that": Treasury Department investigation files, p. 39, "Foreign Funds Control," box 135, record group 131, Office of Alien Property, National Archives, College Park, MD.

139 Edsel communicated back: Edsel Ford, letter to Dollfus paraphrased in Treasury Department investigation files, p. 56, "Foreign Funds Control," box 135, record group 131, Office of Alien Property, National Archives, College Park, MD.

"I have shown your": Edsel Ford, letter to Maurice Dollfus, July 17, 1942, Treasury Department investigation files, p. 57, "Foreign Funds Control," box 135, record group 131, Office of Alien Property, National Archives, College Park, MD.

"is treated as becoming": Ford Auditing Department, memo to Edsel Ford, November 25, 1942, acc 6, box 167, Edsel B. Ford Office Papers, "General Correspondence, 1942," Benson Ford Research Center, Dearborn, MI.

"It was generally understood": Roscoe Smith, oral history, p. 77, Benson Ford Research Center, Dearborn, MI.

140 "There is no difference": F. Scott Fitzgerald, *The Great Gatsby* (New York: Collier Books, 1980) p. 124.

"This was the worst kind": Charles Sorensen, personal account, pp. 817–18, acc 65, box 69, Benson Ford Research Center, Dearborn, MI.

16. *"Detroit's Worries Are Right Now": Spring to Summer 1942*

141 "Throughout the land": "If Hitler Could See These," *New York Times*, July 12, 1942, p. SM3.

"better than I expected": Charles Sorensen, personal account, pp. 820–21, acc 65, box 69, Benson Ford Research Center, Dearborn, MI.

142 "self-contained 'Arsenals of Democracy'": "GM and Ford Plants Double Output for War," *Hartford Courant*, May 22, 1942, p. 13.

"What may not be generally known": "Rapid Conversion of Detroit Auto Plants Is an Amazing, Heartening Story," *Washington Post*, April 12, 1942, p. B3.

"A terrible burden has fallen": "Detroit," *Fortune*, November 1941, p. 65.

"The scale of Detroit's": "Detroit Is America's Greatest Arsenal," November 9, 1941, p. 29.

143 "Even the American": "The Battle of Detroit," *Time*, March 23, 1942.

"Henry Ford is still": "Detroit Is Dynamite," *Life*, August 17, 1942.

"Once old Henry Ford gets": "Mass Magic in Detroit," *New York Times*, March 1, 1942, p. SM4.

"more than three times": "This Is a Mass Production War," *Christian Science Monitor*, July 11, 1942, p. WM8.

"the greatest single": "Rapid Conversion of Detroit Auto Plants Is an Amazing, Heartening Story."

"All 16 major league": "War Plant Would Make Big Stadium," *Washington Post*, June 11, 1942, p. 33.

"the production miracle": "Biggest War Plant," *Wall Street Journal*, May 26, 1942, p. 1.

"It is a promise of revenge": Robert Lacey, *Ford: The Men and the Machine* (Boston: Little, Brown, 1986), p. 395.

"In one American factory": Sir Arthur Harris, *Bomber Offensive* (New York: Presidio Press, 1990), pp. 117–18.

144 "I guess the pressure got": Edsel Ford, letter to Marvin McIntyre, file 680, Franklin Roosevelt Papers, President's Personal File, FDR Library, Hyde Park, NY.

"He wanted them near": Sorensen, personal account, pp. 790–91.

"This man's navy is": Peter Collier and David Horowitz, *The Fords: An American Epic* (San Francisco: Encounter, 2002), p. 149.

government signs: Charles Lindbergh, *The Wartime Journals of Charles A. Lindbergh* (New York: Harcourt Brace Jovanovich, 1970), p. 685.

145 "the most enormous room": Doris Kearns Goodwin, *No Ordinary Time: Franklin and Eleanor Roosevelt: The Home Front in World War II* (New York: Simon & Schuster, 1994), p. 363.

Sylvania fluorescent bulbs: "Electrical Goods Lead in Diversity," *New York Times*, January 3, 1943, p. A76; see also "Bright Lights," *Wall Street Journal*, February 15, 1943, p. 1.

the Plant Hospital was: "Plant Hospital," acc 435, box 52, "Willow Run Bomber Plant," vol. 17, Benson Ford Research Center, Dearborn, MI.

four 30,000-pound cranes: "Craneways by the Mile," acc 435, box 52, "Willow Run Bomber Plant," vol. 21, Benson Ford Research Center, Dearborn, MI.

In the metal shop: "Forming Bomber Parts," acc 435, box 51, "Ford–Willow Run Bomber Plant," vol. 5, Benson Ford Research Center, Dearborn, MI.

conveyors on the ceiling: "Conveyors," acc 6, box 52, "Willow Run Bomber Plant," vol. 21, Benson Ford Research Center, Dearborn, MI.

147 "an unreasonable burden": Truman Committee hearing, minutes, July 22, 1942, available at: archive.org/stream/investigationofn1112unit/investigationofn1112unit_djvu.txt (accessed October 25, 2013).

"Arrived here about eight": Diary of Mrs. John Castle, excerpted in Lowell Juilliard Carr and James Edson Stermer, *Willow Run* (New York: Arno Press, 1977), pp. 97–107.

148 "If there were any better": Diary of Mrs. Sam Gordon, excerpted in Carr and Stermer, *Willow Run*, p. 116.

"a city of homes well planned": Sidney Hillman, Office of Production Management, file 3217, Franklin Roosevelt Papers, "Official File," FDR Library, Hyde Park, NY.

"Detroit isn't worrying": Jerome Beatty, "A City Gets a New Job," *American Magazine*, acc 6, box 168, Edsel B. Ford Office Papers, "General Correspondence, 1942, CR-CU," Benson Ford Research Center, Dearborn, MI.

"I have been asked by": Frederic A. Delano, letter to Edsel Ford, undated, acc 6, box 264, "1942: Misc.," Benson Ford Research Center, Dearborn, MI.

149 "picked a site for this": Henry Ford, telegram to Franklin Roosevelt, May 19, 1942, file 3217, Franklin Roosevelt Papers, "Official File," FDR Library, Hyde Park, NY.

Harry Bennett sent his men: Harry Bennett, as told to Paul Marcus, *Ford: We Never Called Him Henry* (New York: Tom Doherty Associates, 1987), p. 263.

17. Will It Run?: Spring to Fall 1942

150 "I have seen the science": Charles Lindbergh, *Of Flight and Life* (New York: Scribner's, 1948), p. 51.

151 "I want to contribute": Charles Lindbergh, *The Wartime Journals of Charles A. Lindbergh* (New York: Harcourt Brace Jovanovich, 1970), pp. 566–67.
"He is a ruthless and conscious": A. Scott Berg, *Lindbergh* (New York: Berkley Books, 1999), p. 436.
"The plant has progressed": Lindbergh, *The Wartime Journals*, p. 608.

152 "acres upon acres of machinery": Ibid., p. 613.
"The Ford schedule calls": Ibid., p. 609.
"The rest of the industry": Ibid., p. 610.
"There is no question": Charles Lindbergh, "The Future of the Large Bomber," unpublished memo, April 10, 1942, Lindbergh Papers, Manuscripts and Archives Division, Yale University Library, New Haven, CT.

153 "the man who first put": *Ford Times*, November 12, 1943.
"I am so anti-Hun and anti-Jap": S. W. Raymond of Adrian, MI, letter to Henry Ford, March 26, 1942, acc 38, box 94, "Subject File: 1942, Lindbergh," Benson Ford Research Center, Dearborn, MI.
"as scarce as hen's teeth": Lindbergh, *The Wartime Journals*, p. 650.
"These relationships": Ibid., p. 662.
"Sorensen has the reputation": Ibid., pp. 638–39.

154 Edsel had cancer of the stomach: Ibid., p. 697.
"I came here in hope": Charles Lindbergh, "confidential" letter to Charles Sorensen, June 3, 1942, acc 65, box 69, "Charles Sorensen," Benson Ford Research Center, Dearborn, MI.
"We couldn't retaliate": "Burma Must Be Retaken from Japs: Stilwell," *Sarasota Herald-Tribune*, May 25, 1942, p. 4.

155 "They don't give me": Robert Rankin, oral history, p. 12, Benson Ford Research Center, Dearborn, MI.
"A priority is something": Richard Lingeman, *Don't You Know There's a War On? The American Home Front 1941–1945* (New York: Thunder's Mouth Press, 2003), p. 112.
"Bennett is certainly": Lindbergh, *The Wartime Journals*, p. 490.

156 "I'd just as soon shoot down": William O'Neill, *A Democracy at War: America's Fight at Home and Abroad in World War II* (Cambridge, MA: Harvard University Press, 1995), p. 210.

"You were trying to do a job": Roscoe Smith, oral history, p. 68, Benson Ford Research Center, Dearborn, MI.

"Willow Run, the Largest": Employment leaflet for Willow Run, acc 435, box 51, "Ford–Willow Run Bomber Plant," vol. 6, Benson Ford Research Center, Dearborn, MI.

"They didn't know whether": Anthony Harff, oral history, p. 272, Benson Ford Research Center, Dearborn, MI.

157 "I'd rather see Hitler": "Troops Restore Calm in Detroit; Death Toll 28," *Chicago Daily Tribune,* June 23, 1943, p. 2.

The first woman employed: "Training of Women," acc 435, box 51, "Ford–Willow Run Bomber Plant," vol. 2, Benson Ford Research Center, Dearborn, MI.

Rose Monroe became: Douglas Brinkley, *Wheels for the World* (New York: Penguin, 2003), p. 482.

"All the day long": Doris Weatherford, *American Women During World War II: An Encyclopedia* (New York: Routledge, 2010), p. 399.

158 unskilled male laborers: Employment leaflet for Willow Run.

GENTLEMEN, WATCH YOUR: Robert Todd of Dearborn, MI, who worked at Willow Run during the war, interview with the author.

a nun entered a shack: Lowell Juilliard Carr and James Edson Stermer, *Willow Run* (New York: Arno Press, 1977), p. 76.

Photographs of kids living: "Detroit's Willow Run Area Is a Housing Nightmare," *Washington Post,* March 3, 1943, p. 6.

Senator Harry Truman: All of these numbers are from the minutes of the Truman Committee hearing, July 22, 1942, available at: archive .org/stream/investigationofn1112unit/investigationofn1112unit_ djvu.txt (accessed October 25, 2013).

18. Bomber Ship 01: May 1942

160 "Over all, we feel": Lowell Juilliard Carr and James Edson Stermer, *Willow Run* (New York: Arno Press, 1977), p. 161.

Stermer was pointed: Ibid., pp. 133–82. Stermer's diary is excerpted in this book he wrote on Willow Run.

161 "It is impossible in words": Ibid., p. 161.

"to orientate trainees": Ibid., pp. 162–63.

"It costs about $250": Ibid.

162 360,000 rivets: "Two Billion Rivets," acc 435, box 51, "Ford–Willow Run Bomber Plant," vol. 6, Benson Ford Research Center, Dearborn, MI.

"Riveting is a social": Carr and Stermer, *Willow Run,* p. 164.

"One thing that impressed me": Ibid., p. 172.

163 "the worst mess in the whole": William O'Neill, *A Democracy at War:*

America's Fight at Home and Abroad in World War II (Cambridge, MA: Harvard University Press, 1995), p. 218.

"The powers that control": Alan Clive, *Michigan in World War II* (Ann Arbor: University of Michigan Press, 1979), p. 120; see also Douglas Brinkley, *Wheels for the World* (New York: Penguin, 2003), p. 473.

164 "The B-24 has guts": Stephen E. Ambrose, *The Wild Blue: The Men and Boys Who Flew B-24s over Germany 1944–1945* (New York: Simon & Schuster, 2001), p. 78.

Eighteen rubber fuel cells: "Fuel Cells," acc 435, box 51, "Ford–Willow Run Plant II," Benson Ford Research Center, Dearborn, MI.

the bomb bay was constructed: Ambrose, *The Wild Blue*, p. 80.

165 "The plant itself needs": "Assembly of Ford Bomber 01 Proves New Production Methods," acc 6, box 264, "1942: Misc."; and "Speech by Edsel Ford," acc 6, box 262, Edsel B. Ford Office Papers, "1942: Speeches by Mr. Edsel B. Ford," both at Benson Ford Research Center, Dearborn, MI.

"It was HUGE": Ambrose, *The Wild Blue*, p. 82.

19. Roosevelt Visits Willow Run: September 1942

167 "My feelings against": William L. Shirer, *The Rise and Fall of the Third Reich* (New York: Simon & Schuster, 1960), p. 895 footnote.

Shortly before midnight: Much of this chapter is pieced together from three primary sources: "Memorandum of Information Regarding Visit of President and Mrs. Roosevelt to Willow Run Bomber Plant," September 18, 1942, and "The President's Party," both in container 61, Franklin Roosevelt Papers, "Official File," FDR Library, Hyde Park, NY; and "The President Visits Willow Run," acc 435, box 51, "Ford–Willow Run Bomber Plant," vol. 2, Benson Ford Research Center, Dearborn, MI.

"the winter of disaster": Robert E. Sherwood, *Roosevelt and Hopkins: An Intimate History* (New York: Harper and Brothers, 1948), p. 490.

"The awful realization": Donald M. Nelson, *Arsenal of Democracy: The Story of American War Production* (New York: Harcourt Brace & Co., 1946), p. 3.

168 "The news is going to get": Jon Meacham, *Franklin and Winston: An Intimate Portrait of an Epic Friendship* (New York: Random House, 2004), p. 169.

"I have been deeply": Winston Churchill, *The Grand Alliance* (Boston: Houghton Mifflin, 1950), p. 506.

"We must aim at nothing": Ibid., p. 804.

"The airplane production": Isador Lubin, memorandum to Franklin Roosevelt, August 8, 1942, "Aircraft Production," container 125, Harry L. Hopkins Papers, FDR Library, Hyde Park, NY.

"I am concerned by the figures": Franklin Roosevelt, memorandum to Secretary of War, Secretary of the Navy, and Donald Nelson, August 12, 1942, "Aircraft Production," container 125, Harry L. Hopkins Papers, FDR Library, Hyde Park, NY.

169 "All's Not Well in Detroit": "War Progress Report" (confidential), June 26, 1942, p. 6, "War Production Reports: War Progress," container 254, Harry L. Hopkins Papers, FDR Library, Hyde Park, NY.

"The news from Detroit": "Detroit Is Dynamite," *Life*, August 17, 1942.

170 "I was astonished to find": Charles Sorensen, personal account, p. 865, acc 65, box 69, Benson Ford Research Center, Dearborn, MI.

"It was evident to me": Ibid., p. 868.

171 Any worker who had: Robert Todd, Dearborn, MI, interview with the author.

"We're with you, Frank": "Memorandum of Information Regarding Visit of President and Mrs. Roosevelt to Willow Run Bomber Plant," September 18, 1942, container 61, Franklin Roosevelt Papers, "Official File," FDR Library, Hyde Park, NY.

"How do you like": Ibid.

"Charlie, what is": Sorensen, personal account, p. 866.

"Franklin, look over": Ibid., pp. 866, 904.

172 "And so this is the city": Kenneth S. Davis, *FDR: The War President, 1940–1943* (New York: Random House, 2000), p. 614.

173 "the most severe contraction": Richard Lingeman, *Don't You Know There's a War On? The American Home Front 1941–1945* (New York: Thunder's Mouth Press, 2003), p. 65.

174 "Hitler was the one that": William O'Neill, *A Democracy at War: America's Fight at Home and Abroad in World War II* (Cambridge, MA: Harvard University Press, 1995), p. 245.

"not yet in production": Davis, *FDR: The War President*, p. 613.

20. A Dying Man: Fall 1942 to Winter 1943

175 "This hour I rode the sky": Charles Lindbergh, *The Wartime Journals of Charles A. Lindbergh* (New York: Harcourt Brace Jovanovich, 1970), p. 222.

"a 1930s Mack truck": Stephen E. Ambrose, *The Wild Blue: The Men and Boys Who Flew B-24s over Germany 1944–1945* (New York: Simon & Schuster, 2001), p. 21.

176 Up at 20,000 feet: Ambrose, *The Wild Blue*, pp. 21–22.

"unnecessarily awkward": Lindbergh, *The Wartime Journals,* p. 613.
"more complicated than": Ibid., p. 638.
"Rivets missing": Ibid., p. 644.

177   Lindbergh was hearing: Harry Bennett, as told to Paul Marcus, *Ford: We Never Called Him Henry* (New York: Tom Doherty Associates, 1987), p. 277.
"You'd better be prepared": Ibid.
"We have more than": Lindbergh, *The Wartime Journals,* p. 737.
"We knew it was a tough problem": Ibid., p. 738.
"But a lot of people": Ibid., p. 738.
"What are we going": Bennett, *Ford: We Never Called Him Henry,* p. 277.
"A New Ford Motor": Treasury Department investigation files, "Foreign Funds Control," box 135, record group 131, exhibit 13, National Archives, College Park, MD.

178   his office would conduct: Charles Higham, *Trading with the Enemy: The Nazi-American Money Plot, 1933–1949* (New York: Dell Publishing, 1984).
"You are hereby instructed": Treasury Department warrant, December 7, 1942, Treasury Department investigation files, "Foreign Funds Control," box 135, record group 131, National Archives, College Park, MD.
"extremely curious as to": "Report of Investigation of Ford, Societe Anonyme Francaise, Machinery Suppliers, Inc., Matford S.A., Fordair S.A.," p. 5, Treasury Department investigation files, "Foreign Funds Control," box 135, record group 131, National Archives, College Park, MD.

179   For an hour and a half: Ibid., p. 4.
"I'm sorry, but I can": Irving Bacon, oral history, p. 176, Benson Ford Research Center, Dearborn, MI.
"I do hope you are": J. Edgar Hoover, letter to Edsel Ford, November 19, 1942, acc 6, box 171, Edsel B. Ford Papers, "Gen. Correspondence: 1942," Benson Ford Research Center, Dearborn, MI.
"Dear Edgar, I am": Edsel Ford, letter to J. Edgar Hoover, [date unclear], acc 6, box 171, Edsel B. Ford Papers, "Gen. Correspondence: 1942," Benson Ford Research Center, Dearborn, MI.

180   "Looks bad": Charles Sorensen, personal account, p. 892, acc 65, box 69, Benson Ford Research Center, Dearborn, MI.
"Stress and strain": Henry Dominguez, *Edsel: The Story of Henry Ford's Forgotten Son* (Detroit: Society of Automotive Engineers, 2002), p. 307.
"If Edsel could have": Sorensen, personal account, p. 790.
"What he should have": Dominguez, *Edsel,* p. 308.
"If there is anything": Charles E. Sorensen, with Samuel T. William-

son, *My Forty Years with Ford* (Detroit: Wayne State University Press, 2006), p. 318.

"Grandfather is responsible": Peter Collier and David Horowitz, *The Fords: An American Epic* (San Francisco: Encounter, 2002), p. 151.

"I had no idea": Richard Bak, *Henry and Edsel: The Creation of the Ford Empire* (New York: Wiley, 2003), p. 256.

a letter from Mr. Condé Nast: Condé Nast, letter to Edsel Ford, June–July 1942, acc 6, box 171, Edsel B. Ford Office Papers, "Gen. Correspondence: 1942," Benson Ford Research Center, Dearborn, MI.

181 "The baby is a beauty": Collier and Horowitz, *The Fords,* p. 150.

"I think Edsel Ford was": A. M. Wibel, oral history, p. 128, Benson Ford Research Center, Dearborn, MI.

"I spent all day": Robert Lacey, *Ford: The Men and the Machine* (Boston: Little, Brown, 1986), p. 395.

21. Unconditional Surrender: Winter 1943

185 "We will make Germany": Jorg Friedrich, *The Fire: The Bombing of Germany, 1940–1945* (New York: Columbia University Press, 2006), p. 61.

At midnight on January 11: Captain George E. Durno, AAF Transport Command, "Flight to Africa: A Chronicle of the Casablanca Conference," box 15, Franklin Roosevelt Papers, "Map Room File: Casablanca Trip," FDR Library, Hyde Park, NY; see also Robert E. Sherwood, *Roosevelt and Hopkins: An Intimate History* (New York: Harper and Brothers, 1948), pp. 670–74.

186 "The people are sold on": Michael Sherry, *The Rise of American Airpower: The Creation of Armageddon* (New Haven, CT: Yale University Press, 1987), p. 185.

"Our heavy bomber is our greatest weapon": Ibid., p. 136.

"Despite all the talk": Harry Hopkins, memorandum to Isador Lubin, November 13, 1942, "Aircraft Production," container 125, Harry L. Hopkins Papers, FDR Library, Hyde Park, NY.

"There has been some": H. H. Arnold, memorandum to Harry Hopkins, April 9, 1943, "Aircraft Production Program for 1943," container 125, Harry L. Hopkins Papers, FDR Library, Hyde Park, NY.

187 "One is almost stunned": Edward R. Murrow, *In Search of Light: The Broadcasts of Edward R. Murrow 1938–1961* (New York: Alfred A. Knopf, 1967), p. 56.

"Now all we need is": Andrew Roberts, *Masters and Commanders: How Four Titans Won the War in the West, 1941–1945* (New York: HarperCollins, 2009), p. 316.

188 "de-housing the workers": William O'Neill, *A Democracy at War: America's Fight at Home and Abroad in World War II* (Cambridge, MA: Harvard University Press, 1995), p. 306.

189 "I think it can be said": "President's Press Conference Speech," January 24, 1943, box 15, Franklin Roosevelt Papers, "Map Room File: Casablanca Trip," FDR Library, Hyde Park, NY.

190 "the taproot of German might": James Dugan and Carroll Stewart, *Ploesti: The Great Ground-Air Battle of 1 August 1943* (New York: Bantam, 1963), p. 3.
"by far the most": Ibid., p. 9.
"The Billion Dollar Watchdog": O'Neill, *A Democracy at War*, p. 396.
"an errand runner": United States Senate, "1941–1963: March 1, 1941: The Truman Committee," available at: Senate.gov/artandhistory/history/minute/The_Truman_Committee.htm (accessed October 16, 2013).

191 "100 percent behind": AmericaLive, "Harry S. Truman Biography," CNN iReport, December 19, 2010, available at: ireport.cnn.com/docs/DOC-530565 (accessed October 16, 2013).
"the operation of the program": Donald M. Nelson, *Arsenal of Democracy: The Story of American War Production* (New York: Harcourt Brace & Co., 1946), p. 128.
cover of *Time* magazine: *Time*, March 8, 1943.
"We will get all the facts": "Senate to Probe Lag of Output in Two Plane Plants," *Chicago Daily Tribune*, February 16, 1943, p. 23.

192 "to exert influence": "Prescription for Willow Run," *The New Republic*, April 5, 1943; see also Lowell Juilliard Carr and James Edson Stermer, *Willow Run* (New York: Arno Press, 1977), p. 211.
2,060 workers had left: "Prescription for Willow Run," *The New Republic*, April 5, 1943.
new machine gun turret: "The New Nose Turret," acc 435, box 51, "Ford–Willow Run Bomber Plant," vol. 3, Benson Ford Research Center, Dearborn, MI.
"I'd feel as if I had": Charles E. Sorensen, with Samuel T. Williamson, *My Forty Years with Ford* (Detroit: Wayne State University Press, 2006), p. 299.

193 "Now, look": Mead Bricker, oral history, pp. 337–38, Benson Ford Research Center, Dearborn, MI.
"You affect this whole": Ibid., p. 379.
"Now you may not be": Ibid., p. 338.
"Well, I certainly can": Ibid., p. 339.
"Maybe we should have": William F. Pioch, oral history, pp. 77–78, Benson Ford Research Center, Dearborn, MI.

194 "had not produced": Allan Nevins and Frank Ernest Hill, *Ford: Decline and Rebirth* (New York: Scribner's, 1963), p. 219.

22. Taking Flight: Spring 1943

195 "Show me a hero": F. Scott Fitzgerald, "Lost Fitzgerald Story to Be Published," *New York Times*, February 10, 1988.
5,163 enemy airplanes: Paul Kennedy, *Engineers of Victory: The Problem Solvers Who Turned the Tide in the Second World War* (New York: Random House, 2013), p. 321.
The Colonel passed Edsel: "Ford Aircraft Engine Plant and Workers Get 'E' Flag," *Detroit News*, March 13, 1943.

196 6,491 from Kentucky: "Manpower," acc 435, box 52, "Willow Run Bomber Plant," vol. 22, Benson Ford Research Center, Dearborn, MI.
Edsel employed 4,390 blind: "Medicine: The Able Disabled," *Time*, June 21, 1943.
Time Study Department: "Time Study," acc 435, box 52, "Willow Run Bomber Plant," vol. 20, Benson Ford Research Center, Dearborn, MI.

197 "You will probably understand": Marvin McIntyre, note to Franklin Roosevelt, February 27, 1943, file 3217, Franklin Roosevelt Papers, "Official File," FDR Library, Hyde Park, NY.

198 "Never before in history": Jay Mann, "One Way Ticket: 'Pandemonium' — WWII Glider Pilot Recalls Operations in Germany," US Army, May 12, 2011, available at: http://www.army.mil/article/56415/ (accessed October 16, 2013).
"Our war jobs are": William Knudsen Papers, box 2, National Automotive History Collection, Detroit Public Library.
"a city of homes": Sidney Hillman, Office of Production Management, file 3217, Franklin Roosevelt Papers, "Official File," FDR Library, Hyde Park, NY.

199 "I wander upstairs through": Lowell Juilliard Carr and James Edson Stermer, *Willow Run* (New York: Arno Press, 1977), p. 138.
"Practically every night": Ibid., p. 173.
"Professional gamblers": Richard Lingeman, *Don't You Know There's a War On? The American Home Front 1941–1945* (New York: Thunder's Mouth Press, 2003), p. 83.
"Cattle Car": Carr and Stermer, *Willow Run*, p. 83.

200 more workers died or were injured: Arthur Herman, *Freedom's Forge: How American Business Produced Victory in World War II* (New York: Random House, 2012), p. x.
"very old and very young": Agnes Meyer, "Changes in Design Caused Initial Production Delay," *Washington Post*, March 5, 1943, p. 1.
"the automobile was still": Ibid.

201 Forty-one thousand feet up: Charles Lindbergh, *Of Flight and Life* (New York: Scribner's, 1948), pp. 3–8.

202 *Returning from the border:* Ibid., p. 8.

203 "Now, it seemed a terrible": Ibid., p. 9.
The airfield would see over: "Flight Operations," acc 435, box 52, "Willow Run Bomber Plant," vol. 14, Benson Ford Research Center, Dearborn, MI.
In Germany, Heinrich Himmler: William L. Shirer, *The Rise and Fall of the Third Reich* (New York: Simon & Schuster, 1960), pp. 984–86.
204 "the enemy will very likely": Winston Churchill, *The Grand Alliance* (Boston: Houghton Mifflin, 1950), p. 808.
altitude chamber built by: "Altitude Chamber," acc 435, box 2, "Ford and the War Effort," vol. 8, Benson Ford Research Center, Dearborn, MI.
"Forty-three thousand feet": Charles Lindbergh, *The Wartime Journals of Charles A. Lindbergh* (New York: Harcourt Brace Jovanovich, 1970), p. 765.
205 "anxious to find out": Ibid.

23. "The Arsenal of Democracy Is Making Good": Winter to Summer 1943

206 "The criminal, corrupt": "Fireside Chat 25: On the Fall of Mussolini," July 28, 1943, Miller Center of the University of Virginia, available at: http://millercenter.org/president/speeches/detail/3331 (accessed October 17, 2013).
"glorious goals": "Roosevelt Sees Allies Nearing Victory in '43," *Washington Post*, January 8, 1943, p. 1.
"bomb [the Japanese]": "Text of President's Annual Message to Congress," *New York Times*, January 8, 1943, p. 12.
207 "Military strength was": Jorg Friedrich, *The Fire: The Bombing of Germany, 1940–1945* (New York: Columbia University Press, 2006), p. 54.
208 "The war has finally": Doris Kearns Goodwin, *No Ordinary Time: Franklin and Eleanor Roosevelt: The Home Front in World War II* (New York: Simon & Schuster, 1994), p. 482.
When he delivered his report: Excerpted in Norman Beasley, *Knudsen: A Biography* (New York: Whittlesey House, 1947), pp. 357–61.
209 makeshift laboratory for its: Wesley Sout, *Secret* (Detroit: Chrysler Corporation, 1947), pp. 1–66.
According to a public poll: David Lanier Lewis, *The Public Image of Henry Ford* (Detroit: Wayne State University Press, 1987), p. 363; see also Robert Lacey, *Ford: The Men and the Machine* (Boston: Little, Brown, 1986), p. 392.
210 "It's going to be about": The American Presidency Project, "FDR: Excerpts from the Press Conference, July 27, 1943," available at: www

.presidency.ucsb.edu/ws/index.php?pid=16436#axzz2i0Sgv3Dh (accessed October 17, 2013); see also Doris Kearns Goodwin, *No Ordinary Time: Franklin and Eleanor Roosevelt: The Home Front in World War II* (New York: Simon & Schuster, 1994), p. 448.

"Yes, the Nazis and Fascists": "Text of President's Annual Message to Congress," *New York Times*, January 8, 1943, p. 12.

"Last night at five": "JCG," letter to A. J. Lepine, September 4, 1941, acc 6, box 254, "1941: Defense," Benson Ford Research Center, Dearborn, MI.

211 "If anybody made a complaint": Mead Bricker, oral history, p. 57, Benson Ford Research Center, Dearborn, MI.

"I don't have any idea": Douglas Brinkley, *Wheels for the World* (New York: Penguin, 2003), p. 497.

"On numerous occasions": Lacey, *Ford*, p. 373.

212 John Bugas first joined: FOIA FBI file of John S. Bugas, various biographical information.

"Guns, tough situations": Robin Beaver, "From FBI to Ford Motor: John Bugas' Sense of Law and Order Served Him Well," Made in Wyoming, available at: http://madeinwyoming.net/profiles/bugas.php (last accessed October 17, 2013).

more than doubling his pay: FOIA FBI file of John S. Bugas, various biographical information.

"In no city was there": Victor G. Reuther, *The Brothers Reuther and the Story of the UAW* (Boston: Houghton Mifflin, 1976), p. 270.

"the biggest wartime boomtown": Nelson Lichtenstein, *The Most Dangerous Man in Detroit: Walter Reuther and the Fate of American Labor* (New York: Basic Books, 1995), p. 176.

forty "dangerous aliens": "Professor at U. of D. in Custody," *Detroit News*, December 11, 1941, p. 1.

213 "This is all I can": J. Edgar Hoover, memorandum, May 25, 1940, in Henry Morgenthau's diaries, microfilm roll 72, FDR Library, Hyde Park, NY.

"a bizarre plot": "Espionage: Story Book Reading," *Time*, September 6, 1943.

Liebold had close ties: FOIA FBI file of Ernest Liebold, memo by John Bugas, May 15, 1941.

"blow the hell out of London": FOIA FBI file of Ernest Liebold, memo by James J. Hayes, November 4, 1943.

President Roosevelt "a Jew": Ibid.

"When Hitler comes here": Ibid.

access to the blueprints: Ibid.

214 "sick and tired of having": Harry Bennett, as told to Paul Marcus, *Ford: We Never Called Him Henry* (New York: Tom Doherty Associates, 1987), p. 258.

"of sufficient volume": J. Edgar Hoover, letter to Edsel Ford, December 29, 1941, acc 6, box 169, "Gen. Correspondence, 1942: FBI," Benson Ford Research Center, Dearborn, MI.

24. Death in Dearborn: Spring to Summer 1943

215 "I do miss him so": Peter Collier and David Horowitz, *The Fords: An American Epic* (San Francisco: Encounter, 2002), p. 153.
"There were people": A. M. Wibel, oral history, p. 351, Benson Ford Research Center, Dearborn, MI.
216 "You know Edsel is sick": Ibid.
"Wibel was one of the Ford greats": Charles Sorensen, personal account, p. 922, acc 65, box 69, Benson Ford Research Center, Dearborn, MI.
"From then on, events": Charles E. Sorensen, with Samuel T. Williamson, *My Forty Years with Ford* (Detroit: Wayne State University Press, 2006), p. 320.
"Looks like a sick man": Sorensen, personal account, p. 918.
"change his attitude": Ibid.
"Discord over handling": Ibid., p. 919.
"I feel I can be helpful": Sorensen, *My Forty Years with Ford*, p. 321.
"The best thing for me": Sorensen, personal account, p. 920.
"If you go, I go": Sorensen, *My Forty Years with Ford*, p. 321.
217 "He didn't complain": Henry Dominguez, *Edsel: The Story of Henry Ford's Forgotten Son* (Detroit: Society of Automotive Engineers, 2002), p. 313.
218 "Kanzler doesn't know": Ibid.
"I expect you to keep": Sorensen, personal account, p. 989.
"We must expect Henry Ford": Sorensen, *My Forty Years with Ford*, p. 324.
219 "I didn't even know": Collier and Horowitz, *The Fords*, p. 152.
"I think he willed": William Clay Ford, oral history, Automobile in American Life and Society, pp. 11–12.
"As we drove through": Dominguez, *Edsel*, p. 313.
"very well composed": Sorensen, personal account, p. 926.
"My dear Mrs. Ford": Franklin Roosevelt, letter to Mrs. Edsel Ford, May 26, 1943, file 680, Franklin Roosevelt Papers, "Personal File," FDR Library, Hyde Park, NY.
220 "heartfelt sympathy": Ibid.
"When the plant shut down": Dominguez, *Edsel*, p. 316.
"That last year he lived": Sorensen, personal account, p. 927.
221 "What Is a Boy?": Ibid., p. 760.
"totally at sea": Collier and Horowitz, *The Fords*, p. 158.

222 "My dear Mr. President": Morgenthau, memo to FDR, May 25, 1943, p. 213, "Ford Motor Company, Foreign Funds Control," box 636, FDR Library, Hyde Park, NY.
"the good work that you": Ibid.
"There would seem to be": "Report of Investigation of Ford, Societe Anonyme Francaise, Machinery Suppliers, Inc., Matford S.A., Ford-air S.A.," p. 68, "Foreign Funds Control," box 135, record group 131, Office of Alien Property, National Archives, College Park, MD.
"Probably the loss": "Death of Edsel Ford Poses Problems of Management, Taxes," *Wall Street Journal*, May 27, 1943, p. 1.
223 "Well, Harry, you know": Harry Bennett, as told to Paul Marcus, *Ford: We Never Called Him Henry* (New York: Tom Doherty Associates, 1987), p. 287.
"Now, we aren't going": Collier and Horowitz, *The Fords*, p. 154.
"I just can't get over": Ibid.
"Harry, do you honestly": Bennett, *Ford: We Never Called Him Henry*, p. 292.
"I never know where": Collier and Horowitz, *The Fords*, p. 158.
Impossible: Sorensen, *My Forty Years with Ford*, p. 324.
224 "You, Mr. Ford": Dominguez, *Edsel*, p. 321; Robert Lacey, *Ford: The Men and the Machine* (Boston: Little, Brown, 1986), p. 403.
"Most of us were": Sorensen, *My Forty Years with Ford*, p. 326.
"You've got a job now": Ibid.
"Charlie, everything is": Sorensen, personal account, p. 932.
"My Dear Mr. Ford": Walter Hayes, *Henry: A Life of Henry Ford II* (New York: Grove Weidenfeld, 1990), p. 12.
225 "He was a saint": Collier and Horowitz, *The Fords*, p. 156.

25. Operation Tidal Wave: August 1, 1943

229 "We flew through sheets": Donald L. Miller, *Masters of the Air: America's Bomber Boys Who Fought the Air War Against Nazi Germany* (New York: Simon & Schuster, 2006), p. 191.
"Get up! Get up": James Dugan and Carroll Stewart, *Ploesti: The Great Ground-Air Battle of 1 August 1943* (New York: Bantam, 1963), p. 76.
230 "more killing power": Ibid., p. 82.
"I looked around in": Duane Schultz, *Into the Fire: Ploesti, the Most Fateful Mission of World War II* (Yardley, UK: Westholme, 2007), p. 104.
231 "For days, you could": "Ploesti: A Pilot's Diary," *American Heritage*, October-November 1983.
"When you go 200 miles": Philip Ardery, *Bomber Pilot: A Memoir of World War II* (Lexington: University of Kentucky Press, 1978), p. 97.

"the most complete and detailed": Schultz, *Into the Fire*, p. 84.
232 "Now the object of this operation": "USAAF Training Film for Ploesti Part I," available at: www.youtube.com/watch?v=xCbwzdTE1Zw (accessed October 18, 2013).
"[Gerstenberg] was a dedicated": Schultz, *Into the Fire*, p. 64.
233 "mathematical probabilities": Dwight D. Eisenhower, *Crusade in Europe* (Garden City, NY: Doubleday, 1952), p. 187.
"We dreaded this mission": Schultz, *Into the Fire*, p. 93.
"If you do your job": Ibid., p. 95.
234 "It is unclear what": Dugan and Stewart, *Ploesti*, p. 3.
"A cold chill went down": Schultz, *Into the Fire*, pp. 109–10.
235 "If this is the correct turn": Dugan and Stewart, *Ploesti*, p. 131.
"In the distance toward": Schultz, *Into the Fire*, p. 142.
"everything but the kitchen sink": Dugan and Stewart, *Ploesti*, p. 161.
"a bedlam of bombers": Ardery, *Bomber Pilot*, p. 106.
236 "We had to shoot our way in": Dugan and Stewart, *Ploesti*, p. 161.
"I could see Gooden": Ibid., p. 165.
"Another shell exploded": Schultz, *Into the Fire*, p. 126.
"The bomber crashed": Dugan and Stewart, *Ploesti*, p. 125.
237 "Planes fell in flames": Stephen E. Ambrose, *The Wild Blue: The Men and Boys Who Flew B-24s over Germany 1944–1945* (New York: Simon & Schuster, 2001), p. 213.
"What was your overall": Dugan and Stewart, *Ploesti*, p. 208.
the official tallies: Ibid., p. 211.
238 "but I am certain that": Ibid.

26. The Detroit Race Riot of 1943: Summer 1943

239 "23 Dead in Detroit": "23 Dead in Detroit Rioting," *New York Times*, June 22, 1943, p. 1.
240 "The whole school": Robert Lacey, *Ford: The Men and the Machine* (Boston: Little, Brown, 1986), p. 407.
"We ... were allowed the run": "A Super Existence: The Boyhood of Henry Ford II," *Michigan Quarterly Review* 25, no. 2, Spring 1986.
"Father told me to start": Henry Dominguez, *Edsel: The Story of Henry Ford's Forgotten Son* (Detroit: Society of Automotive Engineers, 2002), p. 322.
"That's amazing, when": Ibid.
"The whole place was": Ibid.
241 "the fat young man": Peter Collier and David Horowitz, *The Fords: An American Epic* (San Francisco: Encounter, 2002), p. 163.
"I am green": Douglas Brinkley, *Wheels for the World* (New York: Penguin, 2003), p. 495.

"All these people": Walter Hayes, *Henry: A Life of Henry Ford II* (New York: Grove Weidenfeld, 1990), p. 7.
"I hope that somehow": Collier and Horowitz, *The Fords,* p. 161.
"like a cryptographer": Ibid.
"Nothing pleased me so": Charles Sorensen, personal account, p. 935, acc 65, box 69, Benson Ford Research Center, Dearborn, MI.

242 "When Mr. Henry Ford II": Anthony Harff, oral history, p. 83, Benson Ford Research Center, Dearborn, MI.
"Something had to be": Sorensen, personal account, p. 962.

243 "Harry Bennett is the dirtiest": Brinkley, *Wheels for the World,* p. 498.
This thing killed my: Robert Coughlin, "Co-captains in Ford's Battle for Supremacy," *Life,* February 28, 1955.
"What do you want to quit": William F. Pioch, oral history, pp. 80–81, Benson Ford Research Center, Dearborn, MI.

244 "In Detroit today": "The Ford Heritage," *Fortune,* June 1944.
"I decided that I": Sorensen, personal account, p. 974.
"Everyone's nerves were": Harry Bennett, as told to Paul Marcus, *Ford: We Never Called Him Henry* (New York: Tom Doherty Associates, 1987), p. 273.

246 "the rising tide": Edward Jeffries, *Detroit and the "Good War": The World War II Letters of Mayor Edward Jeffries and Friends* (Lexington: University Press of Kentucky, 1996), p. 48.
"racial characteristics": Ibid., p. 45.
"It will either blow": Ibid.

247 "Let's go out and kill": Richard Lingeman, *Don't You Know There's a War On? The American Home Front 1941–1945* (New York: Thunder's Mouth Press, 2003), p. 327.
"fresh meat": Ibid.
"Jesus, but it was": Ibid.
"There were about 200": Ibid.
"Not even in the South": Walter White, *A Man Called White* (Athens: University of Georgia Press, 1995), p. 226.

248 "Word got around pretty": Lingeman, *Don't You Know There's a War On?,* p. 328.
"The domestic scene is": Doris Kearns Goodwin, *No Ordinary Time: Franklin and Eleanor Roosevelt: The Home Front in World War II* (New York: Simon & Schuster, 1994), p. 444.
"disperse and retire": "Roosevelt's Proclamation," *Daily Boston Globe,* June 22, 1943, p. 1.

249 "Not long afterward": White, *A Man Called White,* p. 228.
"We have no definite": "Troops Restore Calm in Detroit; Death Toll 28," *Chicago Daily Tribune,* June 23, 1943, p. 2.
"It is blood on your hands": Goodwin, *No Ordinary Time,* p. 446.
"This rioting was": Sorensen, personal account, p. 948.

"When the army leaves": "Troops Restore Calm in Detroit; Death Toll 28," *Chicago Daily Tribune*, June 23, 1943, p. 2.

27. *"The United States Is the Country of Machines":* Fall 1943

250 "We'll not capitulate": Ian Kershaw, *Hitler: 1936–1945 Nemesis* (New York: W. W. Norton, 2000), p. 685.

"I'm nearly dead": Jon Meacham, *Franklin and Winston: An Intimate Portrait of an Epic Friendship* (New York: Random House, 2004), p. 237.

251 "tired, with dark rings": Ibid., p. 236.

"God-awful": Ibid., p. 276.

"a flexible productive": Donald M. Nelson, memo to Franklin Roosevelt, May 31, 1943, container 229, Harry L. Hopkins Papers, FDR Library, Hyde Park, NY.

252 "Donald Nelson has": Joseph Goebbels, *The Goebbels Diaries* (New York: Popular Library, 1948), p. 290.

"Get the planes off": Doris Kearns Goodwin, *No Ordinary Time: Franklin and Eleanor Roosevelt: The Home Front in World War II* (New York: Simon & Schuster, 1994), p. 261.

According to a top-secret: "Total Deliveries, Cumulative," container 240, Harry L. Hopkins Papers, "War Production Board Reports: Aircraft Branch," FDR Library, Hyde Park, NY.

253 "When can you start?": Dwight D. Eisenhower, *Crusade in Europe* (Garden City, NY: Doubleday, 1952), p. 197.

"It's the best handling": Charles Lindbergh, *The Wartime Journals of Charles A. Lindbergh* (New York: Harcourt Brace Jovanovich, 1970), p. 744.

254 "What alarmed us most": Albert Speer, *Inside the Third Reich* (New York: Avon, 1970), p. 377.

"The day raids by American": Goebbels, *The Goebbels Diaries*, p. 435.

255 "Don't let them fool": Speer, *Inside the Third Reich*, p. 378.

256 "Man's desire to be": Goodwin, *No Ordinary Time*, p. 473.

"I think about a hundred": H. H. Arnold, *Global Mission* (Military Classics, 1949), p. 469.

257 "I want to tell you": Meacham, *Franklin and Winston*, p. 264.

"If there was any": Sherwood, *Roosevelt and Hopkins*, p. 799.

"This is my personal": *American Airpower Comes of Age: General Henry H. "Hap" Arnold's World War II Diaries*, edited by Major General John W. Huston (Maxwell AFB, AL: Air University Press, 2002), p. 132.

28. Ford War Production Exceeds Dreams: Winter 1943 to Spring 1944

258 "Detroit, where they stand": Richard Lingeman, *Don't You Know There's a War On? The American Home Front 1941–1945* (New York: Thunder's Mouth Press, 2003), p. 146.
"Declaration by 3 Allied Powers": "Text of Declaration of 3 Allied Powers," *Detroit News*, December 6, 1943, p. 1.
"We have concerted": Ibid.
259 "Ford is making": Doris Kearns Goodwin, *No Ordinary Time: Franklin and Eleanor Roosevelt: The Home Front in World War II* (New York: Simon & Schuster, 1994), pp. 362–63.
"The Toughest Fords": Advertisements collected in V. Dennis Wrynn, *Detroit Goes to War: The American Automobile Industry in World War II* (Minneapolis: Motorbooks International, 1993).
260 "Announcing the New": The advertisement is pictured in Jeffrey D. Shively, *Cadillac: It Came Out Fighting* (Bloomington, IN: AuthorHouse, 2008), no page number.
"They know how to manage": Ed Cray, *Chrome Colossus: General Motors and Its Times* (New York: McGraw-Hill, 1980), pp. 318–19.
"I invented the modern": Richard Snow, "It's Still Henry Ford's World," *Bloomberg*, July 29, 2013.
261 "Long lines of huge": "B-24 Bombers Roll Off Lines at Willow Run," *Chicago Daily Tribune*, June 10, 1943.
"Willow Run Performing": "Big Bomber Output Rate Hinted Vast," *Hartford Courant*, February 6, 1944, p. A1.
"Ford War Production Exceeds": "Ford War Production Exceeds Dreams," *Christian Science Monitor*, May 21, 1942, p. 13.
"She was a strange": Charles Sorensen, personal account, p. 881, acc 65, box 69, Benson Ford Research Center, Dearborn, MI.
"We have been ahead": Charles Lindbergh, *The Wartime Journals of Charles A. Lindbergh* (New York: Harcourt Brace Jovanovich, 1970), p. 772.
"Bring the Germans": David Lanier Lewis, *The Public Image of Henry Ford* (Detroit: Wayne State University Press, 1987), p. 351.
262 "That Ford is producing": "Observational Report Made by Curtiss-Wright Representatives, June 1944," acc 435, box 52, "Willow Run Bomber Plant," vol. 14, Benson Ford Research Center, Dearborn, MI.
"John's the smartest": Henry Dominguez, *Edsel: The Story of Henry Ford's Forgotten Son* (Detroit: Society of Automotive Engineers, 2002), p. 325.
"The offer came as a complete": Peter Collier and David Horowitz,

The Fords: An American Epic (San Francisco: Encounter, 2002), p. 165.

"I had a terrible time": Dominguez, *Edsel*, p. 325.

263 "At first, I didn't": Collier and Horowitz, *The Fords*, p. 165.

"The FBI man was actually": Ibid., p. 164.

264 "Nobody invited Mr. Bennett": Ibid., p. 147.

"That is the way to win": Sorensen, personal account, p. 979.

265 "He's doing fine": Ibid., p. 963.

The boy can take it: Charles E. Sorensen, with Samuel T. Williamson, *My Forty Years with Ford* (Detroit: Wayne State University Press, 2006), pp. 328–29.

"First, get your grandfather": Collier and Horowitz, *The Fords,* p. 166.

"He seemed to sit around": Harry Bennett, as told to Paul Marcus, *Ford: We Never Called Him Henry* (New York: Tom Doherty Associates, 1987), p. 303.

266 "Is someone else taking": Lindbergh, *The Wartime Journals,* p. 774.

"I hope there was no one": Ibid., p. 816.

267 "Henry Ford Fires Sorensen": "Sorensen Out as Ford Chief of Production," *Chicago Daily Tribune,* March 5, 1944.

"I guess there's something": Sorensen, *My Forty Years with Ford,* p. 330.

268 "For months the world-straddling": "The Winner," *Time,* March 13, 1944.

"He was a hard-boiled:" Sorensen, *My Forty Years with Ford,* p. xii.

"For myself, I have": Sorensen, personal account, p. 1020.

29. D-Day: Winter to Spring 1944

269 "In this poignant hour": FDR's D-Day prayer, June 6, 1944, available at: www.youtube.com/watch?v=NAUDj6yQx9U (accessed October 23, 2013).

"Nothing in war history": Jorg Friedrich, *The Fire: The Bombing of Germany, 1940–1945* (New York: Columbia University Press, 2006), p. 126.

270 "The picture that greeted": Ibid.

"What can the USA": Doris Kearns Goodwin, *No Ordinary Time: Franklin and Eleanor Roosevelt: The Home Front in World War II* (New York: Simon & Schuster, 1994), p. 240.

"Blazing fires everywhere": Joseph Goebbels, *The Goebbels Diaries* (New York: Popular Library, 1948), p. 591.

"Berlin was a kind of": Edward R. Murrow, *In Search of Light: The*

Broadcasts of Edward R. Murrow 1938–1961 (New York: Alfred A. Knopf, 1967), p. 76.

"We really clobbered": Jay A. Stout, *Fortress Ploesti: The Campaign to Destroy Hitler's Oil* (Philadelphia: Casemate, 2003), p. 102.

"Along the Kaiserdamm": Goebbels, *The Goebbels Diaries*, p. 599.

271 "absolute failure": Ian Kershaw, *Hitler: 1936–1945 Nemesis* (New York: W. W. Norton, 2001), p. 645.

"I could see the omens": Albert Speer, *Inside the Third Reich* (New York: Avon, 1970), p. 435.

"the enemy has succeeded": Stout, *Fortress Ploesti*, p. 190.

"Flying Box Car": Stephen E. Ambrose, *The Wild Blue: The Men and Boys Who Flew B-24s over Germany 1944–1945* (New York: Simon & Schuster, 2001), p. 80.

"Postwar France must": Dwight D. Eisenhower, *Crusade in Europe* (Garden City, NY: Doubleday, 1952), p. 264.

272 presentation of the Army-Navy: "Army-Navy 'E' Flag Presentation," acc 435, box 51, "Ford–Willow Run Bomber Plant," vol. 4, Benson Ford Research Center, Dearborn, MI.

273 "It is certainly with mixed": Ibid.

"It is just another proof": Ibid.

274 "Heavy bomber production": Container 236, Franklin Roosevelt Papers, "Map Room File," FDR Library, Hyde Park, NY.

"May was a great month": "War Production Reports: War Progress," June 10, 1944, container 254, Harry L. Hopkins Papers, FDR Library, Hyde Park, NY.

"Operations of our Air Forces": Container 236, Franklin Roosevelt Papers, "Map Room File," FDR Library, Hyde Park, NY.

"The 'Big Ten' of the Invasion": "War Production Reports: War Progress," June 10, 1944, container 254, Harry L. Hopkins Papers, FDR Library, Hyde Park, NY.

"every movement of his face": Maury Klein, *A Call to Arms: Mobilizing America for World War II* (London: Bloomsbury, 2013), pp. 673–74.

"We have just heard": Jon Meacham, *Franklin and Winston: An Intimate Portrait of an Epic Friendship* (New York: Random House, 2004), p. 278.

275 "As dawn broke": Stephen E. Ambrose, *D-Day: June 6, 1944, the Climactic Battle of World War II* (New York: Touchstone, 1994), p. 239.

"Rosie the Riveter back": Ambrose, *The Wild Blue*, p. 167.

"Early this morning": Murrow, *In Search of Light*, p. 81.

276 "There was no sight in the war": Eisenhower, *Crusade in Europe*, p. 295.

"You'd never get away": Ambrose, *D-Day*, p. 239 footnote.

277 "Soldiers, sailors and airmen": General Dwight D. Eisenhower,

D-Day speech, June 6, 1944, available at: www.youtube.com/watch?v=SGTWOB3pv6U (accessed October 23, 2013).

30. The Final Battle: Spring to Fall 1945

278 "Don't make the mistake": Collier and Horowitz, *The Fords*, p. 167.
"There was a great change": Douglas Brinkley, *Wheels for the World* (New York: Penguin, 2003), p. 496.

279 "You come in here": Allan Nevins and Frank Ernest Hill, *Ford: Decline and Rebirth* (New York: Scribner's, 1963), p. 266.
"Take this back to Henry": Ibid.
"It wasn't any good": Ibid., p. 112.
"I think it's about time": Brinkley, *Wheels for the World*, p. 499.
"Henry, I think young": Ibid.
"Look, you're not well": Ibid.

280 "There are things going on": Ibid.
"He killed my husband": Robert Lacey, *Ford: The Men and the Machine* (Boston: Little, Brown, 1986), p. 418.
"If this is not done": Nevins and Hill, *Ford: Decline and Rebirth*, p. 268.
"Okay, Henry, you take over": Brinkley, *Wheels for the World*, p. 500.
"I'll take it only if": Collier and Horowitz, *The Fords*, p. 167.

281 "We have just fifteen": Doris Kearns Goodwin, *No Ordinary Time: Franklin and Eleanor Roosevelt: The Home Front in World War II* (New York: Simon & Schuster, 1994), p. 602.
"in a jerky way": Ibid.
"I have a terrific pain": Ibid.
"more of them would come": H. H. Arnold, *Global Mission* (Military Classics, 1949), p. 579.
"Believe me, it will": Ian Kershaw, *Hitler: 1936–1945 Nemesis* (New York: W. W. Norton, 2001), p. 807.

282 "Truman's Proclamation": "Truman's Proclamation — War Ends!" *Detroit News*, August 14, 1945, p. 1.
"To the Employees": "Cessation of Production," acc 435, box 51, "Willow Run Bomber Plant," vol. 4, Benson Ford Research Center, Dearborn, MI.

283 "You're taking over": Harry Bennett, as told to Paul Marcus, *Ford: We Never Called Him Henry* (New York: Tom Doherty Associates, 1987), p. 1.
"I was frightened to death": Brinkley, *Wheels for the World*, p. 500.
"You son of a bitch!": Collier and Horowitz, *The Fords*, p. 167.

284 "just as I planned it": "Former FBI Man Replaces Ford Official," *Chicago Daily Tribune*, September 28, 1945.
"Well, I guess Harry": Collier and Horowitz, *The Fords*, p. 168.

Epilogue

285 "I flew thirty-five missions": Oak Mackey, interview with the author.
"America's record in production": Donald M. Nelson, *Arsenal of Democracy: The Story of American War Production* (New York: Harcourt Brace & Co., 1946), foreword.
"The American war production": Ibid., p. 429.
"The production necessary": Ibid., p. 431.

286 "The number of people": Stephen E. Ambrose, *The Wild Blue: The Men and Boys Who Flew B-24s over Germany 1944–1945* (New York: Simon & Schuster, 2001), pp. 22–23.
Of the total 18,482 Liberators: "Ford Summarization," acc 435, box 52, Benson Ford Research Center, Dearborn, MI.

287 "People think they": Jorg Friedrich, *The Fire: The Bombing of Germany, 1940–1945* (New York: Columbia University Press, 2006), p. 287.
"The end of the world": Ibid., p. 136.
"When you looked at the cities": Charles Lindbergh, *The Wartime Journals of Charles A. Lindbergh* (New York: Harcourt Brace Jovanovich, 1970), p. 943.

288 "Here was a place": Ibid., p. 995.
"In the attack by Allied": "The United States Strategic Bombing Survey (European War, Summary Report)," September 30, 1945, reprinted by Air University Press, Maxwell Air Force Base, Alabama, October 1987.

289 "We too are soldiers": Schneider report, p. 13, box 1032, stack 270, row 69, compartment 69, shelf 6, "Foreign (Occupied) Area Reports" (entry 368B), Records of the Operations Branch of the Administrative Services Division of the Adjutant General's Office (record group 407), National Archives, College Park, MD.
"Until 1939, all important": Ibid., p. 1.
"after the outbreak": Ibid.

290 Cologne factory had 870: *Research Findings About Ford-Werke Under the Nazi Regime,* numerous authors (Dearborn, MI: Ford Motor Co., 2001), p. 128 chart.
"The conditions were terrible": Michael Dobbs, "Ford and GM Scrutinized for Alleged Nazi Collaboration," *Washington Post,* November 30, 1998.

291 "We have progressed": "Ford Sees Menace of Bigger War," *Daily Boston Globe,* May 28, 1944.
"rivals the weirdest": Charles E. Sorensen, with Samuel T. Williamson, *My Forty Years with Ford* (Detroit: Wayne State University Press, 2006), p. 8.

Index

Ford, Henry (*cont.*)
hiring of blacks, 14
Hitler's admiration for, 34, 57, 59–60, 82, 102
labor practices and salaries, 13–14, 43
museum of antique machinery, honoring of EF at, 267
news reports lauding for war production, 142–43
opinion of Kanzler, 135
opposition to Bomber City, 148–49
optimism, v
pacifism, antiwar activism, 21, 102–5, 114, 287, 291
potential presidential run, 34
the Quadricycle, 3–4, 6
refusal to modernize, 32, 36
relationship with Bennett, 37–41, 47, 75, 102, 114, 149, 215–16, 222–23, 283
relationship with EF, 5, 8, 17–19, 23, 25, 31–32, 34, 36–37, 41, 43, 47, 80–81, 180–81, 216, 218
relationship with HF2 and other grandchildren, 41, 240–41, 279–80
relationship with Liebold, 213
relationship with Lindbergh, 102–3, 105, 151, 266
relationship with Sorensen, 11, 18, 31, 37, 75, 88, 120, 216, 223–24, 267–68
response to EF's death, 219–20, 222–23
response to war in Europe, 75–76, 130–31
resumption of Ford presidency after EF's death, 222–24, 241, 264–65
retirement, 23
rumors of codicil about running of Ford, 278
salary, 8
during siting of the Willow Run bomber plant, 99
as teetotaler, 18
work for Edison Illuminating Company, 5–6
Ford, Henry, II
acceptance of the E flag and first public speech, 272–73

appearance, 112, 239
changes in during year after EF's death, 272–73
birth and childhood, 20, 239–40
children, 181
death, 291
decision to remain with Ford, 279
EF's decision to bring into business, 89, 217
at farewell lunch for Lindbergh, 266
first visit to Consolidated Aircraft Corporation, 88–89
first jobs at the Rouge, 112
following Gregorie's firing, 240–41
marriage to Anne McDonnell, 112
memories of learning to drive, 240
move into father's office at Ford headquarters, 241
navy service, 113, 144
presidency of Ford, 144, 221, 280, 282, 291
relationship with Bennett, 39, 41, 113–14, 211, 225, 239, 243, 265, 279, 283–84
relationship with Bugas, 263
relationship with EF, 24–25, 41, 45, 89, 91, 93, 112–14, 144, 181, 217–19, 225
relationship with Ford employees, 112–13, 240–41, 265
relationship with Gregorie, 219
relationship with HF, 41, 45, 48–49, 240–41, 279–80
relationship with Kanzler, 224, 239
relationship with Sorensen, 93, 241–42, 264–65, 268
release from Navy after EF's death, 224–25
response to Detroit Race Riot, 249
response to EF's death, 218, 221, 225
return to Ford, 224–25, 240–42, 265
at the rollout of the final B-24 Liberator, 282
at River Rouge factory opening, 24
twenty-first birthday party, 112

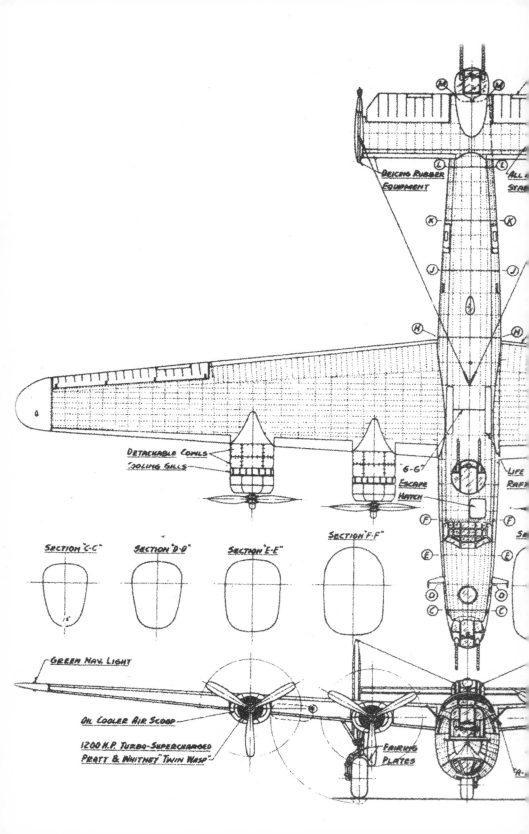

DEICING RUBBER
EQUIPMENT

ALL
STA

DETACHABLE COWLS
COOLING GILLS

6-6"

ESCAPE
HATCH

LIFE
RAF

SECTION "C-C"   SECTION "D-D"   SECTION "E-E"   SECTION "F-F"

SE

GREEN NAV. LIGHT

OIL COOLER AIR SCOOP

1200 H.P. TURBO-SUPERCHARGED
PRATT & WHITNEY "TWIN WASP"

FAIRING
PLATES

A-